Career Pathways

This book is dedicated to the people who have dedicated their lives to the principles of educating our youth, and to all the teachers who have had—and will have—the courage to make the necessary changes in their classrooms to meet the needs of this and future generations of our youth. Two in particular are Marilyn O. Peters and Robert Isenberg, whose love for education and hearts of gold affected many students and professionals and whose work will carry on through many generations.

Career Pathways

PREPARING STUDENTS FOR LIFE

Elaine Makas Howard ■ Pamela J. Ill

CORWIN PRESS
A Sage Publications Company
Thousand Oaks, California

Copyright © 2004 by Corwin Press

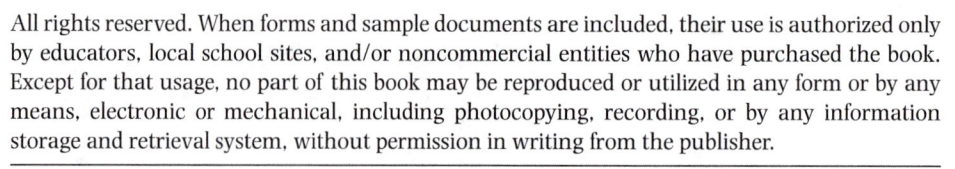

All rights reserved. When forms and sample documents are included, their use is authorized only by educators, local school sites, and/or noncommercial entities who have purchased the book. Except for that usage, no part of this book may be reproduced or utilized in any form or by any means, electronic or mechanical, including photocopying, recording, or by any information storage and retrieval system, without permission in writing from the publisher.

For information:

Corwin Press
A Sage Publications Company
2455 Teller Road
Thousand Oaks, California 91320
www.corwinpress.com

Sage Publications Ltd.
6 Bonhill Street
London EC2A 4PU
United Kingdom

Sage Publications India Pvt. Ltd.
B-42, Panchsheel Enclave
Post Box 4109
New Delhi 110 017 India

Printed in the United States of America

Library of Congress Cataloging-in-Publication Data

Howard, Elaine Makas.
 Career pathways : preparing students for life / by Elaine Makas Howard and Pamela J. Ill.
  p. cm.
 Includes bibliographical references (p.) and index.
 ISBN 0-7619-3970-9 — ISBN 0-7619-3971-7 (pbk.)
  1. Career education—United States. 2. Education, Cooperative—United States.
 I. Ill, Pamela J. II. Title.
 LC1037.5.H67 2004
 370.11´3—dc22

                                2003021578

This book is printed on acid-free paper.

03 04 05 06 07   10 9 8 7 6 5 4 3 2 1

Acquisitions Editor:	Robert D. Clouse
Editorial Assistant:	Jingle Vea
Production Editor:	Kristen Gibson
Copy Editor:	Elizabeth Budd
Proofreader:	Teresa Herlinger
Typesetter:	C&M Digitals (P) Ltd.
Indexer:	Sheila Bodell
Cover Designer:	Tracy E. Miller
Graphic Designer:	Lisa Miller

Contents

Acknowledgments	xiii
About the Authors	xv
Introduction: Student-Centered High Schools	xvii

Part One: Introduction to Career Pathways

1. The What and Why of Career Pathways High Schools — 3
- Scenario: Jacob's Story — 3
- What Is a Pathways High School? — 4
- Why Pathways? — 13
  - Purpose of Public Education — 13
  - Graduate Trends — 13
  - The Village Concept — 15
  - Brain Research — 16
  - State and Federal Findings — 17
  - Action Research — 19
- Two Closing Scenarios — 19
- In Review — 23

2. The Collaborative Career Pathways Model — 24
- Scenario: Nicole's Plan — 24
- Model Structure: The Three Pillars — 25
  - The Counseling Pillar — 26
  - The Classroom Pillar — 27
  - The Community Pillar — 27
- Implementing the Three Pillars — 28
  - Counseling — 29
  - Classroom — 29
  - Community — 31
- Horizontally Integrating the Pillars — 32
  - Grade 9 — 33
  - Grade 10 — 34
  - Grade 11 — 35
  - Grade 12 — 37

	Putting It All Together: The Complete Implementation Chart	38
	Students as the Center of Learning	38
	Pathways and Citizenship	40
	Pathways Myths	44
	Conclusion	45
	In Review	46
3.	**Steps to Implementing the Model**	**47**
	Scenario: A Community Member's Story	47
	Three Steps to Successful Change: A Process Model	48
	Step 1: Focus and Goals	49
	Step 2: Teaming and Collaboration	51
	Step 3: Collecting Data	57
	A Time Line for Implementation	57
	Year 1	57
	Year 2	59
	Year 3	59
	Year 4	60
	Year 5	60
	Funding	65
	Reallocation	66
	Grants and Awards	68
	Community Involvement	68
	Conclusion	69
	In Review	70

Part Two: Building a Foundation

4.	**District Vision and School Leadership:**	
	The Pathways Foundation	**73**
	Scenario: In Order to Form a More Perfect Union . . .	73
	Vision, Mission, Goals, and Values	74
	Presenting a Solid Example	75
	A Common Experience	80
	A Common Process	80
	In Review	81
5.	**Comprehensive Guidance to Prepare**	
	and Assist Pathways Students	**83**
	Scenario: A Day in the Life of a Career Pathways Counselor	83
	The Importance of Comprehensive Guidance	85
	Career Pathways and Traditional	
	High School Guidance Programs	87
	Pathways Comprehensive Guidance and	
	National Counseling Standards	91
	Scheduling in a Career Pathways High School	91
	Educational Development Plans and Portfolios	97
	Educational Development Plans	97

Portfolios	99
Student Testing and Data Collection	102
Creating an Avenue for Pathways Flexibility	104
Conclusion	105
In Review	106

6. Curriculum in a Career Pathways High School: A Rationale for Standards, Mapping, and Integration — **107**

Scenario: Sarah and Ethan's Curriculum Experience	107
The Importance of Curriculum in a Collaborative Career Pathways High School	110
What Is Curriculum?	111
Curriculum Vision and Outcomes	111
Standards and Benchmarks	112
Curriculum Alignment	115
Curriculum Mapping	116
Focusing on Key Content Skills and Department Goals	116
The Basics of Brain-Based Learning—Content Versus Context	118
The What and How of Integrating Your Curriculum	120
Integrating Technology	125
The Definition of a Technologically Literate Learner	125
Embedded Technology at All Four Levels	127
Assessment Systems and Predictors of Success	129
Curriculum and Pathways Connections	131
In Review	131

Part Three: School Structure

7. Pathways Classes for Each Level of Collaborative Career Pathways — **137**

Scenario: Elizabeth's Postsecondary Preparation	137
What Is a Pathways Class and Why Do We Have Them?	138
Pathways Classes: Key Concepts and Placement	139
What Does Each Pathways Class Look Like?	140
Freshman Explorations: The Cornerstone	146
Unit I: Exploring Who I Am	146
Unit II–V: Exploring the Pathways	146
Unit VI: Making the Great Decision	147
The Five-Year Plan	148
Sophomore Selections: The Great Balancing Act	148
Unit I: Who I Am (Intra)	149
Unit II: Whom I Project to Others (Inter)	149
Unit III: My Plan to Succeed	149
Unit IV: Myself and the World of Work	150
Unit V: Myself and Others (Pathway-Specific Integrated Project)	150

Unit VI: Making an Informed Decision	151
Junior Judgments: The Stepping Stone	152
Unit I: Self-Preparation	152
Unit II: Deciding on the Internship	153
Unit III: Work World Preparation	153
Unit IV: Stepping Into the Work World	154
Unit V: Judging the Experience	154
Unit VI: Self-Managing the Plan	155
Senior Transitions: Moving Forward	156
Unit I: A Little Help From My Friends	157
Unit II: Tools of the Trade	157
Unit III: Making the Most of Senior Year	158
Unit IV: Designing the Senior Project	158
Unit V: Implementing the Project	159
Unit VI: Presenting the Project	159
Unit VII: Giving Back (Optional)	160
How Are Pathways Classes Delivered?	160
Curriculum Placement of Pathways Classes	161
Pathways Change Process	161
The Long-Term Results of Pathways Class Work	162
In Review	162

8. Scheduling in a Collaborative Career Pathways High School — 164

Scenario: Two High School Stories	164
The Need to Address Scheduling	165
Major Types of Scheduling and Career Pathways High Schools	166
An Ideal Collaborative Career Pathways Schedule	169
Schedules, Teaching Styles, and Professional Development	172
Creating a Schedule That Is Right for Your School	173
Conclusion	175
In Review	175

Part Four: Classroom Processes

9. Freshman Explorations: The Cornerstone of Pathways Instruction — 179

Scenario: Two Freshman Experiences	179
The Important Connections	180
Freshman Explorations: The Curriculum	181
Connections to Self	181
Connections to School	187
Connecting Students to the World Around Them	189
Integrated Thematic Units	190
Pathway Exploration	194
Researching Pathways	194
Chatting With People	195
Site Visits	197

Decision Making	199
In Review	202

10. Pathways Classes for Grades 10 Through 12: Sophomore Selections, Junior Judgments, and Senior Transitions — **203**

Scenario: Joy's Scaffold	203
The Great Scaffold	205
Sophomore Selections	205
Curriculum Issues in Sophomore Selections	207
Counseling Issues in Sophomore Selections	209
Community Issues in Sophomore Selections	209
Junior Judgments	211
Curriculum Issues in Junior Judgments	211
Counseling Issues in Junior Judgments	213
Community Issues in Junior Judgments	215
Senior Transitions	216
Curriculum Issues in Senior Transitions	216
Counseling Issues in Senior Transitions	220
Community Issues in Senior Transitions	221
The Scaffold Works	222
In Review	223

11. Core and Elective Teachers as Support for the Career Pathways Instructional Process — **224**

Scenario: Transformation to a Pathways Teacher	224
Gaining the Support of the Entire Faculty	225
Core and Elective Teachers as Part of the Team	226
Staff Inclusion	226
Communication	228
Continuous Staff Development and In-Servicing	230
Teaming and Collaboration	232
Career Technology and Academy Teachers	
Versus Collaborative Pathways Teachers	233
Working With the Core Teachers	233
Working With the Elective Teachers	235
How Pathways Teachers Differ From	
Traditional Classroom Teachers	235
In Review	236

Part Five: Culture, Community, and Technology

12. Public Relations, Parents, and Pathways — **239**

Scenario: A Role for Everyone	239
Gathering the Stakeholders	241
The Public Relations Strategy	242
Talking to Parents	243
Talking to Students	244

Talking to the School Community	246
School Board and Administration	246
Counselors	247
Teachers	248
Staff	250
Talking to Community Members	251
Working With Technical Centers and Academic Sources	252
Myths About Pathways	254
The Ongoing Public Relations Mission	257
In Review	258

13. The School Community: The True Classroom of Pathways — 259

Scenario: Hannah's Story	259
Involving the Community	261
Focus of Guest Visits	261
Speakers in the Classroom	263
Site Visit Locations	267
Designing Field Trips to Accommodate Hosts	268
Designing Job Shadows	269
Service Learning	270
Internships and Senior Projects	271
Support Through the Academic Community	272
Conclusion	274
In Review	275

14. School Culture and Climate in a Pathways High School — 276

Scenario: Miguel's First Day	276
What Are School Culture and Climate?	277
Why Are School Culture and Climate Important?	279
A Key Finding: School Connectedness	279
The Pathways Solution to Key Finding 1: School Connectedness	281
Other Key Findings: School Prejudice and Codes of Silence	283
School Prejudice	283
Codes of Silence and Other Indicators of Violence	285
Solutions and Suggestions for Climate Control	289
Establish a Working Committee	
for Culture and Climate Issues	290
Assess Your Climate	291
Develop a Schoolwide Plan	292
Addressing Some Key Points of Instruction	292
Pathways as an Avenue to Good Culture and Climate	294
Other Complementary Programs	295
The First-Day-of-School Challenge	296
Concluding Scenario: Miguel's First Day Revisited	296
In Review	299

15. Pathways as a Systematic Philosophy   **300**
    Scenario: A Pathways Graduation   300
    System Change   302
        Creating a Structure With Purpose,
           Collaboration, and Support   303
        Creating Cultural Change Through Process
           and Experience   304
        Key Provisions for Successful Systems Change   305
    Conclusion   307

Resources   **309**

References   **327**

Index   **330**

Acknowledgments

It took a village to "raise" this book. We thank the vision and leadership of the Michigan Office of Career Development for bringing the concept of Career Pathways to Michigan. We also want to thank the vision and leadership of the Michigan Department of Education in the areas of curriculum and best practice. Their work with the Michigan Curriculum Framework and the new direction of the Michigan Education Assessment Program has been instrumental in moving student achievement in Michigan to new heights.

We would like to acknowledge the following school districts for thinking "outside the box" and especially for their participation, input, and dedication to students:

Akron-Fairgrove Schools
Cass City Middle School
Kingston Community Schools
Mayville Community Schools
Unionville-Sebewaing Area Schools
Vassar Public Schools.

We would also like to acknowledge all the principals, counselors, teachers, and community members who have worked with us, given of their time over and above the call of duty, and who "believed" us when we said, "try this, you'll like it." In addition, we acknowledge all the students who are now experiencing our communities in new ways, developing their own plans, and taking charge of their own education.

Of course, we cannot forget to mention our families and friends who stood by us through "thick and thin" and with good nature accepted when we could not always be there for them. We especially want to thank our teenage technology wiz, Jonathan A. Keinath, Barry Sutton, of Sutton Aviation, and Pat Brown, of Young Eagles. We appreciate how Jon and all our friends and family *really understood* that this was important for all "kids" everywhere and therefore made sacrifices for us to complete this book.

Our hearts go out to our village. Thank you.

Corwin Press gratefully acknowledges the contributions of the following individuals:

Steve Olczak
Principal
Reynolds High School
Troutdale, OR

Kenneth C. Gray
Author, Professor
College of Education
Pennsylvania State University
State College, PA

Janet Sampson
School to Career Coordinator
Hudson Public Schools
Hudson, MA

Kirsten Keach
Adult Education Coordinator
St. Johnsbury Academy
St. Johnsbury, VT

Maureen Gevirtz
Lead STC Coordinator
San Diego County Office of Education
San Diego, CA

Greg Williams
STC Grant Coordinator
San Diego High School
San Diego, CA

About the Authors

Elaine Makas Howard has 25 years of experience in education. She has served numerous districts in Michigan in curriculum, career development, and counseling processes as a regional director of instructional services. She is also a systems consultant with Curriculum Connections and Career Pathways Consulting, a business she co-owns. She has a specialist degree from Saginaw Valley State University in Educational Leadership with an emphasis on curriculum. She has a master's degree from Central Michigan University in school guidance and a bachelor's degree from Western Michigan University in history. She is certified in central office and secondary administration, counseling, and Grades 7–12 social studies secondary education. She has held the positions of secondary teacher, community education director, and curriculum consultant. She lives in Cass City, Michigan, with three of her four sons.

Pamela J. Ill has been a devoted classroom teacher for more than 25 years, and is currently an instructional consultant with Career Pathways Consulting and a classroom teacher with the Unionville-Sebewaing Public Schools in Sebewaing, Michigan. During her career, she has taught a variety of secondary subjects, including language arts, French, and psychology. She has a bachelor of arts degree with a major in English and a minor in psychology, along with a secondary education endorsement from Kalamazoo College in Kalamazoo, Michigan. She received her Michigan elementary certification from Saginaw Valley State University. She currently team teaches Freshman Pathways classes and designs Pathways curricula. Her school became a board-certified Pathways High School in 1999. She resides in Vassar, Michigan, with her husband, son, and daughter.

Introduction

STUDENT-CENTERED HIGH SCHOOLS

This book is about learner-centered high schools. It is about teaching to the student, not to the subject. Most of all, it describes our vision of the structure of our high schools as analogous to the universe. The universe was formed in such a way that wherever you are in it, you are at its center; this is because it is shaped like the outside of a balloon. Our belief is that wherever students are in their high school experience, they are at the center of their learning. In a traditional high school, the center of the system is the teaching of content or subject matter, not student learning.

This traditional "center" can be demonstrated by the way that we use language. If you ask high school teachers what they do, they will reply, "I teach history," "I teach math," and so on. They do not say, "I teach students history" or "I teach students math." Traditional high school teachers see themselves as providers of subject knowledge (and the system perpetuates this).

The system we present to promote the shift from traditional content- or subject-centered high schools to student-centered high schools is called Collaborative Career Pathways—a system of organizing student learning interests and aptitudes around career paths. It provides a structure for students to reference their learning and connect each year of their high school experience. It allows students to plan and practice their skills while creating a smooth and successful transition to a postsecondary option.

Even though our quests for system change began separately, we both began to feel discouraged by our profession. Why? Because Pam, a 25-year veteran in the classroom, felt she was reaching fewer students, more of the time. Elaine, both as an administrator dealing with at-risk youth and as a curriculum director, began to see patterns in every high school that were counterproductive to students and society at large.

Working with both teachers and students, the same patterns kept emerging for both of us. These patterns could be put into two categories:

1. Teachers working harder with fewer positive results.

2. Students growing more and more disconnected with school and the learning process.

It seemed as teachers worked harder and students grew more distant, the gap we were experiencing simply grew larger. It was common to hear teachers complain about how much work they were putting into the classroom with less appreciation and engagement from students. It was also common to hear students complain about how what they learned in school had no relevance to them. The school day could not end fast enough for them—they were eager to get back to the Internet, their video games, computers, and what have you to continue to learn—what and how they wanted to learn. If you and your colleagues have felt this distance from students, the Collaborative Career Pathways Model can be of great assistance in closing the gap. It can help teachers reach their students, and it can help students take ownership of their own education.

A key aspect of the acceptance and understanding of Career Pathways for us was our own experiences as educators. Despite the facts and figures concerning the need for change in our high schools that we received, our own emotional connections to kids and our passion for their educational success was what made it possible for us to create change successfully. Change processes can be long and tedious with many roadblocks—some expected and some not.

Our model began in 1999 when Pam's high school, in the rural area of the thumb of Michigan, became a board-certified Pathways High School and piloted the Collaborative Pathways Model. In the fall of that year, Pam, a language arts teacher, and her coteacher Bob Isenberg, designed a Freshman Focus curriculum tailored to the new model. Each year since then, the school's Career Pathways team has added another level of Pathways. In June 2003, the school had its first Pathways graduating class. At the same time, other schools in the county also began to look at Pathways and adapt it to the needs of their districts and students. Elaine began working with administrators, teachers, boards of education, and students in Kingston, Mayville, Akron-Fairgrove, and Vassar High Schools, and Cass City Middle School (all in Michigan) to implement the beginning stages of what was to become the Collaborative Pathways Model. We were astonished that, at every step we took, we found educators and community or board members who saw hope for successful system change that would be for the benefit of their students. Of course, we also met with resistance, but we never expected to see the kind of passion for change that we encountered. So our team has grown with the best and brightest!

To demonstrate this, one day Elaine was working with a well-known staff member; one of the science teachers who had never actively participated in any in-service (and we all have them), he put down his pen (he was correcting papers), took off his glasses, and looked at Elaine. He then said, "This is good for kids, you have me." In another school the principal was afraid to go to the faculty and ask who would take on the Freshman Explorations class in the high school (all members of the faculty already had too much work on their plate). Elaine said, "Who is your best English teacher?" and the principal pointed him out to her. Elaine met with the teacher separately and went over the curriculum and the class purpose. His remark was, "This fits my English standards and will help kids succeed in this school. I'll do it." The English teacher, his inclusion teacher, and the technology teacher worked together to provide a successful program, brought the rest of the staff with them, and then convinced the board two years later to change the schedule and hire two additional teachers.

We have also been astounded at the night-and-day difference between our Pathways students and those who have graduated from a traditional high school. We have found our students to be more focused and connected, more team orientated, better able to work with adults, and the true drivers of their own learning. To be part of such a complete systems change—not in one school but in an entire county—has been an emotional roller coaster but more rewarding and more renewing than anything we have ever experienced in our careers. We are, more than ever, convinced that student-centered systems make a difference, and we are willing to put ourselves on the line professionally over and over again. We fervently believe that if our public high schools are to survive the changes in our world, they must change their paradigm. They must take an honest look at the data, at their students, and at themselves. They must become student-centered, and Collaborative Career Pathways Model will provide a solid road to reach such a destination.

This book is not just from our minds or our experiences; it is from our hearts as educators and as parents. This book is about our successes, our failures—about bringing change to schools. It is our "blood, sweat, and tears" of creating positive change and sharing with our readers how it can be done effectively and efficiently. It is a high school "knight's tale" of heroes and heroines—teachers, counselors, parents, students, and community members—who were willing to take risks and to be criticized for seeing a different vision for our youth and our educational system. This book is for them, for our readers, and, most of all, for students. It can changes lives for students and for educators. And the truth is, that is what being an educator is all about—making a difference in students' lives.

Part One

Introduction to Career Pathways

Chapter One

The What and Why of Career Pathways High Schools

SCENARIO: JACOB'S STORY

Jacob is an average to above average middle school student who is now entering his high school years. He is outgoing, enjoys social situations, and plays the trumpet. Occasionally he has had difficulty in math but has been able to maintain a C average throughout his middle school math classes. During his freshman year, Jacob has a Freshman Explorations class where he is acclimated to his surroundings and spends time learning good study skills, self-management, problem solving, and teamwork. Jacob also does a great deal of self-discovery through interest and aptitude surveys, personality profiles, learning style inventories, and so forth. Jacob then does six integrated units of study with team members centered on the six Career Pathways his school has designated. The units practice workplace skills, technical skills, and language arts skills. In each unit he, along with his teammates, produces a product or completes a process for presentation. Throughout this exploration, many speakers come into the classroom to talk about the different career paths. The class then takes several field trips to visit various sites where Pathway jobs are visible to the students. Jacob always suspected that he liked medicine (he hopes to be a doctor someday); well, this experience helped Jacob to realize that medicine is a main interest, so at the end of his freshman year he elects the Health Pathway to focus his high school study.

In his sophomore year, Jacob delves deeper into the medical field. He does a job shadowing experience in a doctor's office and in a hospital emergency room. He is excited about patient care but realizes that the years of schooling to become a doctor seem like a difficult goal. Also, he realizes that he would like to have a closer relationship with patients. Jacob looks into other aspects of health and builds a program around the nursing aspect of patient care. During this time, Jacob is having problems with math. His school sets up a program for him with a math tutor, and Jacob begins to work on building his algebraic math skills. His tutor gears his math lessons toward that which Jacob would be expected to know as a health professional. In his junior year, Jacob completes an unpaid work experience with a home health care company. During the second semester, he takes a health occupation class at the regional career center and becomes a certified nurse's aide. He then continues to work at the home health care company as a paid employee.

Before his senior year, Jacob has a postsecondary plan of going to a community college to become a licensed professional nurse, transferring to a state university that is articulated with his community college to complete his registered nurse training (and that also offers a nurse practitioner master's program). Jacob plans to be a nurse practitioner in six years. In the meantime, he is working on his high school requirements with an emphasis on science. For his electives, he takes early childhood development and psychology. During his four years of high school, Jacob continues to play the trumpet and participates in marching band. He has a great love of music, so for his senior project Jacob sets up a music therapy program with the local nursing home. During his second semester, he dual enrolls in a psychology class at the community college he will attend the following year. Jacob is graduating with good academic skills and a focused, realistic plan. His chances of success go from 30% to somewhere between 80 and 100% (School to Work, n.d.).

WHAT IS A PATHWAYS HIGH SCHOOL?

So what does this mean for us as educators? What happens in the systems Jacob encounters, how does it happen, and why? To give Jacob and all students a focused high school experience, administrators, faculty members, and the community must take a long, hard look at their students and their system. We must be aware of and accountable for what happens to our students once they leave our realm, just as we expect the auto industry to be responsible for its cars once they leave the assembly plant. One such system of accountability is the Career Pathways High School system. A Career Pathways High School utilizes the school campus and the entire community to prepare students for life. A Pathways High School uses all the systems within a high school—instruction, counseling, extracurricular activities, remediation, career technical education, discipline, student government, community, and so forth. It also individualizes student learning by gearing its programs and philosophy toward a student's interests and aptitudes.

> *In its proper format, a Career Pathways High School will "put it all together" for the student. It is learner centered and self-directed.*

In the chapters that follow, we will take each system within your school and show you how it can be improved and integrated with the Career Pathways Model so that all systems within the school point in the same direction.

This can be accomplished by centering a student's learning and planning around an established set of career paths. A career path is a broad spectrum of careers that share similar characteristics and for which employment requirements call for common interests, strengths, and competencies. The groupings encompass the entire spectrum of career options, providing opportunities for all students and all ability levels (Michigan Department of Career Development, 2001). Each Pathway contains hundreds of jobs at all levels of entry. For example, the Health Pathway consists of careers that center on personal and societal health issues and can include direct and indirect care. In a career ladder, which shows the steps of a career from entry level to ceiling, the direct care ladder will begin with nurse's aide jobs and continue all the way to medical specialists such as brain surgeons.

> *In a Career Pathways High School, the direction of all school systems point toward the development and implementation of individual student plans that focus students' high school coursework to ensure the successful completion of a postsecondary option.*

Career Pathways are derived from Career Clusters and then broken down into Career Fields. This is where it can get confusing for educators because not all organizations, states, or federal programs use the same terms in the same manner. In most frameworks, the highest category can be a Career Cluster, or Industry Sector. The U.S. Department of Education and Office of Vocational and Adult Education (USDE/OVAE) has identified 16 Career Clusters and the National Skill Standards Board 15 Industry Sectors. These Cluster/Sectors are then narrowed down into second-level categories called Career Pathways. Utah, Oregon, Ohio, and Michigan, to name a few, have five to six Pathways; however, they refer to them in such diverse terms as Pathways, Fields, Endorsements, and Clusters. These Career Pathways (our term for all second-level categories) create a more manageable framework for instruction. Pathways can then be broken back out into Career Fields, which reflect occupational categories. To illustrate this, we have charted the USDE/OVAE Clusters and Pathways programs from four states. Please note the inconsistent use of terms throughout the nation. For the purpose of this book and for your understanding as a reader, we use the definition process shown in Figure 1.1.

The U.S. Department of Education (2002) states that "Career Clusters link what students learn in school with the knowledge and skills they need for success in college and careers." They have identified 16 "States' Career Clusters" (Table 1.1). Their

> *"Our sixteen broad Career Clusters will help students enhance the link between the knowledge they acquire in school and the skills they need to pursue their dreams. Without limiting students, Career Clusters help them focus on an area of interest or a possible career path" (Richard W. Riley, U.S. Secretary of Education, USDE, 2002).*

Figure 1.1 Career Clusters, Pathways, and Fields: Definitions

Career Clusters: Groupings of occupations
(e.g., hospitality and tourism)

⇩

Career Pathways: Groupings of Career Clusters
(e.g., business management and marketing)

⇩

Career Fields: Occupational areas within a Pathway
(e.g., accounting, office administration, business ownership, economics, personnel, hospitality and tourism, marketing sales and finance)

Web site states that the 16 Clusters are an ideal way to organize instruction, academics, work-based learning programs, smaller learning communities, magnet and charter schools, and high schools that are restructuring around career themes (USDE, 2002).

> *Remember, it is important to choose a Pathways system that works best for your school and your community.*

These 16 Clusters can then be combined in various ways to create broader paths for student exploration and instruction. Table 1.2 shows a sample of how four states condense the Clusters into Career Pathways for students.

It is also important that the Pathways you use cover the gamut of careers, both in your area and nationally, and follow any state-legislated educational programs. Your state may have established a set of Career Pathways to bring consistency to its educational process and economic community. There is a reason why different frameworks organize Clusters in different ways. Each Cluster framework reflects the workplace and the economy for which it is intended (Wonacott, 2001, p. 4). State economies can vary tremendously in what industries and occupations are important (Wonacott, 2001). We encourage you to check with your state's Department of Education to find out how and where they stand on their choice of Career Pathways.

The Career Pathways used in our model are a set of six Pathways developed by the state of Michigan. The six Pathways are a manageable number of groupings to demonstrate our model and work well in the alignment and integration of instruction. This model can be used with any set of career paths or clusters, however. Large high schools may be able to manage more Pathways, but for an average to small high school, Pathways may have to be "clumped" to integrate them successfully with classroom instruction and technology-integrated units. Table 1.3 lists the six Career Pathways used in this book.

Table 1.1 The Sixteen Career Clusters

Cluster (Pathway)	Definition
Agriculture, Food, and Natural Resources	Planning, managing, and performing agricultural production and horticulture, and landscaping services and related professional and technical services, mining and extraction operations, and managing and conserving natural resources and related environmental services
Architecture and Construction	Designing, planning, managing, building and maintaining the built environment
Arts, Audiovisual Technology, and Communications	Designing, producing, exhibiting, performing, writing, and publishing multimedia content including visual and performing arts and design, journalism, and entertainment services
Business, Management, and Administration	Planning, organizing, directing, and evaluating business functions essential to efficient and productive business operations (Business management and administration career opportunities are available in every sector of the economy.)
Education and Training	Planning, managing, and providing education and training services, and related learning support services
Finance	Planning, services for financial and investment planning, banking, insurance, and business financial management
Government and Public Administration	Executing governmental functions to include governance, national security, foreign service, planning, revenue and taxation, regulation, and management and administration at the local, state, and federal levels
Health Science	Planning, managing, and providing diagnostic, therapeutic, and information and environmental services in health care
Hospitality and Tourism	Managing, marketing, and operating restaurants and other food services, lodging, attractions, recreation events, and travel-related services
Human Services	Preparing individuals for employment in Career Pathways that relate to families and human needs
Information Technology (IT)	Designing, developing, supporting, and managing hardware, software, multimedia, and systems integration services (In addition to career opportunities in the IT industry, IT careers are available in every sector of the economy, from financial services to manufacturing, transportation to education.)
Public Safety and Security	Planning, managing, and providing judicial, legal, and protective services

(Continued)

Table 1.1 (Continued)

Manufacturing	Planning, managing, and performing the processing of materials into intermediate or final products, and related professional and technical support activities such as production planning and control, maintenance and manufacturing/process engineering
Marketing, Sales, and Service	Planning, managing, and performing wholesaling and retailing services and related marketing and distribution support services including merchandise/product management and promotion
Science, Technology, Engineering, and Mathematics	Planning, managing, and providing scientific research and professional and technical services (e.g., physical science, social science, engineering) including laboratory and testing services and research and development services
Transportation, Distribution, and Logistics	Planning, managing, and moving people, materials, and goods by road, pipeline, air, rail, and water, and related professional and technical support services such as transportation infrastructure planning and management, logistics services, mobile equipment, and facility maintenance

Note: Adapted from The Sixteen Clusters, National Association of State Directors of Career Technical Education Consortium. Copyright 2002.

Table 1.2 Sample State Pathways Chart

Utah's Five Career Fields	*Oregon's Six Endorsement Areas*	*Ohio's Six Career Clusters*	*Michigan's Six Career Pathways*
Artistic	Arts and Communication	Arts and Communication	Arts and Communication
Business	Business and Management	Business and Management	Business, Management, Marketing, and Technology
Scientific	Health Services	Health Services	Health Sciences
Social Humanitarian	Human Resources	Human Resources/ Services	Human Services
Technical	Industrial and Engineering	Industrial and Engineering Systems	Engineering/ Manufacturing and Industrial Technology
	Natural Resources	Environmental and Agricultural Systems	Natural Resources and Agriscience

As previously mentioned, schools can adjust their career paths to match their community needs. In some of our rural schools, agriculture and agribusiness have been combined to make one Pathway. This is because many of the careers and jobs in the area are connected to that Pathway. Also, smaller schools may merge several Pathways such as combining the health and human services field, whereas larger schools may separate the paths such as dividing the health care field into direct and indirect care. This is a process that must be done by the administrator and his or her staff.

Adjusting Pathways to fit a school and community can be illustrated by one of our small rural high schools. This high school combined several Pathways to suit its small size. A farming community, it highlighted agriculture and agribusiness to fit the area's business community and job pool. Its Pathways are as follows:

- Engineering/Manufacturing and Industrial Technology and Business
- Health and Human Services
- Arts and Communication
- Natural Resources, Agriscience, and Agribusiness

Once the Career Pathways are determined in a Career Pathways High School, the work of shifting instruction begins. There are three key changes that will occur:

1. Students will learn about themselves, their interests and aptitudes, and how these relate to school. They will then develop a plan of study and postsecondary choices.

2. Instruction will be geared to a student's plans through the avenues of Pathways Class work and core and elective classes, career technical coursework, and postsecondary articulations.

3. All instructional processes will include the necessary skills for successful employment as set down by the Secretary's Commission on Achieving Necessary Skills Report (SCANS). The SCANS report was presented by a commission established by the U.S. Department of Labor. The commission published the report in 1991 titled *What Work Requires of Schools: A SCANS Report for America 2000* (U.S. Department of Labor, 1991). This report had a significant impact on the 1994 School-to-Work legislation and other federal and state educational funds. The report recommended Five Competencies and a three-part Basic Skills Foundation. The Five Competencies are use of resources, interpersonal skills, use of information, systems thinking, and technology. The three-part educational foundation is basic skills (reading, writing, math, listening, and speaking), thinking skills, and personal qualities.

> *The implications of such an instructional shift are huge. It affects how administrators, teachers, parents, and even students view the classroom process and their role within that process.*

Table 1.3 The Six Pathways Discussed in This Book

Pathway
Arts and Communications

Definition
Careers in this Pathway are related to the humanities and performing, visual, literary, and media arts. These include architecture; graphic, interior, and fashion design; writing; film; fine arts; journalism; languages; media; and advertising and public relations.

Sample Career Categories (Fields)
Advertising and public relations, creative writing, film production, foreign language translation or interpreting, journalism, radio and television broadcasting

Pathway
Business, Management, Marketing, and Technology

Definition
Careers in this Pathway are related to the business environment. These include entrepreneurial careers, sales, marketing, computer and information systems, finance, accounting, human resources, economics, and management.

Sample Career Categories (Fields)
Accounting, office administration, business ownership, economics, human resources, hospitality and tourism management, computer and information systems services, marketing, sales, finance

Pathway
Engineering Manufacturing and Industrial Technology

Definition
Careers in this Pathway are related to technologies necessary to design, develop, install, and maintain physical systems. These include engineering, manufacturing, construction services and related technologies.

Sample Career Categories (Fields)
Architecture, precision production, mechanics and repair, manufacturing technology, engineering and related technologies, drafting, construction

Pathway
Health Sciences

Definition
Careers in this Pathway are related to the promotion of health and treatment of disease. These include research, prevention, treatment, and related health technologies.

Sample Career Categories (Fields)
Dentistry, hygiene, medicine, nursing, nutrition and fitness, therapy and rehabilitation

(Continued)

Table 1.3 (Continued)

Pathway
Human Services

Definition
Careers in this Pathway are related to economic, political, and social systems. These include education, government, law and law enforcement, leisure and recreation, military, religion, child care, social services, and personal services.

Sample Career Categories (Fields)
Education, child and family services, food and beverage service, law and legal studies, law enforcement, cosmetology, social services

Pathway
Natural Resources and Agriscience

Definition
Careers in this Pathway are related to agriculture, the environment, and natural resources. These include agricultural sciences, earth sciences, environmental sciences, fisheries, forestry, horticulture, and wildlife.

Sample Career Categories (Fields)
Agriculture, animal health care, earth sciences, environmental science, fisheries management, wildlife management, horticulture, forestry, life sciences

Note: Adapted from the Michigan Department of Career Development (2001).

Some of these paradigm shifts are described in Table 1.4. In a Career Pathways High School, the shift is always to the student as learner and is reflected in its purpose and mission.

The purpose of a Career Pathways High School is threefold:

1. The achievement of high academic skills
2. The development and implementation of a realistic postsecondary plan
3. The development of democratic citizenship

Therefore the mission of a Career Pathways High School is as follows:

> *The purpose and mission of a Career Pathways High School is always in direct relationship to the concept of the student as lifelong learner and the driver of his or her own educational process.*

> *Every student will focus his or her high school education on a realistic postsecondary plan. The plan needs to match the skills, knowledge, and experience of the student so that it can be completed successfully while allowing the student to become a productive citizen and global resident.*

Table 1.4   Paradigm Shifts in a Career Pathways High School

Traditional Paradigm	Career Pathway Paradigm
Students learn information today to be used in their future.	Students learn information and skills to be applied today to build toward their future.
Students must do their own work.	Students work collaboratively to help each other gain the necessary skills and knowledge.
Grades are competitive.	Grades are performance based.
Curriculum is teacher based.	Curriculum is standard based.
Teachers teach and students learn.	Teachers facilitate student learning.
Rules and school culture are the responsibility of school officials.	School culture and climate are the responsibility of everyone and are facilitated by school officials.
Adults and not students know what is best for every child.	Adults act as guides and mentors to help students find their own path and to make their own choices.
Student adult roles and responsibilities begin after high school.	Student adult roles and responsibilities are practiced throughout the high school years through classroom instruction and work-based learning experiences.
Students narrow their career focus after high school in college or another postsecondary environment.	Students have a clear vision and written plan for postsecondary success.
The focus of instruction is on teachers and teaching.	The focus of instruction is on learning and learners.
High school knowledge is given by subject matter with students making subject connections at a later date.	Students see the connection between content areas and between their schoolwork and their personal goals.
Learning happens only in the classroom.	Learning encompasses the whole community and is connected back to the classroom.
Schools are not accountable for students who do not learn.	The learning bar is set for all students and systems are in place for students who encounter difficulties.
Schools are not accountable for students who are unsuccessful in their next educational level.	Schools hold themselves accountable to the educational and employment success or failure of their graduates.
Stakeholders believe their job is to graduate students.	Stakeholders believe their job is to facilitate students in making a successful transition to their postsecondary plan.

WHY PATHWAYS?

The main purpose of this book is not to make a case for Career Pathways High Schools but to help you implement successful Career Pathways Systems. We do not believe that this can be done unless you and your faculty understand the background of the movement. So let's take a step back and look at several issues that have brought us to this point: the purpose of public education in the United States, current educational and economic trends, the village–child concept, the new field of brain research, state and federal findings, and Career Pathways High Schools' action research projects. All of the above issues add to the puzzle of how and why Career Pathways High Schools make so much sense.

Purpose of Public Education

Historically, the principal reason for public education was the understanding first given to us by Thomas Jefferson: To perpetuate democracy, the nation must have an educated population.

Therefore, the initial purpose of education was the enlightenment of the population to rule themselves successfully. If public education is to guarantee the continuation of our democracy, it must emphasize citizenship. But what is democratic citizenship? In a Career Pathways High School, democratic citizenship is defined as the belief that a person must practice his or her rights as a member of a free society, be productive (which in our technical society requires literacy skills), give back to his or her community, and enjoy life, liberty, and the pursuit of happiness (to quote a famous document). In most current traditional high schools, the purpose is to prepare students for college. The focus of today's traditional high school is limited at best and, if we delve deeper, has been unsuccessful in this "narrow" focus.

> *I know of no safe depository of the ultimate powers of society but the people themselves; and if we think them not enlightened enough to exercise their control with a wholesome discretion, the remedy is not to take it from them, but to inform their discretion by education.*
>
> *Thomas Jefferson (1743–1826)*

> *College is not the goal. College is a choice in a plan—it is only a means to an end.*

Graduate Trends

There are several influential trends that were publicized in the 1990s by both the U.S. Department of Labor and the National School-to-Work Office.

Kenneth Gray, a professor of education in the Workforce Education and Development Program, College of Education, at Penn State recently published a book titled *Getting Real: Helping Teens Find Their Future*. Gray states, "most teenagers who attempt college fail either by not graduating or by not finding commensurate employment if they do" (Gray, 2000, p. 1). Through his research, Gray has concluded that "postsecondary success requires two ingredients: academic skills and commitment that comes from career focus. Going to college without the commitment that stems from a clearly laid-out plan will invariably lead to failure" (Gray, 2000, p. 1). He gives four reasons for this dilemma:

> ***Major Trends:***
> - *A large number of students who are unsuccessful at college*
> - *A large number of students who cannot find employment in their college major*
> - *A large number of students enrolled in a community college after earning a four-year degree*
> - *A larger number of skilled laborers immigrating from other countries*
> - *Youth economically established at increasingly later ages (many researchers have concluded that our youth do not reach economic independence until their late 20s)*

1. Two-thirds of all college students now withdraw at least once before finishing, and 91% of these students never earn a degree (U.S. Department of Labor 1998, cited in Gray, 2000).

2. Although teens said the main reason they were going to college was to get a good job (American Council on Education, 1998, cited in Gray, 2000), few seem to have thought much about the details. Many end up completing degrees that lead to few opportunities.

3. While increasing numbers of college graduates were ending up in low-wage service jobs, the nation's economy was generating record numbers of unfilled positions for technicians in high-skill/high-wage technical jobs.

4. On discovering they had made a mistake, many young adults became "reverse transfers," enrolling in one- and two-year technical programs at community and technical colleges even though many already had four-year degrees and even graduate degrees.

This situation will continue as long as the focus is on college, and not on success (Gray, 2000).

Gray is not the only professional "ringing the bell." The staggering numbers of college dropouts and their lack of gainful employment triggered the National School-to-Work Act and the establishment of the National School-to-Work Office in Washington, D.C. The problem has become so common that comedians make jokes about the "boomerang" effect in which parents send their children out into the world only to get them back down the road! At one of our child's college graduation ceremonies, the president of the college stated that the stereotype of graduates without skills was not true—he challenged any company to hire one of his graduates and train them. We thought that was so ironic—wasn't the college experience supposed to have trained them to enter the workforce? The evidence for this trend is staggering. One night, Elaine was sitting with a superintendent at an evening meeting when we had a guest speaker on information and data. In our discussion, the superintendent made a very potent statement: "I understand what the problem is. What I need to know is what can we do about it."

The Village Concept

The "what we can do about it" begins with a village concept. Career Pathways High Schools utilize the entire community as the school campus. Students are involved in the community and experience site-based educational experiences throughout their four years of high school. These experiences are structured and move from general to specific. For example, freshmen take field trips to view all the Career Pathways, while seniors do a focused senior project in their Pathway with professionals in the field. In a Career Pathways High School, *all* students experience the community in a systematic manner that moves from general to specific. This important aspect of Career Pathways High Schools is grounded in the concept that, as the African proverb says, it takes a village to raise a child.

Within the last decade, research has clearly shown the connection between positive adult intervention and student success. Studies conducted by the Search Institute have produced conclusive evidence that the more positive adult role models that students are exposed to and involved with, the more likely they are to succeed in their adult life—and the less likely they are to indulge in risk-taking behaviors. Following is an excerpt from the book *Developmental Assets: A Synthesis of the Scientific Research on Adolescent Development*:

> Support may be especially important for adolescents because the physical, emotional, social, spiritual, and intellectual changes they are going through may make it more difficult for adults to feel close to them. How important is support? Numerous studies in the 1970's and the 1980's confirmed that social support is associated with better physical and mental health among young adults (Turner, Frankel, and Levin 1983). A large and growing number of studies since that time also have confirmed that a caring and supportive relationship with an adult remains "the most critical variable" predicting health and resiliency throughout childhood and adolescence (Benard 1991; Garmezy 1993). More recently, a national study of more than 12,000 7th–12th graders reported that a high degree of connectedness to families and school significantly protected youth from seven of eight behaviors risky to their health, such as suicidal thoughts and behavior, violence, substance use and having their first intercourse at a young age (Resnick et al. 1997). Unfortunately, large proportions of young people do not seem to experience either enough support or the right kinds of support in their families, school, or communities. (Scales & Leffert, 1999, pp. 21–22)

Another research study done for the period of 1989–1998, cited in "Other Adult Relationships and Caring Neighborhoods," found that students who have positive adult relationships and supportive neighborhoods exhibit the following characteristics:

- Higher grades, more "liking" of school, higher IQ score, higher school completion rates, and higher math test scores
- More prosocial behavior and fewer behavior problems
- Reduced experience of violence
- Less substance use
- Fewer feelings of loneliness, anxiety, or depression
- Greater self-esteem, cheerfulness, and hopes for the future (Scales & Leffert, 1999, p. 27)

One of the main reasons for moving to Career Pathways is the involvement of the community in the lives of students. We share numerous examples of this as we begin to examine each subsystem of the model.

> *It is vital to the success of a Pathways High School to make the community an intricate part of the system.*

You will see more clearly as our model unfolds how the community is integrated as a major component of the system.

Brain Research

Another major area to explore to make the case for Career Pathways High Schools is the current emphasis in education on brain research, which has been called the frontier of the 21st century. Brain research has been able to confirm many of the foundations of learning set down for us by such educational pioneers as Dewey and Bloom.

Key elements of brain research are enmeshed in a Pathways High School and include such important elements as learning through the entire physiology and the importance of spatial learning. Brain research has given us a solid basis for reexamining what we do in the classroom. Kathleen Harris (1996, module 2–7) in *Making Connections: Curriculum Integration Projects* stated the following:

> The greatest challenge of brain research for educators does not lie in understanding the anatomical intricacies of brain functioning but in comprehending the vastness, complexity, and potential of the human brain. What we are beginning to discover about the role of emotions, stress, and threat in learning and about memory systems and motivation is challenging basic assumptions about traditional education. Fully understood, this information requires a major shift in our definitions of testing and grading *and in the organizational structure of classrooms and schools.* (Emphasis added)

Brain research continually points to the organization of information in "big clumps," such as Career Pathways, and then narrowing that information into smaller, manageable portions. It emphasizes experience and close connections to "real life" and real-life objects. These experiences, such as the work-based experiences of site visits and job shadows, prepares a space or pattern in the brain to which students can "hook" academic information, thus retaining what they have learned. Susan Kovalik, founder of the Integrated Thematic Instruction (ITI) Model, stated in her video, *Intelligence Is a Function of Experience* (Susan Kovalik and Associates, 2001), that all educational decisions must be made from brain research—how the brain learns and stores information. Her areas of effective learning strategies begin with real-life experiences, simulated environments, hands-on experience with an actual area of study (e.g., a frog), and hands-on experience with simulated objects (e.g., a plastic frog). According to Kovalik, visuals (e.g., pictures and movies) and symbols (e.g., numbers) are the information sources that are least understood by the brain.

> *Career Pathways High Schools set the stage for using the world as the students' classroom. The Pathways Model sets learning in patterns of Career Clusters and uses academics as the application of skills needed to fulfill students' interest and aptitudes, thus securing education for their individual needs and their future.*

According to Harris (1996, module 2–13), "Learning in context (application) with emotional investment results in long term retention and transferability of knowledge." In Chapter 6, we examine in detail the major principles of brain research and how they relate to instruction in the classroom.

State and Federal Findings

Through the SCANS report (U.S. Department of Labor, 1991), labor market statistics, and other national and state sources, it became apparent that there was a growing gap between the academic skills taught in schools and workforce skills and requirements. The federal School-to-Work Opportunities Act of 1994 was designed to help deal with these growing concerns. The act created three school-to-work components: school-based, work-based, and connecting activities. School-based programs are traditional school academics, work-based activities include students' experiences in the workplace (e.g., job shadowing), and connecting activities are those that make the "connection" between the school- and work-based learning. The act was instrumental in setting aside federal, state, and local funds for education and business partnerships.

Since that time, many states have moved forward with their own educational workforce programs. In Michigan, the Career Development office was established to offer assistance and grants and create regional boards to help close the gap of education and workforce opportunities for students. The Michigan Department of Education, along with the Office of Career Development, has promoted Career Pathways High Schools through their six established Career Pathways. Recently the state's new accreditation program listed three requirements for state school accreditation:

1. All students will read by Grade 3.

2. All students will show one year's growth in one year.

3. All high school students will have focused education centered on a post-secondary plan.

Identifying student-centered high school curriculums, such as Pathways, as part of a state's accreditation program shows the growing priority for such systems. In South Carolina, following a 14-month study, the Governor's Workforce Education Task Force, made up of educators, business leaders, and legislators, called for mandatory Career Clusters. In the October 31, 2001, edition of "What Works in Teaching and Learning," the following conclusion appeared:

> Aiming to bridge an "enormous mismatch" between South Carolina's education system and its workforce needs, a governor's task force is calling for the elimination of college prep and tech prep tracks while implementing career clusters to help prepare all students for work. ("South Carolina Task Force," 2001, n.p.)

The task force made several recommendations, including designing schools around Career Clusters and requiring teachers to take courses in applied learning techniques before becoming certified. "Although our schools are making tremendous strides academically, there is still a serous gap between the skills taught in the classrooms and the skills needed in the 21st-century workplace," states Don Herriott, president of the pharmaceutical company Roche Carolina and chairman of the task force. The report further states gaps on several levels:

> Only 32 percent of ninth-graders will pursue a two-year degree, while 65 percent of jobs will require one; another 28 percent will pursue a four-year degree, while only 20 percent of jobs will require one; and the remaining 40 percent will pursue "unskilled" jobs, because they dropped out of school or lack skills, while only 15 percent of jobs are considered "unskilled." (South Carolina Governor's Workforce Education Task Force, 2001)

Texas high schools also are beginning to implement Career Pathways programs. Fredericksburg High School has implemented outreach programs for off-campus experiences, work-based training, and mentoring programs related to Career Pathways. The successful program, now in its fifth year, was begun to help close the gap in achievement among at-risk students. As school officials note, "Career Pathways have succeeded in making school more meaningful and relevant to students ("At Texas school," 2001). Students design their classes and electives around their own Pathways choices and therefore are in classes not because their friends are, not because they have to be, but because it fits into their own purpose and plan. Fredrickburg's data clearly support the program's success, showing improved SAT scores and a rise in the number of students pursuing postsecondary options. Also, the students' 92% pass rate on the Texas Assessment of Academic Skills (TAAS) far surpasses the state's average of 78% ("At Texas school," 2001).

Action Research

To establish whether Pathways was successful in their own school districts, Michigan Intermediate School Districts (ISDs) have completed several action research projects. Following is a synopsis of data collected by Berrien County ISD (2001), reported in their annual education report, after they implemented a Career Pathways Model. Berrien County ISD serves 16 local districts that have from 60 to 6,000 students. It is a diverse county with rural, suburban, and urban districts. The data centers on four claim statements are measured from 1997–2001 and are shown in Table 1.5. Berrien's data positively reflect that Career Pathways, in line with the national trend data, better prepares students for college, postsecondary programs, and careers while increasing student connections to high school through both improved behavior (attendance) and academic achievement.

In Tuscola County, the Career Pathways Teacher Network conducted a survey on the students' perception of how school relates to their future (Tuscola Intermediate School District, 2003). Tuscola County is a semirural county located in the "Thumb" area of Michigan. It consists of nine local K–12 districts. The purpose of the survey was to

- determine if the program had an effect on students' connection to school and their future, and
- help districts understand where students need more connections.

Four districts participated in the survey. The survey was given to two groups of students: 9th-grade students who had taken the Freshman Explorations Career Pathways Class (the first step in our Pathways Model) and 10th-grade students who had not taken a Pathways course.

Eighteen questions were surveyed with results showing gains from 20 to 60% in every area measured. Table 1.6 offers a sampling of survey results.

These action research results are significant when you realize that students in the 9th and 10th grades, in districts that have only just begun to implement the Pathways System, are reflecting this type of knowledge.

TWO CLOSING SCENARIOS

Following are two examples of students we have encountered whose stories show an integration of the trends and research we have described in this chapter. As you read these samples, we are certain your own student stories will come to mind.

Our first story is about Pam's plumber. Bill was an average student in high school with good social skills and even better athletic skills. He went to college to play football, but that didn't work out as he had planned, although he did finish a four-year degree in sociology. Not finding a market for sociologists and not wanting to go on to earn a master's degree, Bill worked with a local plumber to earn money and pay back his student loans. Bill soon found out he was pretty good at this type of hands-on work. Even though he is not certified or licensed,

Table 1.5 Synopsis of Data Collected by Berrien County Intermediate School District

Claim Statement:
Career Pathways support enriched curricula and high academic standards.

Results:
- High school graduation requirements increased 15%.
- There was a steady increase of students taking an additional third and fourth year of high school mathematics and science.
- There was a substantial increase in the number of advanced placement (AP) course offerings.
- Integrated career-focused curricula have been developed and utilized in 14 schools, creating up to 212 new course offerings.

National References:
Aligning traditional curricula with programs that integrate career preparation into traditional coursework raises student achievement, as cited in the national studies "Choosing Success" (1999) and "School-to-Work" (2001).

Claim Statement:
Career Pathways students are better prepared to define career goals and make plans for their futures.

Results:
- There was a 500% increase in the enrollment of students in career technical education courses.
- There was a 117% increase in the number of students participating in applied learning experiences.

National References:
Students enrolled in Career Pathways believe that learning is meaningful, are more knowledgeable about career options, and may select additional schooling and training, thus remaining in school longer because of their career interests (Hughes, Bailey, & Mecheer 2001; "School-to-Work," 2001; "STW Reporter," 1998).

Claim Statement:
Career Pathways increase student performance and academic achievement.

Results:
- There was a 7.7% increase in the number of students attending a postsecondary program.
- The mean grade point average for all students Grades 9–12 increased.
- Overall high school attendance rates increased steadily.
- More students received endorsements on the Michigan Educational Assessment Program (MEAP) with a sixfold increase in math and a fivefold increase in science.

National References:
National trends have documented that Career Pathways curricula support and increase academic achievement, attendance rates, overall grade point averages, and graduation rates for high school students (Hughes et al., 2001; "School-to-Work," 2001).

(Continued)

Table 1.5 (Continued)

Studies have also indicated that Career Pathways System students are more motivated and engaged in schooling than their age peers due to the relevancy of the course content and career focus of the instructional activities ("School-to-Work," 2001; "Choosing Success," 1999; "STW Reporter," 1998).

Claim Statement:
Career Pathways prepare students for college, career, and the workplace of the future.

Results:
- There was an increase in the use of the workplace as a learning environment.
- There was a 33% increase in the connections between K–12 and postsecondary delivery systems.
- Career and employability skills standards and benchmarks were integrated throughout the K–12 curriculum.
- There was a 9% increase in the number of high school graduates attending postsecondary schools.

National References:
Students learning work-related skills such as job search strategies as part of their career program of studies are better prepared for the world of work and for postsecondary programs ("Choosing Success," 1999; Hughes et al., 2001).

Bill still does most of the plumbing work in our small town. He is good, reliable, and pleasant, and we need a plumber, so no one is terribly concerned about the details. When he works on construction sites, he works under a licensed plumber. No doubt Bill will earn his license one day, but right now he is making a good living for himself and his young family. He is 28 years old and just settling into a career. When he comes to work, we have great conversations about social issues and society; however, we pay Bill because he fixes the plumbing. If Bill had attended a Career Pathways High School, his experience would have been different. He could have pursued his interest in sociological processes while developing a skill. Bill could have participated in an apprenticeship program during his last two years of high school, giving him a head start in his career and the opportunity to be involved in labor and union issues. How can we recreate a different high school scenario for Bill?

Mila is a 35-year-old mother of two with a business degree. She had two business jobs, one in bookkeeping and one in data entry. While raising her small children, she had become involved with her church's youth group and realized that she really enjoyed and could relate to young people. Finding that she wanted to work with people, Mila decided to return to college to become a high school English teacher once her own children entered school. Mila, later in life, finally discovered that she only felt that she was making a contribution to society when she was working with youth. If Mila had attended a Career Pathways High School, her experience would also have been different. In Freshman Explorations, she would have realized that because of her personality and interests, she needed work that directly involved people, most likely in the human

Table 1.6   Tuscola County Survey Results

Student Question	Non-Pathways Students	Pathways Students
My teachers connect what they teach to the world of work or careers.	16%	74%
My teachers connect what I learn to my Career Pathway or my career interest and skills.	10%	63%
Things I learn at school will help me when I have a job or career.	45%	86%
My school provides opportunities to learn about skills used in work-related situations.	29%	77%
My school teaches work-related skills and has projects in problem solving, teamwork, technology, and employability skills.	28%	79%
My Career Pathway will be written in my portfolio or other school records.	22%	70%
My school teaches "people" skills such as problem solving, teamwork, presentation, and organization that will be useful on the job.	36%	84%
I have learned about a broad range of careers at school.	18%	80%
At my school we learn how to explore different careers and what it will take to have a career in a particular field.	17%	83%
I have had the opportunity to listen to workers in different career fields.	28%	75%
I know the type of careers that might be of interest to me based on my interests and abilities.	55%	87%

Note: From Tuscola Intermediate School District, 2003.

service area. In her sophomore and junior years, she could have explored a variety of human service careers (presumably working with youth) and would already have had a plan and direction by the time she entered college. Instead, at the age of 35, she is back in school working toward a second degree while raising two children.

We know every reader can add to this list of stories from his or her own experiences, and from those of family, friends, and students. The question is, how could we as educators have helped Mila and Bill do their explorations and use their high school experience to better prepare them for their future? Could we have saved them several years of economic instability and personal confusion? We believe the answer is yes.

IN REVIEW

- Career Pathways High Schools are learner-centered and self-directed; they require teachers to shift from being knowledge givers to knowledge facilitators.
- A Career Pathway is a broad spectrum of careers that share similar characteristics; the employment requirements for these careers call for common interests, strengths, and competencies. A successful grouping of Career Pathways must encompass the entire spectrum of career options.
- It is key for your school to choose the Pathways system that works best for you and your community.
- The purpose and mission of a Pathways High School is always in direct relationship to the concept of students as lifelong learners and drivers of their own educational processes.
- The mission of a Career Pathways High School is that every student will focus his or her high school education on a realistic postsecondary plan. In designing the plan, the skills, knowledge, and experience of the student must be considered so that students can successfully complete their plans and become productive citizens and global residents.
- Many major labor market trends in the past several decades have led to the establishment of governmental policies to connect academic and workforce learning.
- Research in the areas of adolescent development, brain-based learning, workforce development, and student surveys have all supported the success of the Career Pathways System.

Chapter Two

The Collaborative Career Pathways Model

SCENARIO: NICOLE'S PLAN

Nicole enters her high school years as a quiet girl who has a few close friends. She has average to good academic skills but is shy about the fact that she excels in science and math. Nicole is not competitive but likes to challenge herself. She is not at all sure what she wants to be when she grows up; she may be a teacher like her mom. Nicole takes Freshman Explorations with Jacob. Her experience is very different from his. She loves the flight simulator and designing her own flight school. In fact, she is so good at it that she is the only team member who can successfully takeoff and land a plane. For the first time, Nicole has found her niche. At the end of her freshman year, she chooses the Engineering, Science, and Aviation Pathway.

In her sophomore year, Nicole job shadows a pilot, an air-traffic controller, and an airplane mechanic. Her goal closes in on those "wings." Nicole's parents are excited about her enthusiasm and goals. The summer of her sophomore year, Nicole takes flying lessons and completes a small plane license—by the time she is 16 years old. In her junior year, Nicole enjoys an internship with a flight instructor at a small airport and develops a mentorship relationship. In her math class, Nicole presents her project on how geometry relates to flight. Nicole joins the track team. She knows that as a pilot, it is important for her to be physically fit. She also enjoys challenging herself to get faster and better at running. In government she learns about the judicial system by examining court cases concerning aviation regulations and does research to find out how the government works with the aviation industry.

In her final year of high school, Nicole does her senior project on designing an educational program for upcoming aviation students. She also takes an elective course in mechanics at a local community college to better understand the workings of machinery. Nicole has talked to and visited several flight schools during her junior and senior year and has talked to various branches of the armed forces. She applied to and was accepted at a university. In her senior year, however, Nicole decided to train as a pilot in the U.S. Air Force with the ultimate goal of becoming a flight instructor—we'd say she is well on her way.

MODEL STRUCTURE: THE THREE PILLARS

For students like Nicole and Jacob to reach their goals, they need a high school experience that connects three processes: classroom learning, comprehensive guidance and counseling, and community experiences. We call these the three C's, and they are the pillars of the Collaborative Career Pathways Model. The model is shown in Figure 2.1.

Shared leadership between administration, teacher, community, and students is the foundation of our model. Shared leadership does not mean that administration has no role or the strength to control important school processes. Leadership must still be the main

> *Solid and consistent leadership is the foundation of the model. This leadership must be shared among administration, staff, community, parents, and students.*

responsibility of the administration; however, the administration's primary focus is on the facilitation of a leadership and management process. Like the new teacher model, in a Pathways High School, administrators become the facilitators for leadership and not a "one-man show." This is a significant shift and requires the understanding of such techniques as horizontal versus vertical management. We no longer can exist in a top-down model; if we do, our students and teachers are set up to fail. We are looking at a site-based model in which everyone involved is part of the leadership team. Discipline and student management is not a punitive set of rules and regulations that takes up pages and pages of a student handbook with intricate systems of points and punishment. Rather, it is a system of conduct based on mutual respect and responsibility in which students and community have input into student management issues. Here the understanding of *Professional Learning Communities* management (DuFour & Eaker, 1998) is key to establishing a "shared" process. This process directly affects school culture and climate issues and is an essential process in a solid Pathways foundation.

Yet we cannot emphasize enough the importance of solid and consistent administrative leadership. As in all educational research regarding school leadership, the *principal* as facilitator plays the *pivotal role* in the development, implementation, evaluation, and continuation of an effective and efficient system (Cotton, 2000, p. 8). We have seen high schools revamped through the dedication of one principal, one counselor, and two veteran or lead teachers. We have perceived that sustained change falls directly on the ability of the principal to "hold it all together."

Figure 2.1 The Three C's in the Collaborative Pathways Model

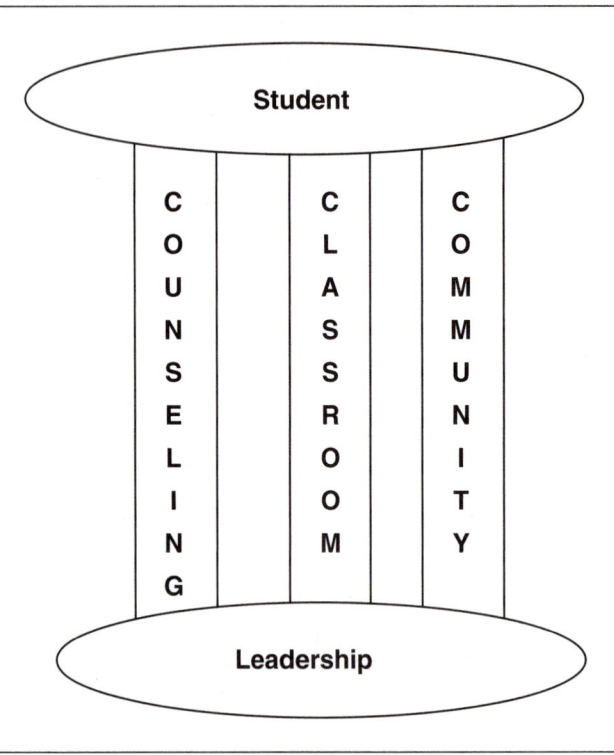

```
                    ┌─────────────────┐
                    │     Student     │
                    └─────────────────┘
                     │    │    │
                     C    C    C
                     O    L    O
                     U    A    M
                     N    S    M
                     S    S    U
                     E    R    N
                     L    O    I
                     I    O    T
                     N    M    Y
                     G
                    ┌─────────────────┐
                    │   Leadership    │
                    └─────────────────┘
```

The Counseling Pillar

The first pillar is the counseling process. In a traditional high school the counseling process runs parallel to instruction; students do not readily make a connection between the work they do with their counselors and what they are learning in the classroom.

Without a strong connection between counseling and classroom experiences, students will see little relevancy in what they are learning.

A comprehensive guidance program has three main areas of focus: academic development, career development, and personal and social development. Implementing a comprehensive guidance model in a Career Pathways High School is discussed in Chapter 5, but the main outcome of the counseling pillar is the completion of a "living" educational plan for every student. Each student, through his or her Pathways classes, will have time to explore and experiment in various career areas and will work together with Pathways teachers and counselors to develop a plan. The counseling process will be involved, inside and outside the classroom, in aptitude testing, personality profiling, interest inventories, learning styles, and so forth. This data will be intricately shared and used by the students and their teachers. All high school class offerings are placed in the proper Pathway(s). The counselor then works with students to build schedules that will help them reach their goals through appropriate class choices. Counselors and teachers will work together to make sure student goals and academic skills align for a successful transition from high school. The counselor will also play a key role as the liaison between the Pathway teacher and the community in building and maintaining work-based learning experiences.

The Classroom Pillar

The classroom, or the instructional process, is the "meat and potatoes" of any educational program. It is our philosophy that if it's not happening in the classroom, it's not happening. We have visited Career Pathways High Schools where teachers are not involved and do not even know that Pathways is happening in their buildings! If they have not been included in the process, how can they integrate into their classrooms important standards and skills necessary for students to make a successful Pathways transition?

In a Collaborative Pathways High School, teachers know how their content is used in the world outside the classroom. They are aware of recent brain research and prepare lessons to be compatible with brain processes using their school's identified Pathways as a theme. Teachers work together to develop interdisciplinary units, content learning, and authentic assessments that connect to real-world applications and processes. It is a major classroom shift and requires commitment, training, and coaching. The teacher now becomes a facilitator for self-directed learning. We address this instructional shift in Chapter 7 and Part III.

> *Here lies the distinction of the Collaborative Model: It is embedded in classroom instruction.*

The Community Pillar

As mentioned in Chapter 1, Susan Kovalik in her Integrated Thematic Instruction (ITI) Model states that "intelligence is a function of experience" (Kovalik, 1994, p. 1). In other words, it is through personal experience that we can acquire depth of understanding of what we are learning.

In essence, the community pillar is what provides the "reality" piece for students in our Pathways Model. It connects, in specific and structured ways, to how students interact with their community. Each year, community persons and industries are intricately woven into a student's experience. During freshman year, for example, many speakers visit the classroom, and group field trips will take place. During sophomore year, students will take smaller group field trips and experience several job shadows. During junior and senior years, students have professional mentors and are involved in internships,

> *The community pillar plays two major roles in the system: It gives students an avenue to try out their interests and aptitudes to develop and implement a realistic plan for their lives, and it uses the community to build support for students and the school.*

volunteer work experience, co-ops, apprenticeships, career technical training, and so on. Every exiting senior will present a senior project to an advisory committee composed of Pathways professionals, teachers, administrators, fellow students, and board members. People in the community—parents, board members, chamber representatives, small business owners, large business representatives, pastors, and so on—fill all of the committee's roles.

The community pillar is an excellent fit with the research concerning at-risk adolescent behaviors. It provides an opportunity for structured experiences that connect students with positive adult role models. The systematic implementation of this pillar is often left out of a Pathways model because we, as educators, are uncomfortable with reaching outside of our domain. Expanding our boundaries are well worth the effort, and sharing student learning and success with the community is a wonderful experience for both educators and community members.

Table 2.1   The Vertical Counseling Process

Grade 9
Interest and aptitude testing
Begin the Educational Development Plan (EDP) and portfolio building
Academic support
Career development
Personal and social skills
Adolescent crisis issues

Grade 10
EDP and portfolio development
Academic support
Career development
Personal and social skills
Adolescent crisis issues

Grade 11
EDP and portfolio development
Begin postsecondary plans
Career development
Academic support
Personal and social skills
Adolescent crisis issues

Grade 12
Portfolio presentation
Applications
Scholarships
Visitations
Academic support
Personal and social skills
Adolescent crisis issues

IMPLEMENTING THE THREE PILLARS

When implementing the three pillars of counseling, classroom, and community, the process must be looked at from both vertical and horizontal perspectives.

Counseling

The counseling process begins with specifically identified activities and skills to be completed and learned in each grade. This book gives you a process for the counseling pillar in Grades 9 through 12; each school, however, must place its counseling needs where they fit best for their students. (See Table 2.1.)

> *Keep in mind that the counseling and personal skills needed to have a good high school experience are skills that transfer to the workplace.*

Classroom

The classroom is the most complicated process to implement because of it includes many factors. When implementing classroom processes, one must deal with personalities, disciplines, teaching styles, and assessment practices. We cannot emphasize enough that without Pathways connections in the classroom, students will not be able to practice important skills and connect their learning to their lives. Therefore, it is extremely important to understand the classroom pillar processes.

To connect the three components of Pathways, core, and elective classes, it is vital that teachers work together in teams to develop lessons that connect (Figure 2.2). This is explained in detail in other chapters.

It is imperative that the flow of instruction be broad at the freshman level and become more specific at each higher level as a student moves toward his or her senior year. Each year adds a new dimension of self along with academic skills, technology, workplace skills, career exploration, and postsecondary planning.

> ***The classroom process, often referred to as instructional processes, has three components:***
>
> ***Pathways Classes:*** *These classes are designed for each grade level to develop and implement students' individual Career Pathways Educational Plan. (Pathways Classes are detailed in Chapter 7.)*
>
> ***Core Classes:*** *These classes continue to teach their subject matter, reinforcing skills learned in the Pathways Classes (teaming, problem solving, and self-management), while utilizing students' interests and aptitudes to reinforce their subject matter with (students' Pathway plans).*
>
> ***Elective Classes:*** *These classes are chosen to coincide with students' interest, aptitude, and plan. They are necessary additions to students' broad concept of the world while enhancing their appreciation of the arts.*

This means that each pillar must have a consistent flow from grades 9 through 12 (vertical) while being integrated with one another (horizontal). To make this clearer, let's look at each vertical process separately.

Figure 2.2 Connecting the Three Components of Pathways Collaboration

Grade 9 →

**Pathways Class:
Freshman Explorations**

- Study skills
- Teaming
- Goal setting
- Self-exploration
- Pathway exploration
- Self-management
- Conflict resolution
- Technical skills: use, transfer, and application of technology

↔

Required	Electives

Grade 10 →

**Pathways Class:
Sophomore Selections**

- Career research
- Career laddering
- Decision making
- Employability skills
- Technical skills: use, transfer, and application of technology in Pathways

↔

Required	Electives

Grade 11 →

Pathways Class: Junior Judgments

- Ethics
- People skills
- Government regulations
- Anger management
- Technical writing
- Time management
- Stress management
- Technical skills: use, transfer, and application of technology in the workplace

↔

Required	Electives

Grade 12 →

Pathways Class: Senior Transitions

- People skills
- Presentation skills
- Applications
- Capstone project
- Portfolio completion
- Technical skills: use, transfer, and application of technology in the workplace

↔

Required	Electives

There must be collaboration among the teachers who teach each grade level (e.g., Grade 9) as well as teachers who teach each subject (e.g., English). For example the 9th-grade teachers work

> *Every new grade level dimension for students requires collaboration among teaching staff.*

together to develop teaming and problem-solving skill units across the curriculum. At the same time, the English department develops identified grade-level skills throughout their units 9 through 12. This English team may develop a unit on problem solving in the 9th grade and goal setting in the 10th grade, both of which are integrated with the year's literature readings. This collaboration takes time and communication and is best implemented by a central curriculum person(s) within the district.

Community

To coincide with the counseling and classroom pillar, the community pillar, as previously mentioned, has structured activities for each year of a student's high school experience. These activities match what is happening in the counseling and classroom processes. The counselor and the teacher, working together to make the necessary community connections, integrate the community pillar into the classroom experience of a student. In some schools, the principal or assistant principal aides in this process. There are a few schools that have the advantage of a Career Pathways coordinator position; this person coordinates all community-based activities. This is ideal but not always possible. We have been surprised to see how many of our teachers do an excellent job making community connections while maintaining their classroom facilitation. We were afraid this job would be too much of an "add on" for teachers; however, many enjoy the contacts and are better able to make academic connections for their students because of them. The structured community or work-based experience for each year takes place out of the Pathways classroom and is indicated by a bold heading in Table 2.2 (individual community activities are explained in more detail in Chapter 13).

Table 2.2 offers wonderful venues for specific, structured experiences to connect the community with students. These venues start with general experiences and move toward more focused activities, each building on the skills of the previous experience. When we first began doing school-to-work activities, so many of our business and community people wanted to be involved but didn't know where to start or what to do. With a structured year-by-year process, community members can pick and choose what they are comfortable with and what they can afford to provide. For example, people at one business may feel they are too small to provide a site visit but are comfortable being a job shadowing site or serving on a board for a senior project. Some industries enjoy doing site visits for small groups of students but because of confidentiality issues are unable to do the more intense shadowing or intern work. This guide gives parents, business and industry, community members, and even retirees specific areas in which they can choose to work with students of different ages and with different career interests.

Table 2.2 Vertical Community Processes

Grade 9
Instructional partners
Pathways guests
Special guests
Site visit hosts
Chat partners
Community organizations

Grade 10
Interview partners
Job-shadowing hosts
Instructional partners
Pathway-specific guests
Community organizations

Grade 11
Internship hosts
Workplace colleagues
Service learning sites
Postsecondary links

Grade 12
Senior project board
Service learning
Community sites for senior projects
Postsecondary links
Pathway mentors and advisors

HORIZONTALLY INTEGRATING THE PILLARS

The ultimate goal of the implementation of the Collaborative Career Pathways Model is the integration of all three pillars at each level of a student's experience Grades 9 through 12. This integration combines for the students their concept of self, work and career skills, academic and technology skills, and real-life experiences. It is important that everyone working within the system understands that the integration of the three pillars allows for students to

1. learn what is necessary to be successful outside of school and
2. have a chance to practice those skills on a regular basis.

Each grade level has key skills and activities in these areas with a specifically designed student outcome for each year.

The key to implementing the Collaborative Model successfully is to integrate the counseling, classroom, and community pillars in a way that gives students a consistent and relevant education to focus their learning while creating a postsecondary plan.

The integration, skills, and outcomes are related in the grade-level charts (Figures 2.3–2.6) and explanations that follow.

Grade 9

The key skills identified and integrated in Grade 9 are the following:

- Study skills
- Teaming
- Goal setting
- Self-exploration
- Pathway exploration
- Self-management
- Conflict resolution
- Use of technology in exploration

The counselor will work in freshman classrooms to administer and explain interest and aptitude testing, teach and practice conflict-resolution skills, and implement a character education framework. The Pathways classes then concentrate on practicing and applying those skills. This is done through team-integrated Pathways projects. These skills are supported in the core and elective classrooms and even extracurricular activities. Let's take teaming for an example. Most of our schools have a teaming process that the faculty has developed and set. Teaming procedures are done the same in all classrooms. All classrooms have posted team procedures, rules, and steps for conflict resolution. The staff has been in-serviced on teaching and practicing teamwork (vs. grouping students) not only in the classroom but also among themselves (see Chapter 7). Teaming concepts are used in science to conduct experiments. The science teachers make proper teaming part of the assessment for student scientific research and experiments. In a speech class, one of our high schools uses the six Pathways as the theme for six types of speeches. Peer teams are used to evaluate student presentations. Teaming can also be taught and reinforced in athletics, marching band, and academic clubs. The community involves themselves in the process through working in Pathways and other classrooms to give realistic input into career explorations and in hosting site visits for students to see careers and teaming in action. Guest speakers and instructors visit the classroom and teach students about teaming in the workplace. The same process is used for study skills, technology integration, and so on. The horizontal alignment in Grade 9 is shown in Figure 2.3.

As previously mentioned, each year has an identified outcome for the students. The entire 9th-grade student experience, through the integration of counseling, classroom, and community, enables the students to have the knowledge, background, and experience to choose a Career Pathway. This Career Pathway complements who they are, what they like to do, and what they are good at doing.

The outcome of Grade 9 is that each student chooses a Career Pathway to focus his or her high school program.

Figure 2.3 Grade 9 Alignment

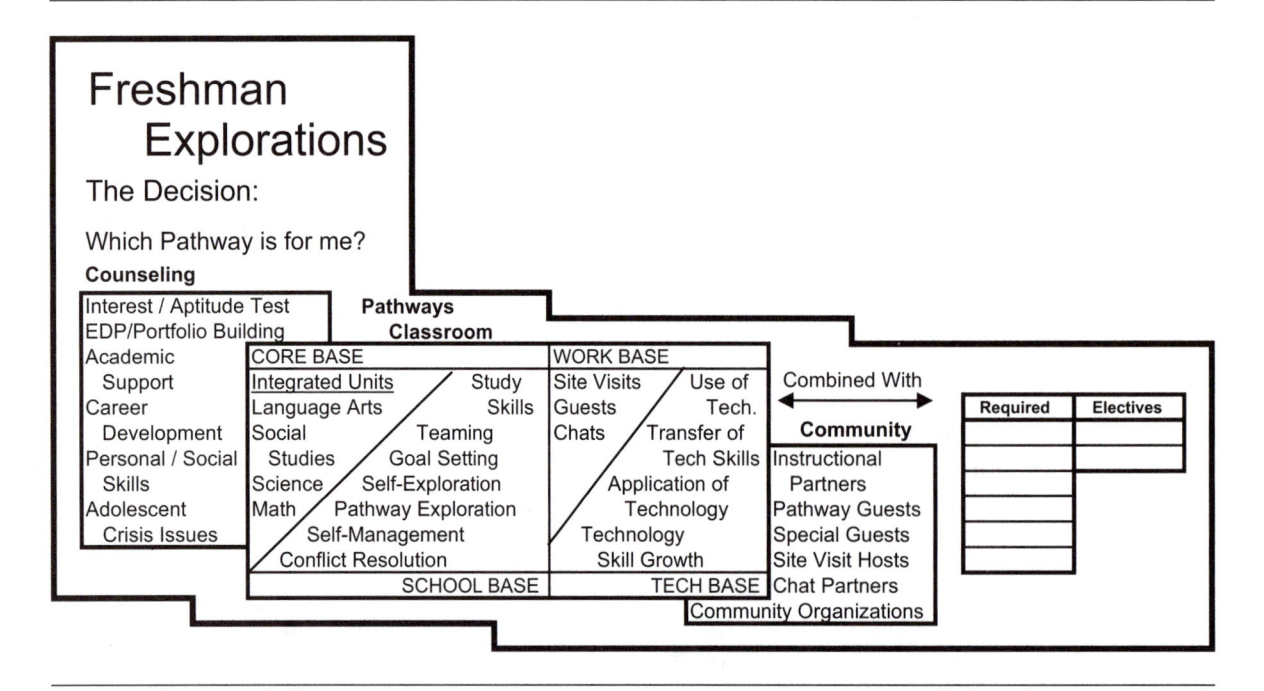

```
Freshman
   Explorations
The Decision:
Which Pathway is for me?
Counseling
Interest / Aptitude Test          Pathways
EDP/Portfolio Building            Classroom
Academic          CORE BASE            WORK BASE
  Support        Integrated Units / Study    Site Visits / Use of      Combined With    Required  Electives
Career           Language Arts  / Skills    Guests       / Tech.
  Development    Social       / Teaming     Chats      / Transfer of   Community
Personal / Social  Studies   / Goal Setting           / Tech Skills    Instructional
  Skills         Science  / Self-Exploration       / Application of      Partners
Adolescent       Math  / Pathway Exploration       / Technology        Pathway Guests
  Crisis Issues      / Self-Management             / Technology         Special Guests
                   / Conflict Resolution          / Skill Growth        Site Visit Hosts
                        SCHOOL BASE               TECH BASE             Chat Partners
                                                                        Community Organizations
```

Grade 10

The key skill areas identified in 10th grade are the following:

- Career research
- Career laddering
- Decision making
- Employability skills
- Use of technology in employability skills

The students work on systems and processes with the outcome of further developing their educational plan and portfolio. Student teams work together in their chosen Pathway doing intensive interviews and technology-integrated projects. The curriculum supports through core and elective classes the chance to practice and apply goal setting and decision making and Career Pathway exploration through assignments and team projects. Technical writing and presentations using technology may be integrated with the language arts class. Research in history or science may be related to famous persons within a student's Pathway. Geometry teachers may use a decision-making model to coincide with the solving of proofs and connect geometry to different Career Pathways such as aviation, carpentry, and architecture. The community pillar offers job-shadowing opportunities through the Sophomore Selections class, giving students a true picture of a number of careers within their Pathway. Community members also participate in intensive interviews with students and student teams. Speakers and guest instructors are used in the classroom to reinforce teacher lessons on employability skills. The 10th-grade pillar alignment is shown in Figure 2.4.

Figure 2.4 Grade 10 Alignment

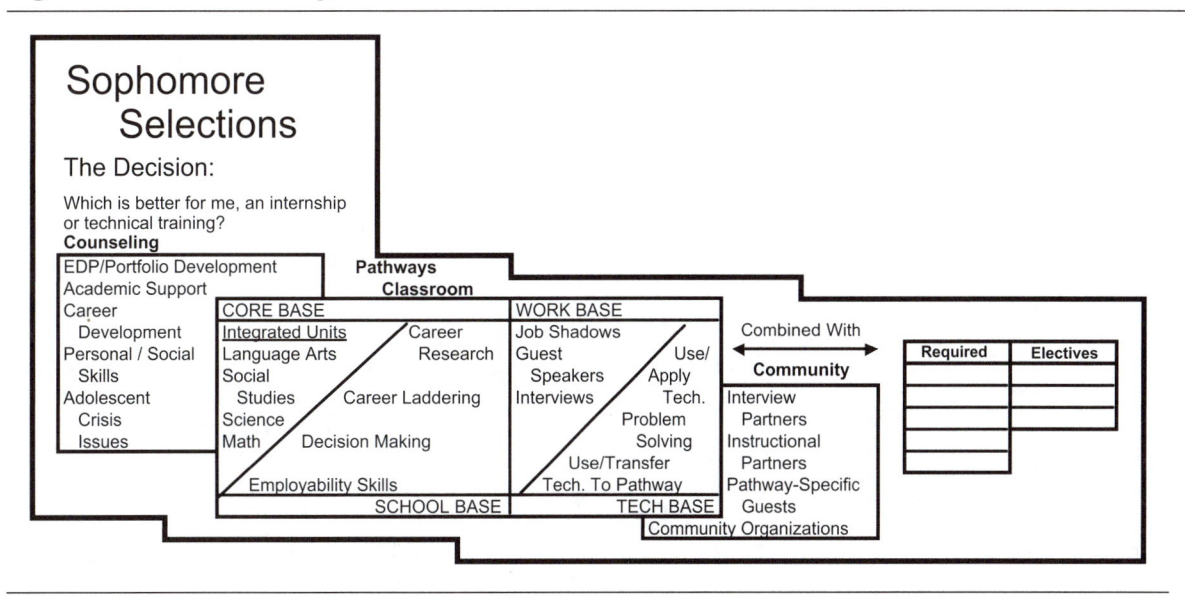

```
Sophomore Selections
The Decision:
Which is better for me, an internship or technical training?
Counseling
  EDP/Portfolio Development          Pathways Classroom
  Academic Support
  Career          CORE BASE                    WORK BASE                Combined With
    Development  Integrated Units  Career      Job Shadows    Use/
  Personal/Social  Language Arts   Research    Guest          Apply     Community      Required    Electives
    Skills         Social                      Speakers       Tech.
  Adolescent        Studies    Career Laddering Interviews   Problem    Interview
    Crisis         Science                                    Solving    Partners
    Issues         Math    Decision Making                    Use/Transfer  Instructional
                                                              Tech. To Pathway  Partners
                     Employability Skills                                Pathway-Specific
                              SCHOOL BASE              TECH BASE         Guests
                                                      Community Organizations
```

The focus of the 10th grade is to prepare students for internship experiences in Grade 11. The background and practice students receive in goal setting, decision making, employability skills, and the experience of job shadows *must* prepare them to make an internship choice that will benefit their studies and postsecondary plan.

> *The outcome of Grade 10 is the preparation of students to choose and successfully complete a relevant internship in Grade 11 or to enter a career-technical or apprentice program.*

Grade 11

The 11th grade sees a significant shift from the learning and practice of skills to the beginning of student transitioning and site-based learning. Counselors begin to work with students on examining postsecondary options and preparing for state and national exams such as the ACT and SAT (American College Test and the Scholastic Assessment Test). It is at this time that students can choose an internship or a career-technical program or apprenticeship. These options will depend on what programs are available to your students.

Here in Michigan, all of our county schools have the advantage of being connected to a career-technical center. Schools south of us have the wonderful opportunity to participate in training programs in the auto industry that are held in manufacturing plants. Many schools will need to develop these connections with postsecondary institutions, business, and industry. The internships are coordinated from the Junior Judgments classroom and follow the guidelines of a traditional cooperative (co-op) education program. Placements are made in areas related to a student's goal, and students move in and out of the classroom, working together to solve workplace problems and concerns. Key skills identified in the 11th grade are the following:

Figure 2.5 Grade 11 Alignment

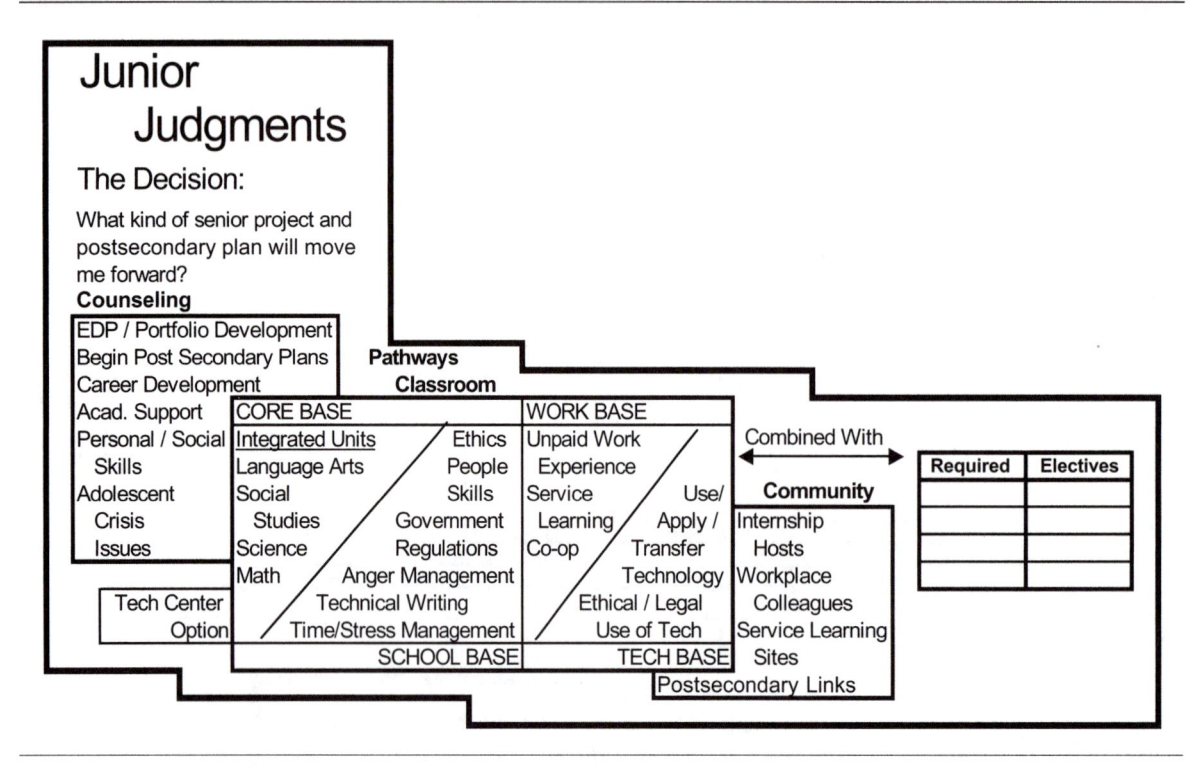

Junior Judgments

The Decision:
What kind of senior project and postsecondary plan will move me forward?

Counseling
- EDP / Portfolio Development
- Begin Post Secondary Plans
- Career Development
- Acad. Support
- Personal / Social Skills
- Adolescent Crisis Issues

Tech Center Option

Pathways Classroom

CORE BASE
- Integrated Units
- Language Arts
- Social Studies
- Science
- Math
- Ethics
- People Skills
- Government Regulations
- Anger Management
- Technical Writing
- Time/Stress Management

SCHOOL BASE

WORK BASE
- Unpaid Work Experience
- Service Learning
- Co-op
- Use/Apply/Transfer
- Ethical / Legal Use of Tech

TECH BASE

Combined With

Community
- Internship Hosts
- Workplace Colleagues
- Service Learning Sites
- Postsecondary Links

Required	Electives

(EDP = Educational Development Plan)

- Ethics
- People skills
- Government regulations
- Anger management
- Technical writing
- Time and stress management
- Use of technology in workplace and in writing

For example, science teachers may examine with Pathways students how the government is involved in protection programs from environment to health issues. The social studies teacher can examine ethics in government, specific court cases that relate to the Pathways, and the consequences of governmental decisions. In the workplace, students will be involved in the use of technology as it relates to their career. This must also be reinforced in core and elective classrooms. The community provides an extensive service in generating positive internships and developing mentor relationships with students. Business mentors have been able to give our students many "pearls of wisdom" that they would not have accepted from parents and teachers. They make remarkable guides and have had significant impact on the futures of our students. It is at this time that Pathway Advisory Committees work with teams of students to help them make successful connections and plans for their transition from high school. The 11th-grade alignment is shown in Figure 2.5.

The outcome of the 11th grade is significant. Students are now, through their own experiences and information passed on to them through mentors, narrowing down their Pathway to a career choice. They are aware of the skills, training time, and actual duties of the careers they have explored. They have begun to gain realistic expectations and plans. They are in control of their own educational processes. Educators, counselors, and community members are now the facilitators and mentors for their own plans, goals, and dreams.

> *The main outcome of Grade 11 is students' readiness to develop a senior project and to implement their educational decisions.*

Grade 12

The senior year is all about transitions. By Grade 12, a student's coursework should be specific to his or her Pathway plan and experiences. We have guided students from a broad understanding of self and career to a narrowed, focused, personalized course of action. Each class and assignment should tie in to the student's individual plan. During their senior year, students will complete their portfolios and through the use of technology have their portfolio in a presentable format. They will make applications, visit postsecondary sites, and complete scholarship searches. Many will complete their career-technical program or have two years completed in an apprenticeship. Some students may be certified in computer software or as nurse's aides, for example. The major event of senior year is the presentation of senior projects, which are integrated with students' career choices. It may be a service learning project, a research project, or product or process that they have designed. Teachers will be involved in helping seniors in the disciplines that directly relate to their career choice and senior project. The community will continue to act as mentors and will serve on presentation boards. The students will also have connections to their postsecondary choice. These connections can be made through virtual trips, distance-learning opportunities, visitations, dual enrollment, mentors from the site or program, or even a pen pal or e-mail connection—the possibilities are endless. In their senior year, students is will have a concrete connection to their first step out of high school. The senior alignment is shown in Figure 2.6.

We do not stop here, however. We feel it is our responsibility to have given the proper skills, guidance, and experiences to enable every one of our students to complete his or her program of study successfully and to be in a position of

Figure 2.6 Grade 12 Alignment

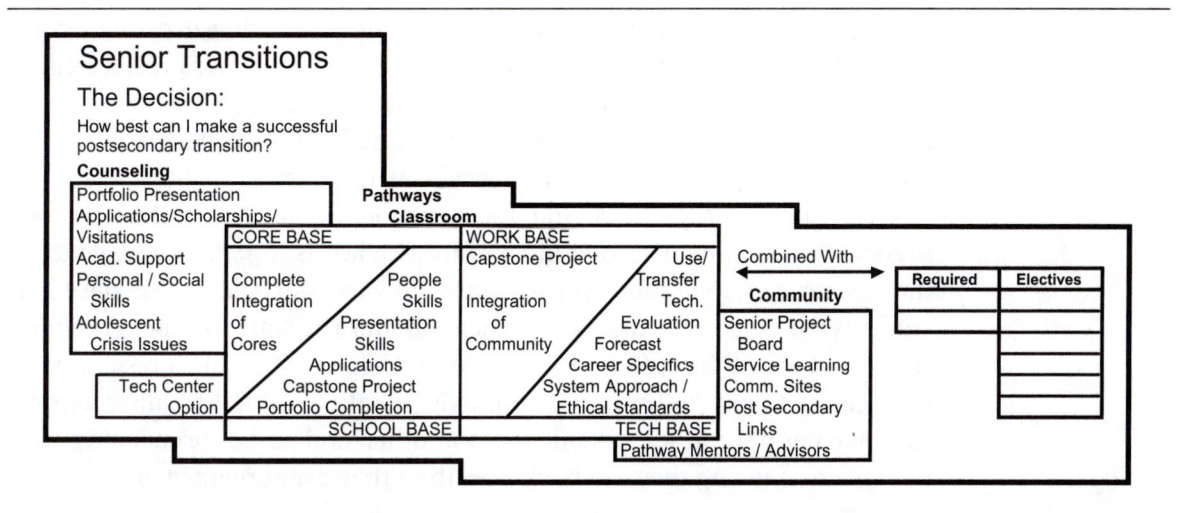

> *The outcome of Grade 12 is a successful transition from high school to a postsecondary choice.*

gainful employment within fives years of completing high school. It is also our responsibility to track and keep data on all our students. We must generate reports on our findings to be brought back to the board and administration for good policymaking decisions. These data must be used to improve instruction, guidance programs, and community connections.

PUTTING IT ALL TOGETHER: THE COMPLETE IMPLEMENTATION CHART

In looking at the complete implementation chart one can see both the vertical and horizontal alignment of the three pillars. (See Figure 2.7)

Students as the Center of Learning

In a Collaborative Career Pathways Model, the shift is always to the student as learner. The purpose is twofold:

1. The achievement of high academic skills

2. The development and implementation of a realistic postsecondary plan.

In a Career Pathways High School all teachers share the information in a student's plan. In one of our high schools, a sheet is developed and distributed to all teachers to update them on what each student has experienced that year. The freshman sheet includes the individual student's personality profile, learning style, aptitude scores, dominant intelligence score, and Pathways choice. The sophomore sheet includes their job-shadowing experiences; the junior sheet, the internship; and the senior sheet, their senior project outline. This information is extremely helpful to teachers in relating to students, focusing assignments to interest and aptitude, and helping students grow in areas that may be difficult for them but important to their goals.

> *How our students perform when they leave our high schools must drive how we implement the three pillars of classroom, counseling, and community.*

A student can go back and redo experiences such as site visits, job shadows, or even do a second internship. The key is to help the students do the necessary exploration during their high school years. We have had students whose parents have taken them all over the state to experience a job shadow in a new field. One of our parents took her student to a site several hours away to look at the career of making dentures. What we have found is that one connection leads students to another and so on, broadening their horizons and giving them more choices than they ever dreamed of.

Figure 2.7 The Complete Pathways Implementation Chart

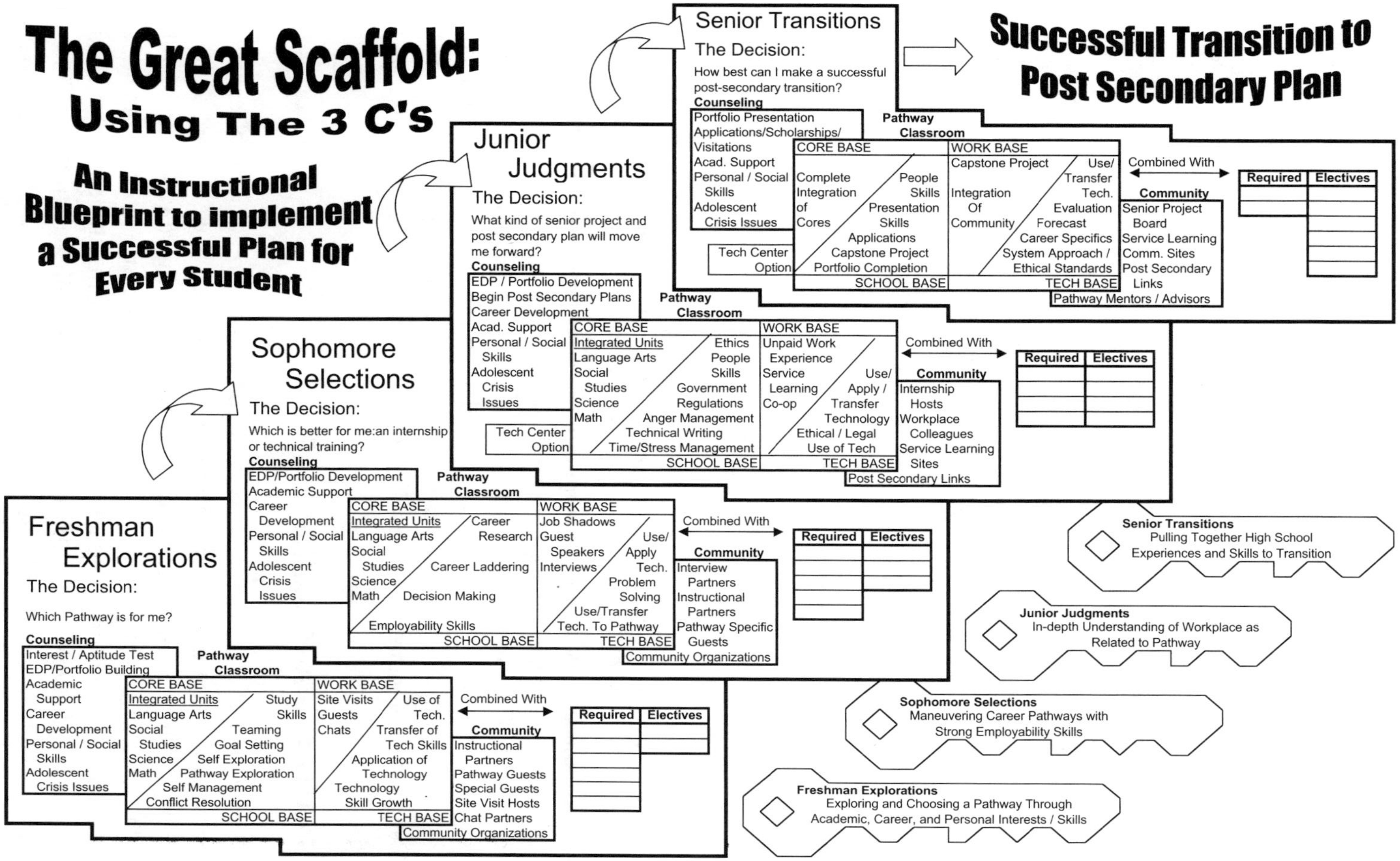

Figure 2.8 Student Educational Web

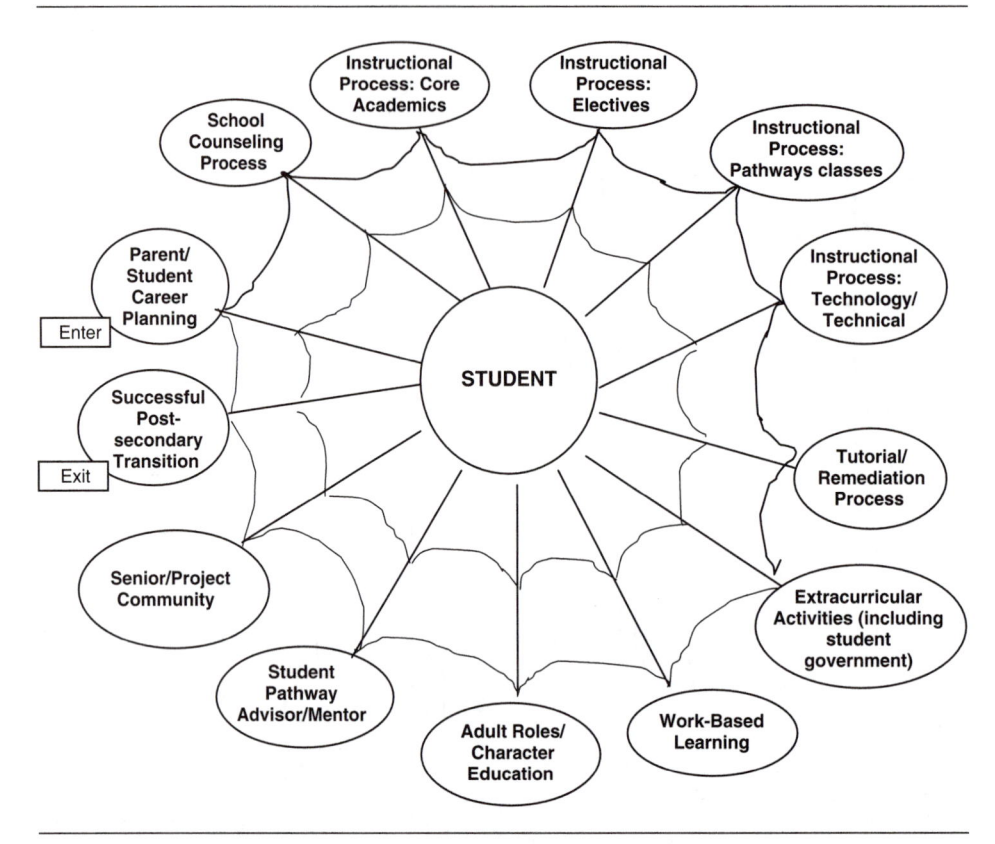

We have designed a student web to help you visualize the student as the center of the implementation process (Figure 2.8). This web will show how the pillars affect the students' education in different areas that they encounter in their school experience. Along with the web is a glossary that defines each student area. The web and glossary (see Figure 2.8 and Table 2.3) illustrate that the student is the center of his or her high school experiences. It also demonstrates that all the components of a high school experience will "catch" all students, thus eliminating the cracks into which many of our students fall.

PATHWAYS AND CITIZENSHIP

As we leave the subject of horizontal and vertical integration of curriculum, counseling, and the classroom we would be remiss if we did not address the thread of citizenship that runs through the Collaborative Model. In our mission statement on Pathways, we talk about citizenship and global residency. Good citizenship is a natural outcome of properly preparing students for their future.

In the Collaborative Pathways Model, student life planning and citizenship are not separated but addressed through integration and practice of personal skills at each level. All of the Pathways Class coursework, reinforced by the core and elective curricula, is involved with citizenship and the practice of skills needed to be an active part of a community or government. The key citizenship skills that are interwoven into the Pathways curriculum are shown in Table 2.4.

Table 2.3 Glossary for Student Web

Process	Definition
Parent and student career planning	In a Pathways Model, student and parent career planning begins with entering freshmen choosing their classes. The process has a formal structure using an educational development plan (EDP). It is different from the process in other high schools because it is accessible to the student through Pathways classes, and the information on the EDP is shared with academic teachers and used in instructional planning.
School counseling process	The school counseling process involves the counselor working with students, parents, and teachers to link instruction to career goals and postsecondary plans. The counseling is involved not only in student testing (i.e., ACT, ASVAB, etc.) and college applications but with the Pathways teachers in both student self-knowledge and work-based experiences.
Instructional process: core academics	Core academic subjects in a high school teach content using cross-content and content standards, thematic instruction, and authentic assessment. Classes are designed to build necessary knowledge and skills through student interest and attributes.
Instructional process: Pathways classes	Pathways Classes are what complete the Pathways High School instructional process. These classes are designed for every year of a student's high school progression to add depth to and help narrow a student's goals and to ensure high school success. Pathways classes add the glue that holds together the larger goals of the entire curriculum—the adult roles such as team worker, problem solver, and self-manager combined with the actual work-based learning experiences.
Instructional process: tutorial	The tutorial processes are the structured processes that a high school has set for the students who are not able to meet the standards set for academic success.
Instructional process: electives	Electives are important in any high school because they give students a chance to broaden their view of the world and to delve deeper into their interests and attributes. In a Pathways school, electives are designed for each Pathway to give students an opportunity to experience more areas and find further success in their educational experience. Such programs as physical education, music, art, and drama add to student career and employability skills through building responsibility, team work, presentation skills, personal health, and so on, while developing important skills for understanding the human experience.
Instructional process: technology and technical	All Pathways classes in the Collaborative Pathways Model use technical processes in their instructional base. Students work together in teams or individually using cameras, computers, software, simulations, and other

(Continued)

Table 2.3 (Continued)

	equipment to research, develop, and present information and systems.
Extracurricular activities	Extracurricular activities in a Pathways Model extend the role of the elective program. The schools, through Pathways advisory committees, teachers, administrators, parents, and students, make sure there are extracurricular clubs, activities, and connections to the school for each designated Pathway.
Work-based learning experiences	Work-based learning experiences are structured throughout the Pathways High School and are directly connected to the classroom. Work-based learning opportunities are never done in isolation from the learning process or from each other and connect to a student's goal and to positive community and adult role models. Examples of work-based learning include guest speakers visits, field trips, job shadowing, mentorships, internships, volunteer work, paid and unpaid work experience, service learning, and senior projects.
Adult roles and cross-curricular standards	In a Pathways High School, curriculum is focused and includes adult role models as set by the state or school improvement plan. This identified and agreed-on set of skills moves curriculum to a higher level and enables the connecting of all disciplines and learning. Examples of adult roles (from the Michigan Curriculum Framework) are literate individuals, involved citizens, productive workers, responsible family members, and healthy and fit people.
Student Pathways advisory committees and mentors	Every designated Pathway in a high school has an advisory committee composed of professionals in that field as well as postsecondary representatives and teachers. Their role is to mentor students and help provide, through networking, the necessary work-based learning experiences. They also have a key role in serving on senior project panels.
Senior projects and community and service learning	Every senior in a Collaborative Pathways High School is responsible for an exit project. This project can range in focus from student vocational organization projects to service learning. All projects must be within a student's Pathway and integrated with technology. Each student is assigned a senior project panel and works with the senior focus teacher.
Successful postsecondary transition	Throughout their high school career, students continually work on their postsecondary plan. These plans include contacting, visiting, and talking to representatives from various post-secondary options. Students are surveyed their first and fifth year out of high school to provide feedback and to make sure their plan is successful thus far.

Note: ACT = American College Test; ASVAB = Armed Services Vocational Aptitude Battery; EDP = Educational Development Plan.

Table 2.4 Key Citizenship Skills in the Pathways Program

Level	Skill	Sample
Freshman	• Responsibility • Making choices • Social awareness	An example of these skills is in the arts and communications unit, in which students must choose a social issue and, using technology, design and present a public service announcement.
Sophomore	• Problem solving • Making informed decisions • Communication skills • Research skills	In the sophomore problem-solving unit, students must identify and use a problem-solving method to solve a social problem. This problem can be school, community, or nationally based. The solution to their problem must be shared with the appropriate audience. For example, a team of students is looking at the problem of water pollution in the nearby wetlands. They design their solutions and discuss them with the local Department of Natural Resources officer and write letters to their congressional representatives.
Junior	• Rules, regulations, and policies • Working within a given structure • Chain of command • Ethical decision making • Confidentiality • Value of self in the community • Gender-equity issues	In the junior year students must examine the rules, regulations, policies, government regulations, and chain of command at their internship experience. They look into how the government interacts with their chosen Pathway or Cluster. For example, how is confidentiality protected in the health field? These findings are then incorporated into the internship presentation given at the end of the class.
Senior	• Giving back to the community through service or volunteering	We have designed into the senior capstone project a "giving back" experience where students give back to the community that supported them during their high school years. This could include volunteer work at the local hospital, park beautification, and so on. This "giving back" is connected to the students' future plans, giving them needed experience, while helping them to experience the rewards of giving to others and to their community.

Interacting with the community also lends support to citizenship. When adolescents only see their community as a "watch dog" and not as a part of their growth, rifts can occur. Positive interaction with their community is the best way for students to understand that their community cares and also how communities and government serve their citizens. It is through real-world experiences and community interactions that adolescents see and learn how citizenship really works.

PATHWAYS MYTHS

The purposes (high achievement and realistic postsecondary plan) of a learner-centered Collaborative Pathways Model are directly related to two myths concerning Pathways High Schools that must be addressed:

- Myth 1: Pathways High Schools track students into jobs.
- Myth 2: Pathways High Schools diminish the importance of the disciplines and academic rigor.

Both of these myths could not be further from the truth. *Never* in a Pathways High School is the focus on jobs—it is on careers and career awareness, and this is the big difference between Pathways and traditional programs. Jobs (e.g., a pilot, a nurse, and so on) are a single-minded, narrow focus; careers are broad and expose students to hundreds of jobs that have similar traits and abilities (e.g., opportunities in aviation, opportunities in medicine). For additional information on Pathways myths, see Chapter 12.

> *What a Pathways High School does do is broaden student choices through planned and actual experiences and coursework, allowing students to make informed decisions on their future based on interest, ability, academic performance, personal experience, financial dictates, future markets, and desired location.*

Instead of narrowing down their future to a few jobs with which they may be familiar (what their parents, family, and neighbors may do for a living) a Pathways System gives *all* students a broad look at the future. It then helps them, year by year, to narrow the goal (through coursework and experience) to create a realistic yet ambitious plan for their own future. In the end, the direction, the goal, and the path become their own quest; Thus students are more likely to succeed. As the data have already shown, students with a goal have half of what they will need to complete a postsecondary program successfully; high academic achievement completes the puzzle.

The second myth is that Pathways High Schools sacrifice academic rigor by watering down their curriculum so that all students can achieve. This could not be further from the truth.

> *When the Pathways Model is implemented correctly, students will perform better, and more of them will take higher-level courses.*

Why? Because they see the need for the work they have to do. None of us wants to do work that has no value to us in the end. When we work with teachers, they can gain a better understanding of this when we discuss their graduate courses.

How many of them take the easiest route to get what they need to go up the pay scale? How many are frustrated with classes they have to take in their planned program for which they see no relevancy? How many of us just pay the tuition without much class enthusiasm because we want to be on the next pay step? Why do we think our students are any different from us? Of course they are going to take the easiest route through high school; they see no reason to do differently. In a Pathways Model, students understand why they are taking the coursework they are taking: because it directly relates to *their* goals. Assignments and course studies are directed toward their interest and aptitudes.

For example, let's take a 9th-grade history class. The unit is on the Civil War. Projects are centered on a Career Cluster, and students are teamed by interest. One group of students interested in the health field may research and present mistakes and breakthroughs that were made in the medical field during the war. Business students may look at industry versus agriculture, and human service students could examine reconstruction programs. Do students learn about the Civil War? Yes. Are they more likely to be engaged and to retain what they have learned? Yes. Other examples include environmental issues, court cases and the judicial system, novels, algebraic equations (which are used by engineers and nurses), and so forth.

Wow! Here again are two processes. These paradigm shifts must be addressed. Most teachers have not used their content in jobs outside the classroom and are therefore uncomfortable making this connection for students. Many traditional high school teachers have only presented content chapter by chapter as in their textbook, teaching only for knowledge and not for depth of understanding,

> *The key here is twofold:*
>
> 1. *Teachers must understand how their content is used outside the classroom.*
>
> 2. *Content must be prepared and presented within themes and connected to the world outside the classroom.*

connections to other subjects, or application. This is a reason students in Pathways High Schools tend to score better on state exams. Many of the state assessment programs require students to apply content and processes, therefore assuming students know and understand content. We talk about programs and ways these issues can be addressed in future chapters.

CONCLUSION

When implementing a Career Pathways Model, it is important to examine and structure your pillars to form a system (or web) for students. Implementation must occur across your curriculum for Grades 9 through 12 and from subject to subject. We must be certain that students understand and connect their academic skills and their interests and aptitudes to a postsecondary focus. We must also address the training needs of our faculty and the community to make the system work. In the chapters that follow, we give you skills and examples to make your "path" to implementing a Pathways Model successful.

IN REVIEW

- The foundation of a successful Career Pathways system is consistent, shared, and focused leadership.
- The three pillars of a Pathways High School are Counseling, Classroom, and Community.
- The three pillars must be aligned vertically (from Grades 9 through 12) and horizontally (subject by subject).
- The Pathways system must create a web for all student activities and learning to prevent any student from falling through the cracks.
- Two myths of Pathways Systems that must be dispelled with your faculty and community are
  - Pathways "track" students into jobs.
  - Pathways waters down academics.
- Good citizenship is a natural outcome of properly preparing students for their futures.
- Successfully implementing a Career Pathways Model requires concise alignment and training for the people involved in each pillar.

Chapter Three

Steps to Implementing the Model

SCENARIO: A COMMUNITY MEMBER'S STORY

Pete is an active community and business member and is extremely supportive of his local school district. From the beginning, he was an involved parent looking for school reform, but he felt like making changes, even in small ways, was next to impossible. He did not know how he could make a difference. He continued to support the school in career endeavors and helped with the school-to-work initiative. As his own children reached high school, he watched as the three of them floundered for career direction and for relevancy in their education. When his oldest daughter, an excellent student in contention for class valedictorian, reached her senior year, she had no clear direction for her transition to the next step. During her senior year, however, a wonderful thing happened: many people came together in the high school to make a difference. It all started when two veteran teachers and a counselor went to a Career Pathways workshop and came back excited about making school relevant for students and truly allowing them to create an individual, ongoing career plan during their high school years. Working hard with the two teachers and the school counselor was a curriculum director (with vision) from the regional district and the high school principal. The collaboration did not stop there; the new Pathways team invited and encouraged participation of parents, community members, and the students. What made real change seem possible was that everyone came together for the good of the students in the district; not only were they working together, but their goal was clearly this: to help students develop a career plan and relate their coursework to that plan.

Throughout that year, Pete and his daughter Amber both worked hard on the new committee. During that time, the entire committee visited schools that had more creative scheduling to allow students time to do integrated coursework and career planning and those that emphasized career education (especially those with Career Pathways programs). After three months of research and results, Pete and Amber, as part of the new committee, devised a four-year plan to implement Pathways at their high school and then presented their plan to become a Pathways High School. After hearing from several people (including Amber, who talked of how scared she was to go on to college with no real plan), reform began that night when the school board voted to become a Pathways High School. Within the next few months, many more things came together. When it came time to hire a new superintendent, the board considered only those candidates who believed in and could support a Career Pathways agenda. In the fall of that year, Pete became a guest speaker for the school's first Freshman Explorations class; toward the end of the year, his business hosted a Freshman Explorations field trip. By the end of that first year, his freshman son John was far ahead of Amber, a college freshman by then, in career planning and people skills. Pete is confident that the school is on the path to true reform; by the time John is a senior, he will know what his next step will be and how his coursework is relevant to that step. Pete is energetic and helpful with committee work because it is focused. He knows how he can help his school district succeed.

This scenario offers a quick glimpse into what a school needs to do to implement, systemically and successfully, the Collaborative Career Pathways Model. The process is not a new one and draws from the data and research that have been shared with us about implementing successful change in any school. Pete, as a parent and community member, was a part of this change process as he came in and out of set and defined processes that were deliberately structured to implement systemic change. This structure had three major arenas:

> *To implement a Collaborative Pathways Model successfully, school stakeholders must choose a model of change, establish a time line, and examine the way in which they obtain and utilize funding.*

1. A chosen process for successful change that included
   - A set focus with defined goals
   - A set process of collaboration and teaming among all stakeholders
   - Accurate student data and experiences
2. An established time line for implementation
3. A reexamination of funding

THREE STEPS TO SUCCESSFUL CHANGE: A PROCESS MODEL

To implement educational reform successfully, an administrator needs to follow a process. The process identified by Schmoker (1999) is well grounded in research. As noted, the process has three components:

1. Focus and goals

2. Teamwork and collaboration

3. Use of data

In this section, we examine how to use these three components to implement a Collaborative Career Pathways Model.

Step 1: Focus and Goals

First let's look at the focus and goals of a Collaborative Pathways High School. *The focus is to connect learning to life.* By this we mean that all students in our school are able to connect what they are learning to their personal plan for life. This establishes that every student has a written, living plan that guides his or her four years of high school and postsecondary education. It also implies that the student has the necessary personal experiences, contacts, and skills to develop and hone such a plan during each year of the high school experience.

Although it is important for every school to develop and implement its own goals to accomplish the vision and focus of a Collaborative Career Pathways High School, every school must include as Goal 1 the implementation of an instructional (classroom) Career Pathways system, integrating the counseling and community processes. It is imperative to this model that it be embedded in the classroom where students use and experience the curriculum on a continual basis.

After that, your school can identify and develop two to four of its own goals to personalize and focus its efforts through faculty teamwork and collaborative efforts with the community. Remember that goal statements must be clear, match the focus, and be measurable (results driven). Table 3.1 features examples of goal statements that complement the Pathways High School's focus and may be used for discussion with your staff and faculty.

Faculty and administrators should choose only three to five goals to begin their work. As each goal reaches completion, they can then begin to add additional goals. It would be discouraging for a faculty to try to tackle the entire

> *The Focus of a Collaborative Career Pathways High School is to*
>
> 1. *Connect learning to life for all students*
>
> 2. *Create an environment and experience for every student to achieve that connection (transition) through high academic skills and a realistic plan*

> *The first and consistent goal of the Collaborative Career Pathways Model is the implementation of an instructional (classroom) Career Pathways system.*

Table 3.1   Sample Goal Statements

1. All students will have a written plan for their lives based on interest, aptitude, and real-life experiences.

2. All students will be able to connect their educational work to their personal plan.

3. All students will be proficient on identified core subject standards and benchmarks.

4. All students will be proficient on state exams and district-identified achievement tests.

5. All students will select coursework and be involved in electives and extracurricular activities as developed by their own individual plans.

6. All students will be proficient in the five critical and three basic skills according to SCANS.

7. All students will take higher-level course work in an area pertinent to their plan.

8. All students will be connected to the community through site visits, job shadowing, internships, mentors, senior project, and service learning.

9. All students will complete high school and will attend a postsecondary program of education, enter an apprenticeship, the armed forces, or another acceptable postsecondary option.

10. All students will make a smooth transition to their postsecondary plan.

11. All students will complete postsecondary or apprenticeship work and will earn above minimum wage within five years of exiting high school.

12. All students, within five years of graduation, will participate as citizens through voting and political or community involvement.

Note: SCANS = Secretary's Commission on Achieving Necessary Skills Report (U.S. Department of Labor, 1991).

vision or too many goals at once, a situation that could easily overwhelm the school teams and cause the group to lose momentum. We do, however, suggest that in determining your early goals, you choose a broad variety, including the counseling, classroom, and community arenas. You might start with the following goals, for example:

- Our school and community will implement an instructional (classroom) Career Pathways System integrating the counseling and community processes.
- All students will have a planned program centered on their chosen Career Pathway.
- All students will be involved in extracurricular activities connected to their planned program.
- All students will have community experiences during each level of their high school experience that are connected to their planned program.

We cannot overemphasize how important it is to have discussions with your team on the focus and goals of your Pathways High School. The focus of the model is clear but has room for personalization. The goals need to be written and agreed on by your team and then shared with the staff at large. It is important to have everyone's input into how the goals can be accomplished. This input is then consolidated and put into your time line, which is discussed later in this chapter.

Step 2: Teaming and Collaboration

The second step is to create an atmosphere of teaming and collaboration among your staff and community. Your efforts will be tedious and slow at best without the buy-in of key people and positions both within and beyond your school building. To begin, create a Pathways fact-finding team. *Remember that teams must have a defined role, set goals and time lines, a process for implementation, and a set meeting time and schedule.* Their work must be validated and important. Most of our team members are paid a stipend for their time, or substitutes may be provided so that they are able to work during regular hours. Every member on the team is given a role such as facilitator, recorder, researcher, staff liaison, community liaison, presenter, and so on. Everyone on a team must feel he or she has a valid role or responsibility. In this way, these teams are no different from the teaming expectations we have for our students. A suggested composition of the team is shown in Table 3.2.

We have also worked with school teams that were composed of a hodgepodge of interested persons who volunteered because they thought the concept would help students. Other groups we have worked with included school improvement teams and parent–teacher organizations. One team was composed completely of English teachers who wanted to revamp their English department to be more learner centered. What we found is that we have begun with all sorts of teams in all sorts of places and have been able to move forward from there. From these meager beginnings we have seen teams grow to include all the necessary players.

> *The initial key players in creating change toward a Pathways system are principals, counselors, and interested teachers.*

It is also essential for team success to have the support of the superintendent. It is best if this support is direct, but even if it is indirect, it is an extremely important component for political and financial reasons. We have seen schools revamped toward a Pathways Model by a principal and a few devoted persons from any of the categories described in Table 3.2.

Once your Pathways team is organized, your initial team tasks should be those listed in Table 3.3.

Table 3.2 Suggested Composition of the Pathways Fact-Finding Team

Team Member	Roles and Responsibilities
High school principal	Building leadership and coordination
Superintendent	District leadership and financial support
Board member	Community leadership and board support
Community business or political member	Employer and employee insight and support
Parent	Parental insight and support
High school counselor(s)	Comprehensive guidance skills and knowledge
High school teachers (three minimum) (core, elective, technology)	Classroom and instructional insight, skills, knowledge, and support
Curriculum director	Coordinates the curriculum efforts
Special education director	Coordinates the special education mandates
Middle school principal or teacher	Helps bridge students from middle to high school
Students (optional)	Students bring a wonderful perspective
Facilitator or consultant	Conducts meetings and puts the team materials together

Table 3.3 Initial Team Member Tasks

Educate themselves about the Collaborative Pathways Model
Educate the staff and board members about the Collaborative Pathways Model
Educate the community, parents, and students
Develop goals, outcomes, and actions
Customize the plan that will fit the school and community for

- Counseling
- Classroom
- Community

Identify key professional development, scheduling, building, and community needs
Develop a time line for implementation
Examine funding issues and seek additional funding sources

We then suggest that you divide the team into three working subteams that line up to our three C's (classroom, counseling, and community):

- Classroom (instruction): prepare faculty for implementation of the model in the classroom through Pathways classes, core and elective support, and professional development needs in curriculum and instruction.
- Counseling (comprehensive guidance): establish counseling processes for student support systems (conflict resolution, peer counseling, etc.), remediation, education development plans (EDP), data collection, and other student services programs.
- Community: establish necessary community commitment, awareness, networks, student placement opportunities, funding opportunities, and support for professional development schedules.

The subteams then complete work shown in Figure 3.1 for their identified area. Figure 3.2 is a sample of a subteam worksheet, and Figure 3.3 shows the same worksheet completed for a classroom subcommittee. Figure 3.4 shows the worksheet completed for the counseling subcommittee, and Figure 3.5 for the community subcommittee.

Figure 3.1 Subteam Tasks

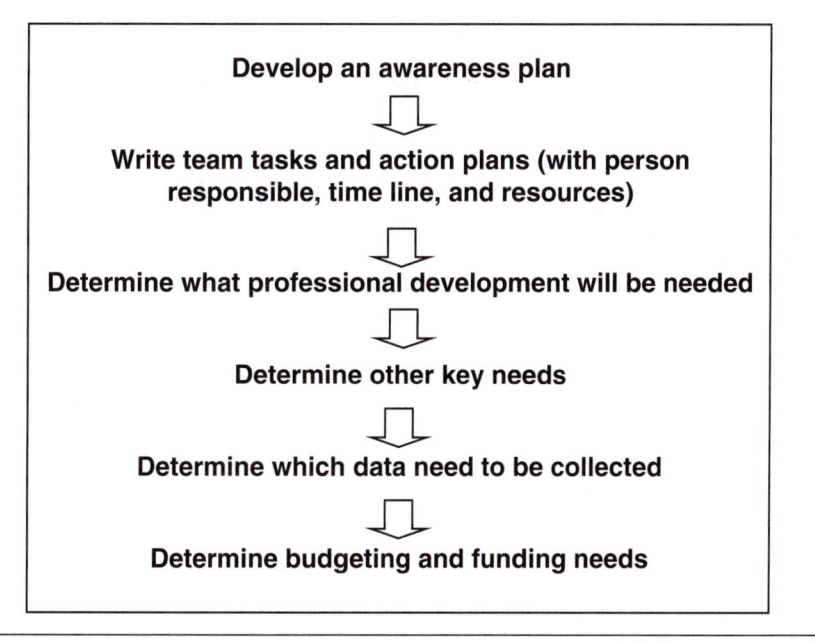

Develop an awareness plan
⇩
Write team tasks and action plans (with person responsible, time line, and resources)
⇩
Determine what professional development will be needed
⇩
Determine other key needs
⇩
Determine which data need to be collected
⇩
Determine budgeting and funding needs

Figure 3.2 Sample Goal Sheet for Classroom Subcommittee

Committee:
Goal:
Task 1:
Action/Outcome:

Person(s) Responsible:	Time Line:	Funding:	Date Completed:

Task 2:
Action/Outcome:

Person(s) Responsible:	Time Line:	Funding:	Date Completed:

Figure 3.3 Sample Completed Goal Sheet for Classroom Subcommittee

Committee: Classroom			
Goal: Implement an Instructional Career Pathways Program			
Task 1: Create an understanding with all staff members on the concepts of a Collaborative Career Pathways High School			
Action/Outcome: Provide needed professional development on Pathways through Team Collaboration			
Person(s) Responsible: – Susie Smith, teacher – Jan Jones, counselor – Mike Miller, teacher	Time Line: Fall in-service	Funding: Professional Development Fund	Date Completed:
Task 2: Find the faculty needed to implement Freshman Explorations Class next year and work with the counseling subteam to place Freshman Explorations in the schedule			
Action/Outcome: To conduct discussions among the team, principals, counselors, and department chairs for placement and staffing of Freshman Explorations. Bring recommendations to faculty.			
Person(s) Responsible: – Tami Todd, principal – Kyle Kieser, counselor – Pam Post, curriculum – Carol Cook, tech teacher	Time Line: Dec. 31	Funding: No cost	Date Completed:
Task 3: Secure Freshman Explorations class materials, etc.			
Action/Outcome: Research, evaluate, and recommend materials			
Person(s) Responsible: – Carol Cook, tech teacher – Susie Smith, teacher – Abe Adams, special ed – Freshman Explorations teachers	Time Line: Jan: recommendations Feb: purchase	Funding: Material	Date Completed:
Task 4: Secure professional development for the new Freshman Explorations teachers			
Action/Outcome: Research and set up professional development			
Person(s) Responsible: – Carol Cook, tech teacher – Susie Smith, teacher – Abe Adams, special ed – Freshman Explorations teachers	Time Line: April–Aug: training	Funding: Training	Date Completed:
Task 5: To work with faculty and undertake professional development so that the core and elective teachers can support the new freshman curriculum			
Action/Outcome: Align and map the curriculum			
Person(s) Responsible: – Pam Post, curriculum – Carol Cook, teacher	Time Line: Jan–May	Funding: Training	Date Completed:

Figure 3.4 Sample Completed Goal Sheet for Counseling Subcommittee

Committee: Counseling				
Goal: Implement an Instructional Career Pathways Program				
Task 1: Implement teaming and conflict-resolution program with teacher				
Action/Outcome: Research programs, make recommendations, train faculty				
Person(s) Responsible: – Jan Jones, counselor – Mike Miller, teacher – Pam Post, curriculum – Rene Roger, student		**Time Line:** Dec: research Jan: recommendations April: Training	**Funding:** Materials and training	**Date Completed:**
Task 2: Identify interest and aptitude tests				
Action/Outcome: Review current practice, research new avenues, and make recommendations				
Person(s) Responsible: – Abe Adams, special ed – Pam Post, curriculum – Kyle Keiser, counselor		**Time Line:** Fall	**Funding:** None	**Date Completed:**
Task 3: Collect baseline data on students				
Action/Outcome: Determine which data to collect, collect data, and present data to staff				
Person(s) Responsible: – Tami Todd, principal – Jan Jones, counselor – Cory Cable, student – Carol Cook, tech teacher – Abe Adams, special ed		**Time Line:** Jan–May	**Funding:** Stipends/materials	**Date Completed:**
Task 4: Plan new freshman parent orientation program				
Action/Outcome: Develop and implement a new freshman orientation program for parents around Pathways				
Person(s) Responsible: – Kyle Keiser, counselor – Rene Roger, student – Bob Baker, parent – Susie Smith, teacher		**Time Line:** Spring	**Funding:** None	**Date Completed:**

Figure 3.5 Sample Completed Goal Sheet for Community Subcommittee

Committee: Community				
Goal: Implement an Instructional Career Pathways Program				
Task 1: Explore and provide additional professional development time for teachers				
Action/Outcome: Work with the school to provide additional time for teachers to receive professional development				
Person(s) Responsible: – Dave Down, board of ed – Ed Evans, superintendent – Tami Todd, principal – Pam Post, curriculum	**Time Line:** Proposals by April	**Funding:** Professional Development Fund	**Date Completed:**
Task 2: Develop a summer teacher job shadowing experience				
Action/Outcome: Provide job-shadowing opportunities for all teachers				
Person(s) Responsible: – Susie Smith, teacher – Greta Gates, business – Kyle Kieser, counselor	**Time Line:** Summer	**Funding:** Stipends	**Date Completed:**
Task 3: Create a database on local resources and site visit possibilities for Freshman Explorations				
Action/Outcome: A list of contacts for all aspects of community involvement and possible site visits for Freshman Explorations				
Person(s) Responsible: – Abe Adams, special ed – Jan Jones, counselor – Greta Gates, business – Cory Cable, student	**Time Line:** Dec–June	**Funding:** None	**Date Completed:**
Task 4: Develop and present board and community presentations				
Action/Outcome: Presentations to parent, community, business, church, school, and industry groups				
Person(s) Responsible: – Dave Downs, board of ed – Tami Todd, principal – Ed Evans, superintendent – Greta Gates, business – Kyle Kieser, counselor – Bob Baker, parent – Cory Cable, student	**Time Line:** Spring	**Funding:** None	**Date Completed:**
Task 5: Create a business and community mini-grant program				
Action/Outcome: Design and implement a mini-grant program for business and industry to give $500–$5,000 for Pathways implementation				
Person(s) Responsible: – Dave Downs, board of ed – Ed Evans, superintendent – Greta Gates, business	**Time Line:** Summer	**Funding:** None	**Date Completed:**

Step 3: Collecting Data

To determine what your exact needs are and to develop a Pathways system for your school, your team will need to collect and look at data. Following is a list of questions that can be helpful to your team in deciding which data you need to collect:

- What percentage of students drop out of your school and why?
- How many of your graduating students go on to college or other postsecondary programs?
- How many of those graduates completed their programs?
- How many of those graduates are working in fields related to their degrees or training?
- How many of your graduates are earning above poverty wages after one, three, and five years?
- How do your statistics match up with national statistics?
- Where are your graduates experiencing the most problems in postsecondary education (English, math, etc.)?
- How many students take upper-level coursework?
- How many students are involved in work-based learning that is connected to their educational plans?
- How many of your students have a written plan for high school that connects to postsecondary education and that they review each year?
- How many of your students are proficient in the Secretary's Commission on Achieving Necessary Skills Report (SCANS; U.S. Department of Labor, 1991) skills?
- How many students, during your Pathways process, have taken coursework that relates to their postsecondary plan? (For example, how many Business and Marketing Pathway students have taken accounting? How many Health Pathway students have taken biology and chemistry? How many Engineering and Trades Pathway students have taken high level math?)
- Do your students see a connection between high school and their life goals? (You will be surprised at how many of them do not!)

Surveys of graduates are helpful, and many schools and state departments of education have such surveys already available.

A TIME LINE FOR IMPLEMENTATION

There are different ways that you can implement the Collaborative Career Pathways Model. If you are starting at the beginning of the process, however, we recommend a five-year implementation plan with the following major tasks described in Table 3.4.

Year 1

The first year sets your foundation. Table 3.5 describes part of your first year plan. Remember that these yearly time lines are a suggestion for your team—they are only a recommendation. Team, faculty, and community discussion is

Table 3.4 A Five-Year Implementation Plan

Year	Major Task or Implementation
Year 1	Planning and preparation
Year 2	Freshman Explorations
Year 3	Sophomore Selections
Year 4	Junior Judgments
Year 5	Senior Transitions

Table 3.5 Recommended Activities for Year 1

- Form a Pathways fact-finding team
- Create awareness and education programs
- Set district or building missions, vision, and goals
- Establish educational standards
- Organize teacher job shadowing
- Build community connections
- Determine which data are to be collected and begin to collect them
- Develop or adopt an Educational Development Plan process for all students
- Develop a one- to five-year faculty development plan
- Research the placement of the Freshman Explorations class and determine teaching personnel
- Train prospective Freshman Explorations teachers
- Begin faculty development on the first step of curriculum: standards, alignment, and mapping

critical to the success of your time line. It is important for your district team to tailor the time line to your individual needs and situation. For example, you may already have a community job shadowing or co-op program—*wonderful!* Use them to help get your faculty out into business and industry. Integrate your existing programs, such as job shadowing, into the time line so it becomes a part of the systemic progress. If your staff has already chosen classroom standards and has aligned your curriculum, *wonderful!* You are ready to use that information to assimilate and implement your Pathways classes and Pathway-specific assignments. The key is to design the program *you* need with the steps you have already taken, your strengths, and your specific school and community needs.

We have recommended certain instructional professional-development activities for each year based on best practices for instruction. In most of the schools with which we have worked, we develop strategic plans for professional development and curriculum with the entire faculty and administration through a facilitated session. This should occur after the faculty members have an understanding of the Collaborative Pathways Model, its focus, and its goals. Every school building is in a different place as far as training in key instructional areas. Use your strengths to help you implement your Pathways system. If your faculty has good background and training in brain-based learning principles, they will have a clearer understanding of what we are trying to accomplish with aligning instruction to interests and aptitudes. If they do not, this is a key area to be addressed early in your implementation program. Refer to Chapter 6 for a recommendation on the stages of instructional improvement.

Year 2

Year 2 is an especially important year. It sets the cornerstone for your instructional Career Pathways program. Remember the difference between a Career Pathways School and our Collaborative Model is the instructional piece. We strongly believe that if it is not happening in the classroom, if it is not a part of a student's learning process and used on a daily basis, it is not coming together for the student. Keep in mind the integration of counseling, classroom, and community (the three C's) for students and staff.

This course will be discussed in detail in future chapters, but for you to understand the second year of implementation, we provide a quick synopsis here. Freshman Explorations is a three-pronged instructional program that integrates personal knowledge and skills, Career Pathways knowledge, and the use of technology. It begins with a student's self-discovery and ends with the selection of a Career Pathway to focus his or her high school course of study. This is achieved through a collaboration of teachers, counselors, technology personnel, and the community. The curriculum for Freshman Explorations is written and available to schools (see Chapter 7). Table 3.6 offers a list of recommended activities for Year 2.

> *The cornerstone of the Pathways instruction program is Freshman Explorations.*

Table 3.6 Recommended Activities for Year 2

- Continue building support
- Implement Freshman Explorations
- Network site visits and visitors for the Freshman Explorations students
- Implement comprehensive guidance components in Freshman Explorations
- Collect and analyze data
- Provide faculty development on technology integration
- Provide faculty development in brain-based teaching and learning and real-world use of subject matter
- Research the placement of Sophomore Selections
- Conduct Sophomore Selections teacher training
- Develop work-based connections for job shadowing

Year 3

During Year 3, the process begins to get easier as the entire school community sees the unfolding of the system and the changes in students. Students who are focused begin to collaborate with teachers to reach their goals. Through their Pathways classes, they have developed good process skills in teaming, presenting, problem solving, and so forth, and this begins to become apparent. Recommended activities for Year 3 are shown in Table 3.7.

Table 3.7   Recommended Activities for Year 3

- Implement Sophomore Selections
- Continue to implement a comprehensive guidance program in Sophomore Selections
- Provide professional development on the assessment system and the integration of disciplines centered on Pathways projects
- Research the placement and staffing of Junior Judgments
- Provide faculty development on workplace technology
- Train Junior Judgment faculty
- Network internship sites for next year's juniors
- Build a mentorship network to connect students and professionals in their fields
- Begin building a postsecondary and apprenticeship network for student transition plans
- Continue collecting and analyzing data

Year 4

Year 4 sees the implementation of Junior Judgments (internship program) and integrated thematic units that use Career Pathways as their venue in all classrooms. Recommended activities for Year 4 are shown in Table 3.8.

Table 3.8   Recommended Activities for Year 4

- Implement Junior Judgments
- Implement comprehensive guidance programs in Junior Judgments
- Implement integrated instruction
- Research the how, where, who, and when of next year's senior projects
- Continue technology integration
- Train Senior Transitions teachers and senior project advisory panels
- Solidify a network with colleges, postsecondary institutions, and apprenticeships as partners in senior projects and postsecondary articulations
- Continue collecting and analyzing data

Year 5

Year 5 sees the final year of implementation with your first graduating class of Pathways students. Recommended activities for Year 5 are shown in Table 3.9.

Table 3.9   Recommended Activities for Year 5

- Implement Senior Transitions with projects and articulations
- Implement comprehensive guidance programs in your Senior Transitions class
- Complete implementation of all classroom instruction through standards, alignment, collective assessment, and integration for the connection of good instruction with students' individualized plans
- Continue collecting and analyzing data
- Continue professional development in the area of technology integration
- Begin tracking graduating seniors

After Year 5 begins the challenge of maintaining your Collaborative Career Pathways system. Areas of continued support and concern fall under the areas of your instructional program: indoctrinating new staff, board, parents, and community members; updating instruction and technology to keep pace with the world outside the classroom; and so forth.

If suddenly the tasks seem overwhelming, stop and think: Any change process contains challenges, and one must stay on course with one's focus, goals, and time line, but be flexible and allow for error and redirection. Anything worthwhile takes time, energy, and devotion. We know that if we are not improving we are getting worse; the implementation of this program has some saving graces, however. The key is that everyone is involved. Everyone has a role, and everyone's role is defined. Counselors work with classroom teachers to develop student-individualized plans and are in charge of data collection. Teachers work with one another to set up classroom instruction. Our technology personnel work with teachers in the classroom to integrate technology. The librarian works on research skills with the students. The community provides work-based sites and mentors. The board and superintendent maintain a solid base of support and financial assistance, and the principal is the hub for all the spokes of the wheel. What makes it a system and not a program is that no one person is responsible for everything. Remember the village and child concept. We are all in this together. Table 3.10 is a comprehensive task chart. Table 3.11 provides recommendations for instructional and faculty staff development implementation.

This implementation time line suggests that you begin implementing Grade 9 through 12 prospectively with a year of foundation building. Integration of the three C's—counseling, classroom, and community—is the focus. We have encountered other Pathways and career development models that have approached implementation from a different angle. Two models that are also common are models that take each of the three C's separately and models that have implemented a single Pathways avenue at a time. In the first alternative model, the comprehensive guidance programs are implemented first, then some sort of community connection, and finally the classroom connection. The problem we have seen with this implementation model is that it rarely makes it to the classroom. The model also creates community connections that tend to be program-orientated and not systematic, meaning not all students at all levels get a community experience.

The second alternative model implements one Pathway at a time. Some schools will implement the counseling, classroom, and community portion first for the Health Pathway, then Engineering, then Natural Resources, and so forth. This model is usually successful in connecting to postsecondary or apprenticeship programs; however, our major concern is the foundational base of all students choosing a Pathway by interest and aptitude that happens in the freshman year. This model promotes program development, and most of the programs become more like career or technical education classes in which instruction is not connected to a student's core and elective subjects such as English or government. Our fear with this implementation model is that not all students are involved in the processes, and it is programmatic instead of systematic.

Table 3.10 Five-Year Recommended Task and Implementation Chart

Year 1	Year 2	Year 3	Year 4	Year 5
Pathways fact-finding team	Continue building support	Implement Sophomore Selections	Implement Junior Judgments	Implement Senior Transitions, senior projects, and articulations
Awareness and education programs	Implement Freshman Explorations	Continue to implement comprehensive guidance program in Sophomore Selections	Implement comprehensive guidance programs in Junior Judgments	Implement comprehensive guidance programs in Senior Transitions class
Set district or building mission, vision, and goals	Network site visits and visitors for the Freshman Explorations students	Provide professional development on assessment systems and the integration of disciplines centered on Pathways projects	Implement integrated instruction	Complete implementation of all classroom instruction through standards, alignment, collective assessment, and integration for the connection of instruction with students' individualized plans
Establish education/classroom standards	Implement comprehensive guidance components in Freshman Explorations	Research the placement and staffing of Junior Judgments	Research the how, where, who, and when of next year's senior projects	Continue collecting and analyzing data
Conduct teacher job shadowing	Collect and analyze data	Train Junior Judgments teachers	Train Senior Transitions teachers	
Build community connections	Provide faculty development in brain-based teaching	Network internship sites for next year's juniors	Solidify a network with colleges, postsecondary	

(Continued)

Table 3.10 (Continued)

Year 1	Year 2	Year 3	Year 4	Year 5
	and learning and real-world use of subject matter		institutions, and apprenticeship partners in senior projects and postsecondary articulations	
Develop or adopt an educational development plan process for all students	Research the placement of Sophomore Selections	Build a mentorship network to connect students and professionals in their upcoming fields	Continue collecting and analyzing data	
Develop a one- to five-year professional development plan	Train Sophomore Selections teachers	Begin to build a postsecondary and apprenticeship network for student transition plans		
Research the placement of Freshman Explorations class and determine teaching personnel	Develop work-based connections for job shadowing	Continue data collection and analysis		
Begin faculty development on the first step of curriculum: standards, alignment, and mapping	Continue data collection and analysis			
Train prospective Freshman Explorations teachers				

63

Table 3.11 Recommended Instructional and Faculty Development Implementation

	Pathways Classes	Processes for Teachers	Curriculum	Technology/ Other
Year 1	• Pathways Class concepts • Freshman Explorations Training/ Processes	Teaming, character development, and conflict-resolution processes	Standards, alignment, mapping, understanding of thematic instruction in the Pathways Classes	Technology software for Freshman Explorations
Year 2	• Freshman Explorations implementation • Sophomore Selections training/ processes	Inclusion programs or other community-building classroom processes and anger management	Focused curriculum and brain-based teaching and learning	Technology integration in instruction
Year 3	• Sophomore Selections implementation • Junior Judgments training/ processes	Peer counseling and student support systems, stress and time management, government regulations	Collective assessment and assessment processes	Technology-based student assessment systems
Year 4	• Junior Judgments implementation • Senior Transitions training/ processes	Service learning programs as a Career Pathways experience, workplace skills	Thematic units and instruction in all subjects	Workplace technology as related to core, electives, and Pathways selection
Year 5	• Senior Transition implementation	Persuasion, problem solving, and presentation skills and in-depth, career-specific knowledge	Cross-curricular thematic connections between subjects	Technology-based senior projects

Again, we are not dictating an implementation model. We are only sharing what we have done and seen work. You must, with your team's help, decide the best implementation process for your particular situation.

In regard to school size, the Collaborative Pathways Model is flexible. If yours is a small school, Pathways can be combined to help place students into Pathways "families." At one of our county schools, the Sophomore Selections class is divided into two sections. The first houses all students interested in arts and communications, business, health, and human services. The second houses the engineering, trades, natural resources, and agriscience students. This model keeps classes full while allowing students to be with other students in their Pathway and in the more closely related paths. This combining of related paths can be done throughout the school in scheduling homerooms, advisory periods, core and elective subjects, and extracurricular activities.

In a larger school, just the opposite can occur. Classes and other scheduling can be done in smaller "families." There may be enough students in the school to have each Pathway be a separate sophomore, junior, and senior class with students of like interests and goals working, planning, and exploring their future as a cohort family. If the school is even larger, Pathways can be divided into Career Clusters, narrowing the focus even more. Again, these "families" can be used for homerooms, advisory sections, classes, extracurricular activities, and so forth. In this way, classes and "families" can be assigned professional mentors to work with them from the fields and professions they represent. A mentor can even follow the group from sophomore year through graduation.

Cohort families work exceptionally well together because students help to build relationships and support each other. They also help in school climate and culture issues, as we review later, by integrating students by interest, not by social class or cliques, thus helping to dispel stereotyping and other behavior issues. The division of students by Pathways does not begin until after their freshman year, when they have had time to explore all the Pathways. Even in the sophomore year, it is advantageous to have students in a class where related paths are included. Remember to start broad and help each student narrow his or her focus over the four-year experience. Cohort groups and "families" are, however, an excellent way to adapt Pathways to your school size, be it small or large.

FUNDING

Although a Pathways system is not expensive to implement, there are still costs involved. The reason the system is low in implementation cost is because it uses existing resources. For example, all districts have some type of instructional funding for teacher salaries, professional development, materials, technology funds for technology integration, counseling, and so on. It is important when designing your system to take all these funds and connect them to one another so they are not being spent in isolation. The idea is to get a roadmap for implementation and then fit funding to merge with your focus and goals. An example of this is the English department that postponed new textbooks to purchase videos and software needed to complement their Pathways English program. Technology needs can be discussed with teachers and the money used to implement the technology units in the Pathways, core, and elective classes as they relate to your new system.

> *The three main funding sources for implementing the Collaborative Career Pathways system are*
>
> - *Reallocation of funds*
> - *Grants*
> - *Community dollars and donations*

As mentioned previously, however, there are still costs to implementing any system. The main costs you may encounter are increased need for professional development dollars, cost for field trips, software and computer costs, team stipends, and, in some cases, one or two additional teachers (if a school chooses to move to a 4 × 4 block schedule). The only new position that schools may choose to establish is a Career Pathways coordinator, who is in charge of all the work-based student experiences and is a liaison between the teachers and the community. This position lifts a great burden off the counselors and Pathways classroom teachers, who are already overloaded.

To examine the cost of your system, you must look at three main funding sources. These funding sources must cover your major costs without causing a great deal of displacement. Major costs you will face are personnel, technology, professional development, field trips, and materials.

Reallocation

In implementing a Career Pathways system, most of the costs are in personnel, which are already being paid by your district. The key is to use the existing personnel in alternative ways. Some of our districts have financed existing and new personnel out of general expenses or grants; however, some positions are even sponsored by the local chamber of commerce or by business and industry. Because the major shift in instruction happens in the Pathways classes (Freshman Explorations, Sophomore Selections, Junior Judgments, and Senior Transitions), some districts have begun the Pathways process by placing these curricula into existing classes. For example, many of our Freshman Explorations classes began in the language arts area and were moved after several years to a stand-alone class. This gave districts time to plan and adjust schedules as people retired or as the success of the new Pathways system spurred enthusiasm. We have always recommended the Freshman Explorations be a stand-alone class so as not to burden other core subject teachers who have many standards and benchmarks to meet for state testing; we have seen schools begin there and be successful, however. The teacher(s) must nonetheless work hard to be able to integrate Pathways curriculum with core subject standards.

The other Pathways classes were many times taught back to back with or integrated into classes such as speech, computer literacy, or service learning. In this model, you only need to fund your Pathways class areas one year at a time if you use the five-year implementation model. Schools have approached this in several ways; you need to use the solution that best fits your situation. Examples of staffing classroom instruction are as follows:

- Eliminate a freshman elective choice and use that teacher and slot for the Freshman Explorations class (this needs to be done between the principal and the departments).
- Implement a block schedule in which students have more opportunities to take more classes.
- Or as previously discussed, implement the Pathways class structure into an existing department such as English or social studies and combine it with the required courses in that department (e.g., Freshman Explorations becomes the freshman English class and is designed to fit the English language arts standards for the freshman year). This option takes time and training for teachers to be able to adjust their instructional process and materials.

The same process would hold true for implementing the next three Pathways classes.

Also to be considered in your reallocation dollars are technology monies. As you further explore this collaborative model, you will discover that all Pathways classes and core and elective Pathways projects have technology integration components. Technology funds need to be used in a way that complements these units. This takes teamwork and collaboration so that no one feels left out of the technology loop.

Counseling funds used for counselors and testing must be aligned with the Pathways class instruction—remember, the classroom is the key. What tests are you currently using for interest and aptitude? These should be the tests used in the Freshman Explorations classroom. Integration of counseling and classroom eliminates the redundancy of students taking a variety of tests and being unable to relate them to one another, their learning, or their future. Use your counseling funds to complement your system.

Dollars for field trips and materials should also be aligned to your system. Are you currently using these monies for random trips on random years with random projects? The freshman year should have the most field trips because they offer a broad experience for students. These dollars can then be narrowed down to shadowing and internships, which are relatively inexpensive because your community absorbs much of the cost.

Reallocation of funds is not easy, but it is possible. Many administrators and teachers are on rigid schedules of textbook adoptions and projects in which they have been involved for many years. The sophomore history teacher who for the last 20 years has taken her class on a field trip to your state capitol may not want to

> *Reallocation is your key funding avenue, but you must be a good communicator, be sensitive to others' traditions, educate your staff, make decisions through teamwork and collaboration, and be willing to make sacrifices yourself.*

give that trip to the freshman program, for example. You are all familiar with "ownership" issues, and many of these programs are valid in their own right. We are looking at creating a system in which all the puzzle pieces fit together for students, however, and this type of shifting can only be done through teaming, collaboration, and understanding. We have seen teachers throw out whole units and classes because they are no longer relevant, but they must come to those conclusions on their own, as professionals who are doing what is best for their students.

Grants and Awards

There are numerous grant opportunities available for programs that connect school and work. This began with the National School-to-Work Opportunity Act of 1994, passed during the Clinton administration. Grants can be public or they may come from private sources such as foundations. Begin looking for grant sources through local and state funding and move on to regional and federally funded programs.

The first place to check is with your regional or intermediate school district, your state department of education, and other state agencies. In Michigan, we received noncompetitive dollars through educational monies allotted for the Michigan Career Preparation System. The state also had set aside $5 million in competitive grants strictly for the implementation of Career Pathways High Schools. Three of our districts received $150,000 for implementation costs. Most areas have local foundations, and for some of you lucky enough to house a large industry, they almost always have foundation monies available. Also check with your state and federal representatives to find out about any public dollars that may be available.

It is a good idea to design your grants in two ways: as a complete package and in smaller mini-grants.

Many times you can receive smaller foundation grants for a student computer lab used to do career research or for multimedia materials used to present student job-shadowing reports. Our local Wal-Mart store gives out educational grants in the amount of $2,000. This can provide the dollars needed to purchase a digital video camera and projector for junior internship presentations.

Also look at educational awards. One of the local districts applied for and received a MACUL (Michigan Association of Computer User Learner) award for the integration of technology in its freshman Pathways classroom. The award came with a $5,000 check with which the school purchased the SmartBoard that was a part of its Career Pathways technology plan. The school also received a $1,000 MASB (Michigan Association of School Board) award for Michigan's Best in Technology Integration, which it used to further enhance teacher professional development.

Community Involvement

Your community is your best resource for the funding of direct and indirect costs. This is because it has a very significant investment in the performance of your school district: its children. Whether you are a rural or urban district, once you begin to build community connections, you will be astonished at what resources are available to you. Personnel, time, and sites are the major resources your community will be able to offer; however, community organizations such as the local Rotary or Lions Clubs have supported our job-shadowing programs and provided transportation to disadvantaged students to get to and from their job shadows. They have also acted as a network to find professionals in fields our students wanted to explore but with which we were unable to make a connection. Business and industry and chambers of commerce have worked with us to teach students teaming, problem-solving, and self-management skills. In addition to time and resources, our communities have also opened their purse strings to provide supplies and materials for student projects. The key is to let community businesses and organizations know what you are doing, why you are doing it, exactly what you need, the cost, and, most important, the projected outcome for both students and their future employers. Chapter 13 provides specific details on how and when to use your community to complement classroom instruction in a Collaborative Career Pathways High School. As an administrator, it is in your students' best interest for you to join a community organization and your local chamber of commerce.

> *The key to good funding opportunities is to have your budget aligned with your system, your goals, and your implementation plan. Then you can fund your system one area at a time.*

CONCLUSION

The implementation of a Collaborative Career Pathways High School is not an easy journey, but it is a rewarding one. The journey sees your school and community coming together as a whole to help students explore, plan, and achieve a great future. It also provides a venue for all areas of the school to integrate with one another and move in the same direction—this is what makes for systemic change: all the arrows of progress moving in the same direction.

It all begins with a fact-finding team studying the focus and goals, teaming, collaborating, and collecting data. The Pathways team then develops plans and goals to include *all* stakeholders and the school community. This is done with a five-year implementation plan that implements year-by-year the instructional Pathways class base needed for students to practice the skills necessary for personal success. The system is then set up according to the size, schedule, and circumstances surrounding your school and community. You and your team must create the final product—your Collaborative Career Pathways School; to achieve this, follow the template for the change process, have a steady and realistic time line, and organize a clear funding and budgetary plan. Remember at every step of your journey to celebrate your successes and be patient with your failures. Change is an ebb and flow process—the key is perseverance.

IN REVIEW

- Establish a change process that includes focus and goals and a process for collaboration, teaming, and data collection.
- Establish a Career Pathways team, making sure that all stakeholders are represented.
- As your team members establish their focus and goals, allow them to create their own plan within the structure of an instructional Career Pathways Model.
- Set a time line for implementation that allows for a year of planning and preparation.
- Set a time line for your instructional program that allows you to add one Pathways class a year, beginning with Freshman Explorations and then adding Sophomore Selections, Junior Judgments, and Senior Transitions.
- Staff development and training is key to the success of your Pathways implementation.
- Reexamine your funding sources through reallocation, grants, and community support.
- Celebrate your successes, understand your failures, and be flexible. Perseverance is the key.

Part Two

Building a Foundation

Chapter Four

District Vision and School Leadership

The Pathways Foundation

SCENARIO: IN ORDER TO FORM A MORE PERFECT UNION...

In May of 1787 a group of delegates met in Philadelphia to set the foundations for a new government. This is a familiar story but nevertheless a remarkable feat. The delegates came from 12 of the 13 newly freed colonies. They were diverse in their needs yet similarly challenged by their new won freedom. They had challenged an empire and won—a small group of men with a vision, with a mission, and with a goal. They had a facilitator named George Washington who presided over the convention and led the group without interfering with the process or dictating the outcome. This attempt at a new government was not the first one. They had tried the Articles of Confederation and had had some success but more failure. They were being scrutinized and ridiculed by the rest of the world. Everyone was waiting to see them fail. The emerging thought of individual rights and colonies uniting as one was absurd.

The delegates began by examining their previous efforts and deciding what was good and bad about their last attempt at forming a successful government. They decided they needed structure and power enough to guarantee a working central government while maintaining the autonomy of individual colonies. Together, these diverse people, designed a document that included the vision of the new government, the mission of the new government, and the goals and values of the new government. Unfortunately, that was just the beginning. They each then had to go back to their constituents and "sell" the new document. Every single delegate had to be successful on his home front. They faced a great battle of selling collaboration while keeping individual identity. They had to convince others to try a new way. They were able achieve this remarkable task, but that was just step one—now they had to make it work. We have witnessed in our history a continual battle to make our Constitution work. We have "tweaked" it with amendments, fought for it, died for it and we continue to interpret it to this day. It is a living document. It is the foundation on which we base all of our decisions.

So now you must be thinking, "What does this have to do with the implementation of a Collaborative Career Pathways High School?" This is the analogy we always use when we teach faculty and staff members about vision, mission, and goals. Without this solid foundation and the buy-in of all parties, you cannot succeed in school reform, just as our forefathers could not have succeeded in creating a nation. We have from the beginning been a nation of compromise and collaboration for the common good *and* for the good of the individual. It can be done. It is a long journey. It must start with a solid foundation. In initiating this change in your district and building you will receive the tasks and battle as did the delegates to Philadelphia in 1787. Many people will tell you that they have tried reform and change before and nothing really changes. There will be those who will sit back and wait for you to fail, and there will be those who will actually work against you. This process of change will always be there "in your face" as we say nowadays. Your cohort group of reformers that we gathered together in Chapter 3 will be your delegation, however. They will make the compromises; they will sell the ideas back on the "home front" and work toward your vision. The key is to have a living document that contains within it the input and collaboration of your staff. This agreed-on document then provides a foundation on which all decisions are based. It becomes the foundation that supports the common good (your school) and the individual rights and needs of students.

The question here is how do you set up vision, mission, goals, and values that will all fit together in a Pathways school, and how do you make it clear and alive for others? We worry about going back to faculty and staff and saying, "Okay, today we are going to work on our vision and mission." At this time, eyes glaze over, heads roll, and the comments begin: "What does this have to do with teaching and kids . . ." The foundation must be set, however, and it must be clear or your staff will be "all over the place" in terms of teaching, learning, and the outcomes for all students. In this chapter, we give you a clear explanation of vision, mission, and goals and how they come together in a Career Pathways School. We will use the Constitution as the example of format because it is so commonly known and easy to understand. We also give you some excellent references on reading and understanding about these concepts in education.

VISION, MISSION, GOALS, AND VALUES

The beginning of the foundation is the vision. A *vision is what you expect the journey to look like at the end.* This is the "beginning with the end in mind" principle. The vision is then followed by the mission. *The mission is how you get to the vision.* The next step is the goals. *Goals are what you have to do to accomplish the mission.*

Vision, mission, and goal statements have been with us for a long time and have become common language in schools, business, and organizations. Recently DuFour and Eaker (1998) have added a new dimension to this concept called value statements. In their book *Professional Learning Communities*, vision, mission, and goals are followed by values statements. Value statements ask people to clarify how they intend to make their shared vision a reality. These statements challenge the people within that organization to identify the specific attitudes, behaviors, and commitments that they must demonstrate to advance toward their vision. An example of a value statement by teachers in a Pathways High School might be the following: *We will know how our subject matter is used in the world outside the classroom.* Value statements, therefore, are what each stakeholder commits to in order to accomplish the goals.

> **VISION**
> *(The end result)*
>
> **MISSION**
> *(How to achieve the vision)*
>
> **GOALS**
> *(What has to be done to accomplish the mission)*
>
> **VALUES**
> *(What each stakeholder must do to see that the goals are accomplished)*

Presenting a Solid Example

Tables 4.1 through 4.4 use the Constitution as an example to clarify what we have discussed thus far and then connect the concepts to the Pathways steps. This explanation works well with staff and faculty, giving them a concrete example of how this process works. Figure 4.1 ties the whole process together.

(Text continues on page 80)

Table 4.1 Vision: What We Are Striving to Become

Constitutional Sample	Pathways Setup
The Vision of the Constitution	The Vision of a Career Pathways High School

Wording

We the people of the United States in order to form a more perfect union, establish justice, insure domestic tranquility, provide for the common defense, promote the general welfare, and secure the blessings of liberty to ourselves and our posterity . . .	Five years after high school *every student* will be gainfully employed[a] in his or her chosen field or will begin postgraduate work and have participated in national or global citizenship.

Outcomes

• A union • Justice • Tranquility • Defense • General welfare • Liberty for future generations	• High school diploma • Postsecondary completion • Gainful employment • Graduate work • Voting or other citizenship and global interaction

[a]Gainfully employed = earning cost-of-living wages or above

Table 4.2 Mission: Why Are We in Existence—Creating a System to Accomplish the Vision

Constitutional Sample	Pathways Setup
The mission of the Constitution as it directly follows the vision	The mission of a Career Pathways High School as introduced in Chapter 1

Wording

. . . do ordain and establish this Constitution for the United Sates of America.	Every student will focus his or her high school education on a realistic postsecondary plan with the skills, knowledge, and experience needed to complete that plan successfully and to be a productive citizen and global resident.

Outcomes

• Agreement on a system of government that provides for the vision • Establishment of a system of government that provides for the vision	Establishment of a school system in which the vision will be accomplished through • Each student having a focused postsecondary plan • Skills and knowledge to complete the plan • Skills and knowledge to be a productive citizen and global resident

Table 4.3 Goals: How the Organization Will Reach the Vision (What) and Mission (Why)

Constitutional Sample	Pathways Setup
The samples use the first three articles as an example of the Constitutional goal statement. The remaining articles can also be used as goal examples. The articles are simplified.	The goal samples are the first goals of any Career Pathways High School as introduced in Chapter 3. Just like the Constitution, which has other articles beyond the establishment of the branches of government, a Career Pathways High School can add other goals to its document.

Wording

• All legislative powers herein granted will be vested in Congress. • The executive power shall be vested in a President. • The judicial power of the United States shall be vested in one Supreme Court and in such inferior courts.	• The integration of a Career Pathways classroom process • The integration of the Career Pathways counseling process • The integration of the Career Pathways community process

Outcomes

• Establishment of a legislative branch • Establishment of an executive branch • Establishment of a judicial branch	• Establishment of the classroom pillar • Establishment of the counseling pillar • Establishment of the community pillar

Table 4.4 Values: What Each Stakeholder Must Do to Complete the Goals (How) Successfully, Therefore Completing the Mission (Why) and Reaching the Vision (What)

Constitutional Sample	Pathways Setup
The Constitutional examples of value statements are listed below in the power vested in each branch of government. Again, this has been simplified to be used as an example.	In a Career Pathways High School, there are a number of stakeholders who will need to develop value statements. These stakeholders include administration, counselors, teachers, parents, paraeducators, and other high school staff such as cooks, custodians, and even students. To provide an idea of the commitment of these stakeholders, we have written sample value statements for a variety of stakeholders under each pillar.

Wording

The Congress shall have the power to . . .
- Levy and collect taxes
- Pay debts
- Provide for the common defense
- Provide for the general welfare
- Make laws
- Declare war, etc.

Teachers:
- Provide an educational experience by which students can link their Career Pathway and future plans to their coursework
- Use methods of instruction that incorporate the SCANS skills for all students
- Incorporate on a regular and consistent basis the use of our community in the classroom
- Reinforce and use the students' structured community experiences in our coursework
- Reinforce the counseling process for teaming and conflict resolution in our classroom policies, procedures, and student activities and lesson plans

Paraeducators:
- Reinforce student postsecondary plans with tutoring practices

Administrators:
- Provide professional development opportunities for teachers to understand how their subject is used in the workplace

(Continued)

Table 4.4 (Continued)

The President shall have the power to ... • Command the armed forces • Grant reprieves and pardons • Make treaties • Appoint ambassadors • Appoint judges to the Supreme Court, etc.	**Counselors:** • Provide a model of teaming and conflict resolution for all students beginning the freshman year and advancing through their senior experience **Hall Monitors:** • Reinforce the steps for conflict resolution with student interaction in the halls
The Supreme Court shall extend to all cases ... • Law and equity under the Constitution • Laws of the United States • Treaties • All cases of ambassadors and maritime • Controversies between states, etc.	**Parents:** • Support our children's community experience and establish high expectations for their behavior off campus **Students:** • Actively participate in our community experiences, formally sharing that experience with our classmates

Outcomes

The operation of the **Legislative Branch** of government, thus completing the goals and mission to accomplish the original vision of liberty for all	The operation of the **Instructional Pillar** of a Career Pathways High School, thus completing the goals and mission to accomplish the original vision of gainful employment and active citizenship for all students
The operation of the **Executive Branch** of government, thus completing the goals and mission to accomplish the original vision of liberty for all	The operation of the **Counseling Pillar** of a Career Pathways High School, thus completing the goals and mission to accomplish the original vision of gainful employment and active citizenship for all students
The operation of the **Judicial Branch** of government, thus completing the goals and mission to accomplish the original vision of liberty for all	The operation of the **Community Pillar** of a Career Pathways High School, thus completing the goals and mission to accomplish the original vision of gainful employment and active citizenship for all students

Note: SCANS = Secretary's Commission on Achieving Necessary Skills (U.S. Department of Labor, 1991).

DISTRICT VISION AND SCHOOL LEADERSHIP

Figure 4.1 The Pathways Process

VISION

Five years after high school **every student** will be gainfully employed in his or her chosen field or beginning postgraduate work and will have participated in national or global citizenship.

⇩

MISSION

Every student will focus his or her high school education on a realistic postsecondary plan with the skills, knowledge, and experience needed to complete that plan successfully and to be a productive citizen and global resident.

⇩

GOALS: The Three Pillars

| The Integration of the Career Pathways Classroom Process | The Integration of the Career Pathways Counseling Process | The Integration of the Career Pathways Community Process |

⇩

Examples of the Classroom Process:

Teachers:
- We will provide educational experiences by which students can link their Career Pathway and future plans to their coursework.
- We will use methods of instruction that incorporate the SCANS skills for all students.

Paraeducators:
- We will reinforce student postsecondary plans with tutoring practices.

Administrators:
- We will provide professional development opportunities for teachers to understand how their subject is used in the workplace.

Examples of the Counseling Process:

Teachers:
- We will reinforce the counseling process for teaming and conflict resolution in our classroom policies, procedures, and student activities and lesson plans.

Counselors:
- We will provide a model of teaming and conflict resolution for all students beginning the freshman year and advancing through their senior experience.

Hall Monitors:
- We will reinforce the steps for conflict resolution with student interaction in the halls.

Examples of the Community Process:

Teachers:
- We will incorporate on a regular and consistent basis the use of our community in the classroom.
- We will reinforce and use the students' structured community experiences in our coursework.

Parents:
- We will support our children's community experience and establish high expectations for their behavior off campus.

Students:
- We will actively participate in our community experiences, formally sharing those experiences with our classmates.

SCANS = Secretary's Commission on Achieving Necessary Skills (U.S. Department of Labor, 1991).

A Common Experience

If you are like most schools, you will not be starting at the beginning of this process (that is, formulating the vision, mission, goals, and value statements). These processes will have been "floating" around your school and district, being set into motion here and there, without any real planning or follow through. When we work with vision and mission in districts, we begin by collecting everything that has been done previously. You do not want to discard the hard work and history of what others have done already. By doing this, you may lose, right off the bat, those who have had and still have great influence in your building. In most districts when we begin to collect vision and mission data, we find ourselves with a vast amount of information and history. Just like the Articles of Confederation, you will find an onslaught of the good and not-so-good stuff that has not been put into a working form or living document—but don't throw it away. This is where you begin.

In one of the districts where we worked, we found the following: school improvement goals, district goals, board goals, North Central Accreditation goals, building goals, department goals, state testing goals, and adult outcomes. We were given mission and vision statements from the board, each building, and the district. Some mission statements read like vision statements and some vision statements read like mission statements. Some goals were measurable, and some were not. We were not able to obtain *any data or evidence* that the goals had been measured, reevaluated, and completed. Nor had the important step been taken to have each stakeholder (teachers, administrators, parents, etc.) determine their roles (value statements) in the written goals. Therefore nobody really knew his or her part in the scheme.

A Common Process

When revisiting and reevaluating your vision, mission, goals, and values, we suggest you use this process. Collect everything that has been done regarding these factors in the past. Compile this information into a working document that will allow your staff to break into groups and find the common threads and needs. Have your Pathways team introduce the new Pathways materials on vision, mission, and goals. Then together with your staff, rework your materials into one living document. After you have redone your vision, mission, and goals, break into your stakeholder groups and develop your value statements. Then recompile your work into a new document—your Constitution. See Table 4.5 for an outline of the process.

This document is now your foundation for all of the other decisions and movement within your school building. How you deal with and solve problems such as diversity, academics and grades, social and personal student needs, socioeconomic inequities, race and gender issues, climate and culture issues, elective and community experiences, and so on will all be determined by your foundation document. All stakeholders and policymakers will refer to it, so it must be evaluated every year for updating and closure by the entire staff. Remember also that data must be collected and presented on your goals. *You should not be revamping or making changes to your document without hard data.*

Table 4.5   Vision Process Chart

Steps to Completing Your Vision Process:	People Involved	Begun	Completed
1. The Pathways committee investigates the Collaborative Career Pathways Vision, Mission, Goals, gaining clarity and understanding.			
2. The committee gathers all previous documents and compiles information.			
3. The Pathways Committee presents Career Pathways vision materials and previously compiled vision data to the faculty.			
4. The faculty breaks into integrated teams and reviews all materials, making recommendations.			
5. All faculty members use the teams' information to compile new vision, mission, and goal statements.			
6. Stakeholder teams are created and value statements developed.			
7. A new vision document, including value statements, is put together for approval of faculty, administration, parent associations, student government, board of education, etc.			
8. The document is published.			
9. The Pathways committee (or school improvement committee, etc.) creates a database and activities for the review and evaluation of the vision, mission, and goals, which will take place on a yearly basis.			
10. Stakeholder groups create a database and activities to measure value statements.			
11. A yearly evaluation of vision document takes place.			

Believe it or not, this process, which will begin with rolling eyes and shoulder shrugs, will be the process that binds your building together and moves everyone in a single, focused direction. If done as a true collaborative effort with staff time and facilitation, the experience will revitalize your school community. Everyone will begin to take ownership of the school's plan, as they begin to help all students take ownership of their plans! Staff and students will then experience the forming of a more perfect union.

IN REVIEW

- To set the foundation for a Collaborative Career Pathways High School, administration and staff must revisit their vision, mission, and goals.

- Vision: Vision is the beginning of the foundation. It is what you expect the journey to look like at the end.
- Mission: Mission is why you exist. It is how you get to the vision.
- Goals: Goals are what you must accomplish to fulfill the mission. Goals must be clear, concise, and measurable.
- Value Statements: Value statements are what each stakeholder must do to see that the goals are accomplished.
- Flow: Your vision–mission–goals–value statements must flow one from the other, providing a solid direction and plan for everyone.
- Common Experience: The staff and faculty of most schools or districts have already dealt with the vision and mission issues of schools, many times unsuccessfully or in a document that has had no effect on instruction.
- Common Process: Begin your review process with what has already been done, moving forward toward the Collaborative Career Pathways High School Model.
- Yearly Review: Remember to review your foundation document yearly, taking a look at hard data. This is the only way to maintain the life of your document. Leave room for change—the founding fathers did!

Chapter Five

Comprehensive Guidance to Prepare and Assist Pathways Students

**SCENARIO: A DAY IN THE LIFE OF
A CAREER PATHWAYS COUNSELOR**

Deondra is a counselor in a 600-student Collaborative Career Pathways High School. Just a few years ago, she felt so frustrated and overwhelmed by her duties as a traditional counselor that she wondered if she was making a difference at all. It seemed as if her counseling strategy was a hit-and-miss approach. Deondra had moved into counseling from the classroom five years earlier because she believed students needed more help with academic, career, and personal support. She quickly became disillusioned, however, when she realized she was only reaching about the top 20% of the class for postsecondary planning and the bottom 10% of the class for academic support; she dealt with adolescent crisis issues only as they "flared up." Deondra wanted a system by which she could help *all* students plan for their postsecondary experience, in which *all* students had reinforced academic skills, and in which *all* students could practice personal and social skills in order to prevent rather than simply react to crisis issues.

In her frustration, Deondra began to look around for a better comprehensive guidance model. She wanted a model that would integrate with students, teachers, and community in a systematic fashion that gave students in advance the skills they would need to succeed at school and in other areas of their lives. Deondra's high school, with her help, adopted a Collaborative Career Pathways

Model. One of the reasons the stakeholders chose this model was because it was a natural fit with her comprehensive guidance needs. Now Deondra feels much more in control of the guidance program and has a system for implementing guidance standards. The system uses a collaborative approach in which Pathways classes are offered as an avenue for academic success skills, career development through exploration and work-based experiences, and as an arena for practicing important personal and social skills such as conflict resolution and self-evaluation. This is how Deondra's guidance system now works.

With teachers Deondra determines where, when, how, and why certain personal and social skills are taught at each level of high school through Pathways classes. She then schedules a time to introduce those skills to all students, and teachers reinforce the skills through classroom assignments. In freshman year, for example, Deondra works with students on conflict resolution and teaming. During sophomore year, she introduces time- and stress-management skills and goal setting. Junior year, Deondra helps students practice a decision-making model and learn about ethical decision making. During senior year, she concentrates on helping students present themselves to schools, universities, and other training environments for acceptance into a postsecondary plan. Each year, Deondra knows which skills she will be working on with each grade level. She also knows that teachers will be reinforcing those skills in their classrooms. Deondra helps teachers secure materials and any training needed for them to integrate the personal and social skills into their classrooms.

Deondra now does student scheduling in the Pathways classrooms. Through a Web-based educational development plan (EDP) software, she works with *groups* of students to help them plan and schedule their next year's classes. Scheduling makes more sense for the students because they schedule their classes through Pathways-recommended coursework. A student who wants to be an engineer knows exactly which classes he or she must take—there is no guess work or decisions being made based on such considerations as "what classes are my friends taking?" Every year Deondra chooses a time to work with students at each of the first three grade levels to help them complete their EDP for the following year, review their portfolios, and schedule their classes.

Career Development is also scaffolded each year for the students. Deondra works with the Pathways teachers to provide exploration during freshman year, career laddering and research sophomore year, focused experiences junior year, and a capstone project senior year. Each year Deondra knows which career- and work-based experiences each student must have, and she works with teachers to help arrange speakers, site visits, job shadows, internships, and senior panels. With Deondra working with students in classroom groups, she is able to connect and get to know all students as they work together. In this manner, students are more likely to come to Deondra with a personal problem. Also, by practicing personal and social skills in the Pathways classes, Deondra and the students are able to use a common language and practice problem-solving skills.

Deondra is still responsible for administering tests and collecting student data. She does this through collaboration with administrators and faculty members, determining which goals they want to measure and how to measure those goals. Together all stakeholders collect data in a focused and direct manner. Following work-based experiences, for example, Deondra asks employers to fill out a quick questionnaire or survey. She also has entrance and exit surveys for students. In this way, she can communicate needs to faculty members and the community.

Deondra would be unable to accomplish all this without a system to support her. Aligned with national counseling standards and integrated with a Career Pathways format, Deondra is able to provide a well-balanced and comprehensive student services program with her limited resources and staff—a feat she found impossible just a few years earlier. Today Deondra is busy as usual, but she has a set purpose. She begins her day with a trip to the Freshman Explorations class to introduce a conflict management process. Just before lunch, she makes a few calls to help the Sophomore Selections teacher set up job shadows. She also looks over the draft of a new internship booklet that the team is preparing for next semester's Junior Judgments. After lunch, Deondra works on compiling data that teachers collected at last week's open house. The data comprise parents' responses to the new Pathways system and will be used as feedback at next month's staff meeting. While Deondra is working, a student, upset about an unexpected breakup, comes by to talk with her. He and Deondra talk about the process they use for problem solving as related to the breakup. She then helps the student to come up with several avenues and sources of support to help him through his crisis.

Just before she leaves for the day, Deondra checks to make sure the ACT (American College Test) booklets are ready for distribution to teachers who have juniors in their classes. She mails the request form with the number of state achievement tests she will need for this year's state exam. On her way out the door, Deondra checks her calendar for the next day. She will be meeting before school with the Pathways teacher team to review first marking period grades and determining the students who need extra academic support. She will then accompany the freshmen on a health and human services field trip. Yes, Deondra knows her job will always be demanding and challenging; however, she now feels she has a true comprehensive guidance system through Career Pathways. She knows that all students receive the necessary services they need to be well on their way to academic, career, and personal success.

THE IMPORTANCE OF COMPREHENSIVE GUIDANCE

The first person you want to "recruit" in the development of a Collaborative Career Pathways High School is your guidance counselor. This stakeholder has more to gain by helping to develop a Pathways High School than any other professional in your building. Why? Because comprehensive guidance programs need to meet the needs of all students, and because our counselors, like Deondra, are so overwhelmed by their tasks that it is a great relief to have the entire staff and community helping to develop student potential in key life areas. According to the American School Counselor Association, this is the way it should be—the counselor facilitating the *systems* that "promote and enhance" student learning (Campbell & Dahir, 1997).

To understand the role of the counselor in a Pathways High School, we first review what a school guidance counselor is and what role these stakeholders play in implementing a comprehensive guidance program in any high school. In 1997, the American School Counselors Association Governing Board adopted a new definition of school counseling:

Counseling is a process of helping people by assisting them in making decisions and changing behavior. School counselors work with all students, school staff, families, and members of the community as an integral part of the education program. School counseling programs promote school success through a focus on academic achievement, prevention and intervention activities, advocacy, and social/emotional and career development. (Campbell & Dahir, 1997)

The ASCA further defines good, comprehensive guidance programs as offering the following:

- Proactive and preventive assistance
- Assistance to help students in acquiring and using lifelong learning skills
- Strategies to enhance academics
- Career awareness
- Employment readiness
- Self-awareness

A common mistake among educators, parents, and the community is to believe that the school counselor is the counseling program. The school counselor and school counseling program use a collaborative model as their foundation. Counselors do not work alone; all educators play a role in creating an environment that promotes the achievement of identified student goals and outcomes. The counselor facilitates communication and establishes links, for the benefit of students, with teaching staff, administration, families, student-service personnel, agencies, businesses, and other members of the community (Campbell & Dahir, 1997).

The goal of a school counseling program is developed from the definition of school guidance programs. The primary goal of the school counseling program is to promote and enhance student learning through the areas of

- Academic development
- Career development
- Personal and social development (Campbell & Dahir, 1997)

The comprehensive school counseling program *integrates* academic, career, and personal and social development. It is important to review honestly whether counselors are able to handle—effectively and efficiently—all of these areas from their offices. It is our observation that traditional guidance counselors will end up spending the majority of their time with the top 20% and the bottom 10% of students in helping with college plans and dealing with crisis issues. This leaves the middle majority with limited services. The job of the traditional high school counselor has grown to such large and diverse proportions that the load cannot be handled with the traditional paradigm. It is obvious to us that the majority of our high schools do not have the resources or the support to add the number of counselors they need to be effective with all students. Counselors in a traditional high school system are overwhelmed by the limited time they have to perform and facilitate the three key components of counseling, as well as by the number of students for which they have responsibility and the diversity of their tasks.

Counselors may traditionally be responsible for student scheduling, testing, career planning, student problems, and crisis issues, and many of the connections to the community such as job shadowing and cooperative programs, but they seldom have a system for which all this can be applied for all students. The Pathways System will tie all these areas together for your counselors, and it will reach 100% of your student population. In fairness, the challenges for the continual improvement of student achievement that high school counselors face are just as steep as those pressed on classroom teachers. The paradigm must change for all students to receive the services they need in their academic, career, and personal and social development.

> *Guidance counselors are the pivotal people in the Pathways High School because they are the ones who will orchestrate the entire operation through the three key areas of a comprehensive guidance program.*

CAREER PATHWAYS AND TRADITIONAL HIGH SCHOOL GUIDANCE PROGRAMS

Career Pathways offers a wonderful solution to the growing need for comprehensive guidance programs in our high school while meeting the needs of the growing challenge to classroom teachers.

In her book *Getting From Here to There... Education for the New Millennium*, Dr. Tommie Radd (2000) addresses the need for school redesign through the integration of academic, career, and social skills. A key point Radd makes is that these skills are taught in isolation; they are not connected to student performance nor practiced. "Student success is viewed as a test score and not a performance skill that includes emotional, personal, social and behavior skills" (Radd, 2000, p. 27).

In the previous chapter, we explained the counseling pillar and its integration to the classroom and community. This pillar is "scaffolded" over four years in the previously mentioned Pathways classes of Freshman Exploration, Sophomore Selections, Junior Judgments, and Senior Transitions. The curriculum of each class is further developed in Chapters 7, 9, and 10. In this chapter, we show you how these classes "blend" with your comprehensive guidance program through counselor–teacher collaboration. We also discuss how EDPs and portfolios are used as the documentation for student success and how data is collected and used to evaluate and reinforce your system.

> *The Pathways Solution: Counselors team with teachers in the classroom and students practice important guidance skills in collaboration with parents and community.*

> *In the Collaborative Career Pathways Model, the integration of the academic, career, and personal and social skills required in a comprehensive guidance program is accomplished by the creation, development, placement, and implementation of the Pathways classes.*

The classes required at each level of a student's high school experience provide the venue for counselors and teachers, as well as parents and the community, to team and to collaborate to meet the needs of all students in the areas of academic, career, and personal and social skills. It also gives students a place to practice the skills being presented to them before they are required to use them outside the classroom. This concept is so important, we must repeat it: *The practice of integrating academic, career, and personal and social skills for students is key to their success during and after their schooling years.*

This is accomplished in three channels. The first of these is through the academic and career skills taught by counselors and teachers and practiced by students in the Pathways classes. The teacher and counselor collaborate to implement the national counseling standards, which are a part of each of the Pathways curricula. These concepts are then reinforced in the second arena, the core and elective classroom, and then experienced by students in the third arena, their community connection. During freshman year, for example, teaming is a key concept that is introduced and taught by the counselor and teacher. It is important at this juncture for counselors to be sure that the teacher is comfortable with the integration and use of teaming skills in the classroom and that the teacher has the materials and training needed to implement this portion of the system successfully. The teacher then continues to teach and reinforce the concept using teaming in the integrated thematic units that explore each Pathway. The students first learn, practice, internalize, and experience teaming in the classroom. It is then reinforced in the workplace through their classroom speakers and their site visits. This understanding of teaming for students is not accidental; it is planned throughout the year and targeted in the community experience, thus achieving the necessary integration of the counseling, classroom, and community pillars through an identified and targeted key area. The same happens with conflict resolution, anger management, negotiation skills, and so on. All this begins in the counselor's arena and weaves through the classroom and the community. If this were a space mission, the counseling office would be the command and control center, the classroom the laboratory, and the community the flight mission.

The second channel by which the counselor implements the Pathways Model is through the scheduling process and the use of educational development plans and portfolios. In a Collaborative Pathways High School, classes are grouped by Pathway to give students an understanding of what they need to take to complete their plan. We discuss how to accomplish this grouping in the next section of the chapter. In brief, the concept is that students start with a broad schedule their first year and focus their course of study each year until the senior year is customized to their transition needs. This broad-to-narrow concept allows students to explore and make decisions each year to enhance their understanding and sound decision making of their future.

> *Your counseling or student services office personnel will be the facilitators of the integration and practice of academic, career, and personal and social skills over a four-year period through the collaboration of counseling, classroom, and community processes.*

Educational Development Plans are the road maps for this journey. EDPs begin at the end of the eighth grade, when students plan their first year of high school, and are then updated each year. The what, where, and how of EDPs is also provided in this chapter. Connected to the EDP is the portfolio. Portfolios are actually documentation of a student's journey through Pathways. It will contain papers, projects, pictures, assessment, and so on for students to use to plan and accomplish each step of their journey and finally as a transition tool.

The last channel for the completion of the Pathways comprehensive guidance program is student testing and data collection. The counseling office is traditionally responsible for state and national testing programs, and some offer some type of aptitude testing. This task is no different in a Pathways High School except that these tests are not just filed away but used in planning and implementing student Pathways decision making. Besides the traditional state and national tests, Pathways High School tests also include interest and aptitude, personality profiles, as well as learning styles, multiple intelligences, and so on. All these tests are then used interactively by students in their Pathways classes to understand themselves, set goals, and plan their own future.

A final important step for the guidance or student services office is data collection. The "central command center" needs to know whether what they are doing is working, retrieve information to fill in the gaps, and make decisions with the staff on documented student needs. This must be done by gathering data and surveys from the students, discussed in more detail later in the chapter.

In summary, the Collaborative Career Pathways High School counseling channels and outcomes are shown in Table 5.1. Table 5.2 highlights the key differences between traditional and Pathways deliveries of the key guidance components.

Table 5.1 Pathways Counseling Channels and Outcomes

Counseling Channels	Outcomes	Key Developmental Area
Pathways Classes and connections to core and elective classrooms	Enhance the teaching and practicing of academic, career, and personal and social skills for all students	• Academic • Career • Personal and social
Scheduling, Educational Development Plans, and portfolios	Creation of an individualized four-year road map and student documentation for each student's high school journey	Career development
Student testing and data collection	Coordination of student testing programs and decision making through data on evaluation and improvement of student success in the areas of academics, career, and personal and social skills	Academic and career development

Table 5.2 Key Differences Between Traditional and Pathways Guidance Components

Category	Traditional	Pathways
Academic development	• Appropriate placement through skill level • Tutoring programs	• Reinforced skills in Pathways classes • Systematic teaching of study skills in Pathways classes • Practice of academic skills in the community • Appropriate placement through interest and aptitude • Tutoring programs
Career development	• Isolated aptitude testing • Isolated plans • Counselor-led processes • Parental input • Statement of needed skills • Sporadic experiences in the community for students • Postsecondary planning for some students • Some transition planning	• Integration of aptitude testing and coursework • Living documented plans • Student-led processes • Parental input • Practice of needed skills • Community-related experiences for all students • Postsecondary plans for all students • Senior projects for all student transitions
Social and personal development	• Isolated character education, peer counseling, or other student programs • Isolated individual outreach • Crisis issues "capped" and referred	• Personal and social skills taught and practiced by all students that are added to and built on each year • Personal and social skills integrated into the curriculum • Personal and social skills practiced in the community • All students have interaction with the counselors, setting the stage for more open communication • Crisis issues "capped" and referred

PATHWAYS COMPREHENSIVE GUIDANCE AND NATIONAL COUNSELING STANDARDS

Your counselor(s), teaming with teachers in the Pathways classes, can systematically develop and implement a comprehensive guidance program. This guidance program will cover all the national standards and benchmarks of the American School Counselor Association for all students. The Pathways curricula are designed to identify, teach, and practice key career and personal and social skills needed for students at each level of their high school career while reinforcing core academic skills. These concepts and skills are aligned with the national counseling standards of the American School Counselor Association.

The academic development standards are hit hardest in the freshman year to ensure continued academic success throughout high school. The Freshman Exploration class works extensively on exploring the Career Pathways through academic development.

The career standards span all four years but are of greatest import during the sophomore and junior years. The personal and social skills must be integrated throughout all four years, each year building on the skills of the year before. Although the comprehensive guidance program is mainly integrated through the Pathways classes, it should be reinforced in all core and elective classes as well. Tables 5.3 and 5.4 help to connect the four-year Pathways process while integrating the national standards and clarifying roles.

> *It is key during freshman year to work with students on study skills, effective learning habits, balancing school and other aspects of life, and the connection to schoolwork and their futures.*

SCHEDULING IN A CAREER PATHWAYS HIGH SCHOOL

As previously mentioned, in a Career Pathways High School, classes are scheduled by Pathway. In this way, students do not pick classes by what their friends are doing, by which they "heard" to take and not take, because they are going to college or because they are not going to college. They choose their classes by what will help them to reach their goals. Students will ask themselves, "I want to be in the health (engineering, art, etc.) field, so what are the best classes for me to take to reach this goal?"

To achieve this type of scheduling, counselors and staff must work together to format classes into the Pathways. Each department must decide which of the classes they offer is a requirement, a recommendation, or an option for each Pathway. Of course, all students still take the requirements for graduation, but their schedules are built around their Pathway. Pathways four-year schedules are developed for each Pathway your school offers. Table 5.5 is a sample of a school's class requirements and recommendations for the Health Pathway. Table 5.6 is a sample of a four-year schedule for a student who plans to pursue a career in pediatrics. Notice that the schedule moves from general to specific.

(Text continues on page 97)

Table 5.3 Integrating the Four-Year Pathways Process and National Standards: Academic, Career, and Personal and Social Development

Academic Development in the Pathways Counseling System

Freshman Explorations	Sophomore Selections	Junior Judgments	Senior Transitions
• Study skills: listening, note taking, skimming and scanning, test taking • Library skills • Working independently and cooperatively (teaming) • Learning styles • Positive learning attitudes • Introduction of the relationship between schoolwork and goals	• Reinforcement of freshman study skills • Stronger relationship between school work and goals • Time management • Interviewing skills • Presentation skills	• Time-management and reliability skills • Connection of schoolwork and postsecondary plan • Government regulations	• Persuasion • Project design • Transition between schoolwork and postsecondary plan

Key Outcomes

• Study skills • Academic confidence	• Academic and career connections	• Academics and career focus • Preliminary senior project plans	• Successful postsecondary transition for academic success

Academic Development National Standards[a]

Standard A: Students will acquire attitudes, knowledge, and skills that contribute to effective learning in school and across the life span.

Standard B: Students will complete school with the academic preparation essential to choose from a wide range of substantial postsecondary options, including college.

Standard C: Students will understand the relationship of academics to the world of work, and to life at home and in the community.

Career Development in the Pathways Counseling System

Freshman Explorations	Sophomore Selections	Junior Judgments	Senior Transitions
• Personality profiling • Interest and aptitude testing • Pathways exploration • Educational Development Plans (EDPs) and introduction of portfolio development	• Employability skills: job seeking, resumes, interviews, job termination, cover letter, applications, thank you letters • EDPs and portfolio development • Career research • Career ladders • Career interviews • Job shadowing	• Workplace experience combinations: job-shadowing series, 2–3 short internships or 1 longer internship • Job maintenance skills • On-the-job problem solving • Transition planning • EDPs and portfolios	• Senior project as related to postsecondary plan or transition • Postsecondary options searches, applications, essays, scholarships, visitations, • Portfolio completion

(Continued)

Table 5.3 (Continued)

Key Outcomes

- Pathway selection
- Introduction of portfolio

- Cluster selection
- Internship or career tech plans
- Portfolio development

- Preliminary postsecondary plan
- Portfolio development

- Portfolio and senior project presentation
- Successful postsecondary transition for career preparation

Career Development National Standards[a]

Standard A: Students will acquire the skills to investigate the world of work in relation to knowledge of self and to make informed career decisions.
Standard B: Students will employ strategies to achieve future career goals with success and satisfaction.
Standard C: Students will understand the relationship between personal qualities, education, training, and the world of work.

Personal and Social Development in a Pathways Counseling System

Freshman Explorations	*Sophomore Selections*	*Junior Judgments*	*Senior Transitions*
- Teaming - Assertiveness training - Conflict resolution - Problem solving - Goal setting - Decision making	- Reinforce teaming and conflict resolutions skills - Character education - Sender–receiver communications - Time and stress management - Writing goal and vision statements - Goal-setting and decision-making process and practice - Self-evaluation skills	- Reinforce teaming and conflict-management skills - Anger-management skills - Personal presentation skills - Ethical decision making - Confidentiality	- Advanced problem solving - Integration of people skills through senior panels

Key Outcomes

Students will be able to
- Work together and resolve conflicts
- Write goals
- Identify problems and brainstorm solutions
- Use a decision-making process

Students will be able to
- Use time- and stress-management skills
- Understand basic communication skills
- Understand and apply positive character traits
- Set goals
- Make decisions
- Self-evaluate

Students will be able to
- Use anger-management techniques
- Present themselves positively to others
- Make ethical decisions
- Understand and apply confidentiality

Students will be able to
- Use personal and social skills to make a successful postsecondary transition

Personal and Social Development National Standards[a]

Standard A: Students will acquire the knowledge, attitudes, and interpersonal skills to help them understand and respect self and others.
Standard B: Students will make decisions, set goals, and take necessary action to achieve goals.
Standard C: Students will understand safety and survival skills.

Note: Standards are from the American School Counselor Association (Campbell & Dahir, 1997).

Table 5.4 Integrating the Four-Year Pathways Process: The Roles of Counselor, Teacher, and the Community

Counselor Role

Freshman Explorations	*Sophomore Selections*	*Junior Judgments*	*Senior Transitions*
• Reinforcement programs for academic needs such as tutoring programs • EDPs • Help with the arrangement of site visits and speakers • Introduction of teaming and conflict resolution, assertiveness training, goal setting, and problem-solving skills • State testing program	• Academic support • EDPs • Help arrange job shadows and interviews • Introduction of career ladders, Career Clusters, and research • Introduction of time management, communication, and character education • American College Testing (ACT)	• Academic support • EDPs • Introduction of anger-management techniques and ethical decision making • Introduction of postsecondary planning and senior projects • Internship support to teachers • ACT	• Academic support • Coordinate with teacher and student postsecondary planning and transitions • Senior data collection • ACT testing

Teacher Role

Freshman Explorations	*Sophomore Selections*	*Junior Judgments*	*Senior Transitions*
• Study skills • Pathway exploration • Speakers and site visits • Practice of personal and social skills • Portfolios • Classroom assessment	• Employability skills • Career ladders, Career Clusters, and research completion • Job shadowing supervision • Practice of time and stress management, character development activities, and communication skills • Portfolios • Assessment	• Student internship experiences and placement • Employment issues • Internship presentation • Preplanning for senior projects • Portfolios • Assessment	• Service learning experience • Mentor teams • Senior project development, portfolios, and presentations • Coordinate with counselor and student postsecondary planning and transitions • Assessment

Community Role

Freshman Explorations	*Sophomore Selections*	*Junior Judgments*	*Senior Transitions*
• Speakers • Site visits	• Interviewees • Job-shadow sites	• Mentors • Job sites	• Mentors • Panels • Advisors

Table 5.5 Required, Recommended, and Optional Pathways Classes for the Health Pathway

Health Pathway (credits required for graduation)[a]	Required[a]	Recommended	Optional
English (4)	English 9 English 10 English 11 English 12	Communications/ public speaking	AP English Journalism Mythology Public speaking Technical English
Math (2)	Algebra Geometry	Advanced algebra Trigonometry Pre-calculus	Calculus Statistics
Science (2)	Physical science Biology	Chemistry Physics Anatomy	Earth science Environmental issues
Social Studies (3)	U.S. history World history Government	Psychology Basic Law	Sociology World cultures World religions
Health (1) Physical education (1)	Health Physical education	—	Personal conditioning Advanced Physical education
Pathway courses (4)	Freshman Explorations Sophomore Selection Junior Judgments Senior Transitions	—	—
Technology (1)	Computer applications		Programming Word processing Advanced applications
Foreign language (1)	Spanish, French, or Japanese	Spanish	French Japanese
Humanities (1)	Music, art, or theatre	—	—
Career/tech education (optional)	—	Nurse's aide training or Health occupations	
Electives (12)	—	Business management Food and nutrition or child development	Art I–IV Music electives Theatre electives Business electives Life management electives Career technical electives

AP = advanced placement.
[a]Total credits for graduation = 32 credits (4 × 4 block)

Table 5.6 Sample Four-Year Schedule for a Pediatric Career

Student: Mark Howard	Grade 9		Grade 10		Grade 11		Grade 12	
	First	*Second*	*First*	*Second*	*First*	*Second*	*First*	*Second*
Block 1	Freshman Explorations	English 9	English 10	Sophomore Selections	Junior Judgments	English 11	Senior Transitions	AP English
Block 2	Geometry	Physical science	Advanced algebra	Biology	Trigonometry	Chemistry	Pre-Calculus	Anatomy
Block 3	U.S. history	Art I	World history	Child development	Government	Psychology	Communications/ public speaking	Business management
Block 4	Spanish	Health	Spanish	Physical education	Spanish	Computer applications	Dual enrollment: Psychology: Human Development (first) Biology: Micro biology (second)	

96

When students begin to choose their classes by their own interests, aptitudes, and dreams, there is a significant shift in extrinsic and intrinsic motivation. This is where teachers, parents, and staff members really see the rewards of their efforts. Students can see the relevance of why they are taking certain classes. This is why it is important, and this will be discussed further in Chapter 11, that all teachers—Pathways, core, and elective—learn how to connect content to Pathways and student plans.

EDUCATIONAL DEVELOPMENT PLANS AND PORTFOLIOS

Educational Development Plans

In the implementation of your counseling program, it is important to have a "road map" or EDP for all students and "documentation" of their trip through portfolios. EDPs are becoming common among high school counselors. The EDP is a documented process that begins at the end of eighth grade and continues throughout high school.

The documents are written or Web based and are a wonderful planning tool for students to become involved in the planning of their own high school experience. As students, counselors, and parents work together to develop and expand each plan year by year, students begin to understand important connections between school and their future plans. This plan therefore must document the connection between a student's high school experience and his or her future plans and goals and set the stage for a smooth transition to postsecondary options. The EDP lists what a student needs to do and documents what he or she has done to achieve his or her goal. This includes students' identifying career goals through assessment testing and work-based experiences and connecting them to their education and educational experiences. We therefore refer to this as a roadmap. A student may show a high interest in and aptitude for science, enjoy his or her work-based experiences in the outdoors, and design a plan to pursue a career in natural resources, for example. We recommend that the components shown in Table 5.7 be included in any EDP.

> *The goal of the EDP is to give students, counselors, teachers, and parents an arena in which to collaborate in the development, documentation, and updating of a student's individualized plan for high school.*

Each student's EDP must be reviewed and updated annually for it to become a "living" document for the student. In a Collaborative Career Pathways High School, your Pathways classes are a natural place to maintain the EDPs. Working with the teacher, the counselor will come to the classroom to help students develop, update, and implement this plan.

The parents must also endorse the plan. When the plan is first begun at the end of the eighth grade, we recommend that each counselor meet with small groups of parents to begin the process. After that time, hard copies of the document should be sent home for signature at the end of each year.

We recommend that you use a Web-based EDP for several reasons. It is more interactive and can be accessed from home or school at any time through

(Text continues on page 99)

Table 5.7 Components of the Educational Development Plan (EDP)

Category	Definition	Example
Personal information	This is where students enter their personal information. If the EDP is Web based, students can use their name with the school's address for security purposes.	Heather Johnson All American School 123 Star Lane Pleasantville, USA Student # 5555
Assessment results	This section allows students to enter information on any assessments given by your school during their high school years. These may include academic, interest, aptitude, and self-knowledge testing such as learning styles.	State exam: proficient ACT: 24 Learning style: Auditory Multiple Intelligence: Spatial Career interest: Science Holland: Creator
Career Pathway choice	This section simply allows students to identify their career Pathway choice. It can also give them a second choice or allow for a Cluster or career.	Pathway: Science, Manufacturing, and Engineering Technology Cluster: Engineering Career: Automotive Engineer
Career preparation activities	This section allows students to keep track of all their career preparation activities. Each year this history helps students to "hone" their career decisions.	Site visit: Manufacturing plants: automotive and pharmaceutical Interviews: civil, automotive, and chemical engineer Job shadows: automotive and chemical engineer, draftsman, foreman
Extracurricular activities and interests	This section helps students to record extracurricular activities or awards earned during their high school years.	Spanish club Spanish Student of the Year Volleyball team Peer counselor Concert band
Plans and preparation: • Short-term goals • Long-term goals • Academic activities • Career activities	This section has students provide information about their goals and objectives. The short- and long-term goals are written in a sentence form. The academic and career activities then list actual activities that must be done to reach those goals.	Short-term goal: to decide between chemical and automotive engineering Long-term goal: to complete a degree in engineering and work in an area that will help to improve the environment Academic activities: take a pre-calculus and calculus class Career Activities: attend career center on automotive technologies, explore option of armed forces engineering program

(Continued)

Table 5.7 (Continued)

Category	Definition	Example
Postsecondary Plan	Students state their current postsecondary plan.	Complete a two-year degree in drafting, a four-year degree in automotive engineering, and a master's degree in environmental engineering through college or armed forces training
Class selection	This section allows students to select their classes for the next school year with the help of their counselors.	Junior English Physics Government Statistics Graphic arts Computer applications
Web site links (if applicable)	If the EDP is Web based, it can be linked to career and college sites for students.	Career site College search site
Endorsements	All EDPs should be signed by the student, parent, and counselor. The EDP can be printed and sent home for signature, or a signature box can be checked by parents on the Web.	Student signature Parent signature Counselor signature

Note: This table was compiled with the assistance of Joan Helwig (personal communication, July 2003), a middle school counselor at Cass City Middle School, in Michigan.

the use of student user IDs and passwords. It is also always accessible to parents. In addition, the Web-based EDP is a wonderful tool for counselors because they can gather data and information on students' needs, plans, and so on through the many reports that can be generated through the EDP. Confidentiality can be ensured through the use of user IDs and passwords, and personal information can list only the student's name and school.

Table 5.8 is a sample of the EDP of a student who is completing his junior year.

The most important points to remember when implementing an EDP process is for that process to be in the hands of students, user-friendly, and easy to access and that it be systematically reviewed and applied.

Portfolios

Portfolios are simply a collection of student work. This work can be collected for a number of reasons, such as assessment, demonstrating academic growth, or even to fulfill a state or local mandate. However you may choose to use portfolios in your school, the goal must be clear to teachers and to students.

Table 5.8 Sample Educational Development Plan for a Student Completing Junior Year

Educational Development Plan: Mark Howard
All-American High School, June 2002

Assessment Results:

Michigan Occupational Information System:	Arts and Communication
Holland:	Creator/Artistic
Hartman Personality:	Blue (Relationships)
Learning Style:	Auditory
Multiple Intelligences:	Musical/Linguistic

State Exam: Proficient in all subjects
ACT: 24

Career Pathway Choice:

Assessment-Based Recommendation: Arts and Communication
Career Pathway Choice: Arts and Communication
Career Choice: Music Teacher

Career Prep Activities:

Interviews: private music teacher, orchestra player, music store owner, disk jockey, teacher, guitar maker
Job Shadows: Instrument repair technician, Music Therapist, Music Teacher
Internships: Disc Jockey (four weeks) and music teacher (five weeks)
Work-related experience: tutor for middle school music students

Extracurricular Activities and Interests:

National Honors Society	Marching Band
Jazz Band	Track

Plans and Preparation:

<u>Short-Term Goals</u>: I would like to examine the differences between teaching music in an elementary school and a high school. I would like to begin training on other instruments, especially keyboard.

<u>Long-Term Goals</u>: I would like to teach music in a public school and to develop a private tutoring program for brass instruments.

<u>Academic Activities</u>:
- Search and apply to colleges
- Design a senior project around music
- Dual enroll in a college music theory class

<u>Career Activities</u>:
- Decide between elementary and secondary teaching
- Take piano/keyboard lessons
- Continue to tutor middle school music students

<u>Postsecondary Plan</u>:
- Bachelor's degree in music
- Teaching certificate

Class Selection Grade 12

First semester	Second semester
Senior English	Senior Transitions
Marching band	Jazz band
Physics	Psychology
Government	College online: Music theory

Signatures

Student: _____ Date _____
Parent: _____ Date _____
Counselor: _____ Date _____

Beginning freshman year, students collect their work as well as information about themselves that show their academic progress, self-exploration, experiences in the workplace, and samples of personal and social skills. This might include a student's interest and aptitude test, personality profile, journal entries on site visits, a sample of an integrated team project, and his or her Pathways choice paper. Each year students add to their portfolios and decide what will remain in the portfolio and what can be eliminated. Sophomore year might include interviews, sample applications, and job-shadowing reports, an assertiveness-training certificate, and an integrated project. Junior year may include an internship presentation, ACT scores, peer counseling credentials, an academic award, and so on.

> *In a Collaborative Career Pathways High School, portfolios are used to document the progress, achievements, and fine-tuning process of students' postsecondary plan as it relates to their academic, career, and social development.*

Student input on the portfolio is important. We suggest a combination of teacher requirements and student choices. This gives students direction and flexibility in their portfolio development. In a Collaborative Career Pathways High School, the portfolio is kept in the Pathways classes and moves with the student each year. This, however, does not discourage students from selecting items from other classes to include in their portfolios. This is especially true for the core and elective classes that are directly related to a student's academic and career plans. Portfolio items would also include awards, certificates, and other items earned or presented to students.

The uses of the Pathways portfolio are

1. To help students make realistic and informed decisions about each level of their postsecondary plan
2. To give students a sense of movement and accomplishment as they build their plan
3. To give students a collection of work for display
4. To aid counselors, teachers, parents, and community in working with students

To begin a portfolio process, sit down with your counselors and teachers and design a required and suggested list for students for each year of their high school experience in your school. Include the EDP, their Pathways work, and their core, elective, and extracurricular activities. We suggest you buy "rolling" carts with student portfolio files to be moved each year as they progress in their Pathways courses. Establish a review process for students, counselors, and teachers to examine and use portfolios at the beginning, middle, and end of each year. By making portfolio presentations a part of each student's senior project and sharing them with parents at open houses and other specified times, portfolios will have the potential to transform instruction powerfully for both students and teachers. In this way, students will have concrete proof of their learning processes and career development.

STUDENT TESTING AND DATA COLLECTION

Your guidance or student services office will be the central location for student testing programs and the collecting and dispersing of data to you, your staff, and your community. Traditionally, high school counseling and student services departments are responsible for state and national testing programs. This is no different in a Career Pathways High School. State achievement tests or assessment programs, as well as nationally normed tests such as the American College Test or Scholastic Assessment Test, fall into the realm of the counselor. Additional tests, such as the Armed Services Vocational Aptitude Battery, will be centrally located in your counseling office. This responsibility also gives counselors a wealth of information about the students in your school. The information that can be obtained through the analysis of these tests can be a great tool in helping your counselors work with administrators and teachers to identify and correct student needs in the areas of academics, career preparation, and personal and social skills. There are many software programs that can take raw data and aggregate it into a useable format. This can also be done by simply charting testing results year by year and by charting the results of each class of students as it progresses through your school.

Data can mean more than just the interpretation and analysis of test scores. There are basically four types of data (Bernhardt, 2003, p. 26):

- Demographic data: describe the students, the school staff, and the surrounding community
- Student learning data: a variety of measurements that show the impact of your education system on your students (from norm-referenced tests to classroom assessments)
- Perceptions data: show what students, parents, teachers, and the community think about the learning environment; gathered through surveys, questionnaires, interviews, and observation
- School processes data: information collected on school programs, instructional strategies, assessment strategies, and classroom practices

In a Career Pathways High School, it is important to collect data in all four of these areas and connect it to your Pathways system. What are your demographics and what specific needs does this imply for your students and your community? What types of business and industry do you have as a resource for your work-based programs? In general, how do demographics affect the process and concentration of your Pathways system? This includes the skills you need to include in your Pathways classes. For example, if your demographics show a large English-as-a-second-language population, the use of English in academic, career, and social skills will be an important aspect of your learning process and your Pathways curriculum.

Student learning data will be an important aspect of your data collection because it will be critical for you to show that your Career Pathways system is not lowering student achievement—in fact you will want to show how your new system is increasing student achievement across the board. Student achievement data will be collected by aggregating (looking at the whole) and disaggregating (looking at specific parts) the information you receive through the multiple measurements you use to determine and report student achievement (local, state, and national tests). This information will be the most powerful in dealing with your academic community.

Perception data will measure how your students, teachers, parents, and the community in general are feeling about the new changes in your system. This perception will be based on your ability to convey what really takes place in a Pathways High School and on the successful experiences of these groups as they go through your system. This data is best gathered by questionnaires, surveys, and interviews. Teacher-parent conferences are a good place to have teachers ask parents a few simple questions about your system and to record parents' responses. Surveys for parents and students at the end of each year can be a quick and precise way to measure the objectives of that year. Student exit surveys will show whether students understand the connection of each year of their high school experience to their feelings of being prepared and confident in their transition plan. Businesses should be asked their opinion after they provide a student work-based experience. This topic of public relations is examined in Chapter 12.

School process data is the examination of the entire system, including follow-up surveys. Follow-up first-year surveys will concentrate on the ability of students to move successfully into their postsecondary plans. The fifth year should show a completion of postsecondary training and a successful transition to the workplace in their chosen field. It should also reflect that students are now making above cost-of-living wages. The tenth year out should show a successful lifestyle with a stable and productive means of income. The surveys should also measure citizen involvement and commitment.

> *It is imperative in a Career Pathways High School that your counseling services conduct follow-up surveys the first, fifth, and tenth years out. If your goal is a smooth and successful transition for all students, you must know that successful transition is happening.*

These data will give your staff a wealth of information in adjusting your system to your students' future needs. Student, parent, and community volunteers, as well as support staff, can conduct student surveys. Remember when conducting senior exit surveys to collect information on how to contact students for follow-up surveys.

> *It is important to ask your former students what they feel helped them, what they feel hindered them, and what they feel was missing from their program.*

Table 5.9 helps to clarify the types of data to collect, the measure to use, when to use the measurement, and how it connects to the Pathways system.

Remember, data are vital to make sound decisions in three areas of student needs—academic development, career development, and personal and social development—and should be continuous throughout and after a student's journey through your school. *Don't overcomplicate the collection of data, however.*

Table 5.9 Data Collection

Type of Data	Measurement Tool	When to Measure	Pathways Connection
Demographics	Description of populations	Continuous examination	To aid in the determination of Pathways skill needs and community connections
Student learning	Local, state, and national assessments	Annual analysis	To show the connection between your Pathways system and student achievement
Perceptions	Questionnaires, surveys, interviews, and observations	Students and staff: at the end of each year Parents: during parent teacher conferences Businesses: after they sponsor a student work-based experience	To be able to deal with perceived and actual "glitches" along your Pathways system
School processes	Follow-up surveys	Entrance and exit student and parent surveys Student follow-up surveys	To measure how well you are achieving the goal of smooth and successful student transitioning and to identify system gaps and needed improvements

Decide what you want to achieve and collect the data to let you know if you are reaching that goal. Schmoker (2003, pp. 22–23), in his recent article *First Things First*, states, "to improve student achievement results, use data to focus on a few simple, specific goals. . . . The most important school improvement processes do not require sophisticated data analysis or special expertise." Your data should answer two simple questions: Are we reaching our goal? What does the data tell us about improving that goal?

CREATING AN AVENUE FOR PATHWAYS FLEXIBILITY

Another issue that your counselors will deal with in a Career Pathways High School is helping students find and "stay the course." We want students to focus their high school experience and to be serious about their choices; however, we do not want to make the system so structured that they do not have the flexibility they need. From the start of high school, students go through four distinct stages of planning for and transitioning to their postsecondary plans:

1. Exploration (of self and the Pathways)

2. Selecting (first the Pathway and then the Cluster or career)

3. Judging (Career Clusters or career possibilities) through internships

4. Transitioning (to the next level) through a capstone culmination project

While this is a wonderful process and all students need to go through these stages, it is critical to remember that it is the student's plan; counselors in particular have to be flexible in allowing students to go through these stages at a speed that is right for them. When students do two or three shadows in Sophomore Selections and feel they may have chosen the wrong path, devising a new plan after consultation and counseling, which may involve more shadows in another Pathway, may be helpful. It may be that a new Cluster will be determined, or the student may need to make a Pathway change. If a student truly does not know what internship he or she wants, perhaps two mini-internships or several weeklong job shadows will be a better approach. When students get to their capstone project, they may need to go back and do a project that allows a comparison of two Clusters or a study of a career ladder within a single Cluster. One of a counselor's most important career development jobs in a Pathways High School is to help the students who need extra guidance in their plans. Although we want to have a system for all students, it is also necessary to build in enough flexibility so that we can move the students forward from where they are.

> *During the first years of operation of a Pathways system, the counselor must continue to reiterate to students, teachers, and parents that it is perfectly acceptable if a student's individual plan does not focus on a single career; each step of the way, the student eliminates some possibilities to move forward in a focused direction.*

If students have a solid experience at each level of high school, the decisions they make will be less likely to need further exploration. You will find that few students actually change their Pathway; they are more likely to change the Cluster or career goal within a Pathway. When students make a Pathway change, it is usually to a related Pathway, such as health to human services. It is recommended that your counselor set a process for making a Pathway change. This process might include a Pathway change application, a meeting with the student and his or her parents, a new Pathway choice paper, and a written plan for a new exploration process. However you deal with Pathway changes, be sure your students are getting solid experiences at each level, that a change process is available to them, and that they never feel locked into any choice but have the flexibility they need to create their own plan.

CONCLUSION

In conclusion, the key to a successful comprehensive guidance program in a Collaborative Career Pathways High School is the counselor–teacher collaboration and the systematic practice of skills by students through the three pillars:

counseling, classroom, and community. The roles of counselors in our schools are enormous, but with these partnerships, counselors can systematically reach all students. By dividing their tasks up into the three national standards of academic support, career preparation, and personal and social skills, and then distributing these skills in a four-year scaffolding Pathways process, counselors, with teachers and community members, can make an unmanageable task not only manageable but successful for all students. We do not deny that this is a great challenge and takes great dedication from our counselors, but it also offers them a system that will support their efforts. In any case, the blending of your comprehensive guidance program and your Career Pathways system is imperative to the success of Pathways implementation and maybe even the sanity of your counselors.

IN REVIEW

- Comprehensive guidance programs and Career Pathways are a natural fit.
- The primary goal of school counseling programs is to promote student learning through academic, career, and personal and social development for all students. This can be done by using the Pathways channel.
- Your guidance counselor is the pivotal person in your Pathways High School system because he or she is the one person who can orchestrate the entire Pathways operation.
- The key to combining comprehensive guidance and Career Pathways is the collaboration of counselors and teachers in the classroom.
- This collaboration is primarily implemented through the Pathways courses that are an intricate part of each year of a student's high school experience.
- All traditional counseling processes are integrated into the Pathways system. This includes scheduling, testing, and postsecondary planning.
- Scheduling in a Career Pathways High Schools is determined by a student's chosen Pathway.
- Educational Development Plans and portfolios are tools used in a Pathways High School to document students' Pathway journey and give credence to their decisions.
- Data are used in a Pathways High School to make informed decisions regarding academic, career, and personal and social achievement.
- Data are collected on demographics, academic success, perceptions, and school processes to maintain and improve the Pathways system.
- The role of any high school counselor is enormous; however, with the collaboration of counselors, teachers, and community members provided by a Career Pathways High School, this challenge can not only be manageable but highly successful in reaching all students.

Chapter Six

Curriculum in a Career Pathways High School

A Rationale for Standards, Mapping, and Integration

SCENARIO: SARAH AND ETHAN'S CURRICULUM EXPERIENCE

As Sarah sits in the empty classroom at the end of the school year on a hot June day, she reflects on this past school year with pride. She team teaches 10th-grade U.S. history with Ethan, trading students in the middle of the year on a 4 × 4 block. She can't believe how far she and Ethan's students have come this year, and she can verify their success. At the start of the year, she and Ethan had pretested the students to see how well they could perform on 8th- and 9th-grade social studies standards (in civics and global studies). The information obtained then helped the two of them come up with a strategy for the U.S. history concepts so that this year's curriculum could review and reinforce those earlier standards and benchmarks on which students had tested poorly. This week Sarah and Ethan posttested the students, and they were thrilled with the achievement the students' posttests had shown. The results are a good indicator of how well they will do on their state and college entrance exams. All of the data collection and analysis of the pre- and posttests will help guide members of the school's social studies department as they make a plan of success for their students.

Sarah reflects back on how she and Ethan have planned this year's lessons, assignments, projects, and tests based on content standards and benchmarks, essential life skills, and career and technology standards. Over the past year, they have used the computer database to see what standards and benchmarks students have mastered, and in the next few days they will add this year's newly mastered standards to the base. They will also add any notes of their own about mastery or tutoring to each student's individual file. Through the use of three sets of rolodex cards throughout the year, they have managed to plan all of their lessons around three key components: content, essential life skills, and career and technology standards. The state set the content standards and benchmarks Ethan and Sarah used. The faculty members selected the essential content and life skills that they thought were best for the students in their district, and the Pathways committee selected the career and technology standards, which were then approved by the entire faculty. So that the standards, and not a textbook, would drive instruction, members of the social studies department teamed to find a textbook and other related materials to best meet the department's goals.

As Sarah files away all the materials for the year, she glances down at the 10th-grade curriculum maps. Sarah and Ethan have had available to them maps not only of their curriculum but those of the other classes in their schools. These invaluable maps have told Sarah and Ethan exactly what their 10th graders have been learning in other classes and when. This allowed them to know that while they were covering post-Revolutionary America, their students were studying thesis statements in language arts, systems of the body in biology, color and contrast in art, goal setting in Sophomore Selections, spread sheets in technology, and blood-borne pathogens in health. This enabled them to support the curriculum of other teachers when possible. For example, to integrate and support the language arts curriculum, Sarah and Ethan had their students develop thesis statements for their project on the Preamble of the Constitution.

Sarah smiles as she puts boxes of integrated projects away in her closet to show to next year's 10th graders. Based on brain-based teaching and learning, the 10th-grade teachers had worked together to design an integrated project that required the use of U.S. history, language arts, Pathways, and technology. This project had students complete a research paper (language arts), based on one or two of their job shadow experiences (Sophomore Selections), that followed their Career Pathway or Cluster though the following eras in U.S. history: colonial, new republic; expansion, Civil War, Reconstruction; Industrial Revolution; World War I, the Great Depression, World War II; Cold War and Contemporary. These papers were then presented to the class through the use of technology (technology class) or art or music (any elective course). Some students presented their papers as a brochure, magazine, or newspaper, and others did theirs through pictures, videos, PowerPoint presentations, commercials, and even the creation of a rap song. All the 10th-grade teachers had worked together first to decide which standards and benchmarks to include from their subject area and then to design a rubric for the project that each student received. This 10th-grade mini-project helped the students practice many of the skills that would be required in the next few years to complete their larger senior capstone projects. It had been the first year of the project, and Sarah remembered how much fun and how much learning had taken place among the students.

Before next school year, the 10th-grade teachers plan to organize a work day to streamline and improve the project. The samples she put away will be invaluable in helping to improve the rubric. Sarah has been amazed at how her school has made a focused and concentrated effort to promote teaming and collaboration. An example of this effort is that she and Ethan share the same daily planning period to promote successful team teaching. In addition, her school has implemented an every-other-week late start time in which students come to school two hours late while teachers work together to improve instruction. During this time her department has a meeting of at least 30 minutes to touch base. At least once a month, the faculty members work together on a curriculum project or issue. In addition, the principal is committed to making certain the faculty has grade-level meetings at which all faculty members share maps and design curricula that integrate and engage students. As a beginning teacher, Sarah has really benefited from her 10th-grade "family" who works with her and supports her classroom endeavors.

Sarah and Ethan both know that they are fortunate young teachers to work in such a solidly curriculum-focused school. Their school has chosen a curriculum (for each department) that develops skills set by the departments and the high school faculty based clearly on their state's standards and benchmarks. *Using standards, alignment, mapping, brain-based learning, integration, and assessment systems weaves a solid base for each subject and expands the school's teaching strategies.* Sarah and Ethan both love teaching in this manner for many reasons:

- It is clear to them and to the students what they are expected to know and be able to do.
- Sarah and Ethan can share units, materials, planning, students, professional support, and ideas.
- Sarah and Ethan feel connected to the entire school faculty and feel that, both academically and professionally, they offer support to and receive support from their colleagues.
- The in-class assessments that Sarah and Ethan provide give them and their students immediate feedback, help in the planning of instruction, and are related to the state accountability system.
- Their subject is connected to their students' Career Pathway plan.
- Students are more engaged in their classroom and see the connections among various subjects.
- Sarah and Ethan, along with the social studies department, have ownership and control of their curriculum while keeping it consistent and meaningful.
- Sarah and Ethan have student data to make predictions and on which to base their instructional decisions.

As Sarah looks around the room and turns out the lights, she is glad this year is over, but she is definitely looking forward to continuing the curriculum process in August—she already has some new ideas.

THE IMPORTANCE OF CURRICULUM IN A COLLABORATIVE CAREER PATHWAYS HIGH SCHOOL

You may be wondering why you are reading about curriculum in the middle of a book on Career Pathways High Schools. The answer to this is simple: The Collaborative Career Pathways Model is instructionally based and therefore happens in the classroom.

> *The Career Pathways system cannot be successful in your school without your willingness to take ownership of your curriculum processes.*

If your teachers use a textbook as their curriculum and you ask them to implement this model, they will have to add it on to everything else they are doing—the results will be disastrous! Teachers cannot put one more thing on their already full plates. They will tell you they cannot teach history, and career skills, and life skills, and character skills—and so on and so forth. The truth is, however, they *can;* other teachers are doing it and doing it well. What we must do is teach the same skills within the same amount of time, but teach these skills *differently*. This can only be done if your faculty takes control of the curriculum.

> *The key to making this happen is for you (as leader) and a curriculum person (as facilitator) to work with teachers so that teachers can take ownership of the entire 9 through 12 curriculum—not only in their own content area, but also in the "broader" skills that all students need.*

The way this is done is to work with your teachers to determine what you want students to know and what they should be able to do, then use the appropriate materials to make that happen. This means that your teachers may have to alter or give up their favorite units for other units that teach the same skills in a different way. For example, an English teacher may teach comparing and contrasting with students examining two Pathways rather than two short stories.

When we work with teachers, we tell them that they are the experts in their field, as well as the experts in interacting with students. From a "big picture" perspective, we discuss what students need and show the teachers how Pathways can help meet these needs. We then facilitate their efforts while allowing them to do the work to make Pathways fit with their curriculum. The key here is threefold: provide the curriculum leadership, the structure (Pathways), and the time necessary to achieve the goals they set.

> *Success depends on giving your teachers a combination of structure, time, empowerment, and flexibility so that they can achieve what they know is important for students in a fashion that will work for them.*

Your teachers are the drivers using the road map you give them. They must have ownership of their curriculum, or the system will not work.

In this chapter, we give you a brief overview of the important curriculum processes or "steps" that you must address in a Pathways High School, or in any other system change or accreditation process. These steps include defining the curriculum, curriculum visions and outcomes, and standards and benchmarks; aligning curricula; mapping curricula; establishing brain-based instruction; and integrating curricula, including technology, assessment systems, and data analysis.

WHAT IS CURRICULUM?

Curriculum can be a "black hole" for many educators, but it is really not that complicated. The key to creating a curriculum is to understand that it is an ongoing process. Just as the human body must eat and rest on a regular basis, so must curriculum be continually addressed. So what is curriculum? *Curriculum is what you want a student to know and be able to do.* What do you want a language arts student in 9th, 10th, 11th, or 12th grade to know and be able to do with language arts concepts? This same question applies to all subjects.

A curriculum starts with a vision, moves to standards and benchmarks, and ends with assessment. The challenge in creating a curriculum is to have the end result meet the beginning vision. To ensure this outcome, there are certain curriculum processes and steps in which everyone must participate. Some processes must be done in order, whereas others can be interwoven throughout the process. For example, a school must begin by developing a vision of literate students and then move to identifying standards and benchmarks. Learning and training on brain-based instruction and expanded teaching strategies, however, can be done throughout the process. In curriculum, the principle of beginning with the end in mind is critical.

Curriculum Vision and Outcomes

The first step in beginning your curriculum processes is to sit down with your faculty and staff to develop a curriculum statement that includes goals for what student learners will look like when they exit your high school. This statement and list of goals are called cross-curricular standards or exit outcomes.

Cross-curricular standards or outcomes are broad, lifelong, and transferable, and they reflect community and workplace standards (Harris, 1996). We call them *life skills* in the Collaborative Career Pathways Model. Here is an example of a school's curriculum vision with cross-curriculum standards or life skills:

> *Cross-curricular standards (or outcomes) connect your entire curriculum and provide a common mission for all teachers.*

> *Cross-Curricular*
> *(Life Skills) Standards*
> *All students will be able to know and apply the necessary skills from their coursework to be able to*
>
> - *Use and apply essential academic skills (as determined by department)*
> - *Set goals and make decisions for themselves*
> - *Resolve conflict and accept diversity*
> - *Be able to work independently and as a team member*
> - *Be an involved citizen*
> - *Understand universal truths and global connections*
> - *Be a self-directed and lifelong learner*
> - *Use and apply technology*
> - *Understand and be able to do systems and critical thinking*

Teachers should be able to see how the life skills listed here can be taught in every content and can pull their subjects together. In the introduction scenario with Sarah and Ethan, every lesson had integrated in its planning and delivery a life skill that was identified by the faculty.

The second step is to do this exercise for each of your core subject areas, Pathways classes, and electives. Ask your teachers two questions: What does a literate social studies (or math, etc.) student look like when he or she leaves our school? What will that student's behavior look like—in other words, what will he or she be able to do? Table 6.1 is an example of a vision and outcome statement in English Language Arts.

What these teachers have done is "come together" to define and "focus" their curriculum. It is critical that faculty continue to discuss and observe the processes of curriculum if they are to understand how important the information in Table 6.1 is to their instruction. This allows them to design common assessments, to align to their state exams, and to use the standards to implement a Career Pathways curriculum using academic skills and rigor.

Standards and Benchmarks

After you have a vision of what a literate student looks like when exiting your school, the standards and benchmarks are where your curriculum begins. A standard is a written statement that describes what a student should know and be able to do in each subject. The benchmarks show at what level students should be able to do various developmental stages of that standard. Note that your curriculum is not your textbooks. Textbooks must only be one of the instruments by which you deliver the established curriculum.

Standards and benchmarks are usually organized first into strands. Strands are standards that have a common theme—for example, for language arts, literature skills; for math, data analysis skills; for social studies, geography skills. The breakdown is as follows (Michigan Department of Education [MDE], 1996):

Strands

Standards

Benchmarks

Table 6.1   A Literate English Language Arts Student

A literate English language arts student can communicate effectively through reading, listening, viewing, writing, and speaking. He or she can convey ideas using sound reasoning and with respect for others' points of view. Language arts students can use language arts effectively in both their career and personal lives.

Top Priority Standards

from the Michigan Curriculum Framework

Meaning and Communication: All students will focus on meaning and communication as they listen, speak, view, read, and write in personal, social, occupational, and civic contexts.

1. Integrate listening, viewing, speaking, reading, and writing skills for multiple purposes and in varied contexts. An example is using all the language arts to complete and present a multimedia project (or senior project) on a national or international issue.

Depth of Understanding: All students will demonstrate understanding of complexity of enduring issues and recurring problems by making connections and generating themes within and across texts.

1. Analyze and reflect on universal themes and substantive issues from oral, visual, and written texts.
2. Develop and extend a thesis by analyzing differing perspectives and resolving inconsistencies in logic to support a position.

Ideas in Action: All students will apply knowledge, ideas, and issues drawn from texts to their lives and the lives of others.

1. Use themes and central ideas in literature and other texts to generate solutions to problems and formulate perspectives on issues in their own lives.
2. Function as literate individuals in varied contexts within their lives in and beyond the classroom.

A sample of several strands for social studies may be as follows (MDE, 1996):

Historical Perspective

Geographic Perspective

Civic Perspective

Under each strand would then be listed standards:

Geographic Perspective:

Content Standard 1: All students will describe, compare, and explain the locations and characteristics of places, cultures, and settlements.

Table 6.2   Sample of Strands, Standards, and Benchmarks

Math Strand: Data Analysis and Statistics

Standard 1: Students collect and explore data, organize data into a useful form, and develop skill in representing and reading data displayed in different formats.

Benchmark 1	Benchmark 2	Benchmark 3	Benchmark 4
Collect and explore data through observation, measurement, surveys, sampling techniques, and simulations	Organize data using tables, charts, graphs, spreadsheets, and databases	Present data using the most appropriate representation and give a rationale for their choices; show how certain representations may skew the data or bias the presentations	Identify what data are needed to answer a particular question or solve a given problem and design and implement strategies to obtain, organize, and present those data

Career and Employability Strand: Teamwork

Standard 1: All students will work cooperatively with people of diverse backgrounds and abilities and will contribute to a group process with ideas, suggestions, and efforts.

Benchmark 1	Benchmark 2	Benchmark 3	Benchmark 4
Exhibit teamwork skills	Take personal responsibility for influencing and accomplishing group goal	Demonstrate understanding of how effective teams operate within organizational and diverse settings	Solve a career- or work-related problem as a member of a team

Under each standard would be listed benchmarks:

Standard 1: All students will describe, compare, and explain the locations and characteristics of places, cultures, and settlements.

Benchmark 1: Describe how major world issues and events affect various people, society, places, and cultures in different ways.

Benchmark 2: Explain now culture might affect women's and men's perceptions (MDE, 1996).

Table 6.2 is a sample of a strand and standard with benchmarks for a core and elective subject area (MDE, 1996).

The strands, standards, and benchmarks in Table 6.2 were taken from the Michigan Curriculum Framework developed by Michigan teachers and educational professionals through the MDE. Members of your faculty do not have to write their own standards and benchmarks. There are many good sets already available. When choosing the standards and benchmarks for your school, the first thing you want to consider is whether your state department of education has a set of standards and benchmarks it recommends. There are also national standards and benchmarks recommended by many of the content and elective areas professional organizations. If your state does not have a set of recommended standards and benchmarks, consider national standards such as those published in *Content Knowledge: A Compendium of Standards and Benchmarks for K-12 Education* (Kendall & Marzano, 2000).

If your state mandates accountability testing, you will want to adopt the standards from which it develops its tests. If you use a nationally normed reference test, check with your testing company or examine standards and benchmarks to determine what best reflects the knowledge and skills that the test measures.

> *The most important consideration when choosing your standards and benchmarks is to pick the set that is the closest aligned with your mandated testing program.*

When working with faculty members, we usually explain standards and benchmarks and their total relationship to curriculum by comparing curriculum to the human body: your standards and benchmarks are the skeleton of your curriculum. They give the curriculum its frame. The curriculum's muscles are the lessons and materials you develop to present and teach the standards. For example, a language arts standard to read and analyze a wide variety of classic and contemporary literature is the reading and comparing of *Romeo and Juliet* with the film *West Side Story*. The curriculum's skin and facial features give it a special appearance and are the events and personality that each teacher brings to his or her classroom. For example, every year a 10th-grade science teacher takes her class on a trip to the wetlands to participate in the catching and tagging of birds with the state wildlife bureau.

Curriculum Alignment

The next step is to align your curriculum. What this means is that you take your adopted standards and benchmarks and decide where they will be taught. This is important in a Collaborative Career Pathways High School because, in order to know where to place your Pathways curricula and when to do your counseling, classroom, and community activities, your must know which skills are currently being taught in which classrooms. An example of an alignment might be as shown in Table 6.3.

Some faculty members have taken curriculum alignment one step further by noting when a standard or benchmark will be introduced, mastered, or reviewed. When you align your standards, however, it is important to be sure that all students master the necessary standards and benchmarks before they take state or national exams. So, if your state exam for social studies comes at the end of Grade 11, ensure that all the standards and benchmarks covered by that test are taught and mastered by that time. This does not mean that in the year that follows, students cannot gain a deeper understanding and contextually practice the standard or benchmark; it does mean that it is unfair to students for them to take a test for which they have not been taught the standards being measured.

Table 6.3   Language Arts Strand: Ideas in Action

Language Arts Strand: Ideas in Action
Standard 1: All students will apply knowledge, ideas, and issues drawn from texts to their lives and the lives of others.

Benchmark 1	*Benchmark 2*	*Benchmark 3*
Students use themes and central ideas in literature and other texts to generate solutions to problems and formulate perspectives on issues in their own lives.	Students function as literate individuals in varied contexts within their lives in and beyond the classroom.	Students utilize the persuasive power of text as an instrument of change in their community, their nation, and the world
Alignment Freshman English Freshman Explorations	*Alignment* Sophomore English Sophomore Selections	*Alignment* Junior English Debate Class

Note: Strand, standard, and benchmarks from Michigan Department of Education (1996). Alignments are the authors'.

Curriculum Mapping

After you align your curriculum, the next step is to make a "road map." This map will tell your faculty *when* in the school year a particular standard, unit, or skill will be taught. The best way to map your curriculum is by the calendar year. Some schools map their curriculum by the month, some by marking periods, some even by weeks. However you choose to create your maps, this is a necessary step for teachers to be able to "piggyback" on each other's lessons and to integrate assignments and projects. Maps of skills and units are also great to share with students and parents, who can then supplement knowledge and skills at home. Maps can also give teachers a visual image of how they may rearrange the order in which they teach their subjects so as to better match what is taught in other classes. For example, teachers might align their schedules to combine a unit on fossil fuels in science class with a unit on the Middle East in social studies; this allows them to connect the two subjects for their students.

The most common mapping processes are those that Heidi Hayes Jacobs (1997) presents in her book and video series, *Mapping the Big Picture*. This series offers procedures for curriculum mapping, explains how to analyze and develop the maps, and shows how to use the maps to generate integration and assessments. Table 6.4 is a sample of a 9th-grade core curriculum map for the first semester in a traditional schedule.

Aligning and mapping curriculum should not stop at your building. This process should be used to create a K–12 curriculum sequence and bridge the gaps for students as they move from one year to the next.

Focusing on Key Content Skills and Department Goals

Once your faculty members have written the vision of literate students and chosen their standards, they can begin to "focus" their curriculum to give depth

Table 6.4 Grade 9 Core Curriculum—First Semester

Content	September	October	November	December	January
Grade 9 Language Arts: Freshman English	Literature and Short Stories	Sentence Structure and Paragraphing	Literature: The Drama	Research: The "I" Paper	Speaking Skills: The Oral Presentation
Grade 9 Science: Physical Science	Physical Science Methods	Energy and Motion	Matter	Substances	Interactions of Matter
Grade 9 Social Studies: Global Studies	Concepts of Geography and Culture	Global regions	Africa	Asia	Middle East
Grade 9 Math: Algebra I	Data and Relationships	Patterns	Functions	Linear Equations and Inequalities	Linear Functions and Graphs

and not just breadth to their teaching. The way this is accomplished is for the members of each department to review their vision, standards, and benchmarks and to choose the "key" standards that all students must master in depth. The key standards are the knowledge and skills that teachers will emphasize throughout the school and in integrated units, which we discuss later in this chapter. In *Professional Learning Communities at Work,* Dufour and Eaker (1998) explain how to focus a curriculum as follows: "a learning community will first identify academic goals, specific standards, and clear benchmarks, and then it will focus, focus, and focus on achieving the articulated results" (p. 163).

They way we suggest you tackle focused curriculum is to have your department teams meet and review their standards and benchmarks and select the "key" or essential skills (Dufour & Eaker, 1998) for their discipline. Then compile these key areas into a document to be shared with all members of the faculty. As content teams plan their instruction, they specifically reinforce the "key" or "essential" skills identified by the other content teams. Thus, your curriculum becomes holistic, and the stage is set for integration. An example of this document is shown in Table 6.5.

An example of the use of the essential skills in Table 6.5 was reflected in Sarah and Ethan's lesson planning in the opening scenario of this chapter, but there are many other examples. Mr. Timm's earth science class presentations on current pollution issues and their potential solutions, for example, can make effective use of both the English language and responsible citizenship, and becomes a graded part of his presentation rubric, thus reinforcing the essential skills of two other content areas. (See Table 6.6)

At this time, we also have members of each department write department goals and action plans to help them with the mastery and in-depth instruction

Table 6.5 Department-Defined Key Skills

Content	Essential Skill 1	Essential Skill 2
Language Arts	Gathers and uses information for research	Uses listening and speaking strategies for different purposes
Math	Uses a variety of strategies in the problem-solving process	Understands and applies advanced concepts of statistic and data analysis
History	Understands the historical perspective	Understands how democratic values came to be and how they have been exemplified by people, events, and symbols
Science	Understands the nature of scientific knowledge	Understands the nature of scientific inquiry
Arts and Humanities	Understands the connections among the various art forms and other disciplines	Understands the merit of one's own artwork and the artwork of others
Health and Physical Education	Knows how to maintain and promote personal health	Understands the social and personal responsibility associated with participation in physical activity

Note: From *Content knowledge: A compendium of standards and benchmarks for K–12 education* (3rd ed.), by J. S. Kendall and R. J. Marzano.

of essential skills and the integration of Pathways into their curriculum. These goals include everything from scheduling to professional development to new materials. A sample of department goals may be as shown in Table 6.6.

The Basics of Brain-Based Learning— Content Versus Context

The most important concept to understand in teaching to the brain is to understand the difference between content learning and context learning. Content learning is the knowledge and skills of a particular content, such as science. Context learning is the use and application of those skills outside of the classroom. How do students use the science they learn in the classroom, and why is that content important? "Why do we have to learn this?" is a relevant question, and one that all teachers should be able to answer. *The brain always learns and retains best in context.* In a Collaborative Career Pathways High School, we use the student's Career Path as the contextual piece. This helps teachers and students to connect and to add relevancy to the classroom. For example, if a science class is studying the uses of energy, a question or assignment might be, "How are energy and its principles used in your Pathway, Career

Table 6.6 Department Goals

Department Goals: Science	Outcome	Time Line	Person(s) Responsible
1. Develop a stronger mastery of earth and environmental science skills before the 10th-grade state science exam.	Work with counselors to schedule a two-year science semester rotation that includes physical and earth sciences.	Current year: plan Next year: implement	Timm Hosea
2. Understand how science concepts are used in the workplace and in the Career Pathways adopted by our school.	All science teachers will job shadow or summer intern in a science-related career.	Current year: half of the department faculty will experience a job shadow Next year: second half of faculty will experience a job shadow Selection process for several teachers for summer internships through the local university program	Smith Yun
3. New technical experimental labs are integrated into the science curriculum.	Work with the administration for budgeting, purchasing, and training for new technical science labs.	Current year: examine labs for recommendation Next year: Lab 1 Following year: Lab 2	Timm Yun
4. Systematically use problem-based and facilitated learning activities in all science classes.	Professional development for conducting problem-based learning and facilitated classes in science.	Current year: examine programs find training, make recommendations to administration Next year: participate in training Following year: participate in training	Hosea Smith

Cluster, or career?" How is energy used in natural resources or engineering? How is energy used in the arts and communication? *Students need to understand why and how knowledge and skills relate to them and their future.*

Brain research is being conducted at the highest level in history. We have learned more about the brain in the last few decades than in all the centuries that came before combined. In education, there are many good materials available on teaching, learning, and the brain. These materials make wonderful study and discussion group materials for teachers, and the materials can be used to help teachers understand why Career Pathways works for students. A few of these include Sousa's (1995) *How the Brain Learns: A Classroom Teacher's Guide,* Jensen's (1998) *Teaching with the Brain in Mind,* and Sprenger's (1999) *Learning and Memory: The Brain in Action.*

Caine and Caine (1991) presented the educational community with 12 principles of brain-based learning. Table 6.7 provides those principles and their relation to Career Pathways. This is also enhanced by Howard Gardner's theory on multiple intelligence, which expands our educational learning processes beyond words and calculations. Table 6.8 is a chart of how the multiple intelligences blend in a Pathways School. For more information and resources on multiple intelligences, see Gardner (1983) and Armstrong (1993).

The What and How of Integrating Your Curriculum

Integrating your curriculum is a critical component of implementing brain-based learning in the classroom. This is especially true for a Career Pathways High School because the curriculum is both applied and based on essential content and life skills.

Once your faculty has been exposed to and understands brain-based learning and has completed the following curriculum steps, you are ready to begin your integration process:

1. Identify life skills to be taught across the curriculum (cross-curriculum standards).

2. Focus on the essential skills in each discipline.

3. Align and map your curriculum so that everyone knows which standards are taught, as well as when they are taught, and where they are taught.

Integration of your curriculum simply means that at certain points in time, you "hook" the curriculum together to help reinforce importance skills so that the curriculum makes sense and allows students to make connections. This does not mean that every teacher—every day and with every lesson—is integrating with all other teachers. There will be lessons or days in which a math teacher is concentrating only on a math skill or unit, and there will be days when he or she can connect to another subject or to the curriculum at large.

For example, it is easy to hook environmental issues in science with citizenship in social studies or to use statistics in math with technical writing for language arts. A language arts teacher may connect with the art or computer teacher to do a brochure or advertisement. The possibilities are endless and can be made to fit your school's curriculum.

> *The fear that many of your teachers may have is that math teachers will have to become "English teachers" or that science teachers will have to become "history teachers." Please dispel this fear immediately. Integrating the curriculum happens only at places at which it makes sense and a natural connection exists.*

Table 6.7 The 12 Principles of Brain-Based Learning in Relation to Career Pathways

Principle	General Definition	Connection to Career Pathways
The brain is a parallel processor.	The brain performs many functions simultaneously, pertaining to thoughts, emotions, imagination, etc.	Collaborative Pathways High Schools use holistic learning and integrated units.
Learning engages the entire physiology.	The brain is connected to all other systems of the body—anything that affects our physiological function affects our capacity to learn.	The model consistently uses technology and "whole-body" learning experiences through teaming and site visits.
The search for meaning is innate.	The search for meaning is survival oriented and basic to the human brain. If the brain cannot find meaning in knowledge, it is not likely to retain it.	There is a strong connection between learning and each student's life through his or her own plans.
The search for meaning occurs through "patterning."	The brain is designed to perceive and generate patterns. The brain resists having isolated pieces of information that are unrelated, and it cannot make "sense" of such data. Its natural capacity is to integrate information.	The Collaborative Pathways Model incorporates integrated units in all classes—Pathways, core, and electives.
Emotions are critical to patterning.	What we learn is influenced and organized by emotions and mind-sets involving expectancy, personal biases and prejudices, self-esteem, and the need for social interaction. Emotion and cognition cannot be separated. Emotions are also critical to memory.	Collaborative Pathways has the power to provide real-world experiences at all four grade levels.
Every brain simultaneously perceives and creates parts and wholes.	In a healthy person, the brain's two hemispheres are inextricably interactive. Educators must understand the requirement to acknowledge separate but simultaneous (whole) tendencies for organizing information. One is to reduce such information into parts; the other is to perceive and work with it as a whole.	In all Pathways classes, there is a combination of integration, multiple intelligences, and real-world experiences.

(Continued)

Table 6.7 (Continued)

Principle	General Definition	Connection to Career Pathways
Learning involves both focused attention and peripheral perception.	The brain absorbs the information of which it is directly aware and to which it is paying attention. It also absorbs information and signals that lie beyond the immediate focus of attention.	Students are aware of so much more than what educators are teaching. In a Pathways high school, students understand that their needs are incorporated into the work of every class.
Learning always involves conscious and unconscious processes.	We learn more than we consciously understand (unconscious processing). We remember what we experience, not just what we are told. For example, students can learn to do division and learn to hate math at the same time.	Students have a wide variety of experiences related to all subject matter, but especially to subject matter that matches their plans.
We have two types of memory: a spatial memory system and a set of systems for rote learning.	The brain has a spatial memory system and a rote memory system. Spatial (real-life) experiences are long term and embedded in the brain. Rote learning is recall and is an inefficient use of the brain and brain storage of information.	Because so much learning takes place spatially in a Career Pathways High School, more learning is long term.
The brain understands and remembers best when facts and skills are embedded in natural spatial memory.	Learning that is shaped by both internal processes and by social interaction becomes embedded in natural spatial memory. Embedding is the single most import element that the new brain-based theories of learning have in common.	The combination of real-world experience, hands-on experiences, teaming, and integration in a Career Pathways High School allows for optimal "embedment."
Learning is enhanced by challenge and inhibited by threat.	The brain learns optimally when appropriately challenged, but "down shifts" under perceived threat. Under perceived threat, we literally lose access to portions of our brain.	Educators at a Career Pathways High School emphasize the importance of academic rigor and collaboration for all students.
Each brain is unique.	Every brain's systems are integrated differently, making every brain unique. In addition, because learning actually changes the structure of the brain, the more we learn, the more unique we become.	Through the importance of teaming, all students will realize that they bring unique gifts to the team, plus each student's postsecondary plan is unique to them.

Note: Principles are from Caine and Caine (1991); general definitions are adapted from Harris (1996).

Table 6.8 Key Elements of the Multiple Intelligences in Relation to Career Pathways

Multiple Intelligence	Definition	Connection to Career Pathways
Linguistic	The capacity to use language. Sample skills: verbalizing, writing, debating, translating. Sample careers: librarian, journalist, lawyer.	• Student exploration of self and learning
Logical-Mathematical	The capacity to understand the underlying principle of a causal system or manipulate numbers and operations. Sample skills: calculating, interpreting data, analyzing, classifying. Sample careers: accountant, statistician mathematician, scientist, economist.	• Broadening of teaching strategies
Spatial	The ability to represent the spatial world internally in one's mind. Sample skills: drawing, designing, drafting, visualizing. Sample careers: engineer, graphic artist, art teacher, photographer.	• Connection of student strengths and career choices
Musical	The capacity to think in music, to be able to hear patterns, recognize, remember, and manipulate them. Sample skills: singing, playing, recording, composing. Sample careers: musician, disc jockey, music therapist, conductor.	• Practice of inter- and intrapersonal skills
Bodily-Kinesthetic	The capacity to use one's whole body or parts of the body to solve a problem, make something, or perform. Sample skills: balancing, assembling, installing, performing. Sample careers: actor, craftsperson, choreographer, recreational worker.	• More body movement involved in course work
Interpersonal	The understanding of other people. Sample skills: serving, empathizing, coaching, counseling, selling, negotiating. Sample careers: administrator, psychologist, nurse, salesperson, travel agent.	
Intrapersonal	The capacity to understand oneself, of knowing who one is, what one can do, and what one wants to do; how to react to things, what to avoid and what to move toward. Sample skills: setting goals, evaluating, planning, working alone. Sample careers: clergyperson, therapist, entrepreneur.	
Naturalist	The ability to discriminate among living things as well as sensitivity to the features of the natural world. Sample skills: examining, detailing, observing, working with plants or animals. Sample careers: biologist, paleontologist, geologist, natural resource officer.	

Note: Column 1 is from Gardner (1983); column 2 is adapted from Armstrong (1993).

Table 6.9 Sample Four-Year Thematic Profession

Theme	Year
Exploration	Freshman
Conflict	Sophomore
Facts and Beliefs	Junior
Achievement	Senior

Integration can happen in several ways. It can be done by a classroom teacher hooking her lessons to the identified life and essential skills, or two or more teachers can develop a unit in which they work on a "concept or theme" together in all their classrooms. This is eventually where you want to be with your curriculum—*specifically developed thematic integrated instruction.* This means that teachers deliberately plan together to choose themes that unite the curriculum, and then they systematically present those themes. Some schools might choose a theme for integration each marking period by looking at their maps and creating connections. Themes can be done by marking period, by grade level, or across the entire school. Themes must be broad and be one step higher than a "topic." For example, a topic might be the American Revolution for which a theme might be conflict. The theme is always the broader concept and can be incorporated into any subject or content area. Table 6.9 is an example of a theme chart that a high school developed. These themes helped to tie the curriculum together for the faculty and students. Teachers worked together to define and develop connections between their content and the larger concept.

> *It is easy to implement thematic instruction in a Collaborative Career Pathways High School because your themes are well established—your themes are the Pathways.*

Career Pathways make natural themes. Not only do they give a common language, but all content areas are connected to careers and occupational skills. They also allow for the tie in of life skills and the application of the essential content skills as students work on problems and projects that require more than just a specific content knowledge or skill. For example, if students present an environmental issue in science as being related to their Pathway, they will need to use English, civics, and math skills as they present their data.

> *It is important for your faculty to be trained in the development and implementation of integrated thematic instruction.*

Integrated thematic instruction is compatible with brain research because it gives the brain whole concepts that are then broken down into parts and restructured back into the whole. Thematic units must be connected to real-life experiences and skills. This is easily accomplished in a Pathways High School where the counseling and community experiences are continually incorporated in the classroom.

In this book, all of our Pathways class curricula are written in a thematic integrated format using the Susan Kovalik ITI Model (Integrated Thematic Instruction; Kovalik, 1994). These samples will give your teachers a template to create other units within their curricula.

There are many good programs and templates available that your faculty can examine. We recommend the work of Susan Kovalik and Associates (Kovalik, 1994) and Heidi Hayes Jacobs (1997).

INTEGRATING TECHNOLOGY

As your school works toward a solidly mapped and integrated curriculum that works well with the Pathways curriculum, technology should be embedded in all the curricula—Pathways, core, and elective coursework. All workplaces in the 21st century include the use of technology, so all students need a systematic approach to become familiar with a variety of technologies and how they are used in the workplace. (See Chapter 7, in which the curricula are discussed in more detail.) Because the Collaborative Pathways Model takes place in the classroom and includes teaming, it is an ideal placement for systematically incorporating technology. In the Pathways classroom, students can see how technology is used in the workplace and in their potential Pathways during their site visits; at the same time, they can begin to explore a variety of real-world uses of technology for each Pathway. During sophomore year, they have the opportunity for more hands-on teaming that allows for use and application of technology; during their junior and senior years, not only can they begin using workplace technology for their chosen field or Cluster, they can also begin to explore ethical uses of technology. In addition, there are many opportunities in their core and elective courses to advance their technology skills. In a Collaborative Pathways High School, you will seldom see an empty computer, and you will see competition among teachers for the lab.

The Definition of a Technologically Literate Learner

As discussed in Chapter 3, when your Pathways Committee begins meeting, one of the first decisions you will need to make is what exit goals you will have for students in your school or district. As you are deciding what you want your students to look like as learners, one of these important areas will be what will qualify them as technologically literate learners. An examination of standards and benchmarks for technology from several states, as well as the national standards, will help you describe what you want your students to look like when they graduate, from a technological viewpoint. While developing the collaborative model, we looked at the standards and benchmarks from Michigan and its definition of technologically literate [(MDE, 1998)]:

A technologically literate learner

- Explores, evaluates, and uses technology to accomplish, independently and cooperatively, real-world tasks

- Develops knowledge, ability, and responsibility in the use of resources, processes, and systems of technology
- Acquires, organizes, analyzes, and presents information
- Expands the range and effectiveness of communication skills
- Solves problems, accomplishes tasks, and expresses individual creativity
- Applies legal and ethical standards

As your district begins to design coursework for the four Pathways classes and integrated units, it will be equally important to look at the national and state standards and benchmarks for technology. National standards (Kendall & Marzano, 2000, p. 600) for technology call for students to

1. Know the characteristics and uses of computer hardware and operating systems
2. Know the characteristics and use of computer software programs
3. Understand the relationships among science, technology, society, and the individual
4. Understand the nature of technological design
5. Understand the nature and operation of systems
6. Understand the nature and use of various forms of technology

Even more detailed and specific are the technology standards of the state of Michigan, so these have been used as the basis of technology embedment in our model. These standards (MDE, 1998) call for students to

1. Use and transfer technological knowledge skills for a life role (family member, citizen, worker, consumer, lifelong learner)
2. Use technologies to input, retrieve, organize, manipulate, evaluate, and communicate information
3. Apply appropriate technologies to critical thinking, creative expression, and decision-making skills
4. Employ a systematic approach to technological solutions by using resources and processes to create, maintain, and improve products, systems, and environments
5. Apply ethical and legal standards in planning, using, and evaluating technology
6. Evaluate the societal and environmental impacts of technology and forecast alternative uses and possible consequences to make informed civic, social, and economic decisions

If you examine the system scaffold found in Chapter 2, you can see that these standards have been built into the four scaffold levels of Pathways, but at the same time, your teachers should continue to weave them into their core and elective coursework on a regular basis.

Pathways and its embedded technology will help your teachers to connect with students in new ways. No longer teaching isolated subject matter, teachers will be able to show students how subject matter integrates with technology in real-world contexts. Students, when using technology in Pathways, core, and elective classes, will no longer need to ask, "Where in the work world could we use this technology?" From the freshman year on, your students are in the workplace and community, where they can see for themselves why it is needed and how it is used.

Embedded Technology at All Four Levels

At the freshman level, there are numerous opportunities for the use of technology. It is easy for teachers and librarians to work together to give students a good research base that uses technology because of the systematic incorporation of study skills. Not only do students in Pathways High Schools learn to use technology as they research, they also have the opportunity to learn how to evaluate online materials and Web sites. This means even at the freshman level, students are beginning to examine the ethical standards and uses of technology. Because of the integrated units that match each Pathway, students have the opportunity to use and explore at least four software programs. In addition, they get to observe the use of a wide variety and scope of technologies at workplace sites. Throughout one freshman's experience, he or she may have the opportunity to see computers or lasers used differently in all of the Pathways, to see a wide variety of software and its scope of use, and to see technology applied to graphic design and drafting.

Students are often comforted when they hear that employees are constantly trained and retrained on new technologies. They realize then that being technology literate will require them to be lifelong learners. With this in mind, students begin using their growing skills to create authentic technical writing for their integrated projects, to design technologically savvy presentations for classmates and other audiences, and to explore their Pathways using the Internet as a base. In addition, core and elective teachers are using software in a variety of ways—digital equipment in computer literacy and art, accelerated reading software and technical writing programs in English, real-life math applications in algebra (such as using equations in a medical formula), and smart board presentations and scanners in computer literacy.

During sophomore year, students have many opportunities to build their technical skills further. In their Pathways class, they have experience with video and video-editing equipment and with problem-solving software in their integrated units. This allows students to see how technology goes hand in hand with problem solving. In the workplace, they have an opportunity to observe up close the uses of technology for their selected Pathway. Most Pathways schools include a section on technology observation in their required job-shadow forms. Core and elective opportunities at the sophomore level may include virtual field trips through volcanoes or virtual dissection of pigs in science;

graphic designing of toys and packaging in art; display board and pamphlet design for specific audiences in language arts; and geometric life application software that relates to flying and architecture. Although most of the standards worked on at the sophomore level are the same as those at the freshman level, the students transcend the level of use and application found during their freshman year.

During junior year, new standards for the embedded technology are applied. At this level, focus moves to the ethical use and legal standards of technology as students begin actually using technology side-by-side with employees in real-life settings. Not only do students observe more technology in use, they actually have the hands-on opportunity to be trained on some of it. In addition, in their junior Pathways class, they continue to use technical writing and presentation technology because each student presents his or her internship experience. Many students include digital pictures and footage in their presentations as they further streamline their technology skills and move forward toward their capstone projects. At the same time, in core and elective classes, they continue to find more uses for technology. For example, in advanced computer coursework, they are using a wide variety of importing and exporting skills as they build and maintain Web pages. In English, students might design entire magazines of their own making. In agriculture classes, they can explore and design landscape plans, which are then carried out on the school grounds and in the community; in economics, students use the Internet to provide "real-time" stock quotes so they can track and calculate changes in the stock market and learn how these changes relate to the current economy. All juniors therefore have the chance to further improve their technology skills.

During senior year, the standards include career usage of technology and forecast and prediction of future use of technology. In their senior-level Pathways class, students are required to have one component of their capstone project focus on the technology integration used in their Pathways Cluster or chosen career. As students return to the workplace for implementation of their capstone project, they will continue to observe and use technology in the workplace and note how it has changed and developed since their freshman site visits. Heavy emphasis will be placed on the use of computer applications as students design their projects and then write and present them to a senior project panel. Some current technology that students might explore include personal digital assistants (PDAs), Web page design programs, and advanced spreadsheets. In addition, their required and elective coursework will include even more specific uses of technology. Senior year is an opportunity for students to pull together all of their technology learning to date and then take it a step further, as they not only use technology but learn to evaluate it and forecast what skills they may need in the future.

Technology embedment is critical in all high schools, and by using Pathways as a venue for reform and systematic implementation, you can ensure that all of your students will exit your building with skills that make them ready for the 21st-century workplace. You and your Pathways team will want to chart exactly which technology skills all students will learn

Table 6.10 A School's Technology Skills

Year	Key Technology Skills
Freshman	• Use and manipulate a variety of software • Work with scanners, digital cameras, and liquid crystal display projectors • Incorporate a variety of technologies when creating technical writing for real-world audiences
Sophomore	• Use more complicated software for video editing or other technical writing projects • Use a variety of technology skills and software for problem solving and critical thinking • Begin to use some technology observed in the Pathway workplaces of each student's choice
Junior	• Be able to use technology in the workplace during internship or technical training experience • Apply ethical and legal standards when planning, using, and evaluating technology
Senior	• Incorporate a wide variety of presentation technology in a senior capstone presentation • Be familiar with workplace technology for the student's chosen career or cluster • Evaluate the societal and environmental impacts of some of these technologies and forecast alternative uses • Examine possible consequences of technology so he or she can make informed civic, social, and economical decisions

Note: Skills are adapted from Michigan Department of Education (1998).

by the time they graduate. Table 6.10 is an example of a school's technology skills chart.

This systematic integration of technology culminates during a student's senior year. The greatest reward of embedded technology in Pathways, in addition to core and electives integration, is that all students in your district become computer-literate learners.

ASSESSMENT SYSTEMS AND PREDICTORS OF SUCCESS

An assessment system that measures the standards you have chosen for your curriculum and that will be able to predict how your students will perform on state and national tests is vital to the success of your program. The assessment system at your school should be aligned both vertically and horizontally. This mean that common testing should be done every year (vertical) and in all content areas (horizontal). The word "system" indicates that the process is the same year after year (vertically) and in all content areas (horizontally).

Vertical testing can be done by giving students pre- and posttests at the beginning and end of each year or class. This enables teachers to know which standards their students have mastered and then plan their future teaching lessons and strategies accordingly. Pre- and posttesting results can be recorded on computer software using a code for the level of mastery a teacher feels a student has achieved for each identified skill. These files are then available to all teachers. In this manner, a teacher does not have to "guess" where a student's skills are in a particular content area.

Horizontal assessment means that "common" assessments are given in all of the same classes. If you have three history teachers, for example, they will all give the same tests and collect the same data on all students. In this way, a student learns history by the curriculum as set down by the entire faculty and not by whom they may have as a history teacher. This guarantees that your teachers are following the curriculum and not just teaching about the Civil War for a semester because that is their favorite topic. This does not mean teachers cannot individualize their lessons; it does mean, however, that what is collectively identified to be important is taught to all students. Think of the saying, "What gets monitored, gets done."

With common assessment, teachers can view how their students did compared with other teachers', students', and share best practices. If History Teacher 1's students do great in the core democratic values, and History Teacher 2's students do great in understanding the chronology and consequences of the events that lead to the core values, these teachers can share their strategies and even work in each other's classrooms to ensure that all students learn at the highest possible level.

> *Teachers need immediate and common feedback on what they are teaching, and the best way to give them this feedback is through commonly developed local assessments.*

This means that teachers need time to get together and develop local assessment tests at each level to measure not how well students know the textbook, but the standards and benchmarks identified as the core of their curriculum. This is not an easy task, and it is time-consuming in the beginning. Once the local assessments have been written, however, they only need to be reviewed and "tweaked" on a yearly basis.

> *The data collected from locally developed assessments, as well as the data from state and national tests, must then be used to make instructional decisions.*

Do our students need more earth science? What can we do to help our students perform better in statistics and probability? Why are our students having difficulty in the reflection portion of the writing process? Why are our students performing so well on core democratic values, and how can we use this technique to raise the achievement in another area? When teachers have data or information on which to make solid instructional decisions, they *make* solid instructional decisions.

The development of a process to complete and update your curriculum along with your data analysis will fit well into any accreditation system that your school is currently certified by or applying for. When looking for a process for curriculum work and data, check your accreditation institution. They may have a recommended process. Many times, schools will be doing curriculum processes and accreditation processes separately when they can be done together.

CURRICULUM AND PATHWAYS CONNECTIONS

Your best friend in developing good and cohesive curriculum is collaboration, and your worst enemy is isolation. The more isolated your teachers are, the more incongruent your curriculum will be; the more collaboration between teachers, the smoother, more consistent, and more relevant your curriculum will be. This will prove true not only in raising assessment scores, but also in integrating Career Pathways into the instructional base of your school.

To help you plan your curriculum journey, complete the quick quiz in Table 6.11 and discuss the results with your superintendent, curriculum director, department heads, and faculty. It can work as a planning tool to help you and your faculty to develop a curriculum action plan.

It is of utmost importance that you understand the connection between curriculum processes and Career Pathways. If your Career Pathways system is to be successful, it cannot be an "add on" for teachers. It must be embedded into the instructional goals of your schools, and your instructional goals must be common to all, have clear standards, be aligned and mapped, be integrated, and be measurable.

In brain-compatible classrooms that use the Pathways system, students will succeed—the work you receive from them will exceed all your expectations.

> *What Pathways can do for you is to take all these curriculum processes and make them relevant for students by connecting coursework to their lives.*

IN REVIEW

- Curriculum is what you want a student to know and be able to do.
- Your faculty need to complete some key curriculum processes or steps to implement Career Pathways successfully in the classroom.
- Implement the Collaborative Career Pathways Model into instruction through curriculum processes, not by simply "adding" it on to teachers' already full plates.
- Important curriculum processes or steps include the following:
  - Identification of curriculum vision, outcomes, and standards
  - Alignment (where) and mapping (when) of the curriculum
  - The focusing of curriculum on key essential content and life skills

- Presenting curriculum in Collaborative Career Pathways High Schools is instructional and applied, therefore teachers must understand the difference between content (information) and contextual (applied) teaching and learning.

Table 6.11 Curriculum Quiz

Curriculum Process or Step	Yes	No
Have you and your faculty developed a curriculum vision statement with goals (life skills) for the student learners that exit your high school?		
Have you and your staff incorporated those goal statements into life skills to be integrated across the curriculum?		
Have you developed curriculum learner statements and goals for each content area in your high school?		
Have you and your faculty identified standards and benchmarks for each of your content areas?		
Have you aligned your content standards and benchmarks to grade levels and coursework?		
Have you aligned your standards and benchmarks to your assessment testing program?		
Have you mapped your curriculum?		
Have you developed essential content skills for the reinforcement of academic skills and rigor throughout the curriculum and as a base for developing integrated units?		
Is your faculty versed in brain-based teaching and learning?		
Does your faculty understand the concept of integrated curriculum and how it can "pull" together learning for students?		
Has your faculty been trained in the development and implementation of integrated themes, units, and curricula?		
Is your faculty trained in the use and integration of technology in instruction?		
Does your faculty know how to create assessments that can work as predictors of success for mastery of standards and state and national tests?		
Does your faculty know how to collect and use data to make instructional decisions?		
Does your faculty understand the connection between curriculum processes and the implementation of Career Pathways?		
Does your faculty understand the connection between curriculum processes and accreditation systems?		

- Curriculum processes need to lead teachers to the understanding and application of brain-compatible teaching and learning principles and strategies, as demonstrated in the use of integrated thematic instruction.
- To ensure the implementation of your planned curriculum, establish an assessment system with common assessments. These assessments will help predict student academic success and give you data and information to be used for instructional decision making and goal setting.
- Professional development and the facilitation of curriculum processes and delivery is a critical part of implementing a Collaborative Career Pathways Model.
- The key to good curriculum and great teaching is giving teachers the time and skills they need for collaboration and empowerment.

Part Three

School Structure

Chapter Seven

Pathways Classes for Each Level of Collaborative Career Pathways

SCENARIO: ELIZABETH'S POSTSECONDARY PREPARATION

One of the remarkable traits that all of Elizabeth's teachers mentioned in her college recommendations was her ability to solve problems in a calm, methodical manner. She hadn't thought much about it, but as she reflected over her high school experiences, she realized that it was not an innate ability but a skill that had been carefully developed through her Pathways classes. It had begun in Freshman Explorations when she had been part of a collaborative team during an integrated unit focusing on problem solving. The real-life problem they tackled, using the same problem steps they used to solve math and science problems, was improving student behavior at pep assemblies. Then, during her sophomore year, one segment of the video on a day in the life of a social worker that her Sophomore Selections team made was about the day-to-day problems a social worker faced on the job and how she went about solving them. During her junior year internship at a local YWCA, Elizabeth was acutely aware of the problems on the job and how her coworkers were not utilizing a methodical problem-solving approach, which made the day-to-day problems continue and worsen. During her senior year, Elizabeth returned to the YWCA and tackled the problems with the free food bank. Using brainstorming and solution implementation, she was able to increase food donations by 30%, and theft of the food was reduced greatly. As Elizabeth prepared for college, she suddenly realized in an "ah-ha" moment that not only had her Pathways classes helped her decide and define a career plan, they had also helped her to hone many important workplace and people skills.

> *Relevancy comes in the connection of learning and experience—this is the important "catch," and it happens in the classroom.*

The Collaborative High School Career Pathways Model is instructionally based. We cannot emphasize this enough. The concepts of Career Pathways—student centered curriculum—must be embedded in instruction; it must happen in the classroom, and this is a huge paradigm shift. All models of career guidance and Pathways that we have encountered are emphasized in the counseling process. This does not allow for students to practice on a regular basis the skills they will use during and after high school; it also does not allow for the student to understand the connection between what they are learning and how those skills will be used.

WHAT ARE PATHWAYS CLASSES AND WHY DO WE HAVE THEM?

Pathways classes are classes specifically designed to integrate the classroom with the counseling and community experiences needed for students to be successful. They are the research and practice grounds for students to find out who they are and how this relates to their learning. In Pathways classes, the skills used in all careers are taught and practiced. These classes systematically and on a regular basis teach and practice the SCANS skills outlined in Chapter 1. These skills include teaming, problem solving, and self-management. Pathways classes also reinforce the core standards and benchmarks as identified by your faculty (see Chapter 6). Therefore, the instructional purposes of Pathways classes are many. They include

- Systematically learning and practicing SCANS skills (U.S. Department of Labor, 1991)
- Emphasizing teaming, problem solving, and self-management
- Reinforcing standards and benchmarks in the core curriculum
- Giving students a real-life laboratory to practice skills and connect them to persons and processes in an area of their interest.

In the Collaborative Model, there are four Pathways classes, one for each year of a student's high school experience:

- Freshman Explorations
- Sophomore Selections
- Junior Judgments
- Senior Transitions

Figure 7.1 The Pathways Classes

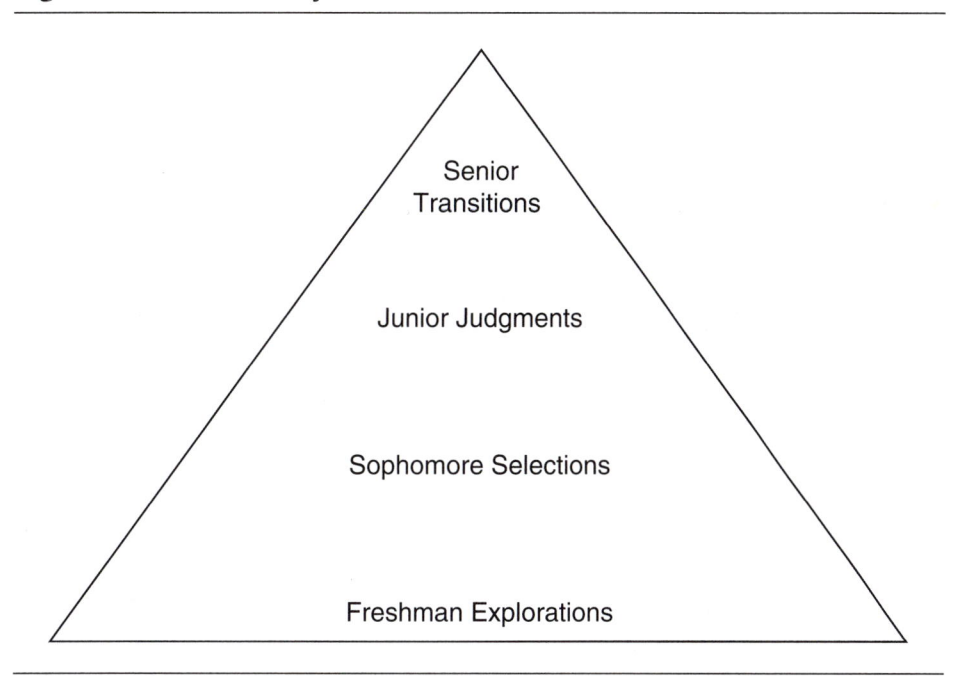

```
            Senior
          Transitions


        Junior Judgments


      Sophomore Selections


    Freshman Explorations
```

Each of the classes is based on the mastering of the skills and experience of the previous class and using a scaffolding method to help a student continually narrow his or her future plans. You can imagine this scaffolding as a pyramid of learning (Figure 7.1) with Freshman Explorations (general) as the broad base and Senior Transitions the focused transition (specific).

PATHWAYS CLASSES: KEY CONCEPTS AND PLACEMENT

The names we have given to our Pathways classes are indicative of where they are placed in a student's experience. These names are not set in stone, and each school should discuss and choose the names for their Pathways classes that best fit their school and community culture. Again, we emphasize that at all steps along the way, it is important to use the templates we give you as a launching pad to creating a Career Pathways System that is right for your school. The key to remember is to keep the model instructional and in the hands of your teaching staff.

> *The goals of the Pathways classes are accomplished with the classroom serving as a "laboratory" for learning. The counselor and community members go into the classroom to work with all students to prepare them for their off-campus community experiences. The community experience then helps them to focus their course of study during high school, based on real-life experiences and knowledge.*

Table 7.1 defines the concepts and rationale for each Pathways class integrated into the three pillars of counseling, classroom, and community.

WHAT DOES EACH PATHWAYS CLASS LOOK LIKE?

Pathways classes are taught by themes. Each year's theme follows the main concept column listed in Table 7.1. The themes are designed to help students gain a deeper understanding of themselves, their relationships, their academic and technical skills, and their future plans and how their learning connects to the workplace. A student's success in each Pathways class depends on a positive, solid experience in the previous class. For example, students cannot choose the proper job-shadowing experience during their sophomore year if they did not gain a solid background of exploration through site visits during their freshman year. They cannot have a successful internship during their junior year without successful job shadows, and so on.

> *All of a student's skills and experiences in the Pathways curriculum depend on those of the previous year. For students to be successful in the community, they must have mastered the necessary, identified skills during the previous year.*

Therefore, the teachers who teach each level of the Pathways curriculum are truly a collaborative team who depend on communication and sharing with one another. In Chapter 10, we discuss further how you can help your teachers to collaborate and grow the skills that students need.

For now, we want to look at the blueprints of each course and show you how they build, one upon the other. Each course was designed around the national counseling standards for that level (Campbell & Dahir, 1997). Figures 7.2 through 7.5 feature maps of each of the Pathways class curricula. They are designed by themes using the Susan Kovalik Integrated Thematic Instruction (ITI) Model (Kovalik & Olsen, 1997, Unit VII).

In this chapter, we provide an overview of the four curricula and how they relate to one other. In Chapter 9, we explore in detail how to implement the Freshman Explorations curriculum as the base for all other Pathways classes. In Chapter 10, we discuss in detail the Sophomore Selections, Junior Judgments, and Senior Transitions curricula and offer specific strategies for implementing them in the classroom.

The maps indicate the central theme of each class by the circle in the center (or hub), each unit of the class being a spoke of that hub and indicated in projecting circles. Specific skills and activities are then listed along the line connecting the spoke to the hub. The off-campus or community activities are boxed, with all integrated units darkened. The class concept, rationale, and course-long activities are boxed separately.

(Text continues on page 146)

Table 7.1 Concepts and Rationale for the Pathways Classes

Class	Concept	Rationale	Key Counseling Concepts	Key Classroom Concepts	Key Community Components
Freshman Explorations	Exploration	Freshmen will begin to view life as a continual adventure that requires exploring options, working with others, and solving problems by making informed decisions.	• Self-exploration (interests and aptitudes) • Conflict resolution • Decision making	• Study skills • Pathway exploration • Technology integration	• General career speakers • Site visits
Sophomore Selections	Relationships	Sophomores will realize that life is a constant balancing of all kinds of relationships; a harmonious life involves the balance of self, relationships, and personal achievement.	• Goal setting • Character education • Relationships • Time and stress management	• Job skills • Career ladders • Career research • Technology integration	• Pathways interviews • Pathway-specific speakers • Job Shadows
Junior Judgments	Knowledge	Juniors will gain knowledge of self within the work world through an internship experience, learning about their values in the workplace while focusing on a future plan.	• Character education • Ethical decision making • Anger management • Postsecondary applications • Scholarship applications	• Workplace skills • Government regulations • Technology integration on the job	• Internship • Pathway mentor
Senior Transitions	Transition	Seniors will design a capstone project that helps them streamline their personal postsecondary plan and then make a smooth transition to their next step.	• Postsecondary visitations • Persuasion • Problem solving • In-depth, career-specific knowledge	• Community interaction • Technology integration (career specific) • Senior project • Service learning	• Pathway mentor • Pathway panel • Postsecondary mentor

Figure 7.2 Freshman Explorations

Freshman Explorations

The Great Adventure

Unit 1 Exploring Who I Am (Identity)
- Rules and Procedures
- Personality Profiles
- Brain-Body Connections
- Examining Skills & Aptitudes
- Intelligences
- Library Skills
- DAT Testing
- Listening
- Charting Interests

Being There: Career Fair

Being There: Pathway Selection Party
- Using the Problem-Solving Matrix
- How to Make a Decision
- Narrow to Two Options

Unit 2 Exploring the Pathways: Engineering/Manufacturing and Industrial Technology and Business (Technology)
- Careers in the Pathway
- Assertiveness
- Listening
- Learning to Team
- Guest Speakers

*Wild Blue Yonder: *Flight Sim 2000* software

Being There: Flight School Fly-In

Unit 3 Exploring the Pathways: Health and Human Services (Human Experience)
- Careers in the Pathway
- Skills & Interests
- Guest Speakers
- Note Taking
- Conflict Resolution

*The Doctor Is In: *Health*

Being There: A Trip to the World of Health

Concept: Exploration
Pattern Shaper: Self/Careers
Rationale: Freshmen will begin to view life as a continual adventure that requires exploring options, working with others, and solving problems by making informed decisions.

Being There: TV Station
- Guest Speakers
- Skills and Interests
- Skimming and Scanning
- Careers in the Pathway

*Multimedia Public Service Team Project: *Movieworks* software

Unit 4 Exploring the Pathways: Arts and Communications (Creativity)

A Focus for Every Student

Being There: Visiting a Co-op or a Business
- Guest Speakers
- Test Taking
- Smooth Sailing in a Team
- Careers in the Pathway

*The Growing Season: A Farm Co-op/Business Co-op: *Sim Farm* software
- Wetlands Preservation

Unit 5 Exploring the Pathways: Natural Resources, Agriscience, and Business (Saving the Population)

Unit 6 Making the Great Decisions (Decision Making)

The Final Commitment: The Pathway Paper

Course Long Activities:
➤ Ongoing Journal and Portfolio
➤ Career Chats
➤ Exploring Options to Decide Pathway
➤ Focus on Study Skills

*Technology-integrated units. *Note:* Pathway exploration is based on the Six Pathways of the State of Michigan.

Four to six integrated units can be offered.

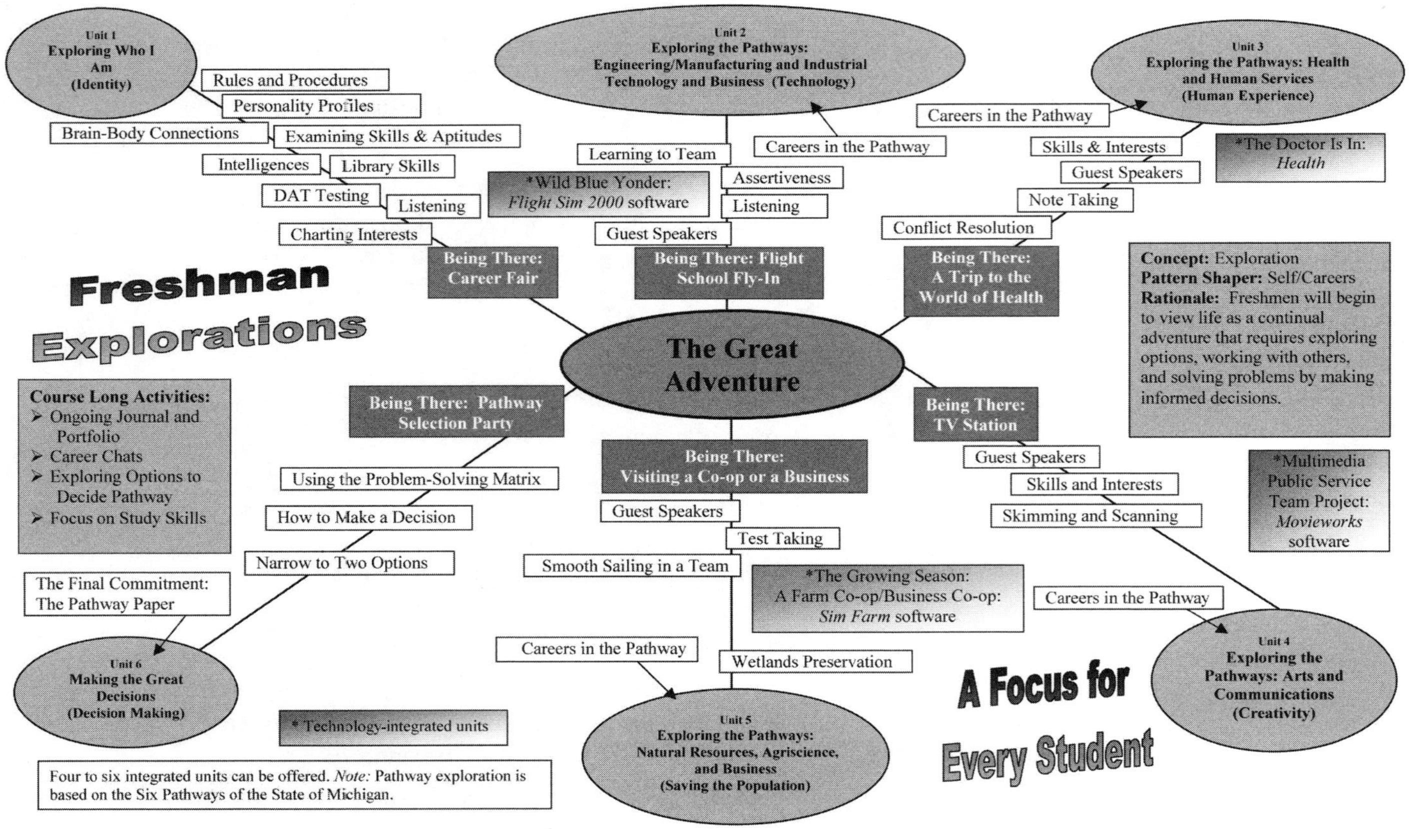

Note: Kovalik (1994) curriculum model template.

Figure 7.3 Sophomore Selections

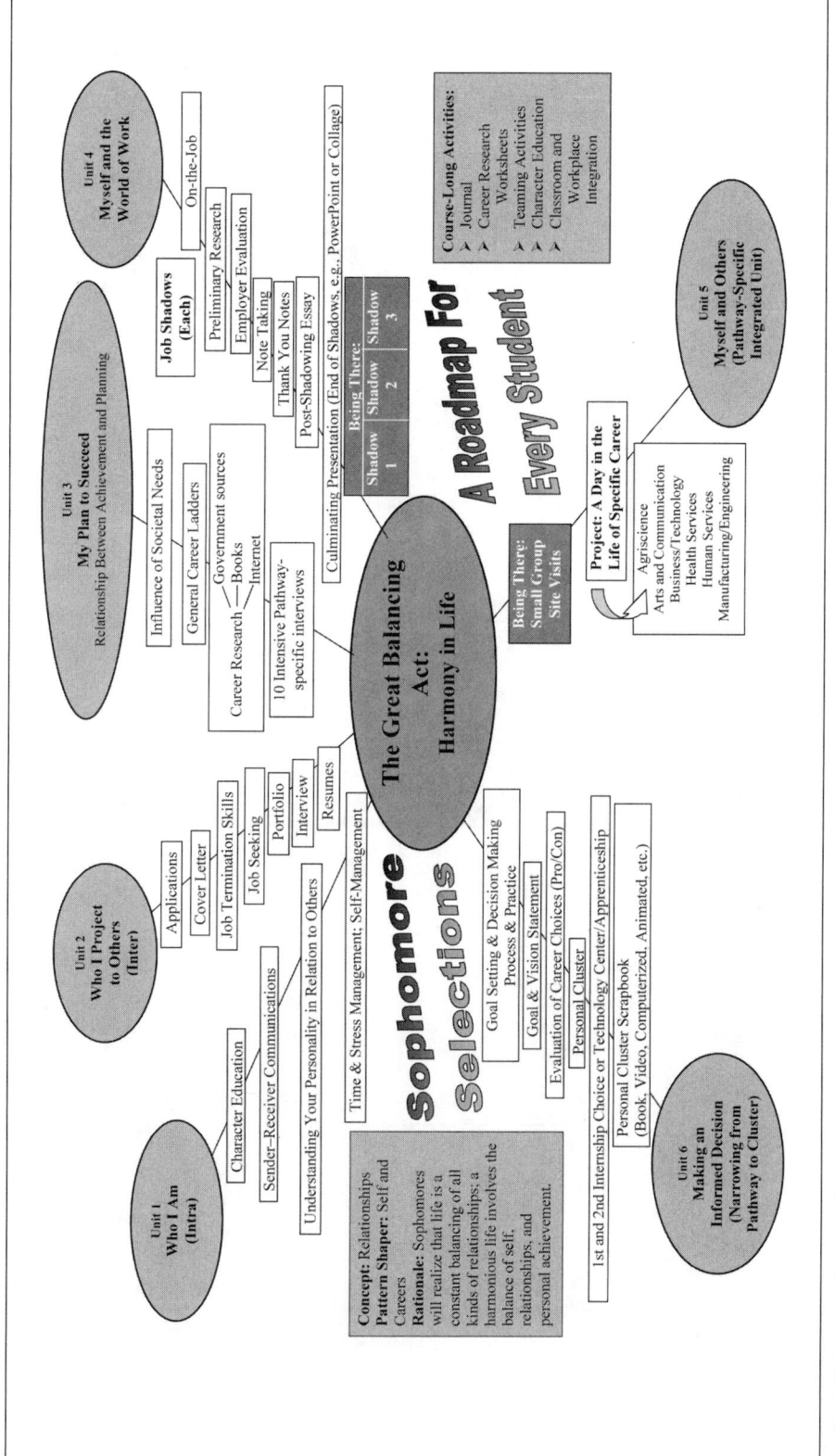

Sophomore Selections

A Roadmap For Every Student

Concept: Relationships
Pattern Shaper: Self and Careers
Rationale: Sophomores will realize that life is a constant balancing of all kinds of relationships; a harmonious life involves the balance of self, relationships, and personal achievement.

Course-Long Activities:
- Journal
- Career Research Worksheets
- Teaming Activities
- Character Education
- Classroom and Workplace Integration

The Great Balancing Act: Harmony in Life

Unit 1 — Who I Am (Intra)
- Character Education
- Sender–Receiver Communications
- Understanding Your Personality in Relation to Others
- Time & Stress Management; Self-Management

Unit 2 — Who I Project to Others (Inter)
- Applications
- Cover Letter
- Job Termination Skills
- Job Seeking
- Portfolio
- Interview
- Resumes

Unit 3 — My Plan to Succeed: Relationship Between Achievement and Planning
- Influence of Societal Needs
- General Career Ladders
- Career Research
  - Government sources
  - Books
  - Internet
- 10 Intensive Pathway-specific interviews
- Culminating Presentation (End of Shadows, e.g., PowerPoint or Collage)

Unit 4 — Myself and the World of Work
- Job Shadows (Each)
  - Preliminary Research
  - Employer Evaluation
  - Note Taking
  - Thank You Notes
  - Post-Shadowing Essay
- On-the-Job
- Being There: Shadow 1 | Shadow 2 | Shadow 3

Unit 5 — Myself and Others (Pathway-Specific Integrated Unit)
- Being There: Small Group Site Visits
- Project: A Day in the Life of Specific Career
  - Agriscience
  - Arts and Communication
  - Business/Technology
  - Health Services
  - Human Services
  - Manufacturing/Engineering

Unit 6 — Making an Informed Decision (Narrowing from Pathway to Cluster)
- Goal Setting & Decision Making Process & Practice
- Goal & Vision Statement
- Evaluation of Career Choices (Pro/Con)
- Personal Cluster
- 1st and 2nd Internship Choice or Technology Center/Apprenticeship
- Personal Cluster Scrapbook (Book, Video, Computerized, Animated, etc.)

Note: Kovalik (1994) curriculum model template.

Figure 7.4 Junior Judgments

Junior Judgments
A Cluster Or
Career Evaluation
For Every Student

Unit 1 Self-Preparation

- Relationship of Individual Characteristics to Personal and Career Goals
- Appearance and Hygiene
- Anger Management
- Stress, Time, and Conflict-Management Techniques
- Interpersonal Skills for Working with Others
- Relationships Between Achievement and Student Planning

Course-Long Activities:
- Work Logs
- Weekly Seminars (Employment Issues)
- Ongoing Instructor and Internship Evaluations
- Self-Reflection (Journaling) and Evaluation
- Internship Presentation
- Expansion of Portfolio and Educational Development Plan (EDP)

Unit 2 Deciding on the Internship

- Student
  - Interviews/Placement
  - Rules and Policies
  - Employability Issues
- Preinternship Packet
- Internship Placement Decision

Unit 3 Work World Preparation

- Ethics and Government Regulations
- Relationships Between Rules, Laws, and Individual Rights
- Chain of Command Issues
- Building a Support Network
- Nontraditional Roles and Occupations
- Job Maintenance

The Stepping Stone: Evaluating the Choices

Pathway Specific Being There
| Internship or |
| Mini Internship | Mini Internship |

Concept: Knowledge
Pattern Shaper: Self/Careers
Rationale: Juniors will evaluate a career or cluster and its relationship to self through one or two mini internship(s); they will gain knowledge of workplace values while focusing on a future plan.

Unit 4 Stepping Into the Work World

- Obligation and Training Agreement
- Attendance
- Confidentiality
- Evaluation Issues
- Work Logs

Internship Packet:

Presentation of Internship Includes:
- Job Duties by Industry
- Hazards and Environmental Conditions
- Impact of Technology on Work Tasks
- Degree of Specialization and Responsibility
- Tools, Machines, Materials, and Academics Used
- Trends and Outlook in the Field

- Life Skills and Teaming Emphasis
- Pathway Specific Gov. Regulations
- Effective Problem Solving and Decision Making in the Workplace

Unit 5 Judging the Experience

Placement Evaluation:
- Likes
- Challenges
- Right Path?
- Right Cluster?
- Right Career?

Employer Expectations Exit Interviews and Thank Yous

EDP and Portfolio Building

Unit 6 Self-Managing the Plan

Where Do I Go Next? Decision Making:
- Evaluate Plan
- Compare/Contrast Two Parts of Plan
- Reevaluate Short- and Long-Term Goals

Brainstorm Senior Project Options for Each Pathway
Student Preliminary Senior Project Plan

Note: Kovalik (1994) curriculum model template.

Figure 7.5 Senior Transitions

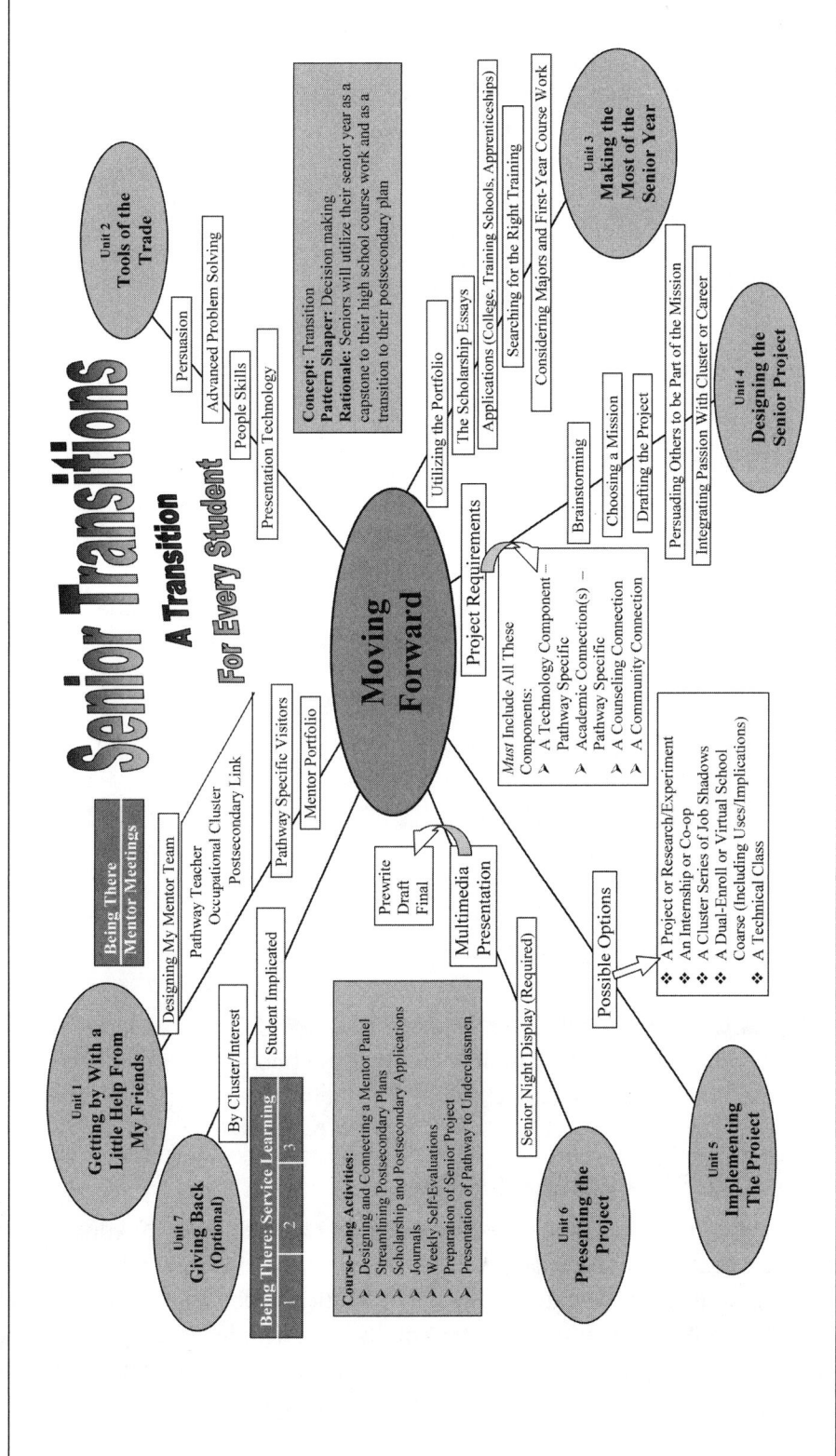

Senior Transitions
A Transition For Every Student

Concept: Transition
Pattern Shaper: Decision making
Rationale: Seniors will utilize their senior year as a capstone to their high school course work and as a transition to their postsecondary plan

Moving Forward

Unit 1 — Getting by With a Little Help From My Friends
- Being There / Mentor Meetings
- Designing My Mentor Team
  - Pathway Teacher
  - Occupational Cluster
  - Postsecondary Link
- Pathway Specific Visitors
- Mentor Portfolio

Unit 2 — Tools of the Trade
- Persuasion
- Advanced Problem Solving
- People Skills
- Presentation Technology

Unit 3 — Making the Most of the Senior Year
- Utilizing the Portfolio
- The Scholarship Essays
- Applications (College, Training Schools, Apprenticeships)
- Searching for the Right Training
- Considering Majors and First-Year Course Work

Unit 4 — Designing the Senior Project
- Brainstorming
- Choosing a Mission
- Drafting the Project
- Persuading Others to be Part of the Mission
- Integrating Passion With Cluster or Career

Project Requirements

Must Include All These Components:
- A Technology Component – Pathway Specific
- Academic Connection(s) – Pathway Specific
- A Counseling Connection
- A Community Connection

Unit 5 — Implementing The Project

Possible Options
- A Project or Research/Experiment
- An Internship or Co-op
- A Cluster Series of Job Shadows
- A Dual-Enroll or Virtual School Coarse (Including Uses/Implications)
- A Technical Class

Unit 6 — Presenting the Project
- Senior Night Display (Required)
- Multimedia Presentation
  - Prewrite
  - Draft
  - Final

Unit 7 — Giving Back (Optional)
- By Cluster/Interest
- Student Implicated

Being There: Service Learning 1 | 2 | 3

Course-Long Activities:
- Designing and Connecting a Mentor Panel
- Streamlining Postsecondary Plans
- Scholarship and Postsecondary Applications
- Journals
- Weekly Self-Evaluations
- Preparation of Senior Project
- Presentation of Pathway to Underclassmen

Note: Kovalik (1994) curriculum model template.

FRESHMAN EXPLORATIONS: THE CORNERSTONE

Freshman Explorations is the foundation of any Collaborative Pathways High School Curriculum. It is team taught usually between an academic teacher and a technology teacher, although we have seen other combinations work as well. The class should be a yearlong course in a traditional or A–B block schedule or a semester-long course in a 4 × 4 block schedule. Later in this chapter, we discuss where and how to integrate the course into your schedule.

The theme of the class is "The Great Adventure," and it focuses on the exploration of the school's established Career Pathways while teaching study and other skills necessary for a freshman to make a smooth transition into high school. It is also The Great Adventure because students have the opportunity to explore multiple facets of themselves. Each unit is organized around a community-based experience. To accomplish this, the following units and activities are set:

Unit I: Exploring Who I Am

In this unit, students gain a strong understanding of themselves through the learning of their interests and aptitudes. The unit also helps students to begin making strong connections not only to their high school, but also to the relevancy of high school studies to their future. Unit activities include

- School rules and procedures
- Library skills
- Listening skills
- Personality profiling
- Brain–body connections
- Learning styles
- Multiple intelligences
- Differential Aptitude Test (1990)
- Examining and charting interests and aptitudes

The unit community connection is a career fair. Our career fair is held at the local community college and involves many schools. If this is not available to you, a school or district can develop its own local career fair.

Unit II–V: Exploring the Pathways

In these units, students explore the chosen Pathways of your school through integrated team projects. Each project centers on a Pathway(s) and uses technology as the avenue for teams to produce a product or process to present to the class. These integrated units are further detailed in Chapter 10. The units, while helping students to explore the Pathways, teach teaming, problem-solving, and self-management skills. Activities include

- Learning to team
- Assertiveness

- Listening
- Conflict resolution
- Note taking
- Skimming and scanning
- Test taking
- Pathways-specific team software projects (e.g., a flight school brochure, a health plan, a public service announcement, and a co-op farm or city plan)

The community connection involves many guest speakers, 75 "chats" with different Pathway professions, and site visits. A school can use these Pathways units or develop its own integrated projects related to the specific school and community. For example, rural schools might develop a co-op farm, whereas city schools develop a city plan.

Unit VI: Making the Great Decision

In this culminating unit, a student chooses his or her Pathway. Activities include

- Using a problem-solving matrix
- Narrowing decisions to a final commitment
- Writing a Pathways paper (The students use an established template to write the paper. The paper describes what they have learned about themselves and their personal Pathways choice, as well as their exploration of the Pathway.)
- Planning for job shadows

At the end of this unit, a Pathways Selection Party is held with special guest speakers, visitors, and a fun activity (such as bowling, dancing, etc.). At this "party" students sign up for the Pathway they believe fits them best. They will then begin to focus and fine-tune their next three high school years around their Pathway. Remember that a single Pathway may comprise hundreds, sometimes thousands, of jobs.

As previously mentioned; although the model needs to be flexible enough that students can change Pathways if they desire, the truth is that it is more likely for a student to change a career within a Pathway than to change the Pathway itself. For example, a student may choose the Health Services Pathway, but in the next few years choose nursing (direct patient care) over medical technology, or blood testing (indirect care). Changes in a Pathway usually result in a change to a related path, such as health to human services or arts and communication to business. It is extremely important for all freshmen to get a solid Freshman Explorations experience. Unless they have a solid understanding

> *The final outcome of the Freshman Explorations class is for every student to be able to make an accurate choice for his or her Pathway.*

of each Pathway, experienced visually and through Pathway practitioners, they will not be able to make a solid and accurate prediction for their future. They will then find themselves floundering through the next three stages of the Pathways curriculum. That is why we call Freshman Explorations the *cornerstone* of any Collaborative Pathways High School and why we so strongly recommend it be team taught.

The Five-Year Plan

As we finish our discussion of Freshman Explorations, we would like to add that some schools have found it more effective to create a five-year Pathways plan. Because the curriculum in Freshman Explorations is heavy, especially for schools that have used an embedding system, some schools split the Freshman Explorations curriculum in half, doing part of it in eighth grade, then finishing it in ninth grade and having students make their Pathway decision at that time. In this way, the Pathways philosophy spans five years, building a natural bridge from junior high or middle school to high school. This option does not work in schools that gain an influx of freshmen from several different feeder or parochial schools.

SOPHOMORE SELECTIONS: THE GREAT BALANCING ACT

Sophomore Selections is an opportunity for each student to further explore his or her Pathway and to observe careers within it. This class also provides an opportunity for students to begin to balance the person they project to others with the person they believe themselves to be. Therefore, the theme of the class is "The Great Balancing Act" (Harmony in Life). Sophomores will realize that life is a constant balancing of all kinds of relationships; a harmonious life involves the balance of self, relationships, and personal achievement. The main purpose of this coursework is to allow students to explore three or four careers within their Pathway by spending a day on each job. Portions of this coursework are already found in many high school curricula, because they include job shadowing and employability skills. Although ideally it would be at least a one-semester stand-alone in a traditional schedule or a nine-week course, in a 4 × 4 block, some schools have found success integrating this coursework into an existing class such as English 10, business/technology, or health.

The six units in this class lead up to the students' next decision about their plans—will they explore one career during an internship the coming fall or will they select technical training in a specific field at the local technical center (or possibly community college)? The community connection for this course is the three to four (hopefully) daylong job-shadowing experiences and several (8 to 10) career interviews (these are longer than the 9th-grade chats and usually lead to job shadows). Shadow experiences can be done in a variety of ways. Some instructors weave these experiences throughout the course, and others choose to do them during the last third of the course as a culmination of the year. Either way, we have seen that fewer than three of these experiences can lead to a breakdown in the entire process because it does not allow students enough true experience to make good choices for their internship or technical program at the end of the course. The units appear as follows.

Unit I: Who I Am (Intra)

This unit allows students to explore further who they are, building on the freshman unit, *Exploring Who I Am.* This unit helps students to define issues of value, character, and integrity and delves deeper into issues of personality, listening, and self- and team management. Unit activities include

- Time and stress management; self-management
- Understanding one's personality as it relates to others
- Sender–receiver communication
- Character education

The community connection can begin during this unit as students review their chat cards (see Chapter 9) from their freshman year and begin to consider which careers might be interesting for interviews and/or daylong visits. Guests might include a psychologist or motivational character-building speaker.

Unit II: Whom I Project to Others (Inter)

After gathering and focusing information about themselves, students are ready to share themselves with potential community contacts and employers. This unit focuses on those skills that will help them become a part of the community. Skills and activities in this unit include

- Job seeking
- Applications
- Cover letters
- Resumes
- Interviews
- Job termination
- Portfolio building (continuation)

The community connection for this unit could include hosting guests in the classroom to discuss successful employability skills and allow students to have mock interviews with practitioners. *It is crucial that students see the link between knowing who they are and who they present to the community through the use of these skills.*

Unit III: My Plan to Succeed

In this unit, students begin to realize the clear relationship between the importance of planning and achieving goals. This unit allows students to look clearly at their chosen Pathway, as well as the Career Clusters and ladders within the Clusters. In addition it gives students an opportunity to undergo several interviews so that they can carefully plan which will be the best job shadows for them. The unit includes the following:

- Influence of societal needs
- General career ladders
- Career research—government sources, books, Internet
- Ten intensive, Pathway-specific interviews

The community connection in this unit is the 10 intensive (45-minute long) interviews. It includes Pathway-specific interviews and additional classroom guests and speakers. Ideally, these classes are Pathway specific, but because of class size or scheduling difficulties, some schools group together several Pathways.

Unit IV: Myself and the World of Work

The most critical part of the course takes place in this unit and can be done all at once or spread throughout the course. After carefully researching the Pathway, students should be ready to spend the day at each of three or four job locales. The unit activities include

- Preliminary research
- On-the-job interview
- Note taking
- Employer evaluation
- Thank you notes
- Post-shadowing essay
- Culminating presentation or project (PowerPoint, scrapbook, display, etc.)

Obviously, the community connection is the job shadows. Although many schools already incorporate job shadows into their curricula, job shadows in a Pathways High School are much more intensive because of the skill and knowledge that students bring to these experiences. They are much more able to evaluate skills being used (or not used) and are able to ask deeper, clearer, more focused questions. The culminating project of Sophomore Selections is crucial because it allows students to see a wide variety of Pathway-specific careers through their classmates' presentations.

Unit V: Myself and Others
(Pathway-Specific Integrated Project)

This unit is actually a chance to further extend the job-shadowing experience, practice teaming and self-management skills, and enhance video-making and editing skills learned in the 9th-grade thematic unit, "Getting the Word Out." Students are teamed in Cluster-specific groups and select a community member to film for a day. They then edit their daylong tape into a short feature, "One day in the life of a _____." If course time permits, students may first attend two or three Pathway-specific group field trips to select the community member whom they wish to follow. This unit emphasizes

- Teaming skills
- Management skills
- Video/editing skills
- Observation skills
- Presentation skills

The community connections involved in this unit allow teams of three or four students to make important, daylong connections—not only with someone in their potential field, but also with the entire career environment and everyone with whom they come in contact (including classmates) during the filming day.

Unit VI: Making an Informed Decision

Building off the last unit of Freshman Explorations, this unit further develops each student's decision-making skills and streamlines his or her plan. In this unit, students compare and contrast several careers and explore the option of a junior internship or technical training. They continue to experience their Pathway while reevaluating their short- and long-term goals. The unit activities include

- Goal setting and decision making—process and practice
- Goal and vision statement
- Evaluation of career choices (pros and cons)
- Personal Cluster
- Personal Cluster scrapbook (book, video, computerized/animated)
- First and second internship choice or technology/apprenticeship program

In this unit, students evaluate and assess all of the community-based experiences they have had during Sophomore Selections. It is a key opportunity for students to start streamlining their plans with the input of their parents, teachers, and mentors. The culmination of this unit comes when students turn in their application to the technical center or an internship. If a school district does not have a technical center or academy or its own career-tech departments, other options are for students to do local junior college coursework or participate in apprenticeships.

The end of Sophomore Selections is an ideal time for students to make changes in their Career Cluster interest or, if necessary, in their Pathway. The stronger the Freshman Explorations and Sophomore Selections programs are, the less likely students will wish to change Pathways. At this level, students will realize that they are personally in charge of their career plan and begin to take critical ownership of it. Therefore, it is critical that students have as many shadowing and community-connecting

> *The final outcome of Sophomore Selections is for every student to begin narrowing his or her plan by deciding on an internship or on technical-center training.*

experiences as possible before they make the important decision concerning internships and technical/apprentice programs. The sophomore level Pathways class is the platform of the Junior Judgments experience. Course-long activities that include career awareness, journaling, and classroom and workplace integration further enhance this course.

JUNIOR JUDGMENTS: THE STEPPING STONE

One of the many items that set a Career Pathways High School apart is the opportunity for every student to go into the work environment on a daily, continuous basis. The junior experience is where the majority of our students have been able to "put it all together"—suddenly they see the connections between the Pathways classes, the community involvement, and the Pathways coursework. The theme then is simply, "The Stepping Stone: Evaluating the Choices" and the main concept shaper is knowledge. In this course, juniors gain knowledge of themselves within the work world, through an internship experience, and about their value in the workplace, while focusing on a future plan.

This course is generally taught at the beginning or end of the day to utilize the community optimally; it is led by a teacher who acts as internship coordinator. The majority of paperwork and rules coincide with that of a traditional co-op program except that internships are usually unpaid. Students spend the first week in the classroom and then intern for the majority of the course (generally four days a week with class seminars on Fridays) and finish back in the classroom for presentations. The internships work best in a 4 × 4 block schedule but can be done in traditional settings by putting class time together for two periods. For example, one 4 × 4 block district may make it a nine-week course backed with speech, while another traditional school might have students take speech and English and Junior Judgments together and have the last nine weeks of the two courses include their internship. Business teachers or teachers who have worked in another field (particularly in the business sector) before becoming teachers are an excellent choice for this position. What sets this course apart is that in addition to traditional co-op instruction, students are also focusing and concentrating all they have learned about teaming, problem solving, conflict and stress management, and ethics and confidentiality. The junior Collaborative Pathways course has much more academic rigor than its traditional co-op counterpart. The units for this course are as follows.

Unit I: Self-Preparation

Before going into the workplace, students will talk about all of the issues that will be important to them in the workplace experience. It is at this point in their Pathways journey that they will realize how valuable their earlier teaming, self- and time-management skills, and problem-solving practice really are. Before beginning their internship or mini-internships, students once again see the relationship between planning and achievement that they learned about in Sophomore Selections. This first unit is a busy time of planning and preparation to help students make a clear connection between their self-preparation and their smooth transition to the workplace setting. Included in this unit are the following:

- Relationship of individual characteristics to personal and career goals
- Appearance and hygiene
- Anger management
- Stress-, time-, and conflict-management techniques
- Interpersonal skills for working with others
- Recognition of relationship between educational achievement and career planning

The community connection during this time may be guest speakers who talk about specific issues concerning working with others in the workplace, such as those issues listed in this unit.

Unit II: Deciding on the Internship

The second important step that Junior Judgment students must take is to actually apply for, go through the policies of, and be placed in an internship. This unit includes

- Student-implemented interviews and placement; rules and policies; employability issues
- Pre-internship packet
- Internship placement decision

The community connections for this unit will include internship hosts who may interview students for a placement in their business. At this time, the internship teacher will want to underscore rules and regulations of the internships. This is the most traditional part of this course. It is at this time that students will need to decide if they will do one longer internship or two shorter ones (in a few specific cases, students may need to step back and do a set of two-day job shadows within their Cluster).

Unit III: Work World Preparation

This part of the course is key to making certain that students will make a smooth transition to the world of work and to their internships. Not only are issues of laws, ethics, and government regulations discussed but also issues of building a strong support system and gender equity. If this unit is taught thoroughly, students will have an easier and smoother transition to their job placements.

- Relationships between rules, laws, and individual rights
- Chain-of-command issues
- Ethics and government regulations
- Building a support network
- Nontraditional roles and occupations
- Job maintenance

Community guests to host at this juncture are many and varied. Employers who can discuss chain-of-command issues, government regulations, and ethics will be key. In addition, employees could visit to talk about the importance of gender equity in the workplace and the importance of support networks and what works best in terms of job maintenance.

Unit IV: Stepping Into the Work World

This is one of the true culminating moments toward which your Pathways faculty works for each student. Freshman Explorations and Sophomore Selections teachers have been preparing students since their first days of high school to step out into the work world on a continuous basis to see if this particular career represents a good fit. It is preferable for students to see the surprises (both good and bad) of an individual career now instead of after spending time, money, and college preparation to reach a goal that may not be right for them. In addition, because of their Pathways coursework, they are in a much better position to evaluate the skills and personality that a career may require. During this "Being There" experience, the following paperwork and agreements are required:

- Internship packet—obligation, training agreement, attendance policies, confidentiality agreement, driving permits, work logs, evaluations, student issues
- Effective problem solving and decision making in the workplace
- Pathway-specific government regulations
- Life skills and teaming emphasis

The community connection during an internship is multifaceted. Students build important relationships not only with their internship hosts, but also with their immediate superiors and their coworkers. They will see many things that may only have been hinted at through their chats, interviews, and job shadows, including the importance of loving what you do, having a strong work ethic, and having good interpersonal and problem-solving skills, in addition to solid academic skills. It will further underscore the importance of relevant schoolwork.

Unit V: Judging the Experience

By now you can begin to see the pattern of every student making a clearer and more focused decision at the end of each Pathways course. The first part of this process comes by preparing a presentation that summarizes what each student has observed and participated in. In addition, this is the time for an exit interview, during which students summarize employer expectations and how well they have met them. It is also an opportunity for students to thank their host employer for the internship experience.

- Presentation
  - Job duties by industry
  - Hazards and environmental conditions
  - Impact of technology on work tasks
  - Degree of specialization and responsibility
  - Tools, machines, materials, academics used
  - Trends and outlook in the field
- Employer expectations
- Exit interview
- Thank you notes to host employers

As students leave their internship placement, they should have the opportunity to see how well they have lived up to employer expectations and to thank their internship hosts and coworkers.

Unit VI: Self-Managing the Plan

The second part of this process comes at the end of Junior Judgments; students first evaluate their internship experience and then work to streamline their plan, using the decision-making process. It is at this point that students need to compare and contrast two parts of their plan so that they can properly develop the senior project that will be the most meaningful to them. The senior project requirements are discussed and students have the opportunity to write a paper that compares and contrasts whichever of the following is most useful: two Pathways, two Clusters, two possible careers, or two types or places for training. The main intent is to answer an important question: *"Where do I go from here?"* At this point, students need to start brainstorming the direction of their senior project. Throughout this process students do the following:

- Educational Development Plan and portfolio building
- Evaluate internship placement (likes and dislikes, challenges, and skills)
- Where do I go next?
- Decision making: compare and contrast two parts of plan, reevaluate short-term and long-term goals
- Senior project requirements presented
- Brainstorm senior project
- Senior project preliminary plan submitted

During this time period students are in communication with their families, their teachers, and their community connections as they begin to narrow their plan further. This is a crucial part of the planning process in which students have a chance to go in a different direction if they need to; for example, an internship at pharmacy could lead a student to decide that although he or she loves health care, pharmacy doesn't allow enough patient contact. The student could then compare other similar careers with more relationship

> *The final outcome of the Junior Judgments course is for every student to develop the beginning of a specific postsecondary plan and then begin the process of designing a meaningful senior project.*

connection opportunities. The other important community connection students develop at this point is postsecondary connections to military recruiters, admissions counselors, trade associations, and possibly postsecondary professors and trainers. Important course-long activities include work logs, internship evaluations, portfolio building, journaling, and multimedia presentation preparation.

The final unit of the Junior Judgments experience cannot be rushed; students need time to assess and evaluate all the important information they have gathered from their internship experiences. In some schools where the Junior Judgments class is only nine weeks of a 4 × 4 block schedule, part of this evaluation can take place in another required course such as English or speech. It is critically important at this juncture that students have time set aside to evaluate thoughtfully and discard parts of their plans that do not work for them. It is equally important that they have time to begin the process of designing a good senior project. Students who wait until their senior year to begin thinking about their projects will struggle, and their projects won't be as in-depth or valuable to them. As is the case with any stepping stone, one of the most important components is taking time to evaluate what has been learned as a result of the experience and then think about how this information can influence the choice of one's future daily life (and in this case, one's career).

SENIOR TRANSITIONS: MOVING FORWARD

Freshman Explorations and Senior Transitions are the two "bookend" courses in a Career Pathways High School. Whereas Freshman Explorations is the base for all that is to come, Senior Transitions is the capstone of the hard work that came before it. The mission in Senior Transitions is twofold: first and foremost, it allows all students to incorporate their problem-solving and teaming skills and the career information that they have gathered in a meaningful final project that pulls together all the parts of their plans (and all of the key self-knowledge they have gained). The second goal of the Senior Transitions course is to provide students with the means to create a smooth transition to their postsecondary plans (or to continue working on that decision if they still have unanswered concerns). The counselor will visit the Senior Transitions classroom on a regular basis, and students will talk to admissions advisors, trade representatives, and military counselors, as well as explore a variety of postsecondary possibilities through field trips. In addition, the Senior Project allows students to showcase and internalize their plans, becoming "plan role models" for upcoming students. This course allows all seniors to use their senior year as the capstone to their high school coursework and experiences as they begin making a smooth transition to their postsecondary plans. The year-long theme of this class is "Moving Forward," and the key concept should be transition. Although the Senior Transitions course generally takes place during one semester in block format or throughout the year in a traditional schedule, some schools have had success integrating it into a required course such as senior English or government. The six necessary units for this coursework are as follows.

Unit I: A Little Help From My Friends

The students begin Senior Transitions with the preliminary senior project plans from the end of their junior year. Students are required to put together their own three-person mentor team. This mentor team helps them throughout the course as they develop and implement their projects. (A separate evaluation panel in addition to the mentorship team can assist in the presentation if desired by the school district.) The mentor team includes a Pathways teacher (most likely the Senior Transitions teacher), someone from the community in the career or Cluster of the student's choice, and a postsecondary link of the student's choosing (an admissions counselor, military enlister, or on-the-job training supervisor). At this time, students are ready to add a specialized mentoring and senior project section to their portfolios.

Crucial parts of this unit are

- Designing the mentor team
- Inviting Pathway-specific guests and speakers to the class
- Streamlining the portfolio
- Organizing a "Being There" activity: mentor meeting (orchestrated and managed by each student)

At this point, the classroom, community, and postsecondary links have merged so that the community (and postsecondary links and opportunities) has become the true classroom. This is discussed in further detail in Chapter 13.

Unit II: Tools of the Trade

In this unit, students have the opportunity to work on the skills that will help them with their projects. Piggy-backing on the learned skills from focused coursework and speech or English, this unit helps to make the senior projects stand out. The topics include

- Persuasion
- Advanced problem solving
- People skills
- Presentation technology

During this unit, community members can become involved as guest speakers to show students how persuasion and presentation technology is used in the work world. Throughout this unit, students continue to work with their mentoring teams.

Unit III: Making the Most of Senior Year

This part of the coursework is geared toward the typical senior transitional activities, but the twist in a Pathways High School is that students really do have a plan. Postsecondary training is part of that plan, not the final goal (no more will you hear the time-honored statement, "I'm going to college but I don't know what I'll study"). In this unit the following topics are covered:

- Utilization of the portfolio
- Scholarship essays
- Searching for the right training
- Applications (college, training schools, apprenticeships)
- Considering majors and first-year coursework

In terms of community connections, this unit can include visits from the school's counseling department, admission counselors and recruiters in the area, and current college students. You will likely find that college students have a significant impact on high school-age students; they can be a key transitional component if their participation is organized properly. This unit is crucial to relieving anxiety for your seniors and helping them to make a smooth transition.

Unit IV: Designing the Senior Project

This unit utilizes all of the skills the Pathways students have learned in their Pathways coursework. Brainstorming, problem solving, and creativity are vital components that students will use as they design a project that incorporates their interests, their Pathway, and their passions. Included in this component are the following.

Part One: Preplanning

- Brainstorming
- Integrating passion and dreams with Cluster or career
- Choosing a mission

Part Two: Preplanning and Designing

- Persuading others to be part of the mission
- Drafting the project

> **Project Requirements**
> - A Pathway-specific technology component
> - A Pathway-specific academic connection(s)
> - A counseling connection
> - A community connection

The community connections to this part of the course are obvious: During the senior year the community, the academic or training postsecondary community, and the counseling department work together to benefit seniors individually as they develop and prepare to initiate their senior project.

Unit V: Implementing the Project

The sky is the limit for the project, but it is imperative that students are aware of the requirements (given out at the end of the Junior Judgments class) and that expectations (including a rubric) are clear from the start. The goal of the project is twofold: to provide an organized culmination of the Pathways learning experience and to position students for a smooth transition.

Possible Options

- *A project or experiment; research*
- *An internship or co-op*
- *A Cluster series of job shadows*
- *A dual-enroll or virtual-school course (including uses and implications)*
- *A Technical class*

Community connections for the senior projects can be endless, but all senior projects (even virtual high school or dual-enroll coursework) must have their roots in the community. *Because we are transitioning students from the school to the "real world," no project should be approved that does not include substantial contact with employees and employers in the student's field of interest.* For example, if a student takes an anatomy course, he or she would then go into the workplace and see knowledge of anatomy applied by x-ray technicians, surgeons, or morticians.

Unit VI: Presenting the Project

Throughout a Pathways High School, and particularly in Pathways classes, there is a continual emphasis on problem solving and on the writing process. The senior project provides the culminating opportunity for students to put to use all of the steps of the writing process in a challenging format. The project requires a presentation to the mentor team (and possibly to an evaluation panel), and each student must also create a display for the school and community at large. In this fashion, students are held to the highest level of accountability. In a Pathways High School, the senior year becomes students' level of highest achievement (and hardest work) and steers them away from "taking a year off" before college or other postsecondary plans. Following is a breakdown of the major steps involved in capstone presentations.

- Multimedia presentation
  - Prewrite
  - Draft
  - Final
- Senior Night Display (required)

The presentations allow community members to see what impact they have had on students and their plans. It is an opportunity for the community to have a final, culminating experience with students they have talked with or for whom they have provided a job shadow or internship opportunity. Not only do community members see what a difference they have made, but many times students are much more likely to stay in the area to work when they have made community connections of this magnitude.

Unit VII: Giving Back (Optional)

School districts that opt to have their senior course as a stand-alone may have time at the end of the year to send students back out into the community to "give back" to those who have helped. These projects may include anything that would be helpful to those employers who have generously given of their time and workplace. It might be landscaping a park or beautifying the community, painting a mural for a school or museum entrance, or working for free on an especially busy day. Students, grouped by Pathway and then teamed by Cluster or interest, brainstorm ideas and are completely in charge of these efforts. Their community work provides service plus connections.

- Service Learning: 1, 2, and 3
    - By Cluster or interest
    - Student designed and implemented

> *Senior Transitions allows students the chance to end their high school career with a culminating piece of work that allows a final, powerful connection to the community. At the same time, it offers all students an opportunity to make a smooth transition to their postsecondary plans.*

Throughout their four-year experience, students in a Pathways High School focus on respect and appreciation, and this is a final opportunity for them to repay and acknowledge community members who have so generously supported them in developing and improving their plans.

Course-long activities include designing and implementing and then presenting a senior project, as well as self-evaluations (weekly), journaling, presentations to underclassmen, and giving back to the community. If the academic challenge, community connections, or individual ownership and design of the senior project are missing, the project will not be a true culminating event nor will the seniors be able to make a smooth transition to their postsecondary plans. It is imperative that the philosophy and mind-set of the school community encourage seniors to make their projects the best work they have done to date.

HOW ARE PATHWAYS CLASSES DELIVERED?

Pathways classes are delivered through facilitated learning in the yearlong thematic integrated units we shared in this chapter. In a Pathways classroom, teachers act as resources, not as "knowledge bearers." They continually set up scenarios in which students explore, work together, and experience the curriculum, achieved through minimal lecturing and paper-and-pencil testing. Hands-on projects, research, guest-speaker forums, work-based experiences, presentations, and technology-integrated units should make up the majority of the coursework. As you read the Pathways class overviews, you may have felt that we were repeating ourselves at times; however, the curricula are purposefully patterned in this fashion to reinforce the practice of key skills. This redundancy is intended to provide a scaffolding for skills, so that students progress to higher levels of each skill during their four years of high school. Again the emphasis is on students interacting with themselves, their peers, and their community. We discuss implementation of facilitated learning in further detail in Chapter 10.

At the end of each course, emphasis should be placed on the transition and setup of the next Pathways class. For example, at the end of Freshman Explorations, students select not only a Pathway but also some potential job-shadow choices. At the end of Junior Judgments, students compare and contrast parts of their plans and then brainstorm a preliminary senior project.

CURRICULUM PLACEMENT OF PATHWAYS CLASSES

Ideally, Pathways classes are offered every year as stand-alones and are required for graduation. They are designed to be implemented with the same time and duration as other classes in your schedule. Make sure the placement of Pathways classes are systematically and consistently delivered in the curriculum. We have seen school districts successfully adapt Pathways classes in a variety of ways; however, these classes must be given the same value as all other classes. Some districts use stand-alone courses for freshman and senior year when the curriculum is particularly heavy; then, in Grades 10 and 11, they divide a semester between Pathways and another course (e.g., Grade 10 will have nine weeks of the Sophomore Selections and nine weeks of health; Grade 11 will have nine weeks of Junior Judgments and nine weeks of speech). Other school districts (particularly those on more traditional schedules) have embedded the curriculum in a variety of places. Sometimes Freshman Explorations coursework is embedded in language arts, social studies, or computer technology, whereas Sophomore Selections coursework has been successfully embedded in business or economics. Junior Judgments can fit into a required speech or social studies courses. In general, it is better not to embed Freshman Explorations (particularly in language arts) because it is the base of everything to come during the students' next four years of high school. Schools that have stronger Freshman Explorations classes end up with students who switch Pathways the least and who have the most well-defined plans. Often schools embed the curriculum at the beginning and then, when teachers, students, and parents see how powerful it is, the school-community Pathways team will go back and look at options to structure it optimally into the school schedule. The counselors are a powerful tool in the positioning of Pathways classes. Their understanding of the Pathways curricula and where the courses can and cannot be placed will be crucial to the optimal success of your Pathways classes.

PATHWAYS CHANGE PROCESS

Because each Pathway is a broad avenue of hundreds or thousands of similar careers, the number of students who actually switch Pathways is minimal. We have noted a correlation between Pathway switching and weaknesses in the Freshman Explorations programs. The stronger your Pathways program, the fewer switches you will have. Even so, one of the most important elements for freshman parents and students is the fact that this plan is fluid and can be adjusted. From the start, changing Pathways must be an option for students. Again, the changes we see are between Clusters or careers within a Pathway, not in the Pathway itself. Your community-school Pathways team members need to sit together and come up with a clear set of rules and requirements for a student's Pathway change. As previously mentioned, we recommend a new Pathway selection paper, an interview with the counselor and current Pathways teacher (and possibly a parent), and a review of the student's file to help ensure a good fit with the new Pathway. In addition, Pathway changes should take place in a systematic fashion—at the beginning or end of each level of Pathways coursework. Even so, it is imperative that the final Pathway decision ultimately belongs to the student. If the student does not see clear ownership of his or her plan, the results will be disastrous.

THE LONG-TERM RESULTS OF PATHWAYS CLASS WORK

In a Pathways High School, the Pathways classes are the glue that binds together the students' learning. The Pathways classes allow a systematic merging of counseling, instructional processes (and systematic delivery of technology), and connections to the community. Students use the teaming, problem-solving, and self- and time-management skills they learn in these classes across the board in all their coursework, community endeavors, and plans. The Pathways classes provide relevance to everything students learn and give them ownership of the Pathways process. This ownership issue is in keeping with current leading educational reform research: Only when people feel true ownership of what they are doing and believe that they are in charge of their learning will our endeavors end in positive, successful results. The long-term result of Pathways classes is clear: We will have students who can team and problem solve (working with others), who can self and time manage, and who follow dreams that incorporate their plans and passions. All teachers are important, but teachers of Pathways classes are particularly fortunate: They can make the most significant, meaningful difference—not just in terms of knowledge but in terms of helping students know the lifelong process of learning and thinking as well.

IN REVIEW

- Pathways classes are the core classes of the Collaborative Pathways Model.
- Pathways classes provide an avenue for students to connect the counseling, classroom, and community process in both academic and real-life experiences.

- Students take a Pathways class during their freshman, sophomore, junior, and senior year of high school.
- Each year the Pathways classes are built on the skills of the previous year and give students general and specific experiences in their community.
- Pathways classes are delivered through facilitated learning in yearlong thematic units that integrate counseling, classroom, and community—the three C's—and technology.
- Pathways classes work best as stand-alone classes but can be incorporated and aligned with other coursework as chosen by the teaching staff.
- Teachers who are willing to train (or who have been trained) in teaming, problem solving, classroom climate, community connections, technology integration, and facilitated learning are best suited to teach the Pathways classes.
- Pathways classes support and reinforce the standards and benchmarks of the school's core curriculum and identified essential learning outcomes.
- Pathways classes result in students being able to focus their educational learning on their personal goals, moving from general to specific experiences.

Chapter Eight

Scheduling in a Collaborative Career Pathways High School

SCENARIO: TWO HIGH SCHOOL STORIES

Sam and Ben go to Pathways High Schools in neighboring towns. They are learning about themselves through Pathways and developing a realistic postsecondary plan. Sam and Ben are experiencing Pathways in two very different ways, however. Sam's school uses a 4 × 4 block schedule in which he has four classes per semester that each meet for 90 minutes per day. Ben's school is on a traditional schedule in which he has six classes per day for 55 minutes each. Although Sam and Ben's experiences in learning may differ, they will both graduate with the skills and road map necessary for a smooth postsecondary transition and with great hope and enthusiasm for their future.

Sam is scheduled into Freshman Explorations during his first semester of freshman year. This class is team taught by a technology teacher and a language arts teacher. Although Career Pathways is the central theme of the class, high school technology and language arts skills are introduced as well. After experiencing Freshman Explorations and developing his plans for sophomore job shadowing, Sam takes freshman English second semester, which focuses on the 9th-grade standards and benchmarks that his school chose. Career Pathways is reinforced and revisited during this class, as well as in his other core and elective classes, and he selects his Pathway at the end of the school year.

Ben is also scheduled into Freshman Explorations as he enters high school; however, his Pathways class is integrated into his 9th-grade language arts class. He takes this class during the entire school year. Ben's teachers use the ideas of Freshman Explorations to teach major language arts standards and benchmarks throughout the year.

The following year, Sam's Sophomore Selections class is nine weeks long in a 4 × 4 block and is backed by a speech class. In this way, the speech and Sophomore Selections teachers work together to integrate their curriculum while alternating half the students on job shadows and half the students in speech class. In Ben's sophomore year, he takes Sophomore Selections for an entire semester. Sophomore Selections is integrated into this 10th-grade speech requirement, and his teacher uses the students' job-shadowing experiences as a base for their class objectives and speeches.

In his junior year, Sam takes Junior Judgments during his second semester. His school has scheduled Freshman Explorations and Sophomore Selections first semester and Junior Judgments and the community half of their Senior Transitions class second semester. This is planned so that the community is not saturated at any one time. In the fall, the community provides field trips and shadows, and in the spring, internships and senior panels. So Sam is scheduled to take his junior internship second semester. His internship is nine weeks and is backed by a nine-week required economics class. Sam's Junior Judgments class is scheduled at the end of the day so he has 90 scheduled minutes plus any additional time he can dedicate to his community internship.

Because Ben's school is on a traditional schedule, the faculty members have to be more creative in embedding Junior Judgments, so they have decided to put two classes at the end of the day together to make a "block" of time for juniors. They combine the 11th-grade required technology class with their 11th-grade language arts class. The two teachers team teach and rotate students into nine-week community internship experiences.

During senior year, Sam takes a nine-week Senior Transitions class in the beginning of the first semester that concentrates on postsecondary application, scholarships, postsecondary visits, and the "setting up" of his senior project. This is backed by an 18-week government class in which Sam learns the government class standards and benchmarks while staying in touch with set time and other guidelines for his project. In the last nine weeks of his senior year, Sam has the second half of his Senior Transitions class in which he prepares and presents his senior project. Ben's Senior Transitions class is a separate class that is required for his senior year. The class meets for one period per day for both semesters. Ben also presents his senior project to his panel in the spring of his graduation from high school.

THE NEED TO ADDRESS SCHEDULING

We have seen the conflict over scheduling do more damage to implementing a Collaborative Career Pathways High School than any other issue. This is because staff and faculty of many schools are more attached to their schedule than they are to their content. Most teachers have "married" their teaching mind-set to a time schedule. It is difficult to separate how a teacher teaches and the time frame into which a class has been embedded. Therefore, making changes in the scheduling and delivery of instruction can be a major undertaking.

Like the chicken and the egg scenario, it will be hard to discover which came first in your school, the philosophy or the schedule. The ability to separate your philosophy of education your from schedule is like trying to separate a mother from her baby. Our advice is not to try to discover where your scheduling tradition began but to move forward with teachers from where your district is currently. As teachers begin to expand their knowledge of best practices and embrace the Career Pathways integration with curriculum, they will begin to let go of some of the older more embedded traditions of your school, the strongest of these being the schedule.

Although a Career Pathways Model can be integrated into any schedule, it is most commonly attached to the block schedule concept. This is because Career Pathways emphasizes more student-directed learning experiences, projects, and community time. Blocks of time are more conducive to this philosophy. As seen in Ben's case, Career Pathways can be implemented successfully into a traditional schedule with small tweaks as needed.

MAJOR TYPES OF SCHEDULING AND CAREER PATHWAYS HIGH SCHOOLS

As seen in the scenario of Sam and Ben, you and your staff can do whatever you want with your schedule—this in itself should be a very freeing thought. Time is the one resource that all schools have in common. So how do we use our time to meet the needs of our students?

For example, recall how Ben's school used a traditional schedule to provide a Junior Judgments experience in which the technology and language arts teacher blocked the last two hours of the day to team teach and provide internship time. Or maybe you are in a 4 × 4 block but want to offer some shorter exploratory or tutoring opportunities; you therefore reduce your four classes by so many minutes and add a "short" class at the beginning of the day or right after lunch. *The possibilities are endless and differ as much as our schools, staffs, students, and communities.*

> *The key to scheduling in a Collaborative Career Pathways High School is to meet the instructional and student work-based needs through flexibility, collaboration, and professional development.*

The most extensive work that has been done on school restructuring through scheduling is by Robert Lynn Canady. Canady asks the important questions of schools, "How well is the time we have now in school being used?" He urges schools to look at alternative schedules, involve others in the process, and determine the best schedule for your school. He notes that it is important to match the scheduling option with the needs and direction of the school (Canady, 1994).

The three main types of scheduling we encounter most often are the 4 × 4 block, the alternative block, and the traditional schedule. The 4 × 4 block sets a school schedule so students have four 90–100 minute blocks of time. The students complete four classes each semester. A 4 × 4 block class covers in one semester what a year-long class covers in a traditional schedule. The advantages of the 4 × 4 block is that it allows students to carry a lighter or less complex load, it allows for in-depth understanding of knowledge and skills and provides the time for facilitated and problem- and project-based learning. It also cuts down on class transition time and student hall contact because they only change classes three times a day. Fewer class transitions mean less opportunity for students to get into trouble. The great advantage for teachers is that they have only three preps and 90–100 minutes of prep time a day to work together to develop and present meaningful instruction. The concern about the 4 × 4 block that faculty and administrators voice most often is that students may have a whole year before they take a subject again. This concern can be eliminated by integrating your curriculum and using the key core subject standards in all classes. English teachers can reinforce core democratic values, for example, by studying universal themes of literature; social studies teachers can reinforce proper sentence and paragraph structure through writing assignments. If used well, the 4 × 4 block schedule is a wonderful tool to improve student achievement and foster student-driven instruction. If, however, teachers are not prepared to use the block effectively and use the lecture and recall techniques of teaching and learning, this schedule can be detrimental to student learning.

> *In a Collaborative Career Pathways High School, the 4 × 4 block gives students the time they need for community interaction, career research, and team projects.*

Table 8.1 is a sample of a 4 × 4 block schedule in a Collaborative Career Pathways High School. Note that math/science and English/social studies are backed with each other to reinforce related skills and keep students proficient in using all subjects.

We have also seen schools add a variation to the 4 × 4 block to allow for some "shorter" classes or remediation and advanced opportunities for students. This is done by reducing minutes in the blocks and adding a short period of time at the beginning of the day or before or after lunch. This provides time for opportunities such as tutoring or remediation, online coursework, advanced placement, band, foreign language, peer counseling, and so on. In other 4 × 4 block schools, this occurs during a seminar period. Remember, your schedule is your tool to do what you need to do to meet the needs of your students.

The alternative block or "A–B" block schedule is really a combination of a 4 × 4 and traditional schedule and tries to combine the best of both worlds. The alternative block uses blocks of time for instruction, thus allowing for in-depth teaching and learning; however, the classes meet every other day and can run for a half or full year. The advantage is that teachers have the "block" of instruction time, but the disadvantage is that students still carry a heavy workload of eight classes. Also, teachers have more preps with blocks of prep time for shared planning only every other day. This schedule does give facilitated learning a root base. Some alternative block schedules will allow for students to have a double block in key subjects such as language arts or math by having those subjects meet every day. We have seen the alternative block schedule used in schools that believe in the philosophy of "chunks" of instruction time but do not have the staff or

Table 8.1 An Example of a 4 × 4 Block Schedule in a Collaborative Career Pathways High School

Freshman First Semester

Freshman Explorations	Math	Art	U.S. History

Freshman Second Semester

Freshman English	Science	Art	Computers

Sophomore First Semester

Sophomore Selections	Sophomore English	Graphic Arts	Math

Sophomore Second Semester

Science	Global Studies	Graphic Arts	Advanced Computers

Junior First Semester

Junior English	Math	Advanced Art	Psychology

Junior Second Semester

Junior Judgments	Science	Advanced Art	Government

Senior First Semester

Senior Transitions (setup)	Math	Dual enrollment: Photography/ English composition	

Senior Second Semester

Senior Transitions (presentations)	Science	Dual enrollment: Photography/ English composition	

dollars to hire the extra staff needed to implement a 4 × 4 block schedule. Even if the alternative block does include some of the advantages of block scheduling, it can be more difficult to implement successfully than a straight block or traditional schedule; in addition, the research is not as positive about its outcome. A sample of an alternative block schedule in a Collaborative Career Pathways High School with blocks meeting every other day is shown in Table 8.2.

In the traditional schedule, a student takes six to seven classes a day for about 50 to 60 minutes. The student follows the same schedule every day. This can be a challenge but is manageable in a Career Pathways School where blocks of time are needed for individual and team projects and community involvement. The traditional schedule lends itself to the lecture–recall mode of teaching and learning and does not allow time for the systematic integration of subjects. In a traditional schedule, however, a great deal of content can be covered, just not in the "depth of understanding" of a block of time. The loss of time in student transitioning from one class to another and the time it takes for attendance and other logistical matters can rob even more time from the short, traditionally scheduled day. Teachers get daily prep time but not the longer blocks of time it takes to do shared planning. Table 8.3 is a sample of a Collaborative Career Pathways Schedule in a traditional high school schedule with all classes meeting every day.

The samples in Tables 8.1 through 8.3 give you an idea of what a Collaborative Career Pathways System could look like in your school. You can see that there are schedules in which the Pathways classes stand alone and other schedules in which they are embedded into other required coursework. In some schedules, Pathways classes are a semester long; in other schedules, they run the full year. Some even combine classes to have the necessary time available to work with the community.

These few examples provide a glimpse of the freedom you have with scheduling, and although the schedules shown here all reflect the two-semester system, a Pathways school schedule could also be used with trimesters or quarters. If your district offers year-round school options, the Pathways course and community involvement could be distributed throughout the year. Also, the Pathways classes can be offered to half the students one semester and half the next, spreading out the amount of students who are out in the community at any given time. Shadows and interns could be scheduled both morning and afternoon to enable time differences in community connections.

> *The key to Pathways scheduling is to design a system that will give you the time you need to teach Pathways course objectives combined with the time needed for the community component.*

AN IDEAL COLLABORATIVE CAREER PATHWAYS SCHEDULE

Let us share with you what we suggest would be an "ideal" schedule for a Collaborative Career Pathways High School. This schedule is a combination of

Table 8.2 An Example of an Alternative Block Schedule in a Collaborative Career Pathways High School

Freshman First Semester

Block A: odd days	Freshman Explorations	Science	Band	Technology
Block B: even days	Math	English	Wood Shop	Civics

Freshman Second Semester

Block A: odd days	Freshman Exploration	Science	Band	Technology
Block B: even days	Math	English	Wood Shop	Civics

Sophomore First Semester

Block A: odd days	English/ Sophomore Selections	Science	Band	Speech
Block B: even days	Math	U.S. History	Machine Shop	Art

Sophomore Second Semester

Block A: odd days	English/ Sophomore Selections	Science	Band	Speech
Block B: even days	Math	U.S. History	Machine Shop	Art

Junior First Semester

Block A: odd days	Junior English	Math	Technology Center: Welding	Junior Judgments
Block B: even days	Science	Band	Technology Center: Welding	Junior Judgments

Junior Second Semester

Block A: odd days	Junior English	Math	Technology Center: Welding	Junior Judgments
Block B: even days	Science	Band	Technology Center: Welding	Junior Judgments

Senior First Semester

Block A: odd days	Senior English/ Transitions	Science	Technology Center: Machining	Technology Center: Machining
Block B: even days	Band	Government Economics	Technology Center: Machining	Technology Center: Machining

Senior Second Semester

Block A: odd days	Senior English/ Transitions	Science	Technology Center: Machining	Technology Center: Machining
Block B: even days	Band	Government Economics	Technology Center: Machining	Technology Center: Machining

Table 8.3 A Example of a Traditional Schedule in a Collaborative Career Pathways High School

Freshman First Semester		*Freshman Second Semester*	
Freshman English/embedded with Explorations	Science	Freshman English/embedded with Explorations	Science
Band	Civics	Band	Health
	Math		Math
	Physical Education		Physical Education

Sophomore First Semester		*Sophomore Second Semester*	
English	Science	English	Science
Band	U.S. History	Band	U.S. History
	Math		Math
	Speech/Embedded with Sophomore Selections		Speech/embedded with Sophomore Selections

Junior First Semester		*Junior Second Semester*	
Science	English	Science	English
	Junior Judgments/ Technology (combining of two class times)		Junior Judgments/ Technology (combining of two class times)
Band	Math	Band	Math

Senior First Semester		*Senior Second Semester*	
Senior Transitions	Science	Senior Transitions	Science
	Advanced Placement English		Advanced Placement English
Band	Math	Band	Math
	Journalism		Journalism

Table 8.4   An Example of an Ideal Schedule in a Collaborative Career Pathways High School

First Semester (17 weeks)	Semester Review (1 week)	Second Semester (17 weeks)	Semester Review (1 week)
Class 1	Student Options	Class 1	Student Options
Class 2		Class 2	
Class 3		Class 3	
Class 4		Class 4	

a Canaday model integrated with the Pathways philosophy. The model is set up in two semesters, although it would also work with trimesters. The students are scheduled into a 4 × 4 block, with the last week of each semester reserved for intense activities. These activities would be designed by the staff and could include remediation, advanced work, career fairs, and every sort of community-student interaction such as job shadows, internships, field trips, speakers, and so on. In this fashion, any student who did not master the essential skills would be given one-on-one time with teachers so that she or he does not fall more than one semester behind. Students who have mastered the standards could do advanced work in an area of their interest or even do more intensive career research. The time could also be used to hold a school career or interview fair. Students who want to do another job shadow to finalize their internship plans or have a shortened internship to compare with their first would have the opportunity to further explore these options. This time could also be used for campus visits and senior project presentations.

This wrap-up week, or two weeks if necessary, would give teachers and students options to improve student achievement and further define a realistic postsecondary plan. A sample of this schedule is shown in Table 8.4.

Of course, the concept of semester reviews, whether they are one or two weeks long, can be used in any scheduling option from 4x4 to traditional and semesters to quarters. The concept gives an advantage to students who need some re-teaching and learning opportunities for difficult concepts or even advanced work in an area of interest. This advantage, coupled with the option of additional time for students to clarify their own educational plans, can be extremely powerful.

> *The key to implementing this review schedule design is to involve teachers and students in the planning and execution of wrap-up options and activities.*

SCHEDULES, TEACHING STYLES, AND PROFESSIONAL DEVELOPMENT

Although we alluded to the interconnectedness of teaching styles and scheduling, it is important to examine the differences. If these concepts are not understood and practiced—in other words, if your schedule choice and your teaching delivery system do not match—it will lead to disaster. You will experience frustration among your faculty, students, and parents, and you will not see a rise in student achievement or properly designed student postsecondary plans. Therefore, it is imperative to work Pathways and your schedule together with expanded teaching strategies and professional development. Table 8.5 explains key schedules and teaching styles.

The importance of professional development for teachers is apparent when reflecting on the information in Table 8.5. It is important to work with your faculty and plan any scheduling changes ahead of time. Before the changes are made, teachers must have professional development in the areas of standards-based education, teacher and student teaming, project- and problem-based learning, integrated curriculum, and assessment systems that include rubrics and self and peer evaluations. This professional development aligns with the recommendation of Chapter 6 in developing staff ownership of the curriculum. It must also be sustained and not a one-time occurrence. Teachers expanding and trying new strategies must be supported, coached, and rewarded.

CREATING A SCHEDULE THAT IS RIGHT FOR YOUR SCHOOL

So how do you create a schedule that is right for your faculty and students? First, ask yourself a few basic questions:

1. What is our current schedule and why do we use it?
2. What is the main teaching style used in our school?
3. What professional development have faculty members had recently, and how open to professional development are they?

Then, with your faculty or a committee of faculty members, explore and review the following:

- What are our goals for students?
- What is the best way to reach those goals in the area of instructional delivery?
- What are our current scheduling options?
- What other scheduling options are available?
- How are other schools implementing these options?
- What does the research show about each option?
- What will fit best with our community?
- What is our recommendation and timeframe?
- What will our faculty need to be successful in making a scheduling change?
- What professional development is needed, and when, how, and with what funds will it be delivered?

Table 8.5 Key Schedules and Teaching Styles

Schedule	Classroom Management	Teaching and Learning Strategies	Assessment	Community
4 × 4 block	Student-managed with complete inclusion strategies	Facilitated learning: student-driven and team-centered projects and integrated subject matter	Authentic: centers on students, rubrics, observation, and self- and peer evaluation	Involved and committed: site visits, chats, interviews, shadows, internships, senior project work sites, and mentor boards
Alternating block (A–B block)	Student managed with complete inclusion strategies	Facilitated learning and student driven, but time is eaten with review of previous activities because it is not continual	Mixed: some authentic with rubrics but also some paper and pencil (because of loss of daily continuity)	Involved and committed but more sporadic: site visits, chats, interviews, shadows, internships, senior project work sites, and mentor boards
Traditional	Teacher centered	Lecture recall, possibly with some student-centered activities; content and textbook driven; short activities and individual assignments	Mostly pen-and-paper testing	Some general site visits and an annual career fair; other community involvement can be integrated but with adjustments to the schedule

In examining where and how to incorporate Pathways classes, ask yourself and your faculty these questions:

- Will they be stand-alone classes or embedded into an existing curriculum?
- Which teachers would be most willing or comfortable with student-based teaching and techniques such as problem- or team-based learning?
- Which teachers like to take risks and can withstand the pressure from status quo supporters?

> *The most important scheduling considerations for you and your faculty in a Collaborative Career Pathways High School is where, when, and how the Pathways classes will be incorporated.*

- How will the incorporation of the Pathways classes affect our core and elective schedule and our graduation requirements?
- How will the Pathways teachers be trained, coached, and supported?

When dealing with all these difficult questions, remember that the implementation of the Collaborative Pathways Model ideally happens over a five-year period, beginning with a planning year, followed by implementation of Pathways in the freshman, sophomore, junior, and senior years. You can deal with change one year a time. This is extremely helpful because not only can you break the change up into smaller pieces, but teachers, students, and parents can begin to see the positive impact on students and the community each year, thus building momentum as you go.

CONCLUSION

You will hear many times that we cannot do "this" or "that" because the schedule will not allow it. *Don't be a slave to your schedule.* Your schedule is a wonderful tool for you to use to implement a system for high student achievement and successful postsecondary plans. As an administrator or educator, don't fall into the trap of being ruled by your schedule. Scheduling changes can be difficult; to be done correctly, they must be collaborative, planned, and well-prepared. You'll find, however, that taking control of your schedule, just like taking control of your curriculum, is freeing and allows for more flexibility in your system. It also will reach more students in more ways. Pathways can work with any schedule if you and your faculty are willing to work outside the box. Our advice is to not be afraid to tackle this monster; it will be well worth it for you, your faculty, students, and community, as well as the success of your Pathways system.

IN REVIEW

- When implementing a Collaborative Career Pathways Model, examine your current scheduling practices carefully.
- Scheduling practices can cause a considerable amount of conflict in the implementation of your Pathways program because teacher delivery systems are intricately connected to the schedule they teach in.
- You and your faculty should examine all avenues of scheduling, including block, traditional, semester, quarters, and so on before making decisions on scheduling changes.
- In implementing a Collaborative Career Pathways program, the most important questions you will answer are, "Where, when, and how will the Pathways classes be implemented?"
- When implementing Pathways classes into your schedule, remember that you only have to implement one year at a time, giving yourself and your faculty the time and flexibility needed to make a successful change.

- The Collaborative Pathways Model best fits into a block type of schedule because it emphasizes student-centered teaching and learning; however, it can be successful in any schedule as long as you and your faculty can incorporate the counseling and community components into the classroom.
- Staff input, professional development, coaching, and continued support are imperative to the successful implementation of any schedule change.
- Remember to use your schedule as a tool and not a trap. Creating a schedule that is right for you and your faculty, students, parents, and community is not easy but is well worth the effort.

Part Four

Classroom Processes

Chapter Nine

Freshman Explorations

The Cornerstone of Pathways Instruction

One of the first and most crucial parts of any Pathways program is the development of a strong Freshman Explorations class. Freshman Explorations is the foundation on which all of the rest of a student's high school coursework is based.

SCENARIO: TWO FRESHMAN EXPERIENCES

Let's begin with another comparison of two freshmen. In Chapter 8, we looked at Sam and Ben, who were both freshman in Pathways high schools, although the school schedules were different. As we start this chapter, let's look at two freshman girls. Kathy is a freshman at a Collaborative Pathways School and Becky is a freshman at a traditional high school. Both students are coming into the system for the first time and know a small pool of people. Both think they may be interested in the health field. Both girls get along well with others and earn good grades.

Kathy takes Freshman Explorations in addition to her other required freshman coursework. By the end of the course, she has examined all of the major Pathways and has learned that there is much overlap. In addition to all of the health opportunities, she has also learned there are several human service occupations that might suit her as well, if not better. She has chatted with people in a wide variety of occupations and more than 30 people in health and human services. She has been to several worksites, including three health sites, and has seen how technology was used in all these workplaces. She has teamed with a variety of classmates and made friends by working with a wide range of students.

Kathy has a good idea of who she is and what she likes to do best when working in groups. She has worked on a variety of integrated projects and learned to deal with diverse problems; she especially loved the project that focused on teen health issues. When she finished Freshman Explorations, Kathy knew that health was truly where she wanted to be and that, by its nature, it would allow her human service opportunities. She had several specific careers in mind that would suit her, and she knew what coursework she needed and why. In addition, she was closely connected to her school and to her classmates.

Becky had a typical freshman year. She took all the required coursework. She liked her math and science courses and worked hard in them, knowing she needed them to prepare for college. (Becky's counselor had told her that these classes would be important to a health career.) Having studied her coursework in isolation, she was not sure how English or technology would be used in a health workplace. She had not actually been to any health environments (except when she went to the dentist or family physician), and she had talked only to her cousin, who was a dentist, about her career. She had a small group of friends who were in most of her classes, and Becky felt as if she was just a small cog in the scheme of her school. If anyone asked about her plans for sophomore year, she would have said she planned to study hard so that she could eventually go to college.

The difference between students completing a Freshman Explorations class and those in a traditional high school setting is night and day. Freshman Explorations gives students all of those important connections that allow them to be in charge of their own plan—connections not only to themselves, but also to their school (and classmates) and to the "real" world.

It is obvious that what we would want for our own children, or for the students in our schools, is the kind of focus, knowledge, and control of the future that Kathy has. Becky, on the other hand, will be one of those students who goes to college, changes majors three times, and graduates in six years instead of four. Even then, she probably won't really have a handle on all of the careers she might have been capable of having or know why she is uncomfortable in the field she eventually chooses.

THE IMPORTANT CONNECTIONS

In Freshman Explorations, a student begins to make the three most important connections that set apart a Pathways education from a traditional one:

- Connections to self
- Connections to school
- Connections to the work world and "real life"

In this chapter, we discuss how students connect to themselves and to their school, to their community and to the real world, through the process of Freshman Explorations. There are several versions of Freshman-type classes, but what makes the Collaborative Model unique is its combination of many key elements—study skills, technology, integrated curriculum, problem solving, and decision making—with career exploration. Figure 9.1 provides a visual example of a typical student's experience in a Collaborative Freshman Explorations class.

Some schools believe that because they have a careers class, they do not need a Freshman Explorations Class (or a systematic exposure to career education for that matter), but the truth is that a collaborative system provides much more support and exploration than a stand-alone career class can (Figure 9.2).

FRESHMAN EXPLORATIONS: THE CURRICULUM

So when designing a Freshman Explorations course, where should it begin? We begin our course with a yearlong theme, "The Great Adventure." Integrated curriculum proponent Susan Kovalik has developed a system of learning in which subjects are taught together in real-life settings based on brain research findings. As in Kovalik's (1994) Integrated Thematic Instruction (ITI), we organize our entire course around a big idea and then break it into smaller themes and then units. If we look at Freshman Explorations in this way, the big idea is diversity. There are so many opportunities at the start of any new undertaking, but at the start of high school, every student starts "clean." Every student has a clean slate in terms of grades and how others perceive them, and in terms of pursuing his or her dreams. Every person is a diverse combination of personality, skills, values, and dreams.

Whereas the course-long map (see Chapter 7) shows the entire journey a freshman will take in a Freshman Explorations Class, we can actually divide the course structure as follows:

> **Phase 1. Getting Acquainted:** The first phase gives students the opportunity to learn more about themselves, their school, and their classmates.
>
> **Phase 2. Exploring:** The second phase allows students to explore a variety of Pathways and careers, as well as teaming and problem-solving strategies.
>
> **Phase 3. Deciding:** The final phase allows students to take everything they have learned in the class and match it to a Pathway decision that works for them.

It is important that the key components of a good Freshman Explorations Class are all adequately covered. Time distribution of the key elements might look something like Figure 9.3.

The teacher of this focus class needs to remember that he or she is only the guide on the journey and that the student is the true explorer.

Connections to Self

Before students can truly discover a Pathway that will suit them, they must first examine themselves. Freshman Explorations is the beginning of the high school career and is a good time for students to spend some time getting to

Figure 9.1 The Freshman Explorations Experience

The Freshman Explorations Experience

Site Visits
- TV Station
- Airport
- Grain Elevator
- Hospital
- Manufacturing Plant

Personality
- Profiles
- Learning Styles
- Aptitudes
- Multiple Intelligences

Journals and Chats

Parental Involvement/Educational Development Plan

Integrated Units
- Problem Solving
- Decision Making
- Teaming
- Conflict Resolution

Varied Technology
- Technical Writing
- Software Skills
- Multimedia Presentations
- Graphic Design

182

Figure 9.2 The Collaborative Model Versus Stand-Alone Career Courses

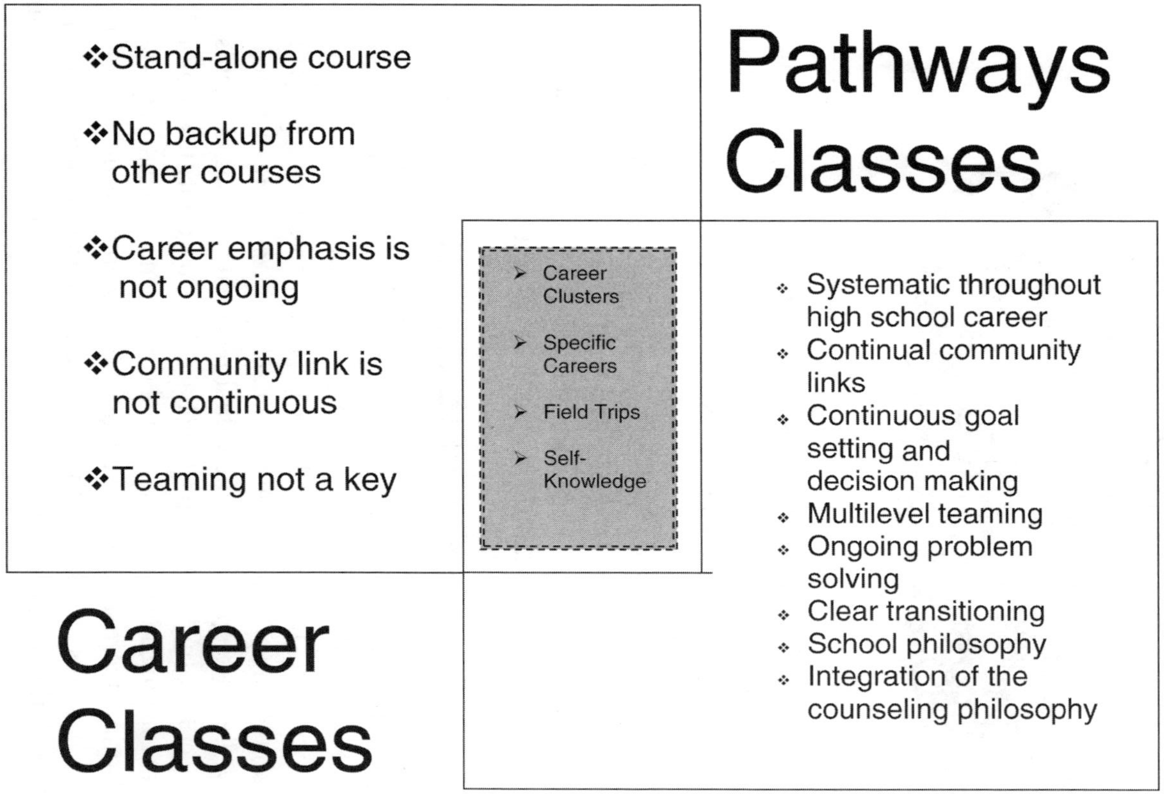

Career Classes

- Stand-alone course
- No backup from other courses
- Career emphasis is not ongoing
- Community link is not continuous
- Teaming not a key

  - Career Clusters
  - Specific Careers
  - Field Trips
  - Self-Knowledge

Pathways Classes

- Systematic throughout high school career
- Continual community links
- Continuous goal setting and decision making
- Multilevel teaming
- Ongoing problem solving
- Clear transitioning
- School philosophy
- Integration of the counseling philosophy

Figure 9.3 Freshman Explorations Class Activities Time Distribution

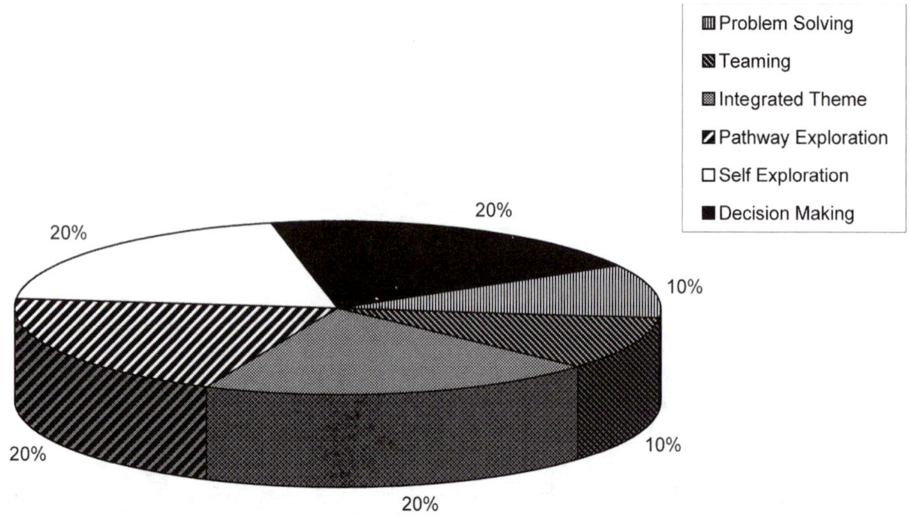

Legend:
- Problem Solving
- Teaming
- Integrated Theme
- Pathway Exploration
- Self Exploration
- Decision Making

20%, 20%, 10%, 10%, 20%, 20%

know who they are, what they like to do, and what is important to them. In a Collaborative Pathways High School, students spend time throughout the course getting to know themselves better.

During the first month of Freshman Explorations, students intensively examine who they are and what makes them special. Students begin the course by taking the Differential Aptitude Test (DAT, 1990) so that they can get a standardized reading of where their strengths lie. The DAT is only one such test, and any test that measures a variety of aptitudes would be helpful. Throughout the semester, students also keep a personal journal and record their thoughts on a variety of topics. Students spend time determining which skills they possess, taking into consideration any jobs they have held such as babysitting, lawn care, and fast food service. They also make lists of what they like to do the most and what they do best. In the first few weeks, we also examine diversity and how that relates to personality. Using the Hartman Color Profile (1999) and the Holland Hexagon (we use the video *Exploring Careers*; Bossert, n.d.), students study the makeup of their individual personality styles. Students are made aware of how the brain learns; they have the opportunity to discover their individual learning style and their multiple intelligence strengths (Gardner, 1983).

During this first month of school while students are making connections to themselves, it is crucial that the Freshman Explorations teachers team continually with the counselors. The counselor comes in and out of the room to help with a variety of testing and to let students know that he or she is available to them. It is also crucial that students begin to develop a rapport with the counselor.

During this first month, in addition to looking at strengths and abilities, students also have the opportunity to examine their

> *As we have continually emphasized, what makes the Collaborative Model so unique is the hand-in-hand incorporation of a counseling model with integrated schoolwide classroom instruction.*

Table 9.1   Freshman Exploration Goals Chart

Goals Today	Goals This Week	Goals This Year	Goals for 10 Years

beliefs. Each student completes a self-survey of his or her belief system; most of the schools in our county use one found in Bingham and Stryker (1993, pp. 31–37). Emphasis throughout the course is placed on helping students clearly define what they stand for and believe in. This is in keeping with Kovalik's (1994) life skills and with the class agreements that are used in the Tribes Program (Ross, 2000, p. 37). The foundation of base values sets the stage for later in high school when students not only look at their values and what connects to them, but also workplace ethics, integrity, and even peer pressure.

Connected to values are the students' goals—both short and long term. One of the interesting things that happens at the beginning of Freshman Explorations is the students' discovery that their goals and the goals that others have for them don't necessarily match. One of the first assignments we give students is for them to list their goals for the year, their goals for high school, and their goals for 10 years from now (Table 9.1).

> *One reason that Freshman Explorations is so crucial is because it allows students to develop their own plans and, at the same time, assists parents and schools in successfully including the young person in decision making.*

During the first year in which Freshman Explorations was instituted, we had a student who raised his hand and said, "Do you want me to list my *real* goals or the goals my parents have for me?"

What enhances our Collaborative Model is that everyone learns to team, not just the student. Within the first month of a Pathways class, the teacher is teaming not just with other Pathways teachers but also with parents, counselors, and the community. When the student realizes how important he is, he feels empowered and begins to develop an intrinsic reward system of his own. At the end of the semester, we do the same chart again, and it is amazing how much more practical and real world their lists become in that short period of time.

Because part of self-exploration is developing self-esteem, we spend time during Freshman Explorations on study skills that can be used not only throughout high school, but in any postsecondary setting as well. Because our school schedule is a 4 × 4 block, Freshman Explorations is 90 minutes long for a full semester. We have approximately four months to work with students, so we break our study skills into four units and work on one skill per month.

Once students have figured out their personality profile and their intelligences, as well as their learning styles, the study units take on more meaning.

Table 9.2   Freshman Explorations Skills: Course Schedule

September: Listening
October: Note taking
November: Skimming and scanning
December: Test taking
January: Review of writing process

Table 9.3   Teaming Card

Name:

Hartman Personality Profile Colors:

   Primary:

   Secondary:

Holland Hexagon Profile (list first three):

   1.

   2.

   3.

Learning Style:

Multiple Intelligences (list first three):

   1.

   2.

   3.

They can better adapt their note-taking, test-taking, and writing skills to match who they are.

At the end of the first month of class, all students fill out a teaming card (Table 9.3). This card is basically a "who you are in a nutshell." It provides the teacher with the most important information at a glance, which helps with teaming and devising lessons and options to meet the student's needs.

This card is helpful for the instructors when they plan teams. It can also be shared with other teachers to enhance their understanding and ability to work with the students from an individual "learner-centered" perspective.

A journal can be useful in allowing students to explore themselves and make connections to what they are learning about themselves. We work on journal entries at least twice (but preferably three times) a week. The journals allow students to reflect on what they are learning about themselves, but they also help to improve language arts and communication skills. Although Freshman Explorations is not a language arts class per se, it continually

Table 9.4   Topics for Journaling

- Do you think the results of your personality profile match the real you?
- Is there another personality or hexagon section that better matches who you are?
- Do your skills and interests match your profile?
- What are your dreams for the future? Are they the same, or do they differ from your long-term goals? How, if at all, do your dreams and goals differ from those your parents have for you?

---

incorporates language and thought together. This is imperative because language arts in some form will be a part of all students' workplace environment. Table 9.4 offers some topics for journaling that we have used in helping students connect to themselves.

The opportunity to reflect on the various phases of Freshman Explorations is critical as students evaluate themselves, their skills, and their Pathways opportunities. Here are some random samples from journals of Pathways students about the importance of journaling:

I feel this class has quite a few good points. I feel it is fun to learn about your personality. It's fun to see how everyone has something different to contribute to a team. It's fun to see what types of jobs you are good at.

One good thing is we are never doing the same thing over and over again. Another thing is we work in groups . . . which is cool and better than just one person thinking about something—[you] have more ideas.

The Freshman Explorations class opens up and gives you a taste of many different jobs. It really opens your eyes to jobs that we have focused on. It may change your mind or opinion on a job. I found out I was a red personality—I had never seen myself as a leader before but now I do.

Connections to School

During the freshman fall semester, it is also important for students to get used to their new learning environment. At some of the schools in our county, as many as half of the freshmen have attended other parochial or private junior high schools, so this is their first experience with a public school and a new school building. It is therefore absolutely crucial in the first few weeks to establish a warm, inclusive environment. This can be done in several ways. In a small school, establishing the learning environment can easily be done within the Freshman Explorations class and throughout the freshman class and school community at large. In a larger school district, establishing individual learning communities that connect to the class can be facilitated best with learning teams that include focus class teachers, counselors, and administrators.

During the first few weeks, it is important to promote inclusion among all of the students. One way to do this is to use a variety of activities called "community builders"; a good resource and program for community building is

Tribes (Gibbs, 2000). In addition, it is important to help students get used to their new school building, the staff and faculty members who run it, and the students with whom they will be working throughout the semester.

The first place this inclusion occurs is at freshman orientation. With grant dollars from the state of Michigan, our pilot school was able to produce a video to show parents at our orientation program. This video explains what a Pathways High School is and how students in the district begin creating their plan in Freshman Explorations. The video includes interviews from the principal, superintendent, and Pathways teachers, but more important, it also features interviews with former students, parents, and the business community.

> *From the start, the emphasis is on the "whole village" approach to helping the young person find his or her plan.*

Although a video may not be feasible for your district, interviews from business members, parents, and Pathways teachers and students (after the first year) can be helpful to the incoming parents and students—not only do the students feel welcome and needed, but so do the parents.

During freshman orientation, we give parents and students a tour of our building and include a visit to the Freshman Explorations classroom. The classroom already displays the Big Picture Plan (Jacobs, 1997; Kovalik, 1997) for the semester and clearly shows the pathways we will be using; we also emphasize the life skills and agreements that we will keep throughout the course. This is the first opportunity for the Pathways teachers to talk to parents and students. Many concerns about the course can be dispelled that evening (Table 9.5).

During the first week of school, it is important to help the students get used to their new environment. One way of doing this is to take them on an extended tour of the school and grounds. Another way is to have an interview day. On one of the first days of school, students can meet in groups to brainstorm interview questions for a special guest. The next day, each group (generally four or five students) will have an opportunity to interview their guest for five to eight minutes and then introduce their guest to the class. Each guest then tells the class briefly about his or her job and any special information the students may need to know; for example, the computer technician may talk about how students can get passwords, and the lunch supervisor may describe how to purchase tickets and make menu suggestions. Some of the school occupations we include are the superintendent, principal, principal's secretary, librarian, athletic director, head accountant, head custodian, cafeteria supervisor, and bus supervisor. By the end of the class period, students have heard from all of the prominent staff members and have been welcomed to the building by all of them. This is an adaptation of a beginning activity from *Focus on Freshmen* (Holmboe & Malone, 1996, p. 24). It is a wonderful way to make the administration and staff part of the Freshman Explorations community right from the start.

During the first month or two, a sense of classroom community can also be built with other activities. The field trips students take from focus class increase

Table 9.5 Common Concerns With the Pathways Program and Responses to Them

Concerns	Reality
• Student will lose control of his or her future	• Student will have more control of his or her future
• Course will require too much time away from traditional academics	• All academics will be better integrated
• Student will make hurried decisions about important issues	• Student will make better-informed decisions
• Student will be pushed into a career	• Student will only make a broad Pathway selection

bonding, as do other extracurricular activities. By the end of the second month, students are comfortable with each other and feel truly included.

A Pathways schools will have fewer documented incidences of violence and bullying and better attendance (Berrien County Intermediate School District, 2001). These connections to school and self are not only paramount for the smooth functioning of the Freshman Explorations class, they also provide a foundation for the rest of the student's Pathways program.

> *Student bonding and a sense of team identity allow Explorations teachers not only to tackle complex, integrated materials but also to address issues of respect and diversity. We cannot overemphasize the importance and long-term rewards of building community among freshman students.*

CONNECTING STUDENTS TO THE WORLD AROUND THEM

In a Pathways High School, students never have to ask, "Why are we studying this?" Instead, they always know how their coursework relates to their personal plan or direction and how it will be relevant. Getting connected to school and self are two important components of Freshman Explorations; however, it is made even more meaningful by adding the real-life or community component. Real-world connections are lacking in the traditional freshman program; they are crucial to an Explorations curriculum in a Collaborative Pathways High School. The three components to good community and real-world connections are the following:

- Integrated thematic units that connect to the pathways
- Exploration of the Career Pathways that connects the student, the community, and the workplace
- Utilization of the decision-making process so that the student can make a thoughtful, informed Pathway decision (following community experiences)

Integrated Thematic Units

One of the reasons Freshman Explorations is the cornerstone of a Pathways High School is because it helps students realize that all of the coursework and skills they are learning will be integrated together in whatever career interest they end up pursuing. Having students team together throughout the semester on integrated projects combines not only key academic areas, but also includes a technology component. In this day and age, all students will need technical skills in any job they may take—from food service to medicine to teaching and so forth.

> *We are not preparing students for one specific career but giving them a host of skills that can be utilized as occupations change.*

The integrated projects also give students the opportunity to work on SCANS skills (Secretary's Commission on Achieving Necessary Skills; U.S. Department of Labor, 1991), such as teaming, problem solving, and self-management; these are critically important for any career a student might wish to pursue. The integrated projects are designed to connect to the exploration of Career Pathways. Connecting to a specific Pathway, the integrated project is an ongoing exploration of a Pathway; therefore, on our block setup, we create several projects over the duration of the course. As we designed the projects, we made sure that they were varied in skills and in the number of team members required for each one. Because students will have to change teams and get used to working with a variety of people in a real workplace, we also created new teams for each integrated project.

In the workplace, students will assimilate their learning to problem solve and manage their daily duties in their given work situation. All of our units include some math, science, language arts, and social studies, but what sets these integrated units apart from others is that they all include the use of technology, teaming, and problem solving. Instead of teaching computer and technology skills in isolation, students *use* the technology to create their projects. To encourage *creativity* and successful teaming and compromise, the projects include choice and design in some components. As in any real-life situation, the projects have roadblocks and problems that need to be solved. In addition, the other crucial element involved in these units is that each one is tied to a Career Pathway—in this manner, all of the units become connected to the real world. These integrated projects can be delivered by one teacher or by a team. They are not true ITI projects because "teacher experts" do not each deliver a single piece. We want students to see that you don't need an expert all the time to integrate subjects matter in life and in the workplace.

One important realization that students come to is that there are occupational possibilities that match their intelligences in all of the Pathways. For example, one student was extremely interested in working with people, working with numbers, and being outside. There were occupational *possibilities* for her in all four of the Pathways she explored (Table 9.6).

When designing the Pathways-integrated units, faculty members will want to use a good planner that includes not only integrated concepts and standards and benchmarks, but also a section for real community activities. We suggest using an organizer like that shown in Figure 9.4.

Table 9.6

Science and Industry	Agriculture and Business	Arts and Communications	Health and Human Services
Glaziers	Forester	Painter	Biology teacher
Marine biologist	Bean co-op marketing agent	Postal clerk	Emergency medical technician
Civil engineer	Real estate agent	Animal park publicist	Spa owner
Telephone repair person	Government inspector	Cruise activities director	Activities therapist

Figure 9.4 The Collaborative Pathways Organizer

Skills	Unit: Pathway: Emphasis:			**Standards**
Cognitive:	\multicolumn{3}{c|}{**Community Links**}	**Science:**
	Research:	Speakers:	Shadows:	**Math:**
	Visits:	Internships:	Projects:	
Technical:	Other:			**Language Arts:**
	\multicolumn{3}{c|}{**Assessment**}	
	Written:	Video:	Oral:	
People:	Skits:	Portfolio:	Journals:	**Social Studies:** (Life Management)
Work Ethic:	Other:			**Other _____:**

Notes:

Let's look specifically at one of the integrated units we designed for Freshman Explorations, an aviation unit. The Pathway we were exploring was Science, and Industry and Technology. The course was team taught by a language arts teacher and a technology teacher. We started researching career opportunities in the Science and Industry Pathway and found that one of the fastest growing areas in that Pathway was aviation. So we decided to design an aviation unit that would match our exploration of Science and Industry. We wanted to make sure that the unit included math, science, and technology because we were connecting it to the Science and Industry Pathway. In addition, this unit emphasizes language arts and life-management skills. Students, in teams of five or six, became the owners and operators of a flight school. Beginning with the end in mind, students visited an airport. Then throughout the unit, we invited several aviation guests to discuss aviation careers, including a flight school owner, a pilot just beginning her flight school experience, and someone from the Michigan Bureau of Aeronautics. In the meantime, students designed and prepared a flight school portfolio that included a brochure, a marketing package, a budget, a "How Planes Fly" project, and valid flying licenses (using a flight simulator) for each owner. After presenting their portfolios, the climax of the unit is a Young Eagles Fly-In that allows all students (who wish to take advantage of it) a free flight. At that same time, we continued to explore a variety of careers in the Pathway and realized that an aviation engineer, or an aviation mechanic, was just a variation of similar occupations found in that Pathway.

In a Collaborative Pathways rubric, the real-world and real-life connections are emphasized. It is these connections that add relevancy to the unit and, according to current brain research, make the processing and retention of the material and the experience more long term. The completed organizer would look like that shown in Figure 9.5. Note that the chart can be revised easily to match specific state standards or the broader national standards (Michigan Department of Education, 1996).

In addition to the flight unit for Science and Industry, students also do three other integrated units, one for each pathway. We have developed two units that can be used for the Health and Human Service Pathway, a unit for the Arts and Communication Pathway, and a unit for the Agriculture and Business Pathway. Units are designed around a software package, a field trip, and meetings with people in the field and a completed project using teaming, technology, and problem solving. Table 9.7 details some of the other projects that we use in Collaborative Freshman Explorations.

The sky is the limit when designing integrated projects that connect to a Pathway. If time permits, students may design another integrated project tied to the Pathway of their choosing. Each Pathways system should eventually include projects that tie into the community's job availability and culture. Most important in the planning of any Freshman Explorations integrated projects for a Pathways High School are the following:

- The project should clearly connect to one, or possibly two, Pathways.
- Have appropriate guest speakers and site visits.

Figure 9.5 Collaborative Pathways rubric

Skills	Unit: Wild Blue Yonder Pathway: Science and Technology Emphasis: Aviation			Standards
Cognitive: Organization, problem solving, decision making, following directions, and assertiveness	**Community Links**			Science: Standard IV: 3-1, 2, 3, 4
	Research: X	Speakers: X	Shadows: X	Math: Standard III: 1-1, 2, 3 Standard III: 2-1, 2, 3, 4, 5
	Visits: X	Internships: X	Projects: X	
Technical: Flight Simulator and *Publisher 2000* software for brochures, computerized poster making, and bumper stickers	Other: Visits: Airport, Fly-in, Engineering Site			Language Arts: Standard 1-1, 2, 3 Standard 2-1, 3, 4 Standard 3-1, 2, 3, 6 Standard 4-1, 4, 5 Standard 8-1, 3, 4, 5 Standard 11-2, 3, 4
	Assessment			
	Written: X	Oral: X	Video: X	
People: Teaming	Skits: X	Portfolio: X	Journals: X	Social Studies: (Life Management) Standard 1 Standard 2 Standard 3
Work Ethic: Initiative, self-direction, reliability, and availability	Other: Individual work log, team evaluation, in-class essay			Technology: (other) Standard 1-6, 7 Standard 2-1, 3, 4 Standard 3-2, 4 Standard 6-1

- The project should include three or four core subjects, plus the use of technology. (Electives such as art, music, or health can also be incorporated.)
- An authentic real-world assessment should be used in place of (or at least in addition to) pen-and-paper essays and tests.
- The unit needs to appeal to a variety of intelligences and learning styles; it may include opportunities for teaming, self-management, and problem solving (SCANS skills).
- Make certain that the unit matches to the student outcomes and standards most important and emphasized in your school district.

Note: SCANS = Secretary's Commission on Achieving Necessary Skills (U.S. Department of Labor, 1991).

Table 9.7   Examples of Collaborative Freshman Explorations Projects

Project Title and Pathway	Scenario	Teaming Outcome	Community Connections	Software
The Doctor Is In *Pathway:* Health	Help a doctor research a health topic	Design pamphlet and presentation	Interviews with health employees and a hospital visit	Health
Getting the Word Out *Pathway:* Arts and Communications	Design a public service announcement	Present announcement and process steps	Library research and TV and radio field trips; guest visit from video editor	Movieworks
The Green Thumb *Pathway:* Business and Agriculture	Design a board report for a farm cooperative	Portfolio and board presentation	Farm interviews and co-op visit; guest visit from organic farmer and banker	Sim Farm
The Election *Pathway:* Human Service and Business	Design an annual report and campaign strategy for a mayor of a city	Design a campaign portfolio and present the annual report	Interviews with mayor and city planner and visit to city hall	Sim City
The Wild Blue Yonder *Pathway:* Science, Industry, and Technology	Operate a flight school, including advertisement and promotion, budget, and pilot "licenses"	Flight school portfolio; sales presentation How Planes Fly demonstration	Guest speakers from the aviation field; field trip to an airport; Young Eagles Flying Experience	Flight Sim 2000

Pathway Exploration

At the same time students are working on an integrated project, they should also be exploring the pathway to which it connects. Pathway exploration should take a variety of forms. Students should not only research which kinds of jobs may be found in the Pathway, but the skills and abilities that this pathway tends to accentuate. There are three kinds of exploration that should occur:

- Researching the wide variety of occupations available in that particular Pathway
- Talking to a wide variety of people within the Pathway
- Participating in on-site field trips for the featured Pathway

Researching Pathways

Researching Pathways should be an ongoing process, and not something done in one way, during one class period. We use a variety of techniques.

Students may use a variety of occupational software or search engines; in Michigan we use the Michigan Occupational Information System (MOIS, 1998). MOIS has created an entire classroom set of masters to reflect on; students may use the wide variety of career information found there. This system is so vast that it can actually be used at all four levels of Pathways Schools' classes and not just in Freshman Explorations. You may also be able to find free online career sites on the Internet that can provide students with a host of information, and sometimes even online career chat partners.

Another good place to have students spend time is in the library. Because we have become a Career Pathways High School, we have a cart library especially for career materials for use in any Pathways classroom (and often borrowed by other classroom teachers as well). Another dog-eared and well-worn library we have in the classroom at all times is our Career Biographies Library, which houses hundreds of career profiles of interesting and unusual jobs (Vocational Biographies, 1999, 2000, 2001, 2002). They are up-to-date, include great data profiles on the occupations, and have wonderful color pictures. Because our school is in a rural area where a wide variety of jobs are not found, the purchase of this text was our answer to parents' concerns that we were featuring only the jobs in our community's vicinity. Our high school library has also continued to expand its career and biography sections for student research.

> *Having a librarian or media specialist who understands Pathways and is supportive of the entire program is a crucial component in the career exploration process.*

Chatting With People

Although both the Internet and libraries are important research venues, much more important, especially during freshman year, is the opportunity for students to chat with people in a wide variety of occupations. To this end, we devised a system in Freshman Explorations classes called "chats." Students are required to chat with a minimum of 75 people throughout the course. We also allow students to obtain "free" chats by having any guest speaker who comes to the classroom do a chat for all students. We also allow some e-mail chats so students may talk to people in a field that might not be available in our area. The chats follow a simple, four-question formula, but usually, when someone starts talking about his or her work, students gain much more than those four pieces of information. The chat format is shown in Table 9.8.

Students write these questions on note cards; on the back, they write a phone number and an address or e-mail for later contact. Many times students find a connection that leads to another job-shadowing experience or even an unpaid internship or co-opportunity. To

> *The most important "aha" that students get from these chat conversations is that liking what you do is the most important prerequisite of being happy with your work.*

Table 9.8   The Chat Format

Name:

Pathway:

Occupation and what you do:

What do you like most about your job?

What are the biggest challenges of your job?

What skills do you use on a daily basis?

What training do you have for this job?

---

make certain that there is a balance in the Pathways exploration, we require students to have at least 15 chats in each Pathway by the semester's end. These chats at the freshman level serve as much more than just an opportunity to explore a variety of careers.

In addition, students learn that although money is an important aspect of work, it should not be the first consideration (this is why we left salary off of the chat questions; however, students almost always end up being told what the average salary would be). Finally, students find out that although college is one path of training for careers, there are a huge variety of ways to train and prepare themselves for different occupations. In this way, the seeds of their personal plan are planted and then can be watered and nurtured in their later Pathways courses.

At the beginning of Freshman Explorations, students always complain about the chats, but by the end of the course, most find it is one of the most valuable tools of exploration. In their journals and evaluations, we have seen just how important chatting is to help students connect their schooling to the real world. Although most workers tell students that interpersonal, problem-solving, and multitasking skills are tremendously important, almost everyone also mentions core academics or particular academic concepts that are needed for their particular fields. Students learn that geometry is crucial for flying, that math and plant science is a must for agriculture, and that language arts are useful in all career venues. When students were asked to journal about how their chats were useful to them, they responded as follows:

> *The Chats we're doing are good. . . . Actually most of the people that I have talked to [say] that the best thing about their jobs is working with people, dealing with people or meeting different people. This came from people in all different fields and occupations. So I've realized that in any field you are going to have to work with people no matter what.*

> *The Chats do help you to realize and make you aware of what is out there. I enjoyed talking with my relatives though and I found out a lot of good things and some stuff that they do not enjoy that I never thought of. I also found out there were jobs that I had never even heard of.*

I learned about a job I have never heard of before that sounded very interesting . . . environmental sanitation.

I also had a chat with an anesthesiologist. I think it is an interesting job but I don't like working with needles and blood. The one thing I may be interested in is a pediatric therapist because that would be great to help hurt kids. Can you help me find one to chat with?

I feel the chats we are doing are a good opportunity. . . . We can pick an exciting job that we find interesting and ask people about the job. These chats are not hard to do. . . . These chats are important for us kids to do.

When the semester is over, the chats are passed on to the next Pathways teacher so that the students have access to their own chats all the way through their high school career. They become each student's own personal resource index for job shadowing, internships and senior projects.

In addition to individual chats, it is key to have a continual stream of visitors to the classroom. Some can come to help with integrated projects, others might be there for special teaming and problem-solving activities; still others might be there to help with sales presentations or interview activities. All of these visitors help make real-world connections and continue to underscore the importance of chatting. Every time a visitor comes, we begin with a chat, which role-plays for the students how to go about conducting them. Students always brainstorm a list of questions and adequately prepare for guests beforehand, and we always send a student-formulated thank-you note with signatures from the entire class. During every Pathways exploration, we attempt to have at least four or five visitors from the featured Pathway. We seek input for the career areas that students want to visit most, and many times our best speakers are ones whom students recommend. We arrange speakers approximately two weeks before they visit and always allow them to pick the day of the week and the time that works best for them. We always make sure they know that the students will prepare for the session. This way, busy people are willing to come and share with the students. It never hurts to ask; in five years we have only been turned down a handful of times. All in all, we try to have between 25 and 40 classroom guests during the course, and early on visitors become a natural flow of our class for both students and teachers.

Site Visits

At the beginning of an integrated unit, we may go and visit a site, soaking up sights, sounds, and impressions without much, if any, advanced classroom preparation. Other times, when we are in the middle of a Pathway exploration, we will go to two or three job sites that connect to that particular Pathway. Many times, there are outstanding career fairs and

> *A Pathway exploration is not complete without actual visits to real-world workplaces.*

career exploration days that we can use as site visits. In our area, we have found a fantastic engineering day visit that is held at a different foundry each year. One of our local community colleges has a Career Day with people from occupations in all of this college's major career areas available to chat with students. Our students always look forward to the site visits because they are a wonderful opportunity for them to get chats. (In fact, after the first visit, we no longer had to remind students to take along their chat note cards and a pen.) The co-op where we visit yearly always sets up a panel of their workers with assorted occupations. Each one gives a quick PowerPoint presentation "chat" to the students, so in relatively few minutes the students realize the wide variety of occupations and levels of training that are available at a single small worksite. We work hard to set the kids up ahead of time for the things we want them to see or the kinds of questions we would like them to ask. By the end of the semester, students have come to the realization that all work sites have the following in common:

- Teaming
- Problem solving
- Multitasking
- Self-management
- Use of core academics

Field trips can be a costly component of a Freshman Explorations program, but they are absolutely essential. There are many ways to cut corners; field trips are not the place to do it.

Current brain research shows the importance of spatial or real-life experience in helping the brain make relevancy connections. As discussed in Chapter 6, we recommend at least one field trip for each Pathway (they can be tied to the integrated units as ours are, or they can be stand-alone trips in areas of interest to the class), and at least one career fair if at all possible. These become vital to students' individual Pathways explorations. At the freshman level in particular, they are not only looking at what fields they are comfortable with, but also the ones that would make them uncomfortable.

In conclusion, as students explore all the Career Pathways, it is important that they do not simply look at careers. Care must be taken to show that all Pathways have occupations at a variety of skill and responsibility levels. This is called a career ladder; in Freshman Explorations we begin to work on this concept, and students actually chart their own career ladders. Career ladders in Sophomore Selections will be discussed in further detail in Chapter 10 as students progress to the sophomore level.

Remember that the emphasis should not be so much on the careers as on the skills that each Pathway is going to emphasize. Students will realize that many careers could be categorized in two Pathways, so what is most important is for them to get a sense of which one or two Pathways match their skills, abilities, and personalities. Your teachers will know they have truly reached students when students realize that they will most enjoy the integrated projects that match their interests and aptitudes. In other words, for most freshman, the truth is that they will enjoy some parts of the course more than other parts.

Decision Making

One of the reasons that the Pathways Collaborative Model works so well is because it puts the student in the driver's seat. The rest of the "tribe" serves as front-seat passengers to watch for obstacles and to help the driver slow down when the speed gets too fast,

> *When students take ownership of their plans, they become invested—in school, in the classroom, and on the job—so that everything they learn becomes enmeshed in their plan.*

but in the end, the driver is in control. The "tribe" includes students, parents and relatives, teachers, community members, and administrators.

Because of this, the last few weeks of Freshman Explorations are critical; it is at this time that students become masters of their plans by choosing their Pathways.

There are four important steps that the teacher needs to guide the students through as they make this first important choice in the formation of their own individual plan:

1. Examining students' short- and long-term goals
2. Narrowing their choices from several Pathways to two
3. Looking at pros and cons of each Pathway for students as individuals
4. Choosing the Pathway that is best for them, based on logical reasoning

We begin this process at the start of the course by talking about general goals, then throughout the course we begin distinguishing long-term goals, short-term goals, and immediate goals. The reason for this is because it is exactly what students do for themselves as they formulate their long-term plan. First they will find a general direction, then they will look at how they can move in that direction throughout high school, and finally they will specifically decide what they can do the rest of *this year* to get them started. The first requirement we have for students when making their Pathway choice is to fill in the chart in Figure 9.6.

Once the decision chart is filled out, it is time for students to ponder thoughtfully what they have written. It is at this point that most students seek the help of their

> *One word of caution: At this point, student and parents will tend to talk about specific careers, so the instructor and the faculty members need to take care to remind both students and parents that at the end of Freshman Explorations, all we are selecting is a general Pathway or avenue of interest.*

"front-seat passengers"—parents, counselors, or teachers. The conclusion to Freshman Explorations is a required Pathways paper. Since *all* freshmen in our school take Freshman Explorations, we have come up with an outline, or rubric, that makes the paper easy to do but also makes thoughtful reflection

Figure 9.6 Pathway Decision Chart

Problem 1: Which Pathway is the best for me?	Immediate Goal
	Short-Term Goal
	Long-Term Goal

Pathway A:	Pathway B:
Pros:	Pros:
Cons:	Cons:
Skill Emphases:	Skill Emphases:

Decision:
Reasons:

about the final decision absolutely mandatory. The paper has an introduction and then includes three main body paragraphs: Paragraph 1 discusses the skills and abilities of the student, paragraph 2 discusses what the student is good at and what he or she likes to do, paragraph 3 discusses the student's goals and what is important to him or her. The conclusion is, of course, the culminating part of the decision process because it is the point when the student declares which Pathway he or she has chosen and why. In his or her reasoning, the student is expected to connect the selection to his or her goals, skills, and interests. This paper is a written profile of the student and his or her plan and becomes a wonderful tool to pass along to the Sophomore Selections teacher as a starting point for career shadowing assignments and class work.

As noted earlier in the book, students seldom change Pathways once they have selected them; they are much more likely to stay in the same Pathway but explore a variety of occupational opportunities (or fields). Nonetheless, the Collaborative Model is built in such a way that if a student does decide to change paths, it is possible to do so. So far in our schools we have only had a handful of students switch their Pathway choice. (The better the Freshman Explorations experience and scaffolding of the Pathways courses, the better the student's choices are, and the less likely it is that changes will be needed later in the program).

Students entering the rest of their high school career can feel confident that they have a direction to travel and because of that, they can more easily make choices about course work, extracurricular activities, and part-time jobs that are relevant to their plans and their futures. Here is a random selection of concluding paragraphs from 9th-grade Pathway papers (please make note of the focus and clear thinking and recognize that these are students of all skill levels):

> *I believe that the best Pathway for me is Arts and Communication. I love drawing and designing things but I have known for a long time that I did not want to be an art teacher. My learning style is tactile and I have a yellow/white (Hartman) personality. My best standardized test scores are English/language arts and my grades are all good, but I love my art classes the most. I had an opportunity to chat with a graphic artist and I loved the Public Service Announcement where I helped with animation. I am looking forward to job shadowing a graphic artist and a film editor next year.*

> *My Pathway is Health and Human Service. I have a Hartman blue personality, which means I like to help people and relationships are important to me. My best subjects are science and math. I am an athlete and pay a lot of attention to health and nutrition. I have several relatives who are in the Health Field so those chats really interested me. I am not sure what I want to do but I am thinking about athletic trainer, paramedic or fire fighter. Whatever I do, I want to help others.*

> *I come from a family of teachers and everyone has assumed I would be a teacher, but now I don't think so. I have never been really comfortable around children and I don't like to get up in front of groups. When we did our flight school project, I really enjoyed hearing all the opportunities. I am a Doer on the Holland Hexagon and a Blue on the Hartman Profile. I like physical science the best because I like to know how things work. My uncle has a race car and I mess with it sometimes. He thinks I would be a good mechanic. Now I am thinking maybe an aviation mechanic. I want to talk to the Air Force Recruiter next year and job shadow several mechanics. Therefore my Pathway is Science/Industry/Technology.*

In accordance with the Focus on Freshmen Model (Holmboe & Malone, 1996), we have a Pathway selection party where all students sign the banner of their chosen Pathway. In this way, they make a final public commitment to their decision. We have an interesting or unusual guest speaker, a selection of teen food favorites, and an activity that the class plans—say, a dance or a bowling party or a skating party. It is important to celebrate this first crucial decision in each student's plan because it is the foundation for the next three phases of a Pathways school: job shadowing, internships, and senior projects (Holmboe & Malone, 1996).

> *A sound and thorough Freshman Explorations class that helps students make connections to themselves, their school, and the real world will set the stage for a solid and realistic personal plan for future success.*

IN REVIEW

- Freshman Explorations serves as a transition for all students leaving middle school and entering the high school environment.
- From the start of high school, the emphasis is on the whole-village approach to raising a child; students receive input from parents, teachers, and the community.
- Important connections to self occur in Freshman Explorations through a variety of sources: personality profiles, aptitude testing, multiple intelligence screening, and learning style evaluation.
- Connections to school happen in Freshman Explorations by helping every student to feel included in the school building, in the classroom, and in the school culture.
- The most critical connections that take place in Freshman Explorations are the connections to the world of work and "real life" through career research, guest speakers, partners in education, and site visits to work environments.
- The use of integrated units allows for the teaching and practical implementation of teaming, problem solving, conflict resolution, and decision making (SCANS skills). These units are crucial in a Career Pathways High School because in "real life," the use of skills and content areas are integrated.
- When students take ownership of their individual plans, they become invested in the classroom and on the job so that everything they learn becomes enmeshed in their plan.

Chapter Ten

Pathways Classes for Grades 10 Through 12

Sophomore Selections, Junior Judgments, and Senior Transitions

SCENARIO: JOY'S SCAFFOLD

Joy is a college freshman who has just finished four years at a Pathways High School. As she starts college, she considers herself to have had an average high school experience. Her teachers, mentors, family, and community have all contributed to her narrowing plan, and even though they have all told her that her educational experience is the exception not the rule, she doesn't really believe them.

After her Freshman Explorations class, which included 8 field trips, 10 work environments, and more than 35 guests and speakers in her classroom, Joy selected the Human Service Pathway. She was particularly intrigued by an integrated project that allowed her to work on a real-life problem. Her three-person team chose to work with the Big Brothers/Big Sisters organization and helped plan an activity that would allow the waiting list children to have a Big Brother/Big Sister for a day while they waited for a long-term match. The team managed to raise enough money to have a bowling and pizza party for 25 unmatched children. Much to their delight, the day led to two long-term matches. Joy also was particularly taken by a trip to a Work and Learn Center that helped rehabilitate inner-city youth.

This led to several job shadows during her 10th-grade year as she explored Clusters within her Pathway in Sophomore Selections. After day-long visits with a psychologist, a social worker, and a third-grade teacher, Joy had narrowed her interest to the psychology Cluster. She spent her internship during Junior Judgments in the office of an adolescent psychologist. Although she could not actually sit in on sessions, she was able to do clerical work, observe the teens and the progress they made (or didn't make) from her vantage point in the waiting room, learn the routine and jargon of the psychologist's office, and talk to a wide variety of therapists and even a couple of psychiatrists. After her internship, as Joy weighed the pros and cons of the different types of therapy, she realized that she wanted to concentrate on child therapy. With that in mind, as she finished her junior year she looked at colleges with strong psychology and social work departments, keeping in mind that elementary education coursework could also be useful to her.

During Joy's senior year, she designed and implemented a senior project in her Senior Transitions class that allowed her to train as a peer mentor and then be a part of her school's mentor program. In addition, she spoke on behalf of the peer mentoring programs at several neighboring high schools. The Senior Transitions mentorship team to help with her project that she put together for herself included the school's psychology teacher, a psychiatrist from her internship experience, and a psychology professor from the local junior college. They helped her to do some intensive research on peer mentoring that further streamlined her project. Her senior project won Best of Show in the Human Service Pathway. During the summer following graduation, she capped off her senior year by working as the assistant to the caseworker in the Big Brother/Big Sister office.

After her first week of college, Joy realizes what a gift her teachers, parents, school, and community have given her. Most of her fellow students have made college their goal and have no idea what the focus of their experience there will be, let alone what they are going to do in their post-college or post-training life. Many are not even certain if they are at the right college; not only have they not declared a major, they aren't even sure what they are good at or what pathway they are most interested in exploring. Joy experienced *a systematic approach* that allowed her to explore herself and the Pathways during her freshman year, her Pathway and Cluster during her sophomore year, to design and streamline her plan during her junior year, and to do a capstone project during her senior year that has helped her to transition to her postsecondary goal.

Joy is well on her way. She has started college knowing that she will get her degree in psychology with a minor in education. During college she plans to work part time in a psychologist's office and volunteer at a local junior high to obtain more firsthand experience with adolescents. Once finished, she plans to get her master's degree in psychology and maybe even open a practice of her own. With that in mind, she also plans to take several business and accounting classes as electives. Once she selected her Pathway, the outstanding facilitated instruction, combined with integrated community and counseling experiences, gave her a real grasp of the direction that she wished to pursue. Her college advisor cannot believe how mature and focused she is. Joy's reply to this is, "I owe it all to my Collaborative Pathways High School!"

THE GREAT SCAFFOLD

One of the most fascinating parts of a Collaborative Pathways High School for educators is to watch students grow and change as each level of skill and experience builds the base for the next. Like Joy, each student in a Collaborative Pathways school has his or her own story to tell. First, a clear foundation is built, and then during their high school experience, in Pathway classrooms and through community experiences, as well as in core and elective coursework, the students enhance and streamline not only their plans, but also their skills. Although this is a true benefit and part of the system design, it can also be a double-edged sword.

> *If there is a breakdown of skills enhancement or loss of any of the three C's (community, counseling, curriculum), it will result in weaker plans and less focus for the students.*

Another component that makes this collaborative system so special is the fact that while the skills begin in the classroom during the freshman and sophomore years, these skills are then honed in real community settings during the junior and senior years. The scaffold that is built develops skills as shown in Table 10.1.

> *As an administrator, it will be important that you stress not only academic rigor but also skill rigor to your faculty. If teaming is not done or is done poorly, if conflict resolution is not completely practiced, or if technology is not integrated at a more complex level each step of the way, the weak link will be apparent because the students' plan or project will lack depth.*

The curricula for these three upper courses were presented in Chapter 7; the goal of this chapter is to discuss ways to make certain that each level of Pathways remains true to the plan so that your school has rigor and strength in the curriculum, counseling, and skill links in its scaffold; in that way, all levels of skill development will lead toward real-world application and complete self-management by the time your students graduate and transition to their post-secondary plan.

SOPHOMORE SELECTIONS

Sophomore Selections is the second block on the Pathways scaffold and allows students to further explore themselves and the Clusters and careers in their Pathway; it also allows them to further develop teaming and self-management skills. (It will be helpful as you read this section to refer back to the Sophomore Selection curriculum found in Chapter 7.) Of all the levels of Pathways instruction, Sophomore Selections is, at the same time, both the easiest and the most difficult to implement. This paradox is true because many of the components of Sophomore Selections are already being done in isolation or as pull-outs within most schools' curricula. Because of this, most schools think that it is just a

Table 10.1 Skills Acquired Through the Collaborative Pathway Model

Pathways Class	Teaming	Problem Solving	Conflict Resolution	Technology	Self-Management
Freshman Explorations	Rainbow teams in integrated units	Software practice and skill growth through teamwork	Basic skills practice during teamwork	Use of technology during integrated units	Self-management in teamwork and during chats
Sophomore Selections	One team project and observation of workplace teaming	Observation of workplace problem solving and integrated unit practice	Observation of conflict resolution in the work settings and practice of this skill in integrated units	Observation of workplace technology and technology practice in integrated units	Focus on time management and stress management in the classroom; self-management observation in workplace settings
Junior Judgments	Teaming during internship or tech center experience	Problem-solving techniques in a workplace or at tech center	Utilization of resolution techniques in workplace or at tech center	Technology application in the workplace or at the tech center	Time and stress management during internship or tech center experience
Senior Transitions	Teaming with mentors and collaborating on senior project	Life application of problem solving during senior project	Life application of conflict resolution during senior project	Application of technology in the workplace and for project presentation	Application of time, self-, and stress management throughout senior project process

> *The truth is that although your school may have a base of job shadows, employability skills, and character education, when you transfer these components to a Pathways curriculum, it needs to be done in a different context and in a facilitated manner.*

matter of continuing current job shadows, character education, and employability skills.

If you use the same teacher to do Sophomore Selections who has been doing a job shadow or two and some employability skills, but do not do enough teacher in-servicing on teaming and the four-year Pathways scaffold, you will end up with a Sophomore Selections program that is a weak link. This then could lead to students being unprepared to make a truly educated decision about internships or technical center involvement; if students do not have opportunities in Sophomore Selections class to continue practicing teaming, they will have difficulty with this component during their junior-year internship. This practice is imperative because it allows for the all-important evolution of good people and SCANS skills (Secretary's Commission on Achieving Necessary Skills; U.S. Department of Labor, 1991) required for successful collaborative internships and senior projects. It is equally important that the character education focus not only on being good citizens and good employees, but also good teammates. Let's examine the curriculum, counseling, and community issues involved in Sophomore Selections implementation.

Curriculum Issues in Sophomore Selections

In Chapter 7, the Selections curriculum was presented as "The Great Balancing Act." In truth it is not only a balancing act for your students but also for your teachers: While students are balancing self (character) and career exploration, the Sophomore Selections teacher is balancing skill training in the classroom with real-world experiences in the community. In the classroom, the teacher has three important jobs to do:

1. Further build on the teaming and self-management skills from Freshman Explorations

2. Help students balance the person they are and the person they project in school and the workplace

3. Help students come to a well-thought-out and informed decision about whether they should select an internship or a tech center experience

In the process of doing this, the Sophomore Selections teacher needs to become a teacher with many hats. One hat is the "Explorer Hat," by which the teacher facilitates students' exploration of the many avenues of the Pathway they have chosen and to look carefully at one or two Clusters that they may be interested in pursuing. Another is the "Character Hat," by which the teacher helps students come to grips with what good citizenship and good character is all about. The third hat is the "Facilitator Hat," by which the teacher facilitates activities that provide good teaming and good self-management skills. In addition in a good Selections class, the teacher will be able to facilitate deep thinking and clear observation at the job shadow sites, so that the student can proceed with the decision-making process without undo stress.

Students in a collaborative setting will gain much more from their job shadows than students from traditional settings who have less background about themselves, the Pathway, and the Career Cluster.

There are many decisions that a Sophomore Selections teacher needs to make about his or her curriculum, and these are influenced by many factors. Selections teachers need to consider how in-depth the Freshman Explorations class has been and how many teamed units students have already had the opportunity to do.

Also important is how long the Selections course is going to be. We recommend one semester on a blocked schedule or a yearlong curriculum in the traditional schedule. Although some schools do this course in nine weeks on a 4 × 4 block schedule or nine weeks of a traditional schedule, they find it difficult to get all three shadow experiences completed. We have found that it takes at least three shadowing opportunities for students to have enough experience to think critically about the pros and cons of several similar careers within one Cluster. Many students really need four or five job shadows to know which one(s) are possibilities and which should be eliminated. There are many "outside-the-box" ways to deal with having insufficient job shadows. A half-day job shadow could take place at the end of freshman year out of an English or family life class; perhaps two shadows could happen in Sophomore Selections and two more in another 10th-grade course (such as health or civics). A third consideration is whether employability skills should stay in the Freshman Explorations class. Some of our schools have the resume–applications–cover letter piece come out of the required computer literacy coursework and then they are just fine-tuned in Sophomore Selections. Finally, it is important for Selections teachers to remember that all of the character education done in Grades 9 and 10 is to help students in preparation for their community experiences.

As you guide your new Sophomore Selections teachers in the implementation of the curriculum, the following checklist may be helpful:

- Where in the delivery of the course will the shadow experiences be placed?
- Who will be responsible for the setup of the shadow experiences?
- What will be the best materials to use for employability skills? Where in the course will they be inserted, or will they be shared with another course?
- What approach to character education will be used, and how does that fit into the larger K–12 character education model or the district's curriculum?
- What kind of facilitated learning, teaming, and technology integration activities will be built into each unit?
- What new materials will students have to use for exploration of Clusters and career ladders within their Pathways?
- What kind of project will be required as part of the decision-making process?
- How will the time line be manipulated if the tech center–internship decision needs to made in March for the next school year, but the course is only half over at that time?
- Will it be possible to set the Sophomore Selections coursework up by Pathway-specific sections (e.g., all students in arts and communications in one section, all students in business and agriculture in another etc.)? This allows for more in-depth exploration and an easier time with focused speakers and mini-field trips.

Counseling Issues in the Sophomore Selections

Sophomore Selections offers many opportunities for the counselors to work with all students out of the Sophomore Selections classroom. We use the term "counselors" loosely because it may include military admissions counselors giving the ASVAB (Armed Forces Vocational Aptitude Battery), school social workers facilitating character activities, and community college admission and counseling departments working on employability skills with students.

> *Generally, the Sophomore Selections portion of the Pathways system is not team taught per se, but this is all the more reason that a good Sophomore Selections teacher must build his or her own collaborative team.*

The shadows teacher needs to work on an ongoing basis with the school counselors, with local admissions departments of junior and four-year colleges, with other teachers who can embed some coursework or shadows, and with experienced Collaborative Model shadow teachers.

Counselors' input is critical to helping students deal with deeper and more complex conflict resolution issues found in teaming situations and observed in on-the-job shadows, as well as to refining anger management and other character issues and building self-esteem. These issues are critical as sophomores begin to project themselves on paper and in person through resumes, applications, and interviews. If there is not enough emphasis on these crucial counseling items in the classroom, students will be uncomfortable and adrift as they interview for tech center and internship placements. *The door of the Selections classroom needs to always be open for counseling opportunities!*

As you help your Selections teachers with counseling implementation, here are some things to remember:

- Make certain that there is enough time between shadow experiences for students to reflect and adequately compare them.
- Help your Selections teachers form a collaborative team of their own.
- If counseling input will be at a minimum because of time restraints, make sure that your teachers get plenty of in-servicing in the areas of teaming, conflict resolution, and character education and self-esteem development.
- If the course length is short, make certain you help facilitate a system in which the entire shadows counseling needs are covered, possibly in some other 10th-grade required course work.

Community Issues in Sophomore Selections

Utilizing the community in Sophomore Selections is similar to the process in Freshman Explorations. The difference is that students become more involved in the self-management of their contacts, and their conversations and observations become more in-depth. If students have built a good base for their chats, selecting 10 interview partners will be simple. The most difficult part for most students is deciding which ten interviews will be the most useful. Many times students will do 10 and then ask to do a couple more if they have not found the answers they seek.

The same decision-making problem also applies to students as they connect themselves to the community through their job shadows. In terms of facilitating good job shadows, your instructors need to help students be observant not only of skills and technology in the workplace, but also of the dynamics of the teamwork taking place daily on the job. Teachers who have done job shadowing in a noncollaborative setting will be particularly surprised by the depth of understanding and thinking that Collaborative job shadow students sustain. We cannot emphasize enough how key the proper execution of these job shadowing experiences is to building a scaffold that will lead to proper focus in the upper-level Pathways classes.

Community is also critical to helping students explore the Clusters within each Pathway during the Sophomore Selections coursework. Especially useful can be a mini-field trip to a worksite for small groups of six to eight students, allowing them to have a more individualized field trip experience. Equally important is continued utilization of community members in the classroom as guest speakers, partners in education during the teaming unit, and as special occasion guests. The use of these guests will be more valuable to your students if it is possible to have your Sophomore Selections classes set up in a Pathway-specific fashion. It becomes easier to focus in on the Clusters of the Pathway, and it allows students the opportunity to be more specific in their observation and questioning of those in their Pathway. A more in-depth examination of job shadows and the community takes place in Chapter 13. In conclusion, it becomes obvious that at each level of a Collaborative Pathways High School the community serves a greater role and functions as a larger part of the classroom.

> *The importance of the community in a Pathways High School is in no place clearer than in the increased community usage that takes place during sophomore year compared with freshman year.*

As you help your Sophomore Selections teachers include the community in the classroom, it is important that many opportunities are available for the Selections and Explorations teachers to collaborate and network on their community contacts. It is important that you not overload the contacts. Schools using the Pathways model would be wise to make certain the community contacts are balanced and not overloaded. For example, in some of our 4 × 4 block schools, Freshman Explorations and Senior Transitions are taught in the fall semester so only those students are in the community at that time; Sophomore Selections and Junior Judgments take place in the spring semester so that the number of students working with community contacts can be spread throughout the year.

Here are some community considerations you will want to share with your Selections teachers:

- Make certain that your Selections hosts are not overloaded with students.
- If there are other area schools doing Selections, make certain the hosts understand what the framework of your shadows is and how it relates to students' Freshman Explorations background.
- While the Selections teachers are an integral part of the course, encourage the use of community members as mini-field trip hosts and as guest speakers.
- Help students fully utilize the opportunities of speaking with employers not only in their Pathway but also within their possible Cluster. Detailed questions about technology usage, teaming, and problem solving should all be part of in-depth interviews.
- Make certain that students, teachers, and the school are appreciative and thankful for the community's involvement both at the school and on the work site.
- Help students to realize that character really does count on the job, and watch for opportunities to point this out to them.

JUNIOR JUDGMENTS

Junior Judgments is the third level of the Collaborative Scaffold and includes unpaid work experience or technical schooling of some sort, along with ethical and legal issue background of the focused Pathway. (While reading this section, it may be helpful to refer to the Junior Judgments curriculum found in Chapter 7.) One of the greatest challenges of a Junior Judgments internship experience is dispelling the fallacy (for student, parents, and teachers) that the internship is a bust if it does not turn out to be "the job." It is extremely important for students, teachers, and parents to remember that the internship experience is built off of the Freshman Explorations and Sophomore Selections scaffold. If the students have not explored who they are and what is important to them, or if they have not thoroughly researched a Cluster or two (through job shadows, interviews, and research), it is likely that they may be exploring a career where there is not an ideal match. This type of internship experience is in no way a waste of time. It gives students an opportunity to really think about what they did like about the career, how it matched them, and then, most important, why it was not a good fit for them. This is key, of course, because this valuable information allows them to explore more careers with a better fit. Junior Judgments is not only about the internship; equally important is the evaluation of that experience and the planning of the student's next step. With this in mind, let's look at the curriculum, counseling, and community issues involved in a Junior Judgments course.

Curriculum Issues in Junior Judgments

The largest curriculum issue we have found in Junior Judgments concerns evaluation not just of the internship but also of the students' plans based on what they have learned from the internship. When our pilot school started its Junior Judgments course, we decided that the students would spend one week in the classroom before the internship began, followed by eight weeks on the job for at least 90 minutes per day. During the internship, students spent four days a week on the job and the fifth day in the classroom. The last week would be reserved for presentation of their internship experience (this school is on a 4 × 4 block). We discovered that time needed to be built in on both sides of this curriculum process. At the end of Sophomore Selections, students needed to have individual interviews with the internship placement advisor (in many of the small schools, this is the Junior Judgments teacher), so that if their first choice could not be filled, the best possible secondary fit could be found. More important, after the first year, we built another arm onto our Junior Judgments curriculum. In our pilot school, we found that it was too large a leap to do a complete evaluation of not only the internship experience but also of how the information gained from it changed or modified a student's plan. So we added a compare-and-contrast project that allows every student to shore up their plan at this point.

Because time was so short in the Junior Judgments class, the pilot school added this branch to its required English course so that every student (even those at the technical center) would be given the same opportunity. We have found this piece invaluable because it allows those who found the internship experience to be "right on" an opportunity to compare colleges or other training opportunities. At the same time, it allows those who are still deciding between two or three careers to go back and compare them again (and most likely do some more job shadowing), or to compare two Clusters or job ladders. In a few particular cases, students have even needed to go back and compare two Pathways.

> *The project must begin at the point the student's plan has reached and then allow for some reflection on what comes next. For example, if the internship was not successful, the student may go back and compare careers or Clusters; if it was successful, the student will go on to compare colleges or other training options.*

Much of the rest of the Junior Judgments curriculum is the same as one would find in any internship program. The same kinds of paperwork and liability forms are used as for co-op experiences and job shadows. As noted before, however, what sets apart the internship experience at a Collaborative Pathways High School is the background and focus that each student can bring to his or her internship. For two years, students have already been practicing people skills through learned teaming, problem solving, conflict resolution, anger management, and assertiveness. When the interns from a Collaborative Pathways High School go into the workplace, employees always marvel at how mature and focused they are. What they don't realize is that these qualities are not uncommon among our students; they are skills we specifically and systematically nurture. The weekly seminar days allow for students to learn from each other's triumphs and mistakes and to analyze how to handle certain situations better in the future. The presentation at the end of the course allows students to show off and practice for next year's senior project presentation.

An additional key to the Junior Judgments curriculum comes in the form of examining ethical behavior and government regulations for the Pathway (and particularly the Cluster) that a student is interested in pursuing. In large schools where classes are Pathway specific, it makes this part of the coursework more manageable. Nonetheless, we have found even in the smaller schools that, because of self-management skills learned in the previous two years, teachers can facilitate this learning for several Pathways simultaneously. For example, the students working in the hospital will learn about patient confidentiality issues firsthand and can then do further research on current ethical and legal standards in the health field. The student interning with a chef will learn about restaurant health standards and can then follow up with research about state and federal standards for restaurants. The student working with a conservation officer will learn about legal considerations for issuing citations and about how wetland and wildlife management laws affect the officer on a day-to-day basis. Learning these ethical and governmental regulation issues will happen naturally on the job—an unsurpassed context for learning.

Finally, the curriculum takes students to a new level of important and serious decision making as they decide whether their plan is progressing well enough to consider schooling or whether they need to go back a step or two and examine more choices that might better suit them. Students learn that all decision making is a process, and if there is insufficient information to make a decision, then one must go back and obtain more information. Junior Judgments is a pivotal course; at this level, the instructor realizes that he or she is only along for the ride—students are truly in the driver's seat. Teachers must be sensitive to a student's need for flexibility in adjusting and exploring his or her plan.

As your Junior Judgments teachers plan their curriculum, they need to think about the following:

- Where will the evaluation of the internship learning fit best for students—within the internship course or embedded some place else within the junior curriculum (e.g., English or social studies class)?
- Who will be placing the students in their internships, and what kind of arrangements can be made for them to meet with Sophomore Selections students at the end of that course work?
- What will be the framework and content of the weekly student discussions?
- In what manner will the legal and ethical issues of the individual Pathways be included in the course work?
- How will the Pathways team collaborate to help each junior streamline his or her plan after the internship experience?

Counseling Issues in Junior Judgments

From a counseling standpoint, the junior year is a crucial turning point for students in all high schools. During the first semester, students are dealing with a variety of tougher and more specific course work; during the second semester, many students have to take their ACT or SAT tests as they begin to ponder which college(s) or training will be best for them. In addition, they must begin to think about scholarships and tuition for their postsecondary plans. Add to that the social concerns of whom to take to the prom, and there is the mix for some highly stressed students.

In a Pathways High School, some of this stress is relieved because students have been working on their Educational Development Plan (EDP) and their individual portfolios since their freshman year. They also began looking at training options through chats in 9th grade, and then interviews, shadows, and career laddering in the 10th grade. This does not dismiss the crucial role of the counselor during this stage of the game, however. Particularly when students are analyzing the information from their internship, the counselor should be ever ready to discuss with the students what they found out about the career in which they interned, what they learned about themselves, and what their next step will be. Equally important at this stage is the Senior Transitions teacher (or coordinator) who, when visiting the Junior Judgments classroom, helps the students (individually and as a class) brainstorm potential capstone projects that can lead to the next step or to the information the student still needs to make an informed postsecondary plan. As the school year ends, every student has a collaborative team helping him or her to go to the next level. This team includes students' Junior Judgments and Senior Transitions teachers, their counselor, their parents, and those community members who have interacted with a student to this point. Unlike their counterparts in the traditional system who talk about college as their goal, Junior Judgments students talk about the college choice as it relates to their entire plan for their futures.

Guiding your staff in regard to the following counseling issues will lay the base for a transition to a wonderful senior year for your students.

1. Make certain students are clear on what they have learned from their internship experience and what information they still need to learn.

2. Help students see the decision process at a new and deeper level. Make sure that they realize it is a process and that it is perfectly permissible to back up to a previous step to obtain more information.

3. Make certain that students know that although they are in charge of their own plan, they have a collaborative team waiting in the wings. The team includes not only the Junior Judgments teacher(s), but also the counselor, parents, and community members and Senior Transitions teachers.

4. Collaborative Pathways Juniors will still feel stress; remind them on a regular basis what they have already achieved and learned (in terms of an evolving portfolio and an educational development plan). Stress to them that sometimes some of the best information comes from the process of elimination. The best guidance they can get is help in figuring out what they need to know or do next.

Community Issues in Junior Judgments

One of the most frequently asked questions about a Pathways High School and sometimes the most difficult is how to incorporate the internship experience. Remember that although every student needs to have a community or internship experience, many of your students (sometimes up to half) are getting these opportunities through technical center or junior college training. For most schools, internships will need to be organized for half to two-thirds of a graduating class. Another way to ease this burden is to balance the flow of students in the community. As noted earlier, in our pilot school, Freshman Explorations and Junior Judgments students are out in the fall semester, Senior Transitions students and Sophomore Selections students in the spring semester. In this manner, workplaces are not overloaded with the upper-level students all at once. Most of the schools place the Judgments class at the end of the day so that students will have an optimal amount of time at the workplace. Because of sports practice, extracurricular activities, and evening obligations, some students require a more flexible schedule for interning, which might include some nights or weekends (depending on the experience).

The Junior Judgments teacher is a facilitator and a guide to the students but also a liaison to the community. Often, second-career teachers who were in business and industry are well suited to this job. They understand the needs of the employer and can try to make certain that the students are a help, not a hindrance, in the workplace. They need to collaborate closely with the Freshman Explorations and Sophomore Selections teachers, as they use their powerful field trip, speaker, and shadow contacts to build an internship contact list of their own. Being a powerful persuader and a "people person" are two important qualities for building good community relationships. The hardest part seems to be talking community members into "trying out" an intern from a Pathways High School. Once this happens and they see how focused and motivated your students are, they are more than willing to become a true partner with the school in this process. Often those same internship contacts turn into mentors or panel members for the Senior Transitions program.

When your Pathways team is designing and streamlining your Junior Judgments class, it is important that you think about how you are going to do it; never allow yourself to think, "It can't be done." Likely there will be some obstacles to overcome, and your team will need a plan that fits you and your community. Make certain that every student gets a systematic chance to be at one workplace and see all the aspects of the job and the daily routine.

Equally important is working hard at placing every student in a situation that, if not the dream job, is at least one that matches many of his or her interests and the chosen Pathway. For example, some of our schools have been extremely creative in transportation—options include having students with no transportation placed at jobs within walking distance, having students catch rides to a neighboring city on tech center buses, and using Rotary and citizen volunteers from the community. The community becomes a key partner in a Collaborative High School from start to finish, but at no place in the scaffold is it more important to have their help than during Junior Judgments. The community's role is discussed more thoroughly in Chapter 13.

You can help your Junior Judgments faculty by making certain your Pathways team considers the following issues:

- Junior Judgments placements and staffing
- Transportation
- Junior Judgments scheduling for optimal internship placement
- Regulatory forms and community member pamphlets
- Internship accountability
- Appreciation of the community

SENIOR TRANSITIONS

Senior Transitions is the top level of the Collaborative Pathways High School scaffold. It has a twofold purpose: first, to serve as a culmination of all of the Pathways learning and experiences to date; second, to help seniors transition successfully to their postsecondary plan (referring to the Senior Transitions curriculum found in Chapter 7 will be helpful while you read this section). Senior Transitions and its capstone projects will be a true test of your school's Pathways system (and core and elective teacher buy-in); any weak links at the Explorations, Selections, or Judgments levels will rear their ugly heads in the form of weak or unfocused projects.

> *In addition, your Senior Pathways teachers must be selected with care. A Senior Transitions teacher needs to be a facilitator, a cheerleader, a mentor, and a liaison to the community. It is not a position for an inexperienced, lecture-recall, or tightly controlled classroom teacher.*

As we've discussed before, the preparation for this course starts way back in the Freshman Explorations and builds throughout the next three years. How well your students do at the senior level will directly depend on how many opportunities they have had to practice teaming, self-management, and problem solving in both the school (in Pathways classes, as well as core and elective chapters; see Chapter 11) and the community. It is also dependent on how well your counseling department has collaborated with the Pathways teachers and has become a part of the daily fabric of the Pathways classrooms. In school districts where there are weak links in the system, it will be much more likely to see unfocused seniors with shallow projects. At these schools, the Senior Transitions teacher's job will be doubly difficult. So that you can avoid some of these pitfalls and have a Senior Transitions course that is truly the strong "matching bookend" to Freshman Explorations, let us examine curriculum, counseling, and community issues in the Senior Transitions classroom.

Curriculum Issues in Senior Transitions

The curriculum in the Senior Transitions classroom is truly an outgrowth of everything learned during the previous three years both in the Pathways classes and in the rest of the students' schooling.

Although all three previous years provide the foundation for Senior Transitions, the first major step of this final Pathways class actually begins in the junior year, when students begin brainstorming a preliminary project. During Senior Transitions, the first step is when the students design their mentor panels.

> *The trick to senior-year content is not to repeat what students have already learned but to take Pathway content to a new level of understanding by applying it.*

Students have "practiced" teaming with other students during Explorations, then observed teaming in the workplace during Selections, followed (hopefully) by becoming part of a teamed situation during their internship experience or at their tech center; now they will have the opportunity to take it to the next level. *They do this by building their own team and then self-managing that team.* In some school districts, part of this management experience is lost because Pathways mentors or community members are assigned to the student. If your students have been going through the process of learning time and self-management, it is important to allow them *to take complete ownership of this project* at this point. (The Senior Transitions teachers should serve as a safety net, helping to guide choices and share contacts if need be.) Throughout their high school years, Pathways students have been told that they are in charge; senior year should be their opportunity to "spread their wings," combine their Pathways interests with their aptitudes and passions, and ultimately do the best (and we hope most enjoyable) work of their high school careers. If your Pathways committee sets clear requirements with a strong rubric, having students self-manage these projects will be rewarding not only for the students, but also for the mentor teams and for the Pathways teachers.

Once the students design their panels, the next step is to help them utilize their presentation and people skills at even higher levels than they have in the past. The challenge here is to make sure your Senior Transitions teachers are not repeating skills that have been taught previously but are enhancing them with new information. If you are working with new or younger teachers that do not know the school and Pathways curriculum well, it is important for them to see how these skills progress (and how the standards and benchmarks align) so they know what has already been taught. For example, persuasion skills are key in getting people to help students with their project and then, most likely, in presenting the project. You need to allow your Senior Transitions teachers to examine what students already have learned about persuasion throughout the previous three years. Maybe students did sales pitches in Freshman Explorations as part of an integrated unit, persuasive brochures in government, and/or persuasive speeches in speech class; there may also have been miscellaneous other persuasive assignments. It is important not to reteach persuasion but to give a few tips and let then let students apply it to their projects. The same will be true with their technology (for presentation), teaming, problem-solving, and conflict-resolution skills. This is where the curriculum alignment and maps discussed in Chapter 6 come into play.

Another tough decision about the Transition curriculum goes hand-in-hand with where the course is placed in the school year to give optimum

Table 10.2 Sample Senior Transitions Scheduling

Part I (9 weeks)	Part II (9 weeks)	Part III (9 weeks)	Part IV (9 weeks)
Psychology, sociology, or philosophy	Senior Transitions Part I	Senior Transitions Part II	Service learning or Advanced psychology

benefit to the seniors. Ideally the projects need to be presented in the late spring so that *students have meaningful work to do their entire senior year,* otherwise they will "finish" early (National Commission on the High School Senior Year, n.d.). The dilemma then is the fact that some parts of the curriculum, particularly the counseling pieces such as college applications and visits, majors and minors, scholarship essays, and utilization of the portfolio, need to happen earlier, generally before Christmas vacation. Some of the schools we have been working with have been creative in dealing with this. Table 10.2 features one school's model.

By using this model, the section of Senior Transitions that deals with scholarships and applications can be taught in the late fall when it is most relevant and senior projects can be presented before the rush of May prom and graduation plans.

Another way to handle this is by embedding the actual project into Senior English or government, but then share some of the presentation skills and work within other classes. As you design your Senior Transitions class, it will be important to think about how placement will affect the curriculum. If your class does not start until second semester, it will be difficult to help students with college decisions and application and scholarship requirements because many are already due by or before the second semester.

Another key element is to make certain that Senior Projects are not just projects but truly individual capstones of each student's four-year Pathways experience; many senior project models we have examined are simply large research papers and therefore do not require individual life application of all of the skills that students have acquired. To achieve this kind of academic and life rigor, it is imperative that all projects are connected to the counseling, the community, Pathway technology, and classroom (academics) needed to be successful in the career or Cluster that the student has chosen. Because students are individuals, not all students will know an "exact" career they want (but instead will have eliminated many choices), but they will at least be able to identify the Cluster. It is imperative that your Transitions teachers realize that their job is to *facilitate* movement forward so that each student can comfortably transition to a postsecondary plan.

You need to help your teachers be clear about the expectations and requirements from the very beginning. The first set of senior projects will be the toughest, because students will fight something this new and challenging. Once they are in place, it will simply become part of the core and fabric of the school. It will take your district two or three years to help teachers learn to guide students into capstone projects rather than simpler senior projects. This tweaking will be a natural process in which students will begin to see the difference themselves as they watch their older friends create true capstone projects. Table 10.3 provides a look at the difference between senior projects and capstone projects.

Table 10.3 Comparison of Collaborative Capstone Projects to Senior Projects

Collaborative Pathways Kathy	Traditional High School Becky
Chosen Pathway: Human Service (selected at the end of Freshman Explorations with a secondary interest in the science Pathways as the best fit to her skills and interests)	**Interest Area:** Health (mom is a nurse, aunt is a physical therapist); she gets good grades in math and chemistry.
Job Shadows: Social worker, science teacher, taxidermist **Interviews:** Speech pathologist, mortician, advanced biology junior college instructor, conservation officer, FBI ballistics expert (these were the ones she liked best of the 10, hour-long conversations she had)	**Job Shadows:** Spent one day at work with mom and one day with aunt; received no background in what to observe and no prepared context for learning **Interviews:** None, but did hear a presentation from nurse and physical therapist at a school career fair and asked a couple of questions
Internship: Nine weeks unpaid at FBI offices with the ballistics department. During the compare–contrast evaluation of internship, she decided to eliminate ballistics because it was not sufficiently people-oriented for her. Haunted by the interview with the mortician, she spent a day with the mortician at a local funeral home. **Summer Job:** Spent the summer as a paid intern at the funeral home.	**Internship:** none **Summer Job:** Fast food, grill work **Volunteer Experience:** Twenty hours in a local medical center as a nurse's aide. Pushed around a book cart and cleaned up after patients. Did not follow a nurse for a full shift but did decide based on her jobs that nursing was not for her. Therefore, she decided to be a physical therapist.
Capstone Project: Followed a funeral from death certificate to final family meeting after the burial. Project presentation was open only to the project evaluation team at the family's request. The project focused on the science and people skills the mortician used, current technology used in the embalming process, schools and coursework for the best education, and a section on the business aspect of the funeral home. Twenty-five hours were spent at the funeral home during the project time.	**Senior Project:** Researched equipment used by a physical therapist and wrote a 10-page paper; sources were from the Internet and books. She interviewed one physical therapist (a friend of her aunt's). Gave a 10-minute presentation with pictures of the equipment. Spent four hours at the physical therapy clinic taking pictures.
Postsecondary Reality: Kathy began the first two years of mortuary study at a local community college and continues to work part time at the funeral home. She is doing well in her coursework and	**Postsecondary Reality:** After her first semester, Becky switched majors to pharmacy because she had not known she needed not only good chemistry and math skills for physical

(Continued)

Table 10.3 (Continued)

Collaborative Pathways Kathy	Traditional High School Becky
is looking forward to transferring to a mortuary program at a state university when she finishes her associate's degree. Her hands-on, day-to-day experience at the funeral home is invaluable not only to her, but to others in her courses who lack the hands-on experience. She has also added a minor in accounting so that she can be prepared for the business aspects of being a mortician.	therapy but also good people skills. She was shy, and her advisor did not think she could get into the competitive program at that university. Because she switched her major and this university did not have a good pharmacy program, she may need to transfer next year. She is not sure if she is sold on pharmacy, so she is taking her required coursework while she "figures it out."

As your Senior Transitions teachers plan their courses, here are some key curriculum questions you can have them ask themselves:

- Are you enhancing earlier curriculum in the areas of people skills, presentation technology, problem solving, teaming, and persuasion, or simply reteaching?
- Are you placing the Senior Transitions curriculum in a place where students can take optimal advantage of it?
- Are you facilitating projects that are true capstones and application of all of a student's learning and not simply a report or paper?
- Are you clear from the start what the project will entail and what each student is responsible for during the project and on presentation day?
- Do you have a clear rubric and set of expectations in the students' hands from the beginning?
- Are you ready as a teacher to take on a wide variety of roles—facilitator, mentor, cheerleader, and drill sergeant if need be?

Counseling Issues in Senior Transitions

Counseling and curriculum merge at the senior level. A Senior Transitions teacher does not have to know huge amounts about every college, military, and training opportunity for students, but he or she does have to know how to put students on the right path to find that information. Ideally what will happen during the senior year is a complete partnership between counseling staff and Senior Transitions teachers. Remember that this is not adding more to the counselors' plate; it simply gives them a systematic and common place to reach all the seniors so that each student has a clear postsecondary plan and clear transitioning to that plan (which is already one of counselors' biggest duties). The biggest challenge in

> *The counseling in Senior Transitions needs to be a clear collaboration between teachers and counselors.*

this is the need for the counselor and teachers to team on the completion of college and postsecondary application's curriculum piece.

During the beginning of the Transitions course, counselors and Transitions teachers should be meeting at least weekly, and the Pathways classroom should have a revolving door, with the counselor coming in and out on a regular basis. Maybe on Mondays, he will come and highlight the scholarship applications due in the next two weeks; on Wednesday he might stop by and talk about the Free Application for Federal Student Aide and the upcoming parent meeting that students should attend. On Friday he might be in with a list from the Rotary or Lions Club of employers willing to help with senior project mentor panels. A well-run Senior Transitions class will make a counselor's job much easier.

Also important to remember is that counseling seniors in a Pathways High School setting will be different from counseling seniors in a traditional system. These students will come with a clear idea of who they are and what they will be studying at college along with knowing what credentials they will need for each career on their career ladders. Because of this focus, being a counselor in a Pathways school should be a wonderful opportunity to truly guide students because they will be ready for their guidance; it should be that truly teachable moment that all teachers and counselors hope for in their dreams.

Community Issues in Senior Transitions

When students design and implement meaningful capstone projects, the joy and pride the community will take in their accomplishment will be amazing. Remember that when students are truly "engaged," making their own "homework," there is no end to the wonderfully creative and detailed projects that they can amass. Also remember that the community has been a partner in these students' educations from the time they were freshmen. They were in the classrooms while students were freshmen exploring paths and careers, and they hosted large group visits; they were with students doing in-depth interviews and then hosting students for job shadows during the sophomore year; during the junior year, many students were in their workplaces as interns. It is only part of a natural progression that the community should be there to help students design meaningful projects that connect to their interests and their future career plans. Most community members perceive helping with the capstone projects as "icing on the cake." Students are now mature and in charge of the project, which means the community member can just guide and serve as a safety net. This might be when a community member hosts a student on four days so he or she can get used to the technology used in the workplace; or it might be the community member who helps in the selection of the best dual-enroll course or virtual high school class and then furnishes possible interviewees who use this coursework in the daily routine of their jobs. The truth is, when students are focused and self-managing with a clear idea of how a community member can help them with their project, there are few who will say no.

As is always the case in utilizing community in a Pathways High School (which will be discussed in detail in Chapter 13), it is key to develop clearly defined ways that the community can help with senior projects. What would work best is if your district (or even better, your intermediate school district or your Pathways School Network) develops a handout packet to give community members that is similar to the packet that most districts give to job shadow hosts. This packet should clearly define the roles of being on a student's mentor team, sitting on a Senior Project evaluation panel, or hosting a student who wants to do his or her project out in the community. Just as is the case at the other three levels, there are many roles—some take a small amount of time and involvement and some take a large commitment to the people of the community. The use of the community is part of a natural progression, but if your system is weak and your students have not done enough job shadows or internships, your district may have a more difficult time getting your community to help at this level. Remember, too, that your community includes the local and neighboring career-technical postsecondary resources, military recruiters, two-year colleges, and local universities. It is extremely important to utilize *all* of your community resources throughout the four years of a Pathways program.

As you help your Senior Transitions teachers examine their use of community, help them to focus on the following:

1. Give students ownership of which community members they will involve in their project, but make sure they have a clear rationale for whom they choose.

2. Make certain that community members are clear on exactly what is involved in the role they have chosen.

3. If the seniors are having difficulty getting help from the community, the Pathways team needs to reevaluate its current usage of the community.

4. Students must express their appreciation to community members—letters, small tokens, or even the optional student-designed service learning projects can be wonderful ways to show that the student appreciates the efforts of the community.

THE SCAFFOLD WORKS

Building a Pathways school is a process that does not happen overnight. When you get to the fourth year and add Senior Transitions, the weaker links in your scaffolding of skills will become apparent, and the Pathways team (faculty and community) must think outside the box to repair those weaknesses. Remember that students from your school will be going into the capstone project with *a true context* to their learning that is not often found among high school students. Often when we talk to employers who work with non-Pathways students about what we are doing with our students, they tell us that students lack focus and work ethic. With the scaffold of skills that your students will bring to their senior projects, you'll never hear community members say this about them. Value and character education have been built into the program, as has the chance for students to eliminate possibilities, which allows them to have more focus at the senior level. They have practiced a wide variety of people skills, and also seen them modeled in the workplace, over their high school experience. The true "proof of the pudding" happens when your students have the opportunity to self-manage and apply all that they have learned through their Collaborative Pathways experience through their capstone projects and then transition to their next steps. The Senior Project should be a highlight of each student's high school career—not just for the students, but for the mentors, the faculty members, the school, and the community.

IN REVIEW

- The three Pathways Classes following Freshman Explorations—Sophomore Selections, Junior Judgments, and Senior Selections—are built on the foundation of the previous class.
- The scaffolding of these classes makes it crucial that there not be a "weak link" anywhere in the system.
- Sophomore Selections is where students narrow their Career Pathways through career laddering, interviews, and job shadowing while learning employability skills.
- The key to Sophomore Selections is to experience enough job shadows to be able to eliminate or select a career Cluster and make an appropriate internship or career center choice.
- Junior Judgments involves unpaid work experience in the community in which students learn about workplace skills, technology, government regulations, and ethics.
- The key to Junior Judgments is for students to get an in-depth understanding of the workplace while narrowing career direction and exploring ideas for a senior project.
- Senior Transitions is the culmination of students' high school experience and the bridge to their postsecondary plans. Students design, implement, and present a senior project to a chosen panel.
- The key to Senior Transitions is for students to be able to pull together their high school experience and skills into a senior project while setting the stage for a smooth transition to a postsecondary plan.
- Pathways staff members must meet on a regular basis to discuss Pathways curriculum, students, and "glitches." It is also important that they communicate with each other and with the community.

Chapter Eleven

Core and Elective Teachers as Support for the Career Pathways Instructional Process

SCENARIO: TRANSFORMATION TO A PATHWAYS TEACHER

As an art teacher, Chris had always been looking for ways to inspire his students to be creative and think outside the box. When the subject of careers in art came up in the past, usually only two or three careers came to mind—that of artist, teacher, or engineer. Over the past three years, Chris's high school has been in the process of becoming a Collaborative Pathways High School. When Chris first heard of the idea, he thought like it sounded like a good opportunity for his students but did not investigate much further because he did not see how it would directly relate to art or to his classroom. Chris had always included writing across the curriculum in his coursework because he believes that art is a form of communication. As he watched students coming through Freshman Explorations, he noticed that many of their integrated team projects included artwork—drawing, graphic design, or photography and other media. Some students came and asked his opinion or asked specific questions about art as they worked on projects.

The next year Chris noticed he had many more students sign up for art and photography then had done so before; many of them were there because they thought that art and photography might be important to or enhance their career aspirations. When school finished that year, Chris had an opportunity to take part in a four day in-service that allowed him to view several careers that used art in the workplace. He spent a half day at a graphic art studio, a half day at a printing shop, a day in a frame and supply shop, and a day in a museum (he had never imagined that there were so many art-related jobs).

Suddenly, as Chris saw the connections between subject relevancy, career pathways, and his students, he became excited. He started to design open-ended assignments that would allow students to examine how art could be used in the work world. He added an assignment in which students designed not only a toy but also the packaging that would properly display and market it. Another assignment called for students to design a store window for a particular holiday. Next, he invited a graphic artist friend into his classroom for a few days. The students had a chance to explore art design as advertisement and to realize that graphic and visual art still has the same base: communication of the artist's perception.

Chris then began going to Pathways Network Meetings for art and humanities teachers in the county; this collaboration gave him the opportunity to share his successes and gain from the success of other Pathways art teachers. The sharing of materials, ideas, and speakers enhanced his classroom greatly as he worked further to help individual students with plans that involved art careers. During this time, Chris did not dilute or drop any of his current standards and benchmarks but rather expanded in more real-world ways their applications.

At the same time, he worked hard in his beginning classes to show students how an artistic sense (an eye for balance and perspective) could be an asset to a wide variety of careers.

Now Chris cannot imagine how he managed to teach art in a non-Pathways high school. He accompanies the Freshman Explorations classes on a one-day Art and Communications Pathway field trip that includes visits to a local art museum, a graphic design business, and a print shop. He collaborates with the art and communication Sophomore Selections teacher and works closely with the art program at the technical center and the local community college. In addition, he mentors several Senior Transitions students and sits on the Senior Project Evaluation Team for art projects. The art department includes a variety of new courses including graphic art, cartooning, and Web page design. He no longer thinks of art as just his passion but as a passion that students can incorporate into their postsecondary lifestyles and careers. He has evolved from being an elective teacher to a Pathways art teacher.

GAINING THE SUPPORT OF THE ENTIRE FACULTY

To become a Pathways School and not just have a pullout Pathways program, your school district needs the continuous support of the entire faculty, including core and elective teachers. Although it is true that two or three veteran teachers, a counselor, and an administrator can begin the Pathways process, the only way the system becomes optimal (and permanent) for students is with the buy-in of the rest of the high school staff. This chapter focuses on how to begin the buy-in process and then on how to encourage your faculty to become not just elective or core teachers but Pathways High School teachers.

Core and Elective Teachers as Part of the Team

Throughout the planning and implementation process, core and elective teachers need to be part of the process. It is crucial that they not be spectators watching others implement the system, but that they see how good this will be for their students. Once they realize that fact, their next question will be, "What should my role in a Pathways High School be?" Becoming a Pathways teacher is a change; change is always terrifying and especially so for teachers who do not feel adequately trained or who are unsure what new expectations you are adding to their plate. In addition, if teachers are not given the opportunity to take ownership of this change (first and foremost in their classrooms), they are much less likely to buy into the entire process. An important point to make to teachers at this stage is not that they will be expected to do more, but that they will be presenting their current curriculum from a "different" angle. Remember, too, that teachers will be phased into the Pathways process over a period of time, just as Chris was in our scenario. To help your teachers during the tough stages of planning and implementation, it is important to focus on four key elements:

1. Total Staff Inclusion
2. Communication
3. Continual Staff Development and In-Service
4. Collaboration and Shared Decision Making

Staff Inclusion

From the start, core and elective teachers should be included in the Pathways process. When a committee is formed, core and elective teacher representation needs to be included (from varying subject areas, if at all possible). These teachers need to be carefully selected. They must be teachers who are truly student centered, who are well respected by their colleagues, and who are open to change. Because of this and the pressure that comes with the change process, it is important not to use beginning teachers.

When we began researching "Pathways" schools, many administrators told us that they were "Pathways High Schools." While visiting the actual schools, however, teachers would be unable to

> *During this stage, professional staff development is critical so that teachers understand why the Pathways system will be the best for students. Equally important is that they know the difference between instruction that includes Career Pathways and Cluster information and a true Collaborative Pathways High School.*

Table 11.1 Becoming Part of a Pathways System: A Progressive Process

Phase 1	*Exposure* to the Collaborative Pathways Model
Phase 2	*Observation* of core and elective Pathways teaching
Phase 3	*Implementation* of Pathway-inclusive coursework
Phase 4	*Integration* of Pathways philosophy into daily curricula

tell us much more about Pathways in their school than, "Oh, the counselors do that" or "I think it is a pull-out three-week unit done in 9th-grade English." Few students could describe to us a true plan; their plan was usually, "I'm going to college"; when asked what they would be studying, they would say, "I'm not sure." In a truly Collaborative Pathways High School, everyone can tell you how Pathways works—students, teachers, administrators, parents, and support staff. This is because in a Collaborative Pathways High School, Pathways becomes a school- and communitywide philosophy, and it becomes personal to everyone. Every child has a plan, every teacher includes some Pathways assignments, every parent helps guide his or her student's plan, every administrator supports the Pathways system, and the entire community becomes connected to helping the students with their plans (see Chapter 13).

Essentially, what happens when a school is implementing a Pathways system is the "trickle down" effect. For most core and elective teachers, this means that becoming part of a Pathways system is a progressive process as shown in Table 11.1.

During Phase 1, teachers are included in the process of learning about Collaborative Pathways and why it is better for students. In addition to an explanation of the Collaborative model, optimally this exposure would include guests from Collaborative schools, as well as a visit to a Collaborative Pathways School. Phase 2 is the opportunity to observe other teachers utilizing Pathways assignments in core and elective classes. Ideally, not only would these teachers be in the same district (or at least in nearby counties or regions) but in their subject area as well. Once teachers have seen Pathways assignments incorporated, they are ready to begin Phase 3. This includes piloting a few Pathways assignments in their own classroom. This may, at first, be awkward for the traditional teacher because the assignments need to be open-ended and facilitated so all students can adapt them to their Pathways plans. It requires the ability on the teacher's part to allow student ownership of the assignment (student centered and teacher facilitated). If the teacher is using mostly traditional teacher-centered techniques, such as lecture and recall, this can be a hard stretch at first. The payoff comes when they see the interest and level of engagement students have in the subject matter taught within the Pathways system. Once students take ownership of these projects, the teacher will see students reaching new levels of effort, growth, and understanding, something that would not happen in a more traditional classroom. The key to this transformation is the relevancy of the student's Pathway and plan. This leads to Phase 4: Integration. After teachers see this kind of growth, they often become hooked. They begin to integrate Pathways work naturally into their curriculum more and more frequently. It is equally interesting that most teachers become engaged in their classroom in a new way. Suddenly, they are looking for opportunities to see their subject used in the workplace. They are seeking opportunities to talk to those who use their subject matter on a daily basis, and they are inspired to come up with assignments and guest speakers that allow for Pathways connections.

Communication

To feel a part of the process while passing through the four phases, core and elective teachers need to be included. The only way this can happen is when communication is taking place in a systematic manner. There are four important components of Pathways communication:

1. *Weekly Pathways Information Sessions.* A portion of each weekly faculty meeting needs to be set aside to discuss the week's guest speakers, integrated units, field trips, and facultywide collaboration of day-to-day Pathways work.

2. *Departmental Planning of Pathways Assignments and Implementation.* Just as all the other curriculum in the department is aligned with standards and benchmarks and divided into appropriate levels, so should the Pathways work that is done by each department be aligned with standards and benchmarks and divided appropriately into various levels. This could happen during in-services, when curriculum alignment is taking place, or on a day set aside for departmental meetings to map the Pathways work.

3. *Sharing of Pathways Materials and Guests.* Some of this will take place naturally in the weekly Pathways meetings, but everyone must make a concentrated effort to get the most "bang for the buck" when utilizing vocational libraries, career software, videos, and the like. Perhaps at the beginning of each school year, everyone should bring the newest and best things that relate to careers and career exploration together so that teachers will have an idea of what the school owns—and possibly be inspired to use it in new ways. If your program becomes truly collaborative on the county or regional level, imagine the possibilities that would arise from the ability to share more costly materials on a countywide basis.

4. *Yearly Evaluation of the Pathways Process by Core and Elective Teachers.* This evaluation could be part of your school's yearly school improvement process, led by the team in charge, or it could be led by your school's Pathways team. Even better would be a rotating system that had a different department take charge of it every year. Designing the rubric would be a great project for your faculty at the beginning of the year as it sets goals for the Pathways program.

Staff work time is an issue in every high school, but Pathways administrators must set aside a few minutes each week for faculty updates; as noted earlier, faculty members use this time to share information about which speakers will be in the building, what field trips will happen (not just in Pathways classes but in core and elective classes as well), and how other departments or teachers might connect to or utilize Pathways coursework. Ideally, every field trip should include two or three chaperone slots so that core and elective teachers may go along and see their subject implemented in the work environment and communicate with those who work in the field. Select the teachers who will most benefit from the event to attend—for example, math and science teachers would be selected as chaperones for a field trip to a foundry; English, speech, and electronics teachers for a trip to a television station.

Time is always part of the issue when not enough communication is taking place. There are many creative ways to resolve this. On Monday, the Pathways coordinator or counselor could print a list of upcoming Pathways events in the building for every teacher. This would require 10 or 15 minutes of staff communication at the prior week's staff meeting. In our experience, schools that build in small amounts of time each week to communicate about the Pathways program run more smoothly than schools that block a large chunk of time (a late start or half day) once a month. It is crucial that this be faculty-driven and part of a systematic routine.

Secondly, when late starts or departmental work time is set aside, some of that time needs to be used by the department to plan Pathways assignments for each course, along with possible implementation time lines. Then these assignments can be coordinated with other departments so that students aren't working on several huge Pathways assignments at the same time. Teachers will accept this concept much more readily when they realize that one or two Pathways assignments a semester will be plenty to augment the coursework done outside the Pathways classroom. Departments can platform their assignments so they build on each other from one required Pathways course to another. During freshman year, for example, students might create a PowerPoint presentation that highlights a Pathway or Cluster in their English class. Sophomore students in computer literacy might design a Web page that explores community opportunities in their respective Pathway. Junior math students might do a statistical presentation that compares and contrasts two Clusters. Senior government students might analyze how current laws affect a career or Cluster in which they have an interest.

The third crucial component is the sharing of materials within and among faculty members. Administrators can support this kind of sharing in several ways. One is to earmark a portion of the professional materials budget to departmental Pathways materials. Another is to coordinate professional development coursework and shared materials and technology with a local Technology Center or community college; this can help direct teachers to useful Pathways-connected materials. In addition, allowing teachers release time for countywide Pathways sharing and in-servicing will give teachers many opportunities to find the materials that they need. Finally, the best way for sharing and communication to happen is through joint partnerships with community members and businesses. They will often know which materials, including software, will most help students; many times they are willing to donate these materials to the school. A flight school owner visiting students who are pretending to run a flight school might donate a manual on how to set up flight schools, for example, or a real estate agent might donate the most recent regulations for realtors.

The fourth component of good communication is to offer faculty members a chance to evaluate together how well they have communicated throughout the year and to assess their improvement not only as a Pathways school, but as individual teachers in a Pathways school. By communicating about their successes and failures, faculty members will be well on their way to streamlining classroom assignments and better coordinating their efforts to help students with their plans. This also allows teachers the opportunity set clear goals for the following year. This model for professional development technique through teacher communication is the key to professional improvement.

In general we have seen that when Pathways communication is improved within a faculty, communication in general is also vastly improved. This positive communication is good not only for teachers and administrators, but—even more important—for students. When teachers do a better job, students succeed.

Continuous Staff Development and In-Servicing

In a Pathways High School, administrators work hard to allow teachers as many staff development and in-servicing opportunities as possible. For these opportunities to be successful, teachers need first to have some buy-in to Pathways. It is also important that these opportunities are not in addition to their daily assignments but simply a part of their schoolwork lifestyle. This occurs when the majority of experiences are woven into the school day and school year rather than occurring in the summers, on weekends, or after school. These opportunities can be broken into three types:

- Workplace exposure
- Teaching technique
- Academic rigor

Workplace exposures can happen in several ways. One is to incorporate teachers into Pathways activities. As stated earlier, taking teachers along on Freshman Explorations field trips is a great starting point. While sophomore students are job shadowing, release some of your teachers to embark on day-long adventures of their own. When Junior Judgments students are interning, release a couple of teachers from the internship subject to observe students on the job. During Senior Transitions projects, teachers have ample opportunities to connect with students' work and postsecondary environments as they work on mentorship and evaluation teams. Another way is to design a county or regional symposium in the summer or as a monthly event (Table 11.2). This four-session program allows teachers to gain background on workplace experiences (Session 1), to be exposed to several work environments (Sessions 2 and 3), and ultimately to make plans to use in their classrooms what they have learned from the institute program (Session 4). This experience might take place before the school year or immediately after it, if it is impossible to incorporate it into the schedule.

Table 11.2 The Four-Session Pathways Institute Symposium Program

Session 1	Pathway or Cluster background	Thematic instruction	Collaborative skills
Session 2	Observation of work environment I	Application of subject matter	Skills used in the workplace
Session 3	Observation of work environment II	Application of subject matter	Skills used in the workplace
Session 4	Evaluation of the field experiences	Design of unit with subject application	Inclusion of collaborative skills in the unit

A third way to sponsor workplace experiences is for core and elective teachers to design field trips of their own, once a semester, that take students to see their subject used in a professional environment. A chemistry teacher might take students to a laboratory or manufacturing plant that makes plastic wrap, for example, whereas an art teacher may take students to a photography studio and an agriculture teacher to an ethanol plant. This is a more traditional approach and may already happen in your district.

> *The key is to get not only students but also faculty members into as many workplaces as possible.*

You will be amazed to find how many members of your faculty have no idea how their subject is used in the workplace. Also, because they have never chatted with people in careers across the board as their Pathways students do, they may have no idea how universal the use of their core skills is. Once teachers see how their subject is used, the sky is the limit for the types of Pathways projects they can design.

The second type of in-service experiences (the Pathways symposium) are those that give exposure to teaching techniques needed in a Pathways school. Because a Pathways school is student centered, teachers need to know how to facilitate teaming and self-management. First and foremost, all teachers must understand the differences between grouping and teaming.

> *Just as Freshman Explorations teachers must teach students to team, administrators need to be dedicated to teaching faculty members to do the same. Once they have learned to collaborate, they are ready to use teaming skills in the classroom on a regular basis.*

It is not enough for students to be taught teaming in Pathways classes and then have no other teachers truly utilize it, nor is it enough for faculty members to be in-serviced in teaming only once. Just as students must be held accountable for their learning, administrators need to be sure that teachers are using and implementing what they learn during in-services. From the start, core and elective teachers must be included in the design of the Pathways program so that they not only see the components but are comfortable using them. During a school's first Freshman Explorations year, core teachers should be included in the design of the first integrated units. At the same time, they should be encouraged to visit the Freshman Explorations classroom so that they can get a feel for the ongoing teaming and problem solving. In this way, they immediately become part of the Pathways team and can begin designing lessons that incorporate teaming and problem solving.

Academic rigor also needs to be emphasized in the in-servicing plans of a Pathways High School. This can happen through many of the curriculum sessions already done by most schools. Included in these in-services should be curriculum alignment, incorporation of standards and benchmarks in all assignments including Pathways assignments, designing thematic units, and creating useful rubrics and assessments. Teachers need to spend time on learning fair grading practices, setting schoolwide teaming and conflict-resolution rules, and maintaining a high level of academic challenge for all students. This process for curriculum flow and academic rigor was explained in Chapter 6.

In a Pathways High School, in-servicing is a continual, ongoing process; because workplaces continue to change as our technology and culture changes, teachers must return again and again to workplaces to see what has changed or been updated. As we learn more from brain research, we also need to revisit issues of classroom management and learning techniques. Finally, we must continue to have high standards for students so that they will make optimal strides in their learning and growth.

Teaming and Collaboration

Entire books have been written on how to help faculties and schools collaborate and team. Here we are only going to discuss what we have seen work in Pathways settings. If your school is truly working on the first three components—staff inclusion, Pathways communication, and ongoing staff development for all teachers—then the facultywide teaming and collaboration will fall into place. When science teachers began to understand what was taking place in the Pathways classes of one high school, they began exploring options for a laboratory with technology that would be closer to workplace technologies. In another school system, once teachers began to realize the implications of Pathways, they pushed for a change in their block scheduling so that students could have more elective opportunities to enhance their plans. Teachers or guests visiting the building may find themselves visiting several classrooms in one day or having lunch with a group of students interested in their careers. Once the staff begins to take ownership of the Career Pathways philosophy, optimal growth will happen. Every teacher will then have experiences that can draw in new community contacts to the school. When all faculty members are teaming and sharing these contacts and building off of each other's assignments, the opportunities and network for students becomes vast. Students also "feel" the consistency of expectations and react accordingly. When a Pathways school reaches this level, it has "self-actualized."

CAREER TECHNOLOGY AND ACADEMY TEACHERS VERSUS COLLABORATIVE PATHWAYS TEACHERS

An important distinction needs to be made concerning the differences between teachers in a career technology or academy system and Collaborative Pathways teachers. Your teachers may be overwhelmed at first, believing that they will be expected to become experts in all or some of the Pathways. The beauty of the Pathways system is that the students take ownership (and self-management) of their Pathways learning. What this means is that in a Pathways High School, core and elective teachers can make open-ended assignments that students can then adjust to their particular Pathway and their own interests. For example, a teacher may assign a paper that focuses on the writing process for college-bound juniors; a student in the art Pathway may choose to do a paper on new photographic technology, whereas a student in the engineering Pathway may write about a prototype car; a student in the health Pathway may focus on the newest technique in laser surgery. This allows teachers to be experts in their subject or elective area while making subject connections with their students. Also, we have found that because the students are in charge of their learning, they often explore further and in greater depth than they would have if they were simply fulfilling a class requirement.

Tech center or academy situations are different in that these teachers are expected to specialize in one career area or Cluster; they generally have been trained or worked in a particular field. The coursework is more focused, with students training in a single career or Cluster of their choice. In theory, this is wonderful, but many times students in a tech center setting may not be truly focused on that career but simply trying it out. They may not have adequately explored their skills and abilities to match them to this field, and there may have been insufficient work environment field trips and job shadows for them to confidently choose this particular program. Sometimes students are placed in these programs not because they are interested in them but because it is a chance for hands-on learning. So while the program should be a perfect "match," many times it is not. A Collaborative Career Pathways High School can assist in this process because students make better connections to what they are learning. By working together as partners, student programs match their entire school experience and plan. Now their high school and technical training experiences are no longer separate entities, but two important and interconnected parts of a student's entire educational experience. When Career Pathways High Schools partner with technology centers or academies, students get the best of both worlds.

WORKING WITH THE CORE TEACHERS

Core teachers have many apprehensions about any change that may affect their content or delivery of material because so much of it is tied to state and national standards and requirements. One of the best parts of the Pathways

Table 11.3 Separating Core Teachers' Fears From Reality During the Pathways Transition

Fear	Reality
➤ Loss of core instruction	➤ More awareness of the relevancy of the core subjects and reinforcement of essential standards and benchmarks
➤ Less student involvement	➤ A better context for learning with hands-on and integrated lessons
➤ Lower achievement scores	➤ Students apply the core learning to their individual plans
➤ All assignments directly connected to career or Pathways	➤ Higher level of learning and application of knowledge

system is that instead of students losing core material opportunities, *they actually gain them.* Within the Collaborative Pathways system, integrated unit are chances to further practice and increase proficiency in core subjects—particularly science, math, English, and social studies. In addition, they provide every student with systematic and continuous delivery of technology standards and benchmarks. Once core teachers realize that this program will be an enhancement and not a loss, they are much more comfortable with the concepts. Furthermore, our experience shows that once a core teacher has had the opportunity to work with Pathways students and compare them to traditional students, they see and experience the difference, thus reinforcing their buy-in. This is because Pathways students are focused, can see clearly how the core subjects are relevant or useful to them, and have a better idea of how to adapt themselves to the learning situation through multiple-intelligence and learning style studies. Speaking from personal experience, we can say the difference is remarkable.

As an administrator, the most important way you can support your core faculty members during this time of change and transition is to help them separate their fears from reality (Table 11.3). Once teachers realize that there is greater potential for growth in core subjects using the Pathways Model, they will be highly supportive of the system and transition themselves through the phases of becoming a true Pathways teacher.

> *Core teachers will find that not all of their work has to connect directly to Pathways. It is the Pathways program's connection to the relevancy of the subject that makes the true difference.*

When students realize that the base or key components of a core subject will be helpful to them, they become more focused and willing to explore the subject area. This allows them to discover how various parts of one subject can fit into different Pathways or career Clusters, ultimately making the teacher's job that much easier because the students understand the context and relevancy of the core subject to their future plans.

WORKING WITH THE ELECTIVE TEACHERS

A key concern for elective teachers anytime that new coursework and programs are added is how it will affect their enrollment. In truth, Collaborative Pathways is every elective teacher's dream. This is particularly true if the coursework is added as stand-alone classes in a 4 × 4 block.

Once students have a focus and a sense of what coursework will be helpful, they will begin to seek courses that will enhance their plan. Because all students' plans will be their own, the electives they choose will be not only subjects that are useful to them, but also those that include interests and passions that they can incorporate into their dreams. For example, take the student who decides to be a minister and has a passion for music. Part of his personal dream may be to write and compose music for brass ensembles in his church. In addition to regular pastoral coursework, this passion may inspire many electives—more band coursework, music theory and conducting classes, and so forth. In addition, he may take creative writing, piano, and singing classes to help him pursue his dream.

To help elective teachers transition into Pathways teachers, it will be important for the administration to support elective teachers with as many field trips and guest speakers as possible. It is also critical for you to help them have ample opportunities to communicate and collaborate with core staff. Hold the elective teachers responsible for one or two Pathways assignments each semester. As they transition into true Pathways teachers, they will begin to incorporate more Pathways-connected work on their own initiatives. Part of the reason this natural incorporation will occur is because elective coursework is naturally closer to Pathways and career Cluster content. The benefit of this is that students can get hooked on the elective content and then connect it to their Pathways plan and career options. An example of this would be an art teacher with passion who hooks students on a variety of electives such as photography, graphic design, and pottery. While taking these electives, students can begin connecting their interests and passion in art to a particular Cluster in the art Pathway. It will then work in reverse, as students revisit the relevancy of core subjects that would be beneficial to them. Once this begins to happen, a natural, ongoing collaboration will take place between your core and elective teachers, and as an administrator you will be able to help dispel their fears of transitioning to a Pathways system (Table 11.4).

HOW PATHWAYS TEACHERS DIFFER FROM TRADITIONAL CLASSROOM TEACHERS

In conclusion, just as the differences between traditional and Pathways students are remarkable, the same holds true for the differences between traditional and Pathways teachers. A Pathways teacher's focus is different from that of a traditional teacher. A traditional secondary teacher focuses first on his or her subject matter and second on the student. In a Pathways High School, teachers focus on the students and then on their individual plans; finally, they help the students to

Table 11.4 Separating Elective Teachers' Fears From Reality During the Pathways Transition

Fears	Reality
➤ Loss of student enrollment	➤ More students enrolled in electives
➤ A weakening of the overall elective program	➤ Students enrolled in electives are more engaged
➤ Only those students interested in the elective for career use will enroll	➤ Clearer and broader connection between core and elective subjects
➤ Loss of elective budget	➤ Better collaboration between core and elective teachers

explore ways of adapting their subject matter to the plan. Also, in a traditional setting, the teacher is the giver of the information; in a Pathways setting, the teacher sets up the students so they can find and utilize information that will be useful to their plans, their passions, and their dreams. Once a teacher becomes a dream facilitator, he or she will never go back to simply being an information source.

IN REVIEW

- Core and elective teachers must know from the beginning that they are not expected to do more, just to do things differently; understanding the workings of a Collaborative Pathways High School is a key component to getting their buy-in.
- From the beginning of the Pathways transition, core and elective teachers need to be included in the process.
- Transitioning from a traditional teacher to a Pathways teacher is a four-stage process that includes exposure, observation, implementation, and integration.
- Communication is a key component of including teachers in the transition process. Small meetings and updates, communication and sharing of materials within departments, and yearly review of Pathways communication are requirements for success.
- Continuous in-servicing in the areas of field experience and environments, student-centered teaching techniques, and tools for academic rigor are essential.
- Proper communication among faculty combined with worthwhile in-servicing lead to teaming and collaboration.
- A Pathways teacher makes open-ended assignments and then puts the students in charge of adapting them to their plans.
- Key to faculty buy-in of Pathways is helping core teachers realize that the system allows opportunities to include more, not less, core subject material, with more opportunities to apply and practice it.
- Elective teachers collaborate more with other teachers and with students because their courses are often more relevant to students' dreams and passions.

Part Five

Culture, Community, and Technology

Chapter Twelve

Public Relations, Parents, and Pathways

SCENARIO: A ROLE FOR EVERYONE

As Dr. Smith enters the school district's board room, he can sense the anticipation of those already in the room, which is filled with a larger audience than attends the usual board meetings. What is interesting to Dr. Smith is the fact that tonight's audience is a diverse group—a handful of students with a wide variety of interests and abilities, several parents, some community members, some core and elective teachers, and some citizens of all ages. As the board members take their seats, they begin their opening rituals of calling roll, reading the minutes, and so forth.

This gives Dr. Smith a few minutes to think about what has led to this night and where they will go from here. Dr. Smith has been to other board meetings because he has his own medical practice in the community and is an active member of the Rotary. His connection with that service organization has allowed him to work with the school on occasion. In addition, as an involved parent of three children (one in elementary, one in middle school, and one ready to enter high school), he has been to other board meetings where the agenda included items that would affect one of his children. What sets this particular meeting apart from others is that the decisions being made tonight will affect all children in the district. In addition, the role he and his wife will have in working with the schools will be altered. The district is looking at making an important change in the high school.

Dr. Smith's interest in the Pathways model peaked about two months ago, when some members of the newly formed school Pathways team spoke at a Rotary luncheon. Two veteran teachers gave the presentation along with current students, the principal, and the counselor. During their presentation, this team of sincere people talked about a new vision for the school. They wanted to use the Pathways model, and although it was about student postsecondary planning and career education, Dr. Smith realized that it would bring many other needed changes to the high school. By adding a series of new classes each year, each class would offer not only a chance for career exploration and decision making, but also a place to teach and reinforce the life skills that he had noticed were missing from many of his employees. There would be opportunities for teaming, problem solving, and other people-related skills. In addition, this new system would allow for parents and community members to become more involved in the career preparation of the district's students through more site visits, guest appearances, internships, and mentoring opportunities.

After the Rotary meeting, he went home and began discussing this new concept with his family. Although it sounded like a good idea, they still had questions and concerns. His daughter wanted her high school to stay the same and did not want "more work to do!" His wife, a nurse in his practice, felt that this had real potential to be a good change but was somewhat skeptical. She had gone to a liberal arts college and believed that if career education was introduced too soon or pushed too hard, that students would lose the opportunity for exploration of a wide variety of subject areas and would not end up with a well-rounded education. Dr. Smith had seen other new programs adopted, on which a small group of people had worked hard, only to see the programs eventually discarded. Because Pathways would take years to implement and hard work on many fronts—by parents, students, teachers, community members, and administration—he wondered if his school district and community would have the determination to stick it out during the tough times until the new concept had a chance to become a complete system.

With all these thoughts in mind, he had attended a parent organization meeting a month earlier, the topic of which was Pathways. It was an open discussion that evening, with many points of view voiced. Many parents who had older children in the high school were concerned that their children would not be getting the Pathways opportunities, and other parents were concerned that if the emphasis was on career development, they would not learn enough to do well on state tests and in the college arena. There had also been students and elective teachers who voiced concerns that the new "required" Pathways classes would not leave enough room in the schedule for students to continue to pursue their courses in music, art, and foreign language, especially if those classes were not part of their career focus.

The committee members' response to all of the questions and concerns was thoughtful and steady. They discussed the possibilities of making several of the Pathways courses nine weeks instead of a semester to save room for more electives. In addition, they discussed the fact that in other places where Pathways was being used (in at least 19 states), students were actually taking more electives, test scores were constant, and students were better prepared for college or other secondary options because they had a focus. The committee also made it clear that it would be the individual student's plan, that he or she could change Pathway, and that this career decision-making process would be alongside of the other coursework, not in place of it. What had left the biggest impression from that evening, however, were the voices of three students who attended that night. One senior, an honors student, had stood up with tears in her eyes and told the audience that they needed to do this for their kids. She was a senior with good grades, going off to college and scared to death because she had no idea of what she wanted to study. Another student, a junior, implored parents to think about this change because school was "boring" and he saw no connection between what he was learning and the real world, and if he could begin making decisions about what kinds of careers to look at and workplaces to try for himself, he *might* be willing to try harder in school. The third student, a sophomore, talked about the need for more help in balancing all of the homework and about having a need for a better study base, which he felt Pathways could give him. As Dr. Smith left the meeting, he was haunted by these student voices, so filled with hope for an improved system that would better meet their needs.

Mr. Smith snapped his attention back to the board meeting at hand, and listened intently to the Pathways committee's presentation to the board. The board members asked many good questions, but they had had many previous questions answered by the board's curriculum subcommittee, which had already had several informal meetings with the Pathways committee. Members of the board and the Pathways committee (including students) had also visited several schools that were already implementing Pathways. There were several members of the board who strongly believed that the changes would be beneficial and were truly necessary. After a long discussion, the board voted 6 to 1 in favor of the new system. The school board president, although pleased, announced to the audience that he felt this would be a "whole village" approach and that if a Pathways system would be best for students, it would only work if all stakeholders were involved in streamlining the system to meet the needs of their district and students.

Dr. Smith knew that what the school board president had said was true—they all needed to be part of the team. When the meeting was over, he congratulated the Pathways team. "Congratulations on your new system. I can see where this will truly be good for all kids. I am willing to serve as a community member or work with students interested in the medical field. I really believe this will be time well spent." Dr. Smith, and soon many others, realized what a gift this system was to the students of his community as he and other became active in the public relations and community experiences of Pathways.

GATHERING THE STAKEHOLDERS

In Chapter 3, we discussed how to begin the implementation process by gathering a committee of stakeholders. It is at this point that your public relations begins. All of your stakeholders have to be valued from the start; you need to listen to every one of them address their concerns. Do not forget from the start, when making decisions that affect students, *primary stakeholders must be the students themselves.* Everything that we decide and do in the school system should reflect back to two questions, "Is this good for students?" and "How will it affect their learning and developmental growth as people?" Many times we talk about what we think is best for students, but we forget to ask them what they need and what they think would be best. One of the reasons that Pathways works so well as an avenue for secondary school reform is because it is student based and student oriented. The students become the center of the school universe, and then when they are put in charge of their plans, they become the center of their own universe.

This is key. Several student representatives need to be placed on your committee because it is their testimony that will truly affect many adults. Students on your Pathways team will then serve as the ambassadors for the program; their buy-in to what is going to happen and why is critical. When selecting students for this panel, you need representation from all aspects of the student body, not just the socially or academically gifted. Here are some suggestions for deciding who these students will be. Keep in mind that this handful of students is really the nucleus for public relations among your student body.

- Include at least one student from each grade level.
- Include a student who does well academically.
- Include an athlete or students interested in a variety of extracurricular activities and leadership roles.
- Include two or three students who are capable but have "checked out" because school doesn't meet their needs.
- Include students interested in technical or trade careers.
- Include a student with special needs.

Obviously one student may fulfill two or three categories, and probably you want no more than a handful (five or six) on your committee to start. Listening to their needs and their desires as your district designs the program will make a huge difference.

> *When students see that they truly have input in what is being done and how, and that the changes are for and about them, their buy-in will follow naturally.*

As you select who the rest of your committee of stakeholders will include, you are also selecting the rest of your public relations team. It is important to choose a representative from every area, including administrators, counselor(s), teachers, community members, and parents who are respected and listened to by all strata of your community. In addition, you need to include veteran faculty members as well as beginning teachers. Remember, your team members will make up your primary spokespeople.

> *Your team's sincere belief that this is best for the students in your district is what will propel your program forward.*

THE PUBLIC RELATIONS STRATEGY

From the beginning, selling the changes that need to take place in your high school will be an exercise in the art of persuasion. As a committee you must collaborate on how to streamline your plan to meet the needs of your school and community. It is necessary to present your model in a variety of places and a variety of ways. There will be informal opportunities (such as in the local coffee shop, talking with senior citizens and the custodians on coffee break), more formal opportunities (such as speaking to a parent group, student council meeting, or curriculum council), and then very formal opportunities (such as speaking to the school board or local technical-school board). As your public relations spokespeople approach these situations, they must be able to describe how Pathways will meet the needs of the audience whom they are addressing. No matter whom they are talking to, there are four basic questions that should be answered for every single group, from that group's point of view:

- Why is this good for students?
- What is in it for me?
- How can I help?
- What will the challenges be—for me, for the school, for the students?

In addition, every time your spokespeople speak, they need to be armed with all of the information they will need. We suggest you make a handout they can use when sharing with each group. It should include information about how you plan to insert the Pathways coursework and where you are planning to embed it in curricula, information about the flexible schedule(s) you are considering, Web sites of Pathways schools, and phone numbers of districts already involved in the Collaborative Model. When possible, also include where funding or academic support may come from for fields trips, professional development, and technology.

Whenever possible, try to conduct site visits to schools that are in the later stages of change in the Pathways Model process. All your stakeholders will see what a positive difference it can make and what role they will need to play in the process to make it happen at your school.

> *It is crucial that your core committee be well educated about Pathways and flexible scheduling issues because it will be their job to educate the rest of your district, your students, and the community.*

TALKING TO PARENTS

Parents have both the most to gain and the most to lose when your district moves to a Pathways system. They gain focused students who are better acquainted with their own special skills, talents, and interests, and also students with plans for what training they need. Pathways can offer peace of mind to parents about their children's futures. What is difficult for some parents, however, is giving up control of a child's plan. In some instances, parents have already decided what their child is going to do; when the student explores the training, skills, and work environment for that carrer, he or she may decide it is not a match and wish to choose something else. We have seen this happen on several occasions. So when speaking to parents it is important to stress the flexibility of the plan and all of the ways that parents can be involved in developing the plan and giving input to their children. Before the first course begins, it is important to address the parent group and explain why the change is needed, how it will be better for their children, and what will be involved in the change. Once you get buy-in from a few parents, they can become some of your best assets in the public relations campaign to other parents.

From the start of the Pathways program, parents can be made more comfortable by being included and involved in the Freshman Explorations course. It is critical that your Freshman Explorations teachers make a concerted effort to be in contact with parents on a regular basis. This can be done through a Web page or a biweekly or monthly newsletter. Equally important is that your parents be involved in your students' explorations and experiences. Make sure you invite parents on the field trips, to be guest speakers on their careers, or to help with special occasions such as the Pathways Selection Party. Make sure parents know when their children are going to make Pathways decisions and how important parental input and help with these decisions will be (at all four levels).

Table 12.1 features sample responses to parents for the four key questions they will have.

TALKING TO STUDENTS

Students are of course the pivotal point of everything you are doing to change and improve the school. The culture and climate of the school will not completely change until the last class who remembers "the old way" is gone. Even so, students can see from the start that the Pathways system has many positive aspects for them. Often students may be vocally negative at first because, just as it is for adults, change is scary. Add to that the fact that teachers are also becoming Pathways teachers for the first time, and the first couple of years can be a tough go for everyone. Therefore, although it is important to listen to your student population from the start, it is also important not to get too nervous when not all students are happy. Much of the coursework requires a teaming and life-skill focus that students are not used to. The Pathways classes will stretch them in new ways that are sometimes uncomfortable but nonetheless necessary.

We have found that the best way to do public relations for students is student to student, and this is why students must be included from the start—in the decision-making process, on the site visits, and in the streamlining of the model. Students who are already on a flexible schedule can easily explain the advantages and discuss the disadvantages with students from your district. Very effective for both parents and students is to have a student panel from a Collaborative school come and talk about their experiences. When both parents and students hear of the wonderfully wide range of opportunity there is for students in a Pathways school, they are completely amazed.

Public relations for students is an ongoing process, and eventually your older students will be your best representatives for the younger ones. When

Table 12.1 Responses to Parents' Questions About Pathways

Why is this good for kids?

Pathways is good for kids because it allows them to begin exploring and experiencing a wide variety of career options while studying in high school. Students become the owner of their individual plans. This makes all of their coursework more relevant, gives them the opportunity to view related skills and workplaces, and lets them eliminate those Pathways that are not a good match for them. It is a system in which every student has access to the practice of teaming, problem-solving, conflict-resolution, and decision-making skills they will need, no matter what postsecondary plan they decide to pursue.

What's in it for me?

Students will have the opportunity to use a step-by-step system that lets them begin a career process in high school rather than doing this exploration in college in a more haphazard fashion and at substantial cost while parents pay tuition.

How can I help?

There are many ways for parents to be involved in the Pathways system. It is important for you to support your student as he or she searches for chat and interview partners. We also are always looking for parents to speak, attend field trips, and help in the Pathways classroom. Finally, at the end of each Pathways course, your student will be making an important decision, and your input and guidance are absolutely needed.

We also need parents and the parent organization to be collaborative partners in finding creative ways to fund field trips, professional development for teachers, and new technology.

What will the challenges be?

One challenge will be to allow your children to explore and to let them be in charge of the plan. Another challenge will be to support your school as it goes through this four-year change process, realizing that it takes time for everyone to adjust to a different or more flexible scheduling or embedment system. Make sure that you communicate concerns with your school and with the Pathways team, and be quick to offer help when you see that your time and talents can make a difference.

---

schools have their freshman orientation, inviting older students to talk about what new students can expect in high school and from the Pathways philosophy will be crucial. Include some sort of a slide show, video, or live presentation, for parents and students alike, that helps to educate them on what Pathways involves for the student. Throughout the change process, it is important that the Pathways team listens to the student body (and makes adjustments as necessary), both through student government and from student opinion in Pathways classes. Table 12.2 offers sample responses to four important questions as you talk to your student body.

> *In many of our schools, the most powerful part of any presentation is when students speak about why Pathways is needed and why what is currently being done is not working.*

Table 12.2 Responses to Students' Questions About Pathways

Why is this good for kids?

Pathways will be good for you and your classmates because it will put you "in the driver's seat." This is good for you because *you* are in charge but will have the support and help of your school, your parents, the community, and local postsecondary institutions. Pathways will allow you to have a focus so that you know how and why the things you are studying in high school can be important to you later. You will also have the chance to practice the life skills you will need for any career area, skills that were not previously included in the school curriculum.

What's in it for me?

You will be making important decisions about your own life, but you will be given many chances to explore and learn at each step of the way. In your freshman year, you will decide on a Pathway; in your sophomore year, you will select the focus of your internship or Cluster or choose to pursue skill training; in your junior year, you will narrow your Cluster or possibly your career field; and as a senior, you will narrow down your postsecondary plans.

How can I help?

You can help by keeping an open mind and trying hard in your new Pathways courses. In addition, taking your opportunities in the community seriously will make a difference for you. Careful observation of skills and workplaces from the start of your freshman year on will be important. Open communication with your school and teachers about how they can help you as you narrow your postsecondary plan is equally important.

What will the challenges be?

If your school is going to a new, more flexible schedule or you are having new coursework embedded in a class that is already required, you need to view this as an opportunity for you to grow rather than as a negative change. Although anything new has some drawbacks, it has many plusses too, and this is particularly true of the Pathways system. It will be important for you to put forth your best effort in your new coursework and help the teachers rather than sabotage them. Looking at change as a glass that is half full rather than half empty will be important.

TALKING TO THE SCHOOL COMMUNITY

From the start, your entire school community needs to be brought on board as you begin this ambitious endeavor. Everyone involved with the school on a day-to-day basis must realize how Pathways will affect their job, the climate of the school, and the way the school will relate to the community. For example, there will be more visitors in the building on a regular basis; more students will be out of the building on field trips, projects, and shadows or placements; and other stakeholders will be directly involved in student projects and explorations.

School Board and Administration

Early on, your school board must be involved in the process and updated on a regular basis. That is why it is important to have two or three board members on your Pathways committee so that they can visit other schools and see Pathways function firsthand. It is critical that board members see what this means for students, so as to be reassured that there are creative ways the district can afford to fund and implement the new program. Board member representatives will play an important role in working with other board members and with your community. Equally important is that your team makes certain everyone on the board has adequate information and background on Pathways and how it can improve the high school. Setting up the Pathways system is just the beginning of the support you will need from your school board and administration, however. You will need to provide Pathways updates to the board on a regular basis.

Obviously, support from administrators—building principals and assistants as well as the superintendent—is equally imperative. Schools where building principals understand the Pathways system and the positive impact it

> *Once your district becomes a board-approved Pathways school district, public relations endeavors will be more important than ever.*

will have on their student body in terms of classroom behavior, engagement, and attendance are the first to embrace the Collaborative Pathways Model. Conversely, we have found that when principals only give surface support to Pathways, the process takes much longer and will not be completed at a deeper level. Support can come in many ways: offering flexibility in allowing field trips and projects, providing as many professional development opportunities as possible, and focusing on the needs of the faculty as each level of Pathways is implemented. From a public relations standpoint, the principal is the Pathways figurehead who is on the front lines, continually helping to educate staff, parents, and the community on why we need Pathways in the district and how it works. A supportive superintendent will also serve as the district spokesperson on Pathways and keep the momentum going by continually emphasizing the importance of the Pathways philosophy to the district and the community. This is an important public relations link because it is only with a true commitment from the entire district that Pathways can continue to move forward as each level is implemented. Table 12.3 offers responses to four important questions for administrators and school boards.

Counselors

As reflected in Chapter 5, counselors are one of the biggest winners among all of the stakeholders. Over the past several years, the counselor's job has taken on more and more duties to the point that no counselor can ever do all the things he or she may want and need to do for students. The Collaborative Pathways Model allows counselors systematic access to students at each of the four levels of their high school development. When counselors become a collaborative partner with the classroom teachers and the administration, they have more time to work directly with students. It is in school districts where the counselors team with Pathways stakeholders that the greatest strides have

Table 12.3 Responses to Administrator's and School Board's Questions About Pathways

Why is this good for kids?
The Pathways model helps students become self-managing and at the same time gives focus and relevance to students' high school experience. It is a system for all students and will affect our high school in a very positive fashion.

What's in it for me?
Our students will become better engaged in the classroom, attendance will go up, discipline referrals will go down, and we will have fewer dropouts. Our school will become a better place for learning. We will have a better system of technology integration. Our students will not only be prepared for the postsecondary world but will have a plan for what to study when they reach it. Because of positive community experiences, more students will elect to stay in the community.

How can I help?
Support is needed for those on the front line of these changes, particularly the counselors and teachers who step out of the traditional mode to deliver the new coursework. We need you to be a positive force in the parent and work community and to serve as liaisons for the program. As much as possible, we need your support in terms of funding and policies.

What will the challenges be?
There will be two large challenges. The first will be to remain steadfast in your belief that this is good for the kids of our district even though many who are frightened of change will doggedly fight all reform. The second challenge will be for you to be creative in finding positive ways to support your staff, students, and parents as they become your collaborative partners. For school boards and administrators, the toughest part of this model is giving up total control of the school and, instead, collaborating with the "whole village," allowing other stakeholders partnership status.

---

been made. Make sure counselors feel included and valued, because their role is essential to Pathways success. Table 12.4 provides responses to four questions counselors may have about Pathways.

Teachers

Pathways change can begin with a small nucleus of teachers, but it must include one or two veterans who believe in student-centered education. They must be willing to take risks and make changes in their teaching style to reach students more effectively. In Chapter 11, we discussed how to go about obtaining teacher buy-in. In terms of public relations, it is important to explain that instead of losing students in higher level and elective classes, more students will consciously choose those courses. In addition, students will be more interested and engaged in the classroom, and the buy-in and commitment to Pathways will be a natural and gradual process. Where the challenge comes for some teachers is in terms of change. Many of the more veteran teachers are so comfortable in their current scheduling venue and are so used to being the "giver of

Table 12.4 Responses to Counselors' Questions About Pathways

Why is this good for kids?

This will be good for kids because all students will get to develop a future plan based on information about themselves and on systematic exploration. No longer will college or military be *the* plan but only part of the plan for the student's overall goal. Students will have access to a variety of life skills of which counselors are traditionally in charge but never manage to oversee completely. Now, instead of students simply being giving information on these skills, they will continually have opportunities to practice them throughout the four years of high school.

What's in it for me?

Pathways offers counselors a system to reach all students. As a counselor, you will be more able to do what you are trained for: provide a support system and a curriculum that develops personal and social skills to all students. It also allows counselors to lay the groundwork for all stakeholders to work together to support that system.

How can I help?

You can support your faculty and the students by getting professional development for yourself and other staff members; by serving as a liaison to the community in terms of contacts for site visits, job shadows, and internships; and by providing support and help for the counseling strand of the program. In addition, you will need to serve as coordinator of the testing, data collection, Educational Development Plans, and portfolio development.

What will the challenges be?

Your challenge will be the same as that of administrators: to give up the absolute control of all counseling activities (which is truly more than any one person can oversee) and to share these duties with faculty members and students by collaborating with them. You need to be a visible and positive force in the community even during those tough implementation years when you are overcoming a variety of obstacles. A key component of your challenge will be dealing with the flexible scheduling necessary to make Pathways work.

---

information" that shifting schedules and giving students the responsibility for their own learning is a tough change. Classrooms go from orderly and quiet to student-oriented and noisy. Also difficult for seasoned teachers who have not received professional development or taken college-level coursework recently is the heavy emphasis on technology and on brain-based learning. These obstacles can be overcome by continual emphasis and opportunity given by the administration on focused professional development, and by their listening to what the teachers need most in order to make a gradual shift to a Pathways High School. When teachers experience student learning that is much more focused, combined with getting active support from parents and community members, they are more willing to diversify their teaching style and adjust to a

> *In the end, what will sell teachers on Pathways is the fact that it is a systematic exposure for all students and that it is not an add-on.*

Table 12.5 Responses to Teachers' Questions About Pathways

Why is this good for kids?

Collaborative Pathways is good for kids because it puts them in charge of their learning and their career plan. Students learn and practice important life skills, learn important information about themselves, and match these to possible career choices. Students then get to see these life skills in use in real workplaces. It makes their education relevant and focused. They will no longer ask, "Why do I need this class?" They will know why. All of this is done while maintaining academic rigor.

What's in it for me?

You will have students who are engaged and focused. They will see your content in a new light. Their projects will take on new levels of sophistication and meaning. Your students will become self-managing. Most of all, what is really in it for you is the fact that you truly make a difference for every student as you help each one streamline his or her plan.

How can I help?

One way you can help is by moving away from a traditional teaching style and toward a facilitated learning style. Give opportunities for students to practice teaming, problem solving, time and stress management, and conflict resolution while learning subject matter skills and knowledge. Go on several job shadows to learn about interesting careers within your field. Seek as much professional development as possible in the area of brain research, and implement its recommendations in your classroom. Take time to gather information about careers in your field, foster contacts for some of these careers, and seek out information about training for careers in your area.

What will the challenges be?

Your challenge is twofold. It is important to maintain academic rigor and, at the same time, to teach to a variety of learning styles and multiple intelligences. In addition, you need to meet all students individually at the point they have reached in their plan and help them to move forward. Obtaining knowledge about how your subject area is used in the workplace and what technologies go along with it is critical, so you will need to stay current by going on field trips and participating in shadowing experiences on a continual basis.

---

more flexible schedule. It also helps that no new standards and benchmarks are added to their curriculum, but instead delivery of some units may change by using Pathways activities. Table 12.5 offers responses to four questions teachers may ask.

Staff

Many times administrators do not realize that when a major new program or philosophy is introduced, one important effect it has is on those silent warriors, the members of the support staff, who are often forgotten in the shuffle. The support staff needs to be included in the Pathways philosophy from the beginning because they are going to be one of the first links with your students' Pathways emphasis. They will need to be part of the process as students reach

each level. Freshman students will wander the halls looking for a staff member who might have time to chat with them, a secretary may be asked if she can be shadowed for a day by a Sophomore Selections student, a Junior Judgments student may want to do an internship with the technology coordinator, and perhaps an accounting student in Senior Transitions will want to base his senior project on part of the school budget. Cooks will have to adjust menus on field trip days and come up with a system of providing meals to the many guests who come to tour the building. When students are working on a service learning project, they may want to "pick the brain" of the custodians as they try to solve the problem of leaky drinking fountains in the hallway or rebuild a broken sofa in one of the classrooms. Often the support staff is the first to see the changes that come with the Pathways philosophy: more respect for school property and more respect toward each other. It is important to include your staff in all the phases of professional development. When the rest of the staff is taking the selected personality profile your students are using, make sure the support staff is included as well. We highly recommend the inclusion of a support staff member on your committee because he or she can become your public relations link back to the rest of the staff and community. When students begin collaborating with staff for the first time, the staff will be pleased and impressed. Table 12.6 offers responses to four questions your support staff may ask of you.

TALKING TO COMMUNITY MEMBERS

In Chapter 13, we closely examine the relationship of the community to the Collaborative Pathways High School and talk about a variety of ways that community members (and parents) can become involved in the school and in the students' individual plans. Community members have much to gain from a Collaborative Model. In the past we have always asked for the help of the community but have not had a system by which they could clearly see what roles they could play and when or how they could make an ongoing, systematic difference. Almost every community member who comes to visit as a speaker, or gives an intensive interview, or becomes involved in hosting students says, "I wish my high school had had a program like this. It would have helped me to save time in training," or "to train for a different career," or "to know myself better," and so on.

Employers recognize right away that students who are in the community settings on a regular basis are much more likely to stay in the area or come back once they have been trained. They also realize that many of these students will one day be their employees, and the better versed students are in teaming, conflict resolution, and other life skills, the better trained the future employee pool will be. In addition, they realize that if students see what they do, how they do it, and what technology they use, they will be better trained and focused employees some day. Just like teachers and support staff, employers want to make a difference. Collaborative Pathways gives them the chance to do just that. From a public relations standpoint, selling Pathways to the community is much easier than selling it to staff; there are so many levels of involvement available and community members see the personal benefits. An important

Table 12.6 Responses to Support Staff Members' Questions About Pathways

Why is this good for kids?

Pathways puts kids in charge of their learning and teaches them important life skills. It gives them a better base for what happens after they graduate so they will know what they want to do and how to go about getting the schooling or training they need.

What's in it for me?

Students who are learning and practicing more life skills will be more respectful of each other, of their elders, and of school property. The school climate will drastically improve. Students will begin to view you as another avenue to gain information and experience for their plans.

How can I help?

You can help by being open and patient with students. Take the time to chat with them about your career and answer their questions about problem solving, time management, and so on. Be helpful and flexible when teachers are trying to create new learning environments and when they are working to give students a wide variety of community experiences. Be open to having students interview you, shadow you, and possibly be your intern.

What will the challenges be?

The school will be going through many changes, and this may affect parts of your day-to-day job, for example, because of changes to classroom furniture and room setup. It may be a little tougher to clean, or attendance may be harder to take, because of field trips and internships, and there may be extra work because of continual guests and visitors to your school. When your job is different or more difficult, try to remember that you are helping to make a difference for these kids because they will be better focused and better able to transition to the next part of the plan. Remember that you are an important part of the high school team and of student success.

---

word of caution: public relations with the community is an ongoing process in which all of your Pathways teachers and students will be involved every time they make a connection, go to a job site, or ask an employer to help. Table 12.7 offers responses to four questions community members may ask.

WORKING WITH TECHNICAL CENTERS AND ACADEMIC SOURCES

An important group you will need to talk to, and connect with, are the members of your career technical training centers and key postsecondary sources. In our state, our training centers are designed primarily for 11th- and 12th-grade students and have a great deal to gain from a Pathways philosophy. Most technical training centers are ahead of the traditional high school because they cluster their training programs and make significant connections to business and industry; however, they have not always aligned themselves well with the traditional, academically focused high schools. In other words, technical centers have

Table 12.7 Responses to Community Members' Questions About Pathways

Why is this good for kids?

Pathways is good for kids because by being involved with the community throughout their four years of high school, they will have a more secure base and find positive role models for their lives. In addition, they will see how subject matter is applied, how life skills are used, and what training and technology are needed for a variety of careers.

What's in it for me?

You will eventually have employees from the area who have better life skills—including time and self-management, problem solving, conflict resolution, and assertiveness training. As you host students, you will be able to select those who may eventually fit into your business to train as interns or utilize in part-time positions. Eventually, more students will feel deeply connected to our community and stay in the area. You will also be able to pass on your knowledge and wisdom to another generation, and that feels great.

How can I help?

You can help by selecting a level of commitment you are comfortable with and by offering your time and expertise through interacting with students, hosting visits and internships, helping with senior projects, and so on.

What will the challenges be?

One challenge is finding a balance that you are comfortable with as an employer. For some employers, having a one-afternoon site visit is preferable to proctoring or mentoring an older student on a day-to-day basis for several weeks. Other community members find it easier to do an intensive interview for a group of several students. Probably the largest challenge will be to make sure your relationship with the district is balanced and reciprocal.

---

traditionally taken the students who were not planning to go on to college but who wanted, instead, to go directly into on-the-job training or trade sites. With Pathways, the door is open for more students to experience technical career programs on their career ladder. For example, a student interested in an architectural degree would gain from taking a drafting program; a student interested in automotive engineering would gain from an auto mechanics course. With the new types of flexible scheduling available, students can afford to take their college prep coursework and experience a career and technical program. Also, students who choose to go into the trades benefit significantly because they are more focused on their plan and make better decisions as to what trade is best for them. This type of self-directed learner benefits career centers as well as postsecondary institutions.

The same can be said for our postsecondary partners. They have much to gain from students who know why they are attending their school and what they want to achieve. They gain from students completing their programs and finding jobs in their field. It is important that these people are a part of your team because they are essential to a smooth transition for students. Once they understand how your system will work, they can work that to their advantage. Showing students their programs by using the same Pathways system and

Table 12.8 Responses to Technical Center and Academic Sources Questions About Pathways

Why is this good for kids?

Students will understand why they are going to your site and what they are trying to accomplish. They will enter with the necessary skills they will need to be successful and the motivation needed to complete their plan.

What's in it for me?

More focused students! Plus, more students interested in your programs and in going on to and completing postsecondary options.

How can I help?

Align your programs with our school's Pathways Model so that students understand how they fit together. Use our common language with students. Be there and involved in the development of their plans and serve as mentors and senior panel participants.

What will the challenges be?

Some people think centers and colleges gain by students not knowing what they want and by their exploring options on their sites. This is not true; statistics show that more students drop out of postsecondary schools within the first two years because of indecision and lack of skills. The challenge is to understand the benefits of the system for students and your institution and to capitalize on those benefits.

---

career ladders will help student see the continuous flow from high school to tech school to postsecondary options, and this is what we want—a continuous flow for students from one educational phase to another. Table 12.8 features responses to questions your technical center and postsecondary partners may ask.

MYTHS ABOUT PATHWAYS

As your committee members speak to a variety of groups and individuals, they will find positive support from those who see how good this system can be for students. At the same time, those who are fearful of change or are comfortable with the status quo will be less receptive. From our speaking and public relations events, we have found that there are three basic myths all audiences bring up. These myths (with small variations of theme) are as follows.

Myth 1. In a Pathways High School, students do not have the opportunity to take a variety of coursework, and the program lacks the academic rigor needed to provide a well-rounded education. In other words, liberal arts are discouraged.

Myth 2. The Pathways Model is just a system of tracking students for jobs. In addition, students will not be lifelong learners, but will focus only on materials related to their careers.

Myth 3. High school students are too young to be making life decisions.

Table 12.9 offers possible answers to each of these myths.

Table 12.9 Responses to the Three Myths

Myth 1. Students do not have the opportunity to take a variety of coursework and the program lacks academic rigor.

The truth is actually the opposite. Students' plans make it much more likely that they will take high level courses and related electives. Also, because Pathways schools often feature flexible scheduling of some sort, they are more likely to offer more room in students' schedules for exploration of a wide variety of coursework related both to student interests and to possible career choices.

When responding to this question, remind your audience that in Freshman Explorations every student spends a long time exploring his or her interests and aptitudes. Most likely the career will somehow connect to students' personal interests, either directly or indirectly. In addition, as more time opens in students' schedules, they can explore a wider variety of coursework, even in small schools, because of dual-enroll, virtual high school, and skill center and training opportunities. Many times when visiting workplaces, students gain new ideas about subject areas that may interest them, or they have a new or indirect connection to the career they are observing. When students visit with employees and employers, they will often stress that gaining a wide and balanced background will be extremely helpful for their field.

Myth 2. Pathways is just another system of tracking students for jobs.

In a Pathways High School, students are actually much less likely to be tracked. Students are often put in Pathways classes that are Pathway specific, in which a wide variety of academic levels will work together and which will include students who are looking at careers all the way up and down the ladder (from those simply requiring a diploma all the way up to careers in a Pathway or Cluster that require a doctorate). In addition, with the flexible scheduling of most Pathways High Schools, you will find many more students taking career technical work and college-bound courses. More students in a Pathways school see the need for both components because they hear this over and over again from teachers, counselors, and community members.

Myth 3. High School students are too young to be making life decisions.

High school students make life-altering decisions all the time—some of them much more risky than the choice of career path. *A career focus will actually help them to be involved in less risky behavior because they can visualize their futures.* In terms of career focus, what people who believe this argument forget is that high school students are already required to decide their next step after high school. We are not asking for any decision that they are not required to make already; we are just asking them to make decisions one step at a time, as they are given information for each step, and breaking down the process for them. How can you decide to pursue the military, technical training, or college if you do not have a focus for your studies? Many postsecondary institutions communicate to students (and parents) that they don't need to make a career choice until their junior or senior year of college. One factor that leads to students dropping out during their freshman year at college is that they are taking "required" coursework, not knowing how it will be relevant, when they will use it, or why they are there in the first place.

When answering this question, it is also important to remind your audience that students in a Collaborative Pathways High School are learning goal setting and decision making as a step-by-step process. Refer them to the scaffold, and show them how only one step is required each year and how, throughout each Pathways class, students are given opportunities and skills to ensure they will be ready to make each decision with the help of their individual village (parents and relatives, teachers, counselors, and community members). With "village" support, they will be ready for each step.

Table 12.10 Public Relations Considerations for the First Five Years

Design and Planning	Focus: • Why do we need Career Pathways? • Why is the Collaborative Model a good one for us? • How can we streamline it to fit our needs? • What kind of flexible scheduling or embedment system would be best for our district? • How can we compensate for any domino effects?
Freshman Explorations	Focus: • How is each part of this curriculum valuable? • How can we communicate well with the community and parents so that we remain a collaborative team? • How can we make this curriculum possible within our district? • How will we solve problems with this course when it arrives? • How can we include the field trips? • How will we make sure that all the parts of the "village" get educated for their roles?
Sophomore Selections	Focus: • How does the sophomore level connect to the freshman level and why? • How do community roles change for the sophomore level? • Are we going to make this course Pathway-specific sections and if so, how can we do that? • How are we going to handle students who want to make a Pathway change? • How will we help students who move into our district and have not had a Freshman Explorations class? • How are we going to implement the job-shadowing component? • What do we need to do at the end of Sophomore Selections to get ready for Junior Judgments?
Junior Judgments	Focus: • How do we design a "sales presentation" for employers to explain to them why their involvement in internships is a win–win situation? • How do we make certain that employer time for Junior Judgments does not conflict with Freshman Explorations and Sophomore Selections opportunities? • What alternatives will we give students who cannot be placed in their first choice or who need more time to explore before they are ready for an internship? • How do we make our internship hosts feel appreciated and valued? • How do we make sure we are not overusing some of our community members (e.g., make sure we are not asking for site visits, shadows, and internships all at the same time)?

(Continued)

Table 12.10 (Continued)

	• How do we make certain students have time to evaluate their junior experience adequately, set up ideas for their senior projects, and then transition to the senior level? • How do we explain to students and the community what mentors are, who they should be, and how they can help?
Senior Transitions	Focus: • How do we help our entire village see the difference between capstone projects and the more traditional senior projects? • How are we going to recruit help for our students in the four required elements of their project: academics, counseling, technology, and community? • What will our presentation day(s) look like and how will we get the help we need? • How do we help those students who need more exploration before selecting their Cluster or career focus integrate their needs into their capstone projects? • How will we deal with transportation and possible funding issues? • What will our Pathways graduation look like?

When doing public relations, there will always be those who say "I can't," or "This won't work." Remember that you are planting seeds and that some will sprout and some will not.

THE ONGOING PUBLIC RELATIONS MISSION

Although public relations begins at the moment your Pathways committee expresses a desire to enhance your high school, it will be an ongoing and never-ending process. One bit of comfort is the fact that by using a five-year implementation process, it can be done one step at a time. Also, as each level is added and streamlined, you add more people—students, parents, administrators, community members, counselors, and staff—to your arsenal of believers, and therefore to your public relations team. As you implement the levels of your program, your public relations push for each year will change. Table 12.10 features a time line of what public relation questions may need to be considered and answered for your district during the first five years.

As you are implementing each year, your team will also need to be answering questions—for the team, for the new level planners, for the community, and for the next level students. This means that while you are answering the questions for your "village" during the year the implementation takes place, you are also making decisions and arrangements for the next year of implementation.

Public relations is an ongoing process and truly an exercise in what we are trying to teach our students—good listening, communication, conflict-resolution, problem-solving, and decision-making skills. Keeping the public informed and included, valuing and appreciating everyone who helps, and using an inclusive style of decision making will make your public relations more effective and easier. Because this Collaborative Pathways Model is all about students and because the system is so good for students, sincerity and enthusiasm will bring you a long way when speaking to all the stakeholders in your "village."

IN REVIEW

- When planning your public relations campaign, remember that you must include all of your stakeholders but that your primary stakeholder is the student.
- Your public relations begins at the moment the desire to change your school is made known.
- All stakeholders must be represented in your Pathways committee so that they can be educated in the Pathways process via their respective representatives.
- Stakeholders include parents, students, the school community (school board and administration, counselors, teachers, staff, and counselors), the larger community, and academic sources and technology centers.
- Your public relations team needs to have answers to these four questions for each stakeholder: (1) Why is this good for kids? (2) What is in it for me? (3) How can I help? (4) What will the challenges be?
- Your public relations team needs to be able to respond to the three key myths about Pathways. The Myths are the following: (1) Pathways does not offer enough variety and balance for a well-rounded education. (2) Pathways is just another form of tracking. (3) High school students are too young to be making these decisions.
- Public relations is an ongoing mission, and as you implement each new year, you need to prepare answers for your entire "village" about the next level of implementation.
- Sincerity, enthusiasm, and the fact that this program is for and about students will propel your public relations positively forward.

Chapter Thirteen

The School Community

The True Classroom of Pathways

SCENARIO: HANNAH'S STORY

The community is the final pillar in our model. *The Collaborative Model cannot be truly successful without a solid community process.* For you to gain a true understanding of how important the community process is to a Collaborative Pathways High School, we would like to tell you a student's true story. Her name is Hannah, and her experience will bring home to you how serious our work with students can be.

Hannah was an exceptional student. She ranked in the top of her class in a very large urban high school, which had an excellent reputation for academics. The high school also hosted several academies within the school, one of which was a health and medical Pathway academy. Hannah scored very highly in math and science, and was encouraged to join the health academy. She was also extremely involved in sports and was a good athlete. Hannah's counselors, parents, and teachers worked with Hannah to develop a good plan. They combined her high academic skills, her love for sports, and her aptitude in math and science to create a plan for Hannah to work in sports medicine. In her career ladder she would begin at a four-year college in physical therapy and later move on to a higher degree in the medical field. Her work would be centered on working with injured athletes. Everyone was excited about the plan.

Hannah finished her senior year with honors in both academics and sports. She had taken several advanced placement classes, earning college credits; her high marks in advanced science and math courses allowed her to be accepted into one of the most prestigious universities in her state.

According to all we have been professing, this is exactly what we want for all students. The plan went amiss, however. Something happened during Hannah's freshman year at the university. She was injured and was sent to physical therapy. *She hated it.* So, what did Hannah do? Well you might assume that she changed her major or that she found aspects of the career to which she could adjust. No, instead Hannah dropped out of school. Why? Because the stakes were too high. The conflict and pressure was just too much for her to handle. She was never quite sure about this medical "thing," but that was what everyone else was telling her "matched" her skills and interests; being an all A student, she believed what the system told her. Talking to Hannah, the most important question was, "Well Hannah, what do *you* like to do?" After pondering for a few minutes, she replied that while she was at school, she had worked in a clothing store and had really enjoyed helping customers find the "right outfit." Then she added that she didn't think there was much of a living in that. Well, quite the contrary—there is the entire business Pathway with careers in fashion merchandising and retail.

So, what went wrong with Hannah's plan? She had good counseling—she had taken interest and aptitude tests, she had been given achievement tests, focused scheduling, and good postsecondary planning. She had excellent academic training—she had rigorous and challenging curriculum, advanced classes, and coursework focused on her future course of study in the health sciences. On top of that, she had involved and caring parents. What was missing? The community process! Hannah did not know what physical therapy looked like, smelled like, felt like, or involved. She had no "spatial" understanding of her path through real-life experiences. She had never "chatted" with healthcare workers or interviewed health professionals. She had never done a job shadow or an internship, nor had she completed a senior project to connect her studies with the actual field she was entering. Whatever she had imagined in her mind was the only reality she had.

We must remember that our students have little life experience. We must also remember what we have learned from brain research and the brain's need to actually experience the environment from which it is learning. Hannah gave up because we put many important changes in motion (self-exploration, a Pathway, focused curricula, and parental involvement) to give her an advantage in the competitive professional world, but we forgot to expose her to that reality. No one ever thought they would be hurting Hannah or other students. We must look at the total picture. *Without the community, students are getting a false image of what is out there.* It is our responsibility as educators to be sure they understand the world outside the classroom.

Fortunately, Hannah's story has a happy ending. With guidance she decided to transfer to a community college to study business, where she will have the opportunity to study in Paris (a great place for fashion). After finishing at the community college, she will be transferring to a four-year college in retailing. She currently works at a dress boutique and loves it. *She knows she fits in her path because she fits into the environment.*

Working the community into the Pathways process is not as difficult as most educators think. This is one area most educators do not feel comfortable in and in which they are more likely to give less than 100 percent. Yet our communities are eager to be a part of educating students—let's face it, our students will become their employees one day. To facilitate the process, you must give community members specific roles that they can fulfill for students and teachers. Table 13.1 offers a list of roles, which we have integrated into the four-year Pathways process. Figure 13.1 depicts the community's role in a visual format. Now, let's further examine each part of the community's involvement in Collaborative Pathways High Schools.

INVOLVING THE COMMUNITY

In a Collaborative Pathways High School, there is no separation between school and "real life" because the community is a continual part of the students' daily learning. In a Pathways High School, from the start of Freshman Explorations until graduation, students know that the adults around them are a resource waiting to be tapped. At the same time, the community takes ownership of the education for their district because they are continually in and out of the building, mentoring and advising students in the classroom and the workplace, cheering the students on as they complete one successful rung after another on their personal ladders to success. What follows is a description of the countless ways in which community members can be involved in the Collaborative Pathways High School.

Focus of Guest Visits

Beginning freshman year, there is a wealth of opportunities for community members to come to school and be guest speakers in the classroom. In Freshman Explorations at the county's pilot high school, we generally have between 25 and 35 guests in the classroom throughout the year. These guests tend to fall into three general categories:

1. Guest speakers with particular expertise that focuses on a particular assignment or integrated project

2. Short chat visits in which people from a variety of occupations within the Pathway on which we are currently focusing come and talk about their fields

3. Community in partnership visits in which community leaders come help with a special lesson or come as a speaker for a special occasion

When speakers come to support a particular integrated project, they generally stay for the entire class period. Speakers who come to visit about careers usually stay for about half an hour per class, and because we know how valuable their time is, we schedule them at the end of one class and the beginning of another; this way, by visiting for one hour, they have made contact with approximately 60 students. Once in awhile, we also have community members who partner with the classroom teachers for special teaming and self-management

Table 13.1 The Role of the Community in the Pathways Model

Role	Definition	Proposed Year
Chat and interview partners	Employees from a wide variety of fields who are willing to be open and honest about their careers	Freshman/Sophomore
Guest speakers	Career-oriented employees comfortable in a classroom setting	Freshman/Sophomore
Special occasion support guests	Community members willing to be involved in special activities, usually as speakers	Freshman/Sophomore
Site visit hosts	Local businesses willing to host students for a tour of their facilities and to display the wide variety of career opportunities available within their business	Freshman/Sophomore
Job shadowing hosts	Community members and businesses willing to allow students to "shadow" them for a half or whole day	Sophomore
Service learning hosts	Community members and businesses willing to provide community service experiences (and at times supervision) for local students.	Junior/Senior
Advisory committee members	Members of a focused Pathway field who evaluate and give advice to students as they streamline their senior projects (and their overall plans)	Junior/Senior
Internship and co-op sites	Employers willing to host unpaid and paid co-ops so students can be exposed to the work environment	Junior/Senior
Educational partners	Community members who are willing to partner with teachers in the instructional process, giving their particular expertise to a topic or integrated unit	All Years
Senior project associates and evaluation team	Business and community members, along with academic partners in the Pathway-specific field, that assist in the development of senior projects or sit as a review committee for senior projects in that specified Pathway	Senior
Pathways support groups	Parents and parent organizations, board members, service organizations, local government, and school support staff	All Years

Figure 13.1 The community's involvement in Collaborative Pathways High Schools

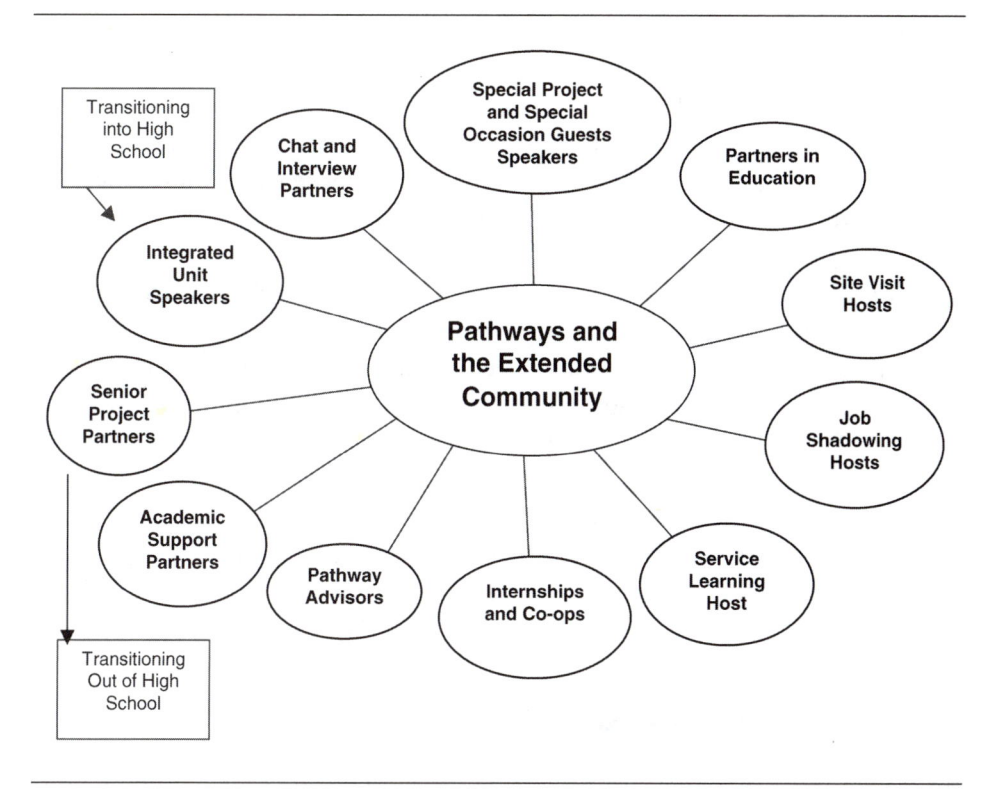

Figure diagram: "Pathways and the Extended Community" at center, connected to: Special Project and Special Occasion Guests Speakers, Chat and Interview Partners, Integrated Unit Speakers, Senior Project Partners, Academic Support Partners, Pathway Advisors, Internships and Co-ops, Service Learning Host, Job Shadowing Hosts, Site Visit Hosts, Partners in Education. Side boxes: "Transitioning into High School" and "Transitioning Out of High School."

activities or to speak at special occasions such as our Pathway Selection Party or Job Shadow Celebration.

When visitors come to the classroom, faculty members should remember the following:

> *What truly sets a collaborative high school apart is that the community's role in the student's education is equal to the role of the counseling and instructional process.*

1. The guest's time is his or her biggest gift, and every minute of the visit is valuable.

2. These guests are here for the students so it is imperative that the students take ownership of the visit.

3. Classroom visits offer students an opportunity not only to learn from the guest speaker's experiences but also to practice professional people skills.

4. All guests must be made to feel that their contribution is valuable and appreciated (by both students and faculty) so that they will want to be a continuing partner with the Pathways school.

Speakers in the Classroom

Now let us talk about deciding how your faculty may use a particular guest speaker. If we have a speaker who may be shy in front of groups or self-conscious, we need to make certain he or she is comfortable. For that person, coming on a day when the class is designing containers for shipping or doing a marketing presentation for a new product might be preferable to a straight conversation or presentation. The longer we have worked within the Pathways Model, the easier it has become to find guests who can engage the students and to find ways to help our speakers feel at ease. Because our classes are set in 90-minute blocks, we generally don't ask the guest to talk for more than 30 minutes at a time. In our flight unit, for example, we have two flight school instructors visit the classroom a week apart. The first flight school instructor comes at the beginning of the unit (after students have read an article about learning to fly and flight schools); this instructor answers their flight school questions. The day before the guest visits, the students gather in flight school teams and brainstorm a list of questions about flight schools that they might ask. They share their best five questions with the rest of the class, so that even teams who have had difficulties have some good questions available. It also allows us the opportunity to weed out inappropriate questions. When we have integrated unit speakers, we have found that if we allow students to create their own questions and don't restrict them to questions about the career itself, students find out not only about the job but also about the kind of person who does the job, and, in addition, the information they need for their projects.

> *If the guest is a person who is truly passionate about his or her career, the visit to the classroom will flow naturally.*

We are fortunate to have a flight school owner–flight license evaluator as one of our favorite guest speakers. He has a real sense of how to grab the students' attention. This year he brought with him his ground school instructor, who is a bank vice president in charge of corporate loans to aviation businesses. After students walked out to the helicopter to greet our guests, they returned to the classroom and began the visit by asking each gentleman for a career "chat"; we start all guests' visits in this way. This has a twofold purpose. First, it puts our guest at ease from the start because the focus becomes the job and not the person. It also puts the students in control of the visit because they are comfortable with a chat, which means it immediately becomes a student-led visit. After the chats, we had a question-and-answer session in which students got to ask all of their flight school questions. We ended with an examination of the helicopter so that the owner could show us the propellers and the engine and explain how helicopters differ from airplanes. It is no surprise that this year our "flight schools" had helicopters in 12 of the 14 fleets!

We followed this visit with one the next week featuring a small, new flight school in our area; it is owned and completely operated by a local woman. Her flight school is in direct contrast to the first speaker's; it is smaller, and she serves as both owner and instructor. This contrast is why we have both flight schools visit the classroom. She is another of our very favorite visitors because she has such enthusiasm not only for flying but also for helping beginners learn to fly. Because of the contrast between the two schools, the students get to observe both ends of the flight school spectrum; in addition, they have an opportunity to meet both a woman and a man doing similar jobs. On the day of the second visit, our speaker also began with a chat, and then she entertained questions for a few minutes. After that, students broke into their flight teams. She visited each team, examining the drafts of their brochures, admiring their work, and offering suggestions. Her visit ended with a short video clip of how planes fly that she uses in her ground school; this helped set up students for the next phase of the integrated project, a demonstration of aerodynamics. At the end of the unit, when we have a Saturday morning fly-in, students have the opportunity to visit with the wide variety of Young Eagle pilots who bring their planes to the local airport. On that day, students have a chance to see the cockpits and styles of several airplanes and to actually go flying. In addition, our aviation guests often bring handouts with them; these might include lists of aviation careers, pamphlets on how planes fly, trade want-ads for helicopters and planes, and Web site listings for more information. As you can see, this variety of guests connected to the integrated aviation unit brings a rich and varied wealth of experience and knowledge to the classroom.

Equally important for integrated units are the guests who help us explore the Pathways. We ask these guests to be 30-minute interview speakers. For each Pathway, we try to have guests from at least five diverse careers. We have a suggestion box in our room in which students can suggest careers that they would like to know more about or provide the names of people (usually friends and family) who would be willing to come to the classroom. Many of our best guests came the first time because a student wanted them to visit. Among the varied careers we have had represented in this manner are a supervisor from a hog farrowing operation, a diesel truck mechanic, a home care nurse, a stockbroker, a motorcycle racer, a photographer, and a post office supervisor.

> *In this way, guests become an integral part of the daily classroom but do not become the only focus of a given day.*

In addition to featuring Pathways guests whom the students suggest, as teachers, we continually strive to make certain a wide variety of careers are represented in the classroom. We often use professional organizations such as the American Foundry Association, the American Bureau of Insurance Agents, and the Healthcare Home-Providers League as sources of speakers. We draw on speakers from our school community as well, including our grounds supervisor, our attendance coordinator, and our budget director. We use these colleagues for our 30-minute interviews, but they also help us in other ways, for example, as special-projects visitors. The budget director, for example, comes in to assist the students when they are creating budgets for their flight schools. Our superintendent and school librarian pretend to be potential investors in our flight school when students are doing sales pitches. We use our attendance director at the beginning of the year when we play an interview game. When we make public service announcements in the Arts and Communications Pathway, one of our guests is the webmaster from our Regional Educational

Media Center (REMC), who helps students with media software. In the Human Service Pathway, we have our school social worker come for a 30-minute interview. The bottom line is that the more exposure students have to a wide variety of careers and personalities, the better the Pathways Model will work.

One of our favorite ways to utilize guests is to have them be a partner in education. What we do with these guests is have them help us design a block-long activity that will focus on skills needed in their workplace. Focus generally includes teaming, problem solving, self- (and team) management, and time management. We have a bean cooperative vice president who visits when students are designing containers for eggs that, when dropped from seven-foot ladders, allow the raw eggs to remain intact. The main skills focused on for that day are teaming and problem solving. We have a bank mortgage lender who comes and helps us put together a presentation for an amusement park or a rock star's mansion. The theme for her day is teaming, but also time management and persuasion. We have an engineer who visits on a day when the project is to make roller-coasters for marbles out of toilet paper and paper towel tubes. Obviously, the focus here is problem solving, but also time management and teaming because the roller-coaster not only has to work but also come in at the lowest cost possible. We use these projects to try out our teams at the start of new integrated units. These one-time practice days ensure that the teams work well together. Our rule is that once an integrated project starts, students cannot switch to other teams. If problems arise, they must use conflict-resolution techniques to solve them. Teachers should have one day to evaluate the teams and make certain that none have significant problems that can't be resolved. In Freshman Explorations, we do approximately four of these days. In Sophomore Selections, students generally do only one or two because that course is only a nine-week or one-semester block (or embedded into a six-period day).

As you can see, when considering which speakers to invite to the classroom and how to put them to work once they get there, the sky is the limit!

Guests can also be included in many other creative ways; these are our special-occasion guests. We always have a keynote speaker at our Pathways selection party. One year it was a psychologist with a Ph.D. who moonlights as a balloon clown at children's parties. Another year, it was a business consultant who has a commitment to Pathways High Schools. This year's speaker was an investment broker who talked to students about striving for their dreams. During one of our first years, we had a teacher who owns a videography business as an ongoing guest; he took video on several occasions (including our selection party) for our Pathways video. One year we redesigned our learning environment so that our guests could include a brain researcher and an interior design artist.

Our final advice is to encourage your faculty not to be afraid to ask guests to come. Generally, everyone is flattered by the request, and when they realize all they have to do is come and the kids will carry the majority of the visit, they are more than willing to participate. We can count on one hand the number of times we have been turned down. As we leave the topic of classroom guests, here are some questions you can encourage your faculty to ask when planning Pathways visits from the community:

- Would several students be interested in this career?
- Does this career connect to an integrated unit?
- How can we make the best use of the guest's expertise and maximize the visit?
- During which week would the visit make the most sense?
- Are there students who should hear this speaker who may not be available for the presentation? Who are they, and can they be released from an obligation in order to attend the visit?
- Would this speaker's workplace provide a potential job shadowing or internship site?
- Would this speaker be interested in sitting on a Pathways advisory board?

Site Visit Locations

Another way that the community can be involved with a Pathways High School is to provide "host sites" for school visits. In a Collaborative High School, from the freshman year on, students view and analyze work environments on a regular basis. The more experience we, the educators, have in organizing site visits, the better we are able to help our hosts know what works and what we need from them. The focus of site visits changes as students progress in their planned development. Students in Freshman Explorations participate in five to seven site visits during their course. We strive to have one for each Pathway; ideally, students would go on one at the beginning of the Pathway unit and then another at the end of the integrated unit section. In Sophomore Selections, students observe the environment of the three occupations that they shadow. During Junior Judgments, students gain an in-depth understanding of a single environment and have a chance to observe how that environment changes on a day-to-day basis. During Senior Transitions, students have a variety of opportunities that allow them to visit their career environment. If a student's plan is to become a pharmacist, for example, she might have a co-op job as a pharmacy assistant that allows her to work side-by-side with a pharmacist in a drug store environment for the first quarter. Then, during the second quarter, she might co-op in a hospital pharmacy. When completing her senior project, these experiences would allow her to compare and contrast the work environments and the skills involved in the two situations.

In a Pathways High School, the challenge for your faculty when setting up site visits is to make them match the needs of the students at that particular point in their plans. Site visits for freshmen are very different from job-shadow site visits or internship placements. Although the contacts are often the same, the role of the site host changes; the Pathways teacher must be clear about the goals of the visits when talking to the community site hosts. Table 13.2 shows how the goals change throughout the Pathways process.

Table 13.2 How Goals Change During the Pathways Process

Grade Level	Purpose	Time Duration
Grade 9: Field trips	To explore sights, sounds, and smells of the workplace environment; to observe a variety of occupations	Thirty-five minutes to one hour; slightly longer if a panel of employees does "chats" with students
Grade 10: Job shadows	To be immersed in a specific job; to observe the specific skills and techniques involved in that career field; to observe differences between jobs within a Career Cluster	Four-hour minimum; a full day is preferable
Grades 11 and 12: Internships, co-ops, and senior projects	To perform and "try on" parts of the job so that students know if the work environment and the work skills will fit with their personality, aptitudes, and interests	A systematic schedule over a period of time (one month or more) that allows students to view and participate in the ongoing work process

Designing Field Trips to Accommodate Hosts

One of the most important parts of arranging field trips is preparing the hosts. We have found that the longer we have been a Collaborative Pathways High School, the easier this becomes. First, it is crucial that your hosts understand what a Collaborative Pathways High School is and that they realize these students will be trained to look for very specific items, as well as just absorbing the sites, sounds, and smells of the workplace. Second, we also explain that we need to see people performing their jobs, not just talking about them. Finally, we talk to the hosts about chats and prepare them to be asked to "chat."

> We always make certain employers know the five major emphases of our classroom:
> 1. Skills
> 2. Teaming
> 3. Problem solving
> 4. Conflict resolution
> 5. Time management and multitasking

To ensure that we do not interrupt the flow of the workplace, employers often prefer to expose students to a panel of "chat" guests at the beginning or end of the tour. Usually this panel consists of a variety of career descriptions, genders, and training levels. Some are so familiar with doing chats with us that they use a PowerPoint presentation to make it easier for students to write down the chats. Prized chats from this year's class included those obtained at local television and radio stations. At the television station, students sat on the empty set with five employees: a producer, a news anchor, a weather reporter or sportscaster, an electrician, and a publicist. Because we made several site visits to the television station, the organizers alternated the chat speakers according to the time of day and the convenience of their work schedules. At the radio station, the students' most adored teen DJ gave them a chat in his studio while on air (during a song)! Needless to say, no student gets on a bus for a field trip without a wad of note cards for chats.

By explaining the Collaborative Pathways High School to your hosts, faculty members clearly describe what the visit will entail, but in addition, this process continues to sell the community on the value of your program—value both for the students and for the hosts, who may employ these students one day. Once we have explained our Pathways system to employers, their reactions are usually as follows. First, they invariably say, "I sure wish I had gone to a high school like that!" Next, we usually hear stories of people who switched careers two or three times later in life, and sometimes even stories of people who feel they would be in different careers had they had more and earlier opportunities to consider options. Almost always, the conversation ends with this: "How can we help?"

In conclusion, designing field trips to accommodate hosts is an important aspect of the 9th- and 10th-grade curricula. It is also may provide an important connection to many community employers. Following are questions your staff might be encouraged to use when designing a field trip.

> *Remember that when the contact is made on behalf of the school, we are setting up an ongoing connection and relationship with this community partner. It may open the door to an important resource. Many of the places we go on freshman field trips later become job-shadowing and internship sites, and often employers and employees become partners in other ways—as guest speakers, special-occasion guests, or even mentors and senior advisory panel members.*

- Will this job site fit well into the Pathways emphasis for this unit?
- Is this a Career Cluster in which students are interested or to which they should be exposed?
- Will this be an interesting or different work environment (especially compared with students' expectations)?
- Is this a job site that students can be passionate about?
- What skills, teaming, problem solving, conflict resolution, time management, and multitasking will students be able to observe at this worksite?
- How can this visit fit the needs of the employer?
- What careers at this job site would be good for a panel chat?
- Are there other ways that this employer could help our students in the future?

Designing Job Shadows

During sophomore year, students have the opportunity to visit several work environments for half- or full-day exposure. Many times we find that even students at the junior and senior levels are choosing to do more job shadow experiences so that they can compare careers that they are considering. Once students determine which careers they would like to view, finding and setting up the visit is the easy part. It is important that both students and hosts are clear on what they expect from the visit. Many districts and states have job shadowing opportunities already arranged for their students.

In a Collaborative Pathways High School, sophomore students are continually linked to the community through their intensive interview projects and job shadows. While doing job shadows, students first select a Career Cluster and then build a career ladder for themselves. At this point, they need to find 10 intensive interview partners who are in careers within their Cluster. The students sit with their interview partner for about an hour and a half and have a thorough discussion about that particular career.

> *One key to successful job shadow experiences and intensive interviews is preparation—not only of the student but also of the job site host or interviewed guest.*

Many successful job shadows transition into internship and senior project destinations. Following are some tips for involving the community in job shadowing and intensive interviews.

- Have students do intensive interviews and some career laddering to help them select the sites that are most interesting to and compatible with them.
- Make sure your students are well prepared before they go.
- Be careful to prepare the hosts adequately (not only your contact at the company, but also the students' immediate supervisors and coworkers).
- Make sure that the hosts feel appreciated and valued. They are making an important contribution to help students focus their individual plans.
- Ask yourself what careers at this job site would be good for a panel chat.
- Think about ways that this employer could help students in the future.

Service Learning

Service Learning is becoming a key part of most high schools in the 21st century and links to the concepts of democratic citizenship. Community service is a key part of most college and scholarship applications, as well as a criterion for National Honor Society and a host of other awards and honors at the high school level. In a Pathways High School, service learning naturally evolves from the continual use of the community as part of the learning process.

> *What makes service learning special in a Collaborative Pathways High School is that it is connected to student interest and aptitude and is available to all students.*

Service learning hosts allow the students an opportunity to become valuable and useful citizens of their community. In addition to giving students a chance to practice teaming and leadership skills in a "real-world" setting, service learning also gives students the opportunity to give back to the community that is giving so much to them. Service learning experiences can be found in a variety of core classes as parts of integrated projects or unit reviews. In a freshman English class, students might go to the elementary school and do short units with first and second graders on personalities and careers, or work with middle school students on collecting money for a play or showcase. Science students might go to the local zoo and clean cages to help cut costs in the zoo's financially strapped budget. Social studies students could work with veterans to design a Memorial Day service or collect money for flag cases. In Pathways classes, sophomores might spend a day helping their career shadow hosts with small projects, and seniors might voluntarily give time beyond their co-op hours.

The service learning experience is different from the job shadow. Although students may perform a few small tasks during a job shadow, they are mainly in the work environment to experience its sights, sounds, and smells and to examine the variety of skills and academics needed for that career. During service learning, a student is giving—giving whatever the service learning host might need. This may include filing, environmental clean up, or collecting money or food donations. In any Pathways High School, service learning can add depth to a student's understanding of his or her Pathway while promoting good citizenship.

Internships and Senior Projects

There are many ways for the community to help students at the junior and senior level. No longer is the community just a link to the classroom; it actually becomes the classroom. An internship host needs to be well prepared beforehand, and a successful Junior Judgments teacher will actually be a salesperson not just for Pathways and the school, but also for his or her students. During an internship, many members of the community, not only the internship host, will be involved. All of the workers at the internship site become a part of the student's learning experience—including the immediate supervisor and coworkers (and customers in many cases). A large part of the Junior Judgment teacher's job is to prepare the student for the situation and to prepare the host and his or her employees for the student.

The sky is the limit when it comes to creative and unusual senior projects. The possibilities for community help and support are endless. Senior project partners can be supervisors in a co-op situation that is the result of a successful internship. They might help a student set up a senior project. Jacob from Chapter 1, for example, might work with the nursing home's occupational therapist while he designs his music therapy program. If a student is comparing two careers on a career ladder, he or she may spend several days at each place and then, using a Venn diagram, highlight the similarities and differences of the two environments, the two job descriptions, and the two resulting lifestyles. For example, Craig is interested in pharmaceuticals and did his internship at a drugstore in the pharmacy department. Now he is unsure that working in a pharmacy is right for him, because he discovered there is too much structure and little variety in the job. So Craig works with two senior project partners as he compares and contrasts the careers of pharmaceutical sales and sports therapy. For two weeks, he spends time with his first senior project partner, a pharmaceutical salesperson, making calls, doing bookwork, and filling orders. During the next two weeks, Craig works with his other partner, a sports trainer for a local hockey team. He goes to games with him, helps in the training room, and even listens in on client consultations. After this month of immersion in the two careers, he will have a wealth of firsthand knowledge for use in his Venn diagram, a compare-and-contrast chart. Senior project partners can help a student with a dual-enroll class, work on research, design a project, or aid in a virtual high school class.

Another way that community members can support junior and senior Pathways students is by becoming Pathways advisors. As in career and technical centers, each Pathway has an advisory committee that meets twice yearly to help develop curriculum and introduce new concepts in the chosen field. In a Pathways High School, community members of the advisory panel also give career advice to students as they refine their plans. In addition, these Pathway-specific advisors often sit on the senior project presentation committees that evaluate required senior projects just before graduation.

In conclusion, the community becomes the teacher. The roles for the community at this level evolve from their work with students during the freshman and sophomore years. No longer does the teacher or school ask the community to become involved; now the student is the driving force, hunting for the advice and expertise he or she needs to make informed decisions for a smooth transition to the postsecondary level. Also, remember that when the community works hand-in-hand with students at this level, the employers are helping to develop and create opportunity for students who wish to remain in the local area. Working with junior and senior students from a Pathways High School can be a rewarding experience for members of the community.

Support Through the Academic Community

Just as no man is an island, no school is a country unto itself. The larger academic community is an important part of the expanded high school arena. There is a vast amount of resources for students and teachers in our regional or intermediate districts, career centers, community colleges, universities, apprenticeship programs, math and science centers, and even our new virtual courses and schools. Take a look at the 25-mile radius around your school. Define the larger educational community that can serve your school. Table 13.3 is a list of educational community options and how your students and your staff can utilize them.

Just like your high school and employment community, each academic community is different. Being in a rural area, we have limited access to universities but excellent career centers. Utilize the academic communities that are available to you. As with the other aspects of our program, you can customize how you use your academic community to fit students' needs, their educational Pathways, and their postsecondary plans.

Table 13.3 Options in the Educational Community

Academic Community Member	Support for School and Staff	Support for Students
Regional School Districts, also referred to as intermediate school districts, are state sponsored and offer instructional, special education, and career and technical services to local school districts.	• Professional development • Curriculum consulting • Grant writing • Networking and support • Resource information • Grant dollars	• Special education services • Job shadowing opportunities • Classroom guests/speakers • Student mentors • Advisory members • Senior project options for human services
Math and Science Centers are centers sponsored by state, regional, or college districts to help promote learning in math and the physical sciences.	• Curriculum support • Professional development • Materials • Math and science standards • Classroom activities	• Speakers • Internship sites • Advisory members • Senior project options in math and science
Regional Media Centers are usually state sponsored and give regional support in the areas of technology, instructional media materials, broadcasting, and distance learning options.	• Professional development • Materials and Resources • Technology support • Media support • Distance learning options	• Classroom activities • Integrated unit speakers • Job shadowing and internship sites • Senior project options in media and broadcasting
Career, Skills, or Technology Centers are usually sponsored by state, regional, or community colleges and offer skilled trades and other hands-on career training to students during their last two years of high school.	• Applications of the core curriculum • Resources for setting up co-op programs, employability skills materials, placement services, developing integrated units with specific skill lists, etc.	• Specific skill training • Employability skills • Co-op • Student organizations in occupational areas
Community Colleges are two-year state institutions that offer certificate and skilled trades degrees and training, associate degrees, and two-year university preparation programs.	• Align curriculum to higher education • Support academic counseling services	• Classroom speakers • Postsecondary advisors • Dual-enrollment options • Articulation agreements • Advisory members • Senior project review committees
Colleges and Universities are four-year and graduate degree institutions (state	• Professional development • Grant services	• Postsecondary advisors • Dual-enrollment options

(Continued)

Table 13.3 (Continued)

Academic Community Member	Support for School and Staff	Support for Students
and private) focusing course of study at an academic or professional level of job entry.	• Placement services • Graduate degree options • Support academic counseling services	• Articulation agreements • Advisory members • Senior project review committees
Trade and Apprenticeship Programs are programs sponsored by unions and trade organizations for students in high school and beyond.	• Classroom support materials • Skills applications • Materials and networking • Support academic counseling services	• Unit and guest speakers • Site hosts • Job shadowing hosts • Internship hosts • Pathway advisors • Co-op sponsors • Senior project advisory committee
State Departments of Education are the connection between districts and state and federal government mandates and educational support programming	• Funding • Grant dollars • Awards and recognitions • Laws and regulations • Networking	• Potential student placement resource
Virtual High Schools and Distance Learning Opportunities are state and privately sponsored educational services that are available over the Internet.	• Professional development • Classroom activities	• Independent study (in courses not available at the high school or in cases when there is a scheduling conflict) • Specific career study options • Dual enrollment • Remediation

CONCLUSION

In conclusion, think a minute about a student you have personally known who reminds you of Hannah. We have all known both academically talented and remedial students who have suffered along a path of uncertainty, dropping out and then resuming postsecondary options. As discussed earlier in this book, the U.S. Department of Labor statistics verify how many of our students complete a four-year degree before pursuing educational options which will lead to a living. The community pillar is essential for our students if they are to gain a clear and realistic understanding of their plans. Using the community in the classroom, for job-shadowing and internship opportunities, for service-learning opportunities, for co-op experiences, for academic support, and for senior projects is not simply important—*it is critical*. Let us all take a lesson from Hannah: Take the time to integrate your community into the learning process—for the future of all students.

IN REVIEW

- Without the community process, students are getting a "false" image of what life and careers are like outside of the classroom.
- The community process expands the high school campus and allows for easy transitions for students.
- The community process is where most Pathways High Schools fail because educators are uncomfortable and unfamiliar with utilizing their community.
- The community process works best when community members are given specific roles.
- Student community experiences are scaffolded, beginning with short and easy contacts (such as chats) and developing into deeper relationships (such as mentorships and advisors).
- To utilize your community successfully, customize your program to fit what it has to offer.

Chapter Fourteen

School Culture and Climate in a Pathways High School

SCENARIO: MIGUEL'S FIRST DAY

Miguel was excited yet apprehensive about his first day of high school—and so were Miguel's parents. Yet everyone kept a positive and supportive attitude about this adolescent milestone. That morning he was sent off with a smile, a hug, and a "go get 'em, tiger" farewell. When Miguel arrived at school, all freshmen were guided to the gym for an assembly. There Miguel was welcomed to the school and told how lucky he was to have such a great school and to live in such a great nation. He was then presented with the school's infamous handbook, and the revered "point" system of discipline was explained to him. It was complicated and detailed, and Miguel felt immediately lost. He was a little worried as he left the assembly, wondering whether he would do something he didn't know was wrong and get sent to the office to be given a "point." (In fact, several days later, Miguel forgot he could not chew gum in computer class; he was sent down to the office, assessed "one point," and asked whether he was usually a troublemaker!) Next, Miguel was given his locker and locker combination, and he and the other freshmen settled into their lockers before heading to their new classes. Because of the assembly, he would spend only a few minutes in each of his upcoming classes. Of course, Miguel had trouble with his locker, but he was not the only one—everyone seemed nervous, and that just made simple tasks more difficult.

Miguel's first class was band. There he was given the band room rules and grading procedures and the regulations for being in the high school band.

Miguel's second class was science. Miguel was given a different set of rules for this class and its grading procedures. He was then assigned a science textbook. He was told what would be expected of him in science, and the teacher told the kids a few jokes to make them more comfortable. Next Miguel went to English. He was given a different set of rules for the English class and the grading procedures. He was then assigned an English textbook. He was told how important English was to ensuring he passed the state exam, earned a scholarship, and graduated from high school. Miguel then went to lunch. He couldn't find his buddies, so he stuck to the "sidelines" and skipped eating all together. Next, Miguel went to his computer-literacy class, where he was given yet another set of class rules and grading procedures. The teacher then went over the district's technology and Internet use contract and told students what they could and could not do on the computers. Miguel was then given his first high school assignment: a 101-question quiz the next day on the student handbook. After computer class, Miguel went to algebra where he was given his fifth set of class rules and grading procedures, all different from the last four, and again assigned a textbook. The last hour of the day, Miguel went to Spanish, where he received the Spanish class rules, grading procedures, a textbook, and a Spanish–English dictionary. At the end of the day, Miguel had trouble with his locker again, so he just carried all his books home.

When Miguel's parents got home from work that evening, they were excited to hear about their son's first day of high school. "So, how did it go, Miguel?" "It was okay," Miguel replied. "Well, what did you learn, what did you do? Do you like the school?" Miguel's reply was, "Yeah, I guess so, but there are lots and lots of rules and I can't remember them all and I have a 101 quiz tomorrow on the handbook." He then shared with his parents the student handbook and six pages of class rules, six pages of classroom procedures, and his seven textbooks. He later commented to his mother, "Mom, they [the teachers and administrators] made it really clear to us that it was *their* school."

Unfortunately, Miguel's is a true story of one student's first-day experience in a common and traditional high school. We are sure his story is not an isolated incident. The other unfortunate part of this story is that the teachers at this school were doing what they thought was right; they would be surprised and even dismayed at Miguel's experience. This once again reflects the isolation of our high schools and their staffs. No one looked at the "big picture" of Miguel's day. No one specifically addressed the culture and climate of the school building that Miguel and his friends entered that first day of high school.

WHAT ARE SCHOOL CULTURE AND CLIMATE?

School culture and climate are essential for creating an effective learning environment. What are culture and climate, and why are they so important to the educational process? School culture is the broader term. A school's culture is the overall "patterns of norms, values, beliefs, relationships, rituals, traditions, and myths that are shared in varying degrees by members of a school community" (ERIC Wizard, http://ericae.net/scripts/ewiz). American high schools share many of the same cultural experiences—homecoming, sports rivals, school colors and mascots, proms, academics, and so on. Yet even with these similarities, the culture of every school building is also different in many ways and can vary in great degrees from one high school to another. Many components can play into a school's culture, such as the racial composition and cultural subgroups of the community, subgroups within a school, socioeconomic status, geography, population density, and even the school's history and traditions. A school's culture is influenced by the entire community in which it is located.

School climate is a subset of culture. Climate is the "temperature" of your school. Is it cold and unfeeling? Is it hot and volatile? Is it warm and pleasant, and does it feel like a safe harbor for students? School climate is used to refer to the overall psychological and physical atmosphere in a school. What are student expectations for behavior toward themselves and others? What are teacher expectations for behavior toward students and each other? How do students fit in? Is it difficult for them to belong or feel connected? What are the attitudes toward learning—can everyone learn and is everyone expected to achieve? Following is a list of characteristics of a school with a positive climate (Michigan Department of Education, 2002):

- People like to be there; they enjoy working or learning there.
- Everyone in the school is courteous, caring, and respectful of one another.
- Accomplishment and positive social behavior are promoted and celebrated.
- Everyone uses constructive and respectful ways of handling disagreements.
- Everyone accepts individual responsibility for the success of the school and the well-being of others in the school.
- The school's structural organization is research based.
- Respectful behavior toward differences is taught and practiced.
- Students are involved in decision making.
- Family and community members are involved at a number of levels and in a variety of ways.
- Appropriate school- and community-based support services are available to students and staff.
- Adults model sound decision making, clear communication, academic curiosity, and creative problem solving.

School climate is critical to academic success because it is the environment in which learning occurs.

WHY ARE SCHOOL CULTURE AND CLIMATE IMPORTANT?

The main reason a school should address any area of education is for the success of its students. School climate permeates every aspect of your school building and affects every student, faculty member, parent, and community member. It has a huge and sometimes devastating impact on learning and many times is not identified as the culprit because it can be an elusive and unseen entity. Therefore, we must address school climate for what it is: a feeling toward your school that sets the tone for learning. Unfortunately, many educators do not think they have any control over the culture and climate of their school; many administrators share this belief. They do not realize that what they do and say, or don't do or say, has a great impact on culture and climate. Because culture and climate are not generally structured and directly addressed, they are often ignored.

> *Here is the good news: You can affect, set, and control the culture and climate of your school. The key areas of a Pathways High School can help you to do just that.*

In this chapter, we discuss the latest key findings on school culture and climate and how they affect students. We will then show you how using the key components of a Career Pathways High School can help you to have a direct effect on the inner workings and temperature of your school. We will also list related areas that can work in conjunction with your Pathways system. In addressing the most recent research on culture and climate issues, we have narrowed the data down to three major factors:

- A student's feeling of connectedness to school
- School prejudice and acceptance
- Codes of silence

We then give you several references from which you can obtain information to assess your current school culture and climate and develop, along with your Pathways system, a plan to address how students and staff feel when in your building.

A KEY FINDING: SCHOOL CONNECTEDNESS

The number one factor in a school's culture and climate is whether all students feel connected to their school. Just like the story of Miguel, students need to feel that their school belongs to them and that they are welcome there. In a study mandated by Congress in the National Institute of Health Revitalization Act of 1993, the National Institute of Child Health and Human Development developed and conducted a prospective longitudinal study on adolescent health (Blum & Rinehart, 2000). The National

Longitudinal Study of Adolescent Health (called the Add Health Study) determined that only two main factors in a school affect the health and well-being of students. The first, and the one related to our discussion, is "feeling connected to school." The study shows overwhelming evidence that both older and younger students who feel connected to their school report lower levels of emotional distress and are less likely to think about, or attempt, suicide (Blum & Rinehart, 2000). The report went on to define school connectedness as follows:

- Teens feel that teachers treat all students fairly.
- Teens feel close to people at school (other students and adults).
- Teens get along with teachers and students.

Another comprehensive study, *Improving the Odds: The Untapped Power of Schools to Improve the Health of Teens* (Blum, McNeely, & Rinehart, 2002), added classroom management, school size, and integrated friendship groups as key components to effective school connectedness. When students feel they are a part of school, say they are treated fairly by teachers, and feel close to people at school, they are healthier and more likely to succeed. What promotes this connectedness to school? Well-managed classrooms, small school size, and integrated friendship groups (Blum et al., 2002). The study also complements earlier findings that students who feel connected to school

- Are less likely to use alcohol and illegal drugs
- Are less likely to engage in violent or deviant behavior
- Are less likely to become pregnant
- Are less likely to experience emotional distress (Blum et al., 2002).

The study considers why some adolescents feel attached to school and others do not. Table 14.2 provides a definition of what the study indicated for each component of the key findings for classroom management, school size, and integrated friendship groups, and relates these findings to Pathways solutions.

To gain understanding of these concepts, a large sampling of students was asked to respond to the following comments. How would your students respond to these comments?

- I feel close to people at this school.
- I am happy to be at this school.
- I feel like I am a part of this school.
- The teachers at this school treat students fairly.
- I feel safe in my school.

Understanding these key findings, let's look at school connectedness in a Collaborative Career Pathways High School and how it addresses the major needs of all students.

THE PATHWAYS SOLUTION TO KEY FINDING 1: SCHOOL CONNECTEDNESS

In a Collaborative Career Pathways High School, students have *multiple connections* to their school and their community. All students feel that teachers are interested in them because all teachers know specific information about the students that can help them not only to relate to the students but to help them to find the connection to their class. As previously suggested, this is best accomplished by sharing a list of key student information with all teachers. The list consists of each student's interest and aptitudes, personality profile, learning style, work-based experiences, Pathway, and other data pertinent to your school activities.

Table 14.1 offers a sample list of key student information. This list is updated at the end of each semester and distributed to all teachers. In this way, when Miguel enters a teacher's classroom for the first time, the teacher can say, "Miguel, I see you are interested in becoming a lawyer and that you plan to shadow in a law office this year. I think this English course will really help you with the skills you will need to pursue your dream." Or "Miguel, I see you are a natural leader. I hope in our team projects this year you will take a leadership role." In this fashion, the connections teachers can make with students are endless and can be done throughout the year with specific and deliberate connections being made for each student. This works even in the discipline process where teachers take a caregiver role, trying to help students understand how their adverse behavior will affect their own goals and dreams. Making personal connections helps students feel that all teachers treat them and their fellow students fairly and care about their present and future. An excellent exercise that was shared in the document *A Threat Assessment of Schools* (Vossekuil, Reddy, Fein, Borum, & Modzeleski, 2002) suggests that at a staff meeting a list of students be put up on the walls with each teacher putting a star next to the name of the students to whom they feel connected. Any student with no or few stars is then targeted for intervention. Teachers can work together to connect to these identified students using the student's Pathways information and experiences as a base.

In a Pathways High School, adult connections go beyond the teachers. Pathways students from freshman to senior year have regular contact with adults in the community. This reinforces their connections to school and the community, and these connections are solidified by the Developmental Assets work discussed in Chapter 1. Students connect to adults through chats, site visits, speakers, job shadows, internships, senior projects, mentors, and senior boards. The entire school and community take an interest in where the student is at in his or her development and where the student wants to go. This goes a long way in helping students feel connected.

The third area is the ability to get along with teachers and other students. The Pathways curriculum in both Pathways Classes and core and elective work emphasizes teamwork and conflict-resolution skills. During freshman year, the direct teaching and emphasis on teamwork and conflict

Table 14.1 An Example of a List of Key Student Information for Teachers

Name	Miguel	Dottie	Jake
Personality Profile	Blue	Yellow	Red
Learning Style	Visual	Audio	Visual
Multiple Intelligence	Musical, Linguistic	Spatial, Kinetic	Kinetic
Differentiated Aptitude Test—Interest Inventory	Fine Arts, Health Services, Education and Legal Services	Math and Science, Sales, Machine Operations	Transportation, Clerical, Sales
State Test Scores	Proficient in all subjects	Proficient in math and science, average in language arts and social studies	Proficient in language arts and social studies, average in math and science
Interests and Hobbies	Hockey, reading	Volleyball, hiking	Writing, auto mechanics
Pathway Selection	Human services	Engineering trades	Arts, communications
Favorite Subjects	Band, English	Science, math	English, automotive
Job Shadows	Psychologist, teacher, lawyer	Civil Engineer, Carpenter, Environmental Engineer	Public relations firm, newspaper
Intern	Psychology office	Plastics company	Automotive factory's public relations department
Senior Project	Student mental health education program	Plastics and the environment project	Writing a newsletter for an automotive firm

resolution is taught and practiced over and over again with continual reinforcement from not only other class teachers but hall monitors, administrators, parents, bus drivers, and so on. This gives all students the structure and skills to take responsibility for their own behavior toward themselves and others.

Everyone should be aware of and trained in the chosen method for conflict resolution, team rules, character education, and expected school behaviors; once they have learned these methods, all members of the school community must practice them. Every adult in your school (as well as every student) is a part of the climate team, and students must get the same response and instruction from everyone.

> *It is critical that all staff members participate in professional development programs.*

In the classroom, as teachers plan their lessons, the teaming exercises and projects should be designed so that students can meet and work with other students with whom they would normally not have contact and with whom they must work successfully to complete their projects. They should also, on a regular basis, be integrated with other students of their Pathway. When students get to work with other students with whom they share many of the same interests and aptitudes, it allows for the integration of students in positive and diverse ways.

> *These planned and structured classroom interactions help all students feel connected with more students in their school, thus creating a culture and climate of tolerance, acceptance, and diversity.*

Although studies show that students tend to drift to their own race, culture, gender, or socioeconomic groups, through Pathways, they have positive and consistent classroom experiences with others in their school, eliminating barriers, isolation, stereotyping, and hostility. Table 14.3 is a comparative chart of how Career Pathways High Schools address the key components of the Blum, McNeely, and Rinehart (2002) study.

The fact that Career Pathways High Schools establish a plan for every student in itself affects the larger whole. Students' plans connect them to their education and to their school.

OTHER KEY FINDINGS: SCHOOL PREJUDICE AND CODES OF SILENCE

School Prejudice

Another key finding in the development of a safe and healthy school is the elimination of student prejudice toward one another. Do students in your school feel that they are accepted,

> *In a Career Pathways High School, students know that where they are and where they are going are important. In addition, students know that the hopes and dreams of every other student are just as important, thus connecting the entire school community.*

Table 14.2 Addressing the Key Components of the Blum, McNeely, and Rinehart (2002) Study

Component: Friendship Groups

Definition and Indications:
- Students feel more connected to school when friendship groups are integrated in terms of race, gender, and social status; when there are enough students of each racial group to form friendships, racial groups tend to isolate themselves.
- There is a need to go beyond our current integration practices that focus on numeric integration of the school as a whole and neglect integration within a school (such as more minorities being assigned to low-level classes).

Career Pathways Model:
- With teaming and Pathways-specific groupings, students interact and are integrated with many classmates. They work with students from all ethnic and racial groups and skill levels, many of whom they would not normally have had any connection with. This familiarity with many students helps to eliminate barriers and stereotyping through structured learning opportunities and established school practices.

Component: Well-Managed Classrooms

Definition and Indications:
- The school sets clear expectations for individual responsibility and conflict resolution among students.
- Teachers consistently acknowledge all students.
- Students participate in the management of the classroom; they do regular jobs, have input on classroom rules, and help set grading criteria.

Career Pathways Model:
- Students are taught teaming, conflict resolution, individual responsibility, and self-management skills in all Pathways classes beginning during the freshman year. These processes are practiced and reinforced across the entire school curriculum, in the halls, and during extra curricular activities.
- Teachers have specific information to acknowledge all students through the student information sheets.
- All Pathways classes use a facilitated learning model by which students direct both themselves and the classroom, helping to make decisions on speakers, trips, experiences, assignment, class rules, grading, and so on.

Component: School Size

Definition and Indications:
- Students in smaller schools feel more connected to school, on an average, than students in larger schools.
- The optimal school size for increasing school connectedness is under 600 students.

(Continued)

Table 14.2 (Continued)

- Studies on learning report that the optimal high school size for high academic achievement is between 600 and 1,200 students (due to the capacity to offer a wide variety of courses and curricula).
- **Career Pathways Model:**
  - In large schools, the Career Pathways Model can be used to set up schools within schools, giving students a smaller interest group with which to connect. For example, students can be scheduled into homerooms or Pathways classes by Pathway, with each Pathway group remaining together for their four years of high school.
  - Pathways can also be the venue in which students from smaller schools can participate in online learning or dual enrollment for advanced opportunities in their planned program.

---

welcomed, and equal? Do students in your school feel that one particular group is treated better than another? Do they feel that your athletes get special treatment or that students from better homes have a better chance at your school? Does the atmosphere of your school create a hierarchy for students based on race, gender, ability, socioeconomic status, athletics, and so on?

In the Blum and Rinehart (2000) study, students who perceive other students to be prejudiced report high levels of emotional distress. What we need to ask ourselves is, "Are we, through our established school culture and climate, inadvertently adding to the unfair treatment of minorities, at-risk students, socioeconomically deprived students, and teens in general?" In Blum et al. (2002), research was clear that students feel more connected to school when friendship groups are integrated. Does

> *In addition, do students at your school feel that other students buy into these deep and ingrained cultural beliefs, thus assuming there is no hope to break the established culture?*

your school specifically address these issues through classroom instruction, school discipline policies, and other school processes such as counseling and community connections? Does you school have an established and strictly practiced policy of *no tolerance* for bullying and teasing? The positive effect of the following Pathways processes on your school culture and climate is significant, as shown in Table 14.3.

Codes of Silence and Other Indicators of Violence

Codes of silence are perhaps the most dangerous behavior related to your students' safety. Codes of silence are a student's belief that it is better to keep silent than to "rat out" their peers. Vossekuil, Reddy, Fein, Borum, and Modzeleski (2000) identified eight preliminary key findings and implications that we feel are important for all schools to know and understand

Table 14.3 Positive Effects of the Pathways Process on School Culture and Climate

Pathways Process	Culture and Climate Connections
Counseling	• Teaming • Problem solving • Conflict resolution/negotiation skills • Anger management • Character development • Self-management/stress management • Crisis intervention/peer-counseling skills • Goal setting • Decision making • Ethics • Postsecondary planning
Classroom	• Study skills • Community-building attributes in the classroom • The *continual practice* of counseling process skills (conflict resolution, teaming, etc.) in the classroom • Pathways teams • Pathways-integrated projects • Facilitated learning and differentiated instruction • Technology integration • Service learning • Zero tolerance for bullying or teasing in the classroom
Community	• Citizenship • Community members in the classroom • Community-based activities and experiences for students • Community participation as mentors and project advisors • Postsecondary links

to establish preventive measures. Almost all the preliminary findings are related to the culture and climate of your school and can be positively affected by directly addressing and understanding the problems and solutions. The findings are shown in relation to the Pathways system in Table 14.4.

What are the implications of this important study? Students who engaged in targeted violence in school typically did not "just snap." The key is paying attention to grievances and bad feelings about school. In almost no case did students bring that information to an adult's attention, although many friends, classmates, and siblings knew about the attackers' ideas and plans before the attack. Finally, the use of profiles is ineffective and will fail to identify those who may and may not pose a threat. A good offense is the best defense against school violence. There are many ways you can take control of your school culture and climate.

Table 14.4 Findings and Implications from Vossekuil et al. (2000) and the Pathways System

Number 1

Finding	Incidents of targeted violence at school are rarely impulsive.
Implications	The attacks are typically the end result of an understandable and often discernible process of thinking and behavior. Most of the attackers developed their idea at least two weeks prior to an attack, and most were known to hold a grievance at the time of the attack.
Using your Career Pathways system and community network	Use your Pathways classes to teach students how to resolve conflicts when they begin. Use the rapport you have built with students using the student fact sheet to create a bond of trust. Make it comfortable for students to talk with teachers, administrators, and each other about their grievances and seek help and solutions in an appropriate fashion. Assignments can be developed to help students develop a plan of action for them if they feel they have a grievance against another student, teacher, or adult in your building. *Practice resolution and coping skills as part of instruction.*

Number 2

Finding	Prior to most incidents, the attackers told someone about their idea or plan.
Implications	In virtually all studied cases, the person told was a peer, friend, schoolmate, or sibling, and in only two cases did such a peer notify an adult. Almost never did attackers relate their plans to their targets.
Using your Career Pathways system and community network	Students need to be aware of and taught about codes of silence—when it is right to keep a confidence and when it is right to tell someone of impending violence. Your Pathways classes with counselors and teachers working together are a great place to have such conversations, projects, journal writings, and so on.

Number 3

Finding	There is no accurate or useful profile of a school attacker.
Implications	Attackers range in age from 11 to 21 years in age, come from a variety of racial and ethnic backgrounds, have excellent to failing grades, are socially isolated to popular, and give no observed behavioral problems to multiple warnings. Few attackers show any marked change in behavior before the attacks.
Using your Career Pathways system and community network	Because there is no general profile of a school attacker, it is important to go back and make sure that all students feel connected to your school through the processes talked about in this chapter.

(Continued)

Table 14.4 (Continued)

Number 4	
Finding	Most attackers had used guns previously and have access to them.
Implications	Access to weapons among students is common. Attention should be paid not only to weapon access but, more important, to the use of and communication about weapons. Parents should be aware of safe gun storage.
Using your Career Pathways system and community network	It is important to use your parent and community connections to help adults know the risks and responsibilities of firearms in relation to their children. It is an important topic to put on your parent orientation agenda or to discuss with service agencies. Just having adults feel free to discuss firearms behavior with youth can make a big difference. Youth need to know that violence is not the way we choose to settle our differences, and the more adults who talk to them about this, the better.
Number 5	
Finding	Most shooting incidents were not resolved by law enforcement intervention.
Implications	Schools may make the best use of their resources by focusing on prevention, not by relying exclusively on law enforcement to respond to and resolve school-based violence.
Using your Career Pathways system and community network	When the law is called in on school violence, it is too late. It is okay to create your security and safety plan in collaboration with law enforcement officials, but an incident control plan should never be sufficient to make you feel safe. Security plans can be a false security—your best chances of a safe school are preventive measures that let all students know they are important. Make sure all students have a plan for their future and that all students can connect their learning to that plan. It is their future that is important.
Number 6	
Finding	In many cases, other students were involved in some capacity.
Implications	In over three-fourths of the incidents, other students knew about the attack before it occurred. Some knew exactly what the attacker planned to do; others knew something "big" or "bad" was going to happen, and often they knew the time and date it was to occur.
Using your Career Pathways system and community network	Use your Pathways classes, student organizations, and other school opportunities to show students how they are responsible for school violence through their behaviors, reactions, and beliefs. Give your students the skills and responsibility to make the climate of your school best for everyone.

(Continued)

Table 14.4 (Continued)

Number 7	
Finding	In a number of cases, having been bullied played a key role in the attack.
Implications	A significant number of school attackers described experiences of being bullied in terms that approached torment. They told of behaviors that, if they had occurred in the workplace, would meet the legal definitions of harassment. That bullying played a major role in school violence and shootings should strongly support ongoing efforts to combat bullying in U.S. schools.
Using your Career Pathways system and community network	*No-tolerance policies for teasing and bullying must be clear and practical.* All members of the school community need to open their eyes and ears to bullying behaviors among students, and there should be a clear-cut procedure for students, teachers, parents, adults, and staff members to follow to ensure this behavior is addressed and *stopped.*
Number 8	
Finding	Most attackers engaged in some behavior, prior to the incident, that caused concern or indicated a need for help.
Implications	A significant problem in preventing targeted violence in schools is determining how best to respond to students who are already known to be in trouble or needing assistance. Attention should be given to a student's difficulty coping with major losses or perceived failures, particularly when it may have led to feelings of depression and hopelessness.
Using your Career Pathways system and community network	Have set avenues for your students to seek help and feel safe about doing so. Again, all adults in your school must have the skills to identify warning behaviors and refer their observations to the proper channels.

SOLUTIONS AND SUGGESTIONS FOR CLIMATE CONTROL

The number one concept you must remember in solving school culture and climate issues is that you can set a positive culture and climate for your school. It is not out of your control. Following are six steps to help you build the culture and climate you want in your school:

1. Establish a working committee for culture and climate issues.
2. Assess your climate.
3. Develop a schoolwide plan.

4. Conduct professional development for all parties.
5. Make culture and climate building a part of your classroom instruction.
6. Use your Pathways system as the avenue to secure good climate.

Establish a Working Committee for Culture and Climate Issues

The Culture and Climate Committee is the most important committee you will ever establish in your school. We suggest the following composition:

- Class advisors (teachers)
- Class officer(s) (students)
- Student organization sponsor and students (e.g., Ski Club, Chess Club, etc.)
- Athletic director
- Counselors
- Assistant principals or administrators
- Parents
- Community or board members
- Specialty persons: This may be different for each school. Some schools may have social workers, some have Safe and Drug Free School coordinators, some schools have on-site nurses, truancy or law enforcement liaison officers, and so on.

The team should meet at least monthly to develop a written plan, time line, and action plan. We then suggest that the team break into working subcommittees. When the actual work begins, the entire team meets every other month and the working subcommittee on the off months. This gives time for the subcommittees to work and report back to the larger group and keeps the larger group on track. The committee should be facilitated by an administrator or someone who has the time available to keep things in order. Many times, it works well to have cochairs with one chair being from the school and the other from the community. It is also important to have a secretary or someone to take down and then distribute minutes and the action plans.

The following tasks should be assigned to this committee:

1. Assess the current school culture and climate. This includes choosing an instrument for assessment, conducting the assessment, and reporting the results to the administration and school board.

2. Review and make recommendations on the current discipline policies and procedures. Blum and colleagues' (2002) research clearly shows that when schools have harsh or punitive discipline policies, students feel less connected to school. The discipline policy for any particular infraction does not influence connectedness; rather, a harsh discipline climate

in general is what seems to be associated with lower school connectedness (p. 12).

3. Build a three- to five-year building plan for improving the culture and climate. This plan must reflect (a) the data collected by your assessment and (b) the review and recommendation regarding discipline policies and procedures.

4. Attend to selection of and recommendations for celebrations and activities that will enhance the culture and climate of the school. For example, find themes that include all students in school events such as homecoming, school plays, intramurals, school assemblies, and so on.

5. Make recommendations to the administration on trainings and information that staff members, students, and community members need to improve the culture and climate of the school.

6. Plan the first day of school in collaboration with staff members.

7. Suggest programs for student support and school connectedness.

Assess Your Climate

Assessing your school culture and climate may be one of the greatest challenges you will face as an administrator. It takes a great deal of courage for the stakeholders at a school to assess their environment honestly, to admit their weaknesses, and to build a plan to change the climate and culture of a school. It must be led by a strong, key stakeholder (such as a principal or counselor) with support from key persons (such as the superintendent, your board members, and parents). There are some excellent tools available to school districts to assess culture and climate. These tools can be used by your staff, or they can be contracted to an outside firm that will come into your building to conduct the surveys and calculate the results.

The National Association of Secondary School Principals (1990) has a Comprehensive Assessment of School Environments Information Management System that contains a battery summary, a school climate survey, a teacher satisfaction survey, a student satisfaction survey, a parent satisfaction survey, a principal questionnaire, a principal report form, a teacher report form, a student report form, and users' and examiners' manuals.

Masden and Wagner (2002) created a survey-based process that gives immediate evaluation of the current condition of school culture based on responses to a brief series of questions. After a quick assessment, the program engages in a more elaborate and extensive analysis of the school culture and determines the wise allocation of time and resources.

We also suggest that you check with your state department of education and other professional organizations with which you may be affiliated. Currently, the Michigan Department of Education is drafting a School Climate Planning Tool using eight modules with rubrics that include building relationships, student participation, curriculum, staff development, school and district policies and procedures, structure and organization, facilities, and resources to address barriers to learning (MDE). Again, be sure to check with your state's department of education.

Develop a Schoolwide Plan

After your assessment is completed and the data compiled, act on the information. Your culture and climate team need to make a plan the same as you would make a security plan. The plan must be realistic and benchmarked by time, and it must address the issues that were most important on your assessment. In addition, you must communicate it to all parties and your school board must adopt it. Then once you've written and adopted this plan, it must not be shelved! Start your implementation immediately so that the people who spent so much time and effort will not feel their work is for nothing and so that everyone knows you are serious about taking control of your school's culture and climate. Table 14.5 provides a sample of a school climate planning sheet.

ADDRESSING SOME KEY POINTS OF INSTRUCTION

As you read this chapter, discuss culture and climate with your staff, and begin to build a network to address culture and climate issues. There are several key points of culture and climate that must be addressed in the classroom. We have alluded to them throughout this chapter, but they are so important that we want to list them for you so that you can work with staff members directly on these issues:

- **Conduct Professional Development for All Parties:** First and foremost, it is unfair to ask teachers to do anything they have not been trained to do. As you develop plans and choose a program of conflict resolution, team building, and other processes that fall within the counseling realm, all staff must have access to professional development and feel equipped and comfortable with the concepts and procedures. It is ultimately the responsibility of the administration working with either school improvement or professional development teams to ensure this happens.

- **Culture and Climate Issues as Part of Classroom Instruction:** As with Career Pathways curriculum, we believe and have experienced ourselves that *if something is not happening in the classroom, it is not happening.* Simply giving students information does not mean they will have the skills to use that information. Culture and climate processes must be practiced and be a part of everyday instruction. The use of teaming, conflict resolution, listening, negotiation skills, and so forth cannot be practiced enough and must be used in the teaching of important content knowledge and in the mastery of standards and benchmarks. As presented in Chapter 6, essential standards and life skills can be practiced across the curriculum and actually can reinforce content knowledge and skills.

Table 14.5 Culture and Climate Planning Sheet

Relationships	Current Status	What We Need	Action Plan	Time Line
Staff-to-staff relations				
Staff-student relations				
School-community relations				
School rituals and celebrations				

Student Needs	Current Status	What We Need	Action Plan	Time Line
Student social and academic support				
Student connectedness • Self • Students • Teachers • Community				
Student participation				
Student orientations and transitions				
Student avenues to seek help				

Instruction	Current Status	What We Need	Action Plan	Time Line
Well-managed and facilitated classrooms				
Staff development				
Curriculum integration of culture and climate programs[a]				
Culturally appropriate and enhanced curriculum				

Structure	Current Status	What We Need	Action Plan	Time Line
No-tolerance policies and procedures for teasing and bullying				
Simple, consistent rules and procedures (without punitive and tedious discipline polices)				
Conflict-resolution and teaming processes				

[a] Continual practice in the classroom of counseling curriculum skills such as character development, conflict resolution, ethical decision making, and listening skills.

- **Teaching Strategies:** Incorporating essential standards and life skills to enhance climate affects the way teachers plan and present lessons. It is important to help teachers broaden their teaching strategies to include such skills as facilitated learning, problem-based learning, integrated thematic and differentiated instruction, Socratic seminars, community building in the classroom, and so on. Of course, this cannot all be tackled at once. Sit down with your faculty and develop a plan for enhancing teaching strategies and begin where they feel they first need help. You can then build on that base, letting master teachers help new teachers and other teachers needing assistance.

- **Culturally appropriate and enhanced curriculum:** Your curriculum must be relevant, and your student population and community must understand it. If you have a large number of minorities or subcultures in your building, include their history and lifestyles in your history and social studies classes; include their music in band, their art in your humanities program, and so forth. Native Americans, for example, should be able to study and learn all about their wonderful heritage, history, art, music, and culture. This is true for African Americans, Hispanics, and descendants of European immigrants, for students in farm communities, urban centers, and historical sites—the list could go on forever. This does not imply that you do not expand the cultural background of your building to a more national or global interest, but it is always important with curriculum and "connectedness" that you start where the student currently is and expand outward.

PATHWAYS AS AN AVENUE TO GOOD CULTURE AND CLIMATE

There are many ways that using a Collaborative Pathways system in your school can enhance and help ensure a positive culture and climate. The following Pathways processes will, when systematically established, automatically and positively affect your school's culture and climate.

- **Counseling processes in the classroom:** In a Collaborative Pathways High School, the counseling processes are integrated into classroom instruction (both Pathways classes and core and elective classes) with the counselors coming in and out of the classroom. In this way, all students receive counseling services and practice counseling and life skills. In addition, all students feel connected to the counselor and therefore can seek out this resource when they need help.

- **Classroom processes that are student centered:** Facilitated teaching makes student learning more permanent, more relevant, and promotes high-level thinking skills and mastery of standards and benchmarks. Student-centered classrooms are the key to successful Pathways instruction as students take control of their learning and its connection to their future.

- **Community processes as part of instruction:** The broadening of your campus to include the community with positive adult role models moving in and out of the school and providing work-based experiences for students and serving as mentors and advisors connects students to their school and community.

The integration of these three processes in themselves weaves a net under students so that they cannot fall through the cracks and sets a stage of interconnectedness that is the key to all students feeling connected to their school experience.

OTHER COMPLEMENTARY PROGRAMS

There are many other complementary student programs in a school building that can aid schools in building good culture and climate with their students and that complement any Pathways system. Following is a list and the rationale and definitions of a number of programs that we recommend you investigate or implement along with your Pathways system.

- **Peer Counseling:** Peer counseling is based on the fact that teenagers generally go to other teenagers for advice. Peer counseling classes and programs teach students how to listen, problem solve, make decisions, and mediate conflict. After extensive training and adult recommendations, these students serve as peer counselors on identified hours of the day for students to contact and discuss their issues. The peer counselors listen and help their fellow students make positive decisions. They never give advice or solve problems for them and are trained to refer when serious issues (e.g., suicide, drug use) arise. In high schools we work with that have peer counseling programs, administrators, teachers, and parents have seen a marked difference in the number of referral issues and improved student behavior.

- **Team Sports:** Team sports can be a double-edged sword in any high school building. Team sports can teach important teaming concepts, keep students connected to school, and help them maintain their grades. They can also help other students, and the community, feel pride in their school. When sports programs become more important than academics and students' post-secondary plans, however, a great deal of damage can be done. If athletes and coaches get special treatment or have different rules than everyone else, the healthy climate of your school will be affected.

- **Intramural Sports:** Providing before- and after-school sports for all students is a great way to keep students physically and mentally healthy. With intramural sports, all students get to play, and competition is contained. It is a great way for all students to get the benefit of sports and physical activity. Intramural sports are great programs for one of your community organizations, such as Lions or Rotary Clubs or the chamber of commerce, to sponsor.

- **Tutoring Programs:** Requiring students who aren't doing as well as they should be to attend tutoring programs sets high academic standards for all students. Your honor society students can provide tutoring during lunch or before and after school. Other possible tutors include parent volunteers, your library or literacy system, community organizations, or paid teachers and aides. Providing and requiring good tutoring programs for failing students lets them know that you believe in them and that they can learn.

- **Before- and After-School Programming, Pathways Groups, and Other Student Clubs and Organizations:** As we now clearly understand, the more students are involved in extracurricular activities, the more all students will connect to school. This means we need to have activities for all interests and aptitudes. One way to do this is to have Pathway-specific student clubs and student organizations such as computer club for business and video clubs for arts and communication. Parents and community members with special interests can sponsor clubs and organizations. Work with your parent-teacher organization and with community groups. State, federal, and foundation dollars are also available for before- and after-school programming. As you examine all your student activities, make sure you have a variety of activities that at least cover all your school's Pathways.

- **Student government:** All high schools should have a student government system that allows students to help make policy and procedures and decisions on the culture and climate of their own school.

- **Service learning and community service:** These programs work with volunteerism in the community and can be an elective class or student organizations. There is a great deal of information available on service learning from educational associations such as Phi Delta Kappa and the Association for Supervision and Curriculum Development.

- **Health education and drug prevention programs:** Whether it is in your health or physical education classes or integrated with other classes, such as your Pathways classes, it is important to include health and drug prevention programs in your curriculum that are not one-time "information shots" but continually address teen health issues. *Making the Grade: A Guide to School Drug Prevention Programs* is a publication provided by Drug Strategies (1999), a non-profit research institute. This publication gives data on program effectiveness and resources. (To obtain a copy of this important and interesting report, visit http://www.drugstrategies.org/pubs.html.)

The First-Day-of-School Challenge

With your staff and faculty, try the "first-day-of-school challenge" in Table 14.6 to examine your current practices to help you plan a better day for students like Miguel.

Review your responses to the questions and, as a faculty, discuss the positive aspects of your first-day-of-school plan and design an action plan for improvement of your areas of weakness. Finally, implement your action plan for a great first day for everyone.

CONCLUDING SCENARIO: MIGUEL'S FIRST DAY REVISITED

Miguel's first day of high school was for freshmen only; the older students would not attend until the following day. This gave all freshmen a chance to get

Table 14.6 First Day of School Questionnaire

	Yes	No	Response

How are your students welcomed into the building on the first day of school?

What are the first items with which they are presented: rules? discipline policies? positive interactions?

Is it clear that respect, responsibility, and the school environment are a collaborative effort rather than a "them against us" attitude?

Is it clear that no one will be teased or bullied in your school? Is it clear what a student who needs help with teasing and bullying can do?

Are the students made to feel this school belongs to you, to them, or to everyone?

Do you help new and transitioning students to acclimate to your school?

Do you involve community members and parents in a meaningful way on the first day of school?

Does each teacher give his or her students a different set of rules and grading procedures?

Is what you are expecting of students clear and fair for everyone?

Do you make it clear how conflict and anger is expected to be resolved in your building?

Is your discipline policy punitive, or does it have a tedious point system that encourages students to test it or to "play games" with it?

Do you interact with the students on the first day, or do you just "talk" at them?

Do you learn something special about your students the first day and share something special about yourself?

Do you give the students a chance to interact positively with each other?

Do you present your subject and class in a manner the students can relate to and that encourages students to be excited about participating in them?

Does your first day of school really show your students the respect and concern you have for them and their future?

Does your first day reflect unity, teaming, and care among staff and faculty?

Is everyone having fun on the first day of school—including you?

---

acclimated to the school without crowded halls and moments of embarrassment. When Miguel first arrived at school, everyone met in the commons area, where they were greeted by the entire staff and a group of community members. In Miguel's town, they have an active Veterans of Foreign Wars chapter that takes part in the first day of high school. The freshmen were divided into groups by alphabetical order and seated at tables. Each table had about 10 to 15 students, several staff members, and a veteran. The groups spent about an hour with a semistructured discussion that included a testimony from the veteran about his or her experiences as a student, a veteran, and a citizen. The veteran talked about respect and responsibility toward oneself, toward others, and toward their nation. The veteran also talked about the ceremonies the chapter sponsors throughout the year in the town and told the students how they could participate or help with these cultural events. The discussion included the fears, apprehension, and excitement the students felt about coming to high school and some general questions were answered. The teachers assigned to that group then went over the class rules and grading policies, *which were the same for all classes.* They also discussed the "No Tolerance" policy for teasing and bullying and told students how to report or deal with such infringements. After that, cookies and juice were served, and the group said goodbye to their veteran partners.

The group then went together to get their schedules and lockers. They had time to practice opening their lockers and organize them. The teachers reviewed schedules with the students, and then Miguel spent a reduced amount of time in each of his classes. Miguel's first class was Freshman Explorations, his Pathways class. At Miguel's school, this class is a "blocked" class that integrates his English and technology credit. Miguel used a handheld computer to write down three things he liked to do and three things he thought he was good at; he then "beamed" this information to three other students' handhelds to see if there were any matches and to discuss the similarities and differences of their choices. The students then beamed this information to the teacher, who used a computer projector to sort the interests and skills into the six Pathways used by their school.

At lunch, Miguel and three other students were matched with upper classmen from National Honor Society, Students Against Drunk Driving, student council, and the Business Professionals of America who had volunteered to be lunch buddies for freshmen during the first week of school. A student named Jared helped Miguel and his classmates learn about the lunch program—the process, the protocol, open gym during lunch, and so on. He said he would check in with his students during their first week to answer questions they had, reinforce the No Tolerance policy for teasing and bullying, and explain what they should do if they witnessed or experienced such actions. Miguel appreciated Jared's help. He felt comfortable at lunch, and knowing he might see Jared in the halls made him feel at ease.

After lunch, Miguel went to algebra, where the students did a community-building activity. Miguel thought the activity was corny, but it did help him meet and talk to his classmates. After the activity, the teacher presented an overview of the class and offered some ideas for the students to think about as potential projects for the semester. Miguel then went to science, where the class did another community-building activity. By this time, Miguel was getting the hang of these activities, and the students were beginning to have fun with each other. The science teacher gave an overview of the class and talked about the trip they take every year to the nearby wetlands. Next Miguel went to his Spanish class, where they did yet another community-building activity with directions given in Spanish. Miguel left the class already knowing several directions in Spanish! Band was his last class of the day, and it, too, began with a community-building activity with the kids using all sorts of instruments. Miguel knew his band teacher from band camp, so he already felt comfortable. The class talked about the upcoming marching band schedule, concerts, and festivals.

Miguel flew in the door after his first day of school. He couldn't tell his parents enough about all he did, the veteran he met, about Jared, and even about his classes and upcoming trips and projects. During the rest of the first week, Miguel and his teachers continued to build community and began academic work. They also spent time going over the student handbook, looking more in depth at some of the other important details that Jared had reviewed with them at lunch. Miguel felt as though he was an important part of his school; he felt safe and connected. He was well on his way to a successful high school career.

IN REVIEW

- A school's culture is the overall "patterns of norms, values, beliefs, relationships, rituals, tradition, and myths that are shared in varying degrees by members of a school community" (ERIC Wizard).
- Climate is the "temperature," or overall psychological and physical atmosphere in a school.
- Administrators, staff, students, parents, and community can affect, set, and control the culture and climate of their school.
- The key components of establishing good school culture and climate are school connectedness, well-managed classrooms, acceptance of diversity, and the elimination of codes of silence.
- It is vital to your school's culture and climate that you have an enforced "No Tolerance" policy and procedure for teasing and bullying.
- Create an active and empowered school culture and climate committee with working goals.
- Begin your culture and climate system by first assessing your current culture and climate and then developing a three- to five-year school plan.
- Use your Pathways system and other complementary programs to weave a system of culture and climate control that includes the key components for the establishment of school connectedness.
- Plan the first day of school with the big picture for students in mind.

Chapter Fifteen

Pathways as a Systematic Philosophy

SCENARIO: A PATHWAYS GRADUATION

When Natalie begins her stroll into the gym to the tune of "Pomp and Circumstance," she takes a moment to look around. The gym is ablaze with anticipation and excitement. It is graduation day at her Collaborative Pathways High School. One section of the gym has been reserved for all of the business members of the community who have supported Natalie and her classmates throughout their four-year journey. She notices the owners and managers of several local businesses who have allowed her school to do site visits and job shadows, several employees she chatted with as a freshman and job shadowed as a sophomore, two of the hospital workers she collaborated with during her senior project, and the nurses she worked with during her internship. As she looks to her right, she sees several of the academic institutions represented by admissions counselors and professors who have worked with and mentored many of the students, particularly during their junior and senior years. She spies the admissions counselor who sat on her senior project panel and helped her with her postsecondary plan. Natalie waves, and the admissions counselor gives her a "thumbs up." Just in front of the admissions counselor is the section that holds all the staff and counselors who helped her experience and build her plan each step of the way. She feels very connected to her high school teachers and knows they really took an interest in her and in her dreams.

When she looks to the left, she sees a large share of the high school population who has come to support the seniors of their school. Natalie waves at the freshman girl who needed Natalie's help in selecting her Pathway and smiles at the group of junior boys from her Health Pathway that she worked with on a service learning project this year. She never realized before how much truth there was in what her Pathways teachers had been telling her from the beginning of her high school career: It truly has taken the entire "village" to help guide her as she designed her postsecondary plan.

Proud parents watch as their students come down the aisle clad in their black robes. Just as all of the balloons in the gym represent the Pathways colors, all the students wear a cord representing their Pathway—red for business, green for agriculture and natural resources, light blue for human service, dark blue for health, yellow for arts and communication, and grey for science, industry, and technology. In addition, the tassels on their caps represent the Pathway they have pursued over the past three years. The gorgeous flower arrangement in front of the podium includes all six Pathways colors. The students sit down to begin the ceremony seated next to their classmates from the same Pathway; these are the students with whom they have worked side by side as they each developed their individual plans. Natalie notices her parents and grandparents as she sits, and they smile at her. Several of her classmates look up at her dad who has helped them with chats, job shadows, and senior projects.

In a few minutes, after the opening remarks and giving of scholarships from several businesses (who truly know the students, their aspirations, and how far they have progressed in their plans), it comes time for the valedictorian and salutatorian speeches. Dae Soon, the valedictorian, talks about the future and how whatever comes next for the students is what they have worked for and transitioned themselves into over the past four years. As he mentions the many paths that students are taking—colleges and junior colleges, training programs and skill schools, apprenticeships, and the military—it becomes clear that all the students have worked to eliminate what would not work for them and selected a path and a plan that will fit the unique skills, talents, and interests that each one possesses.

Next comes Rochelle, the salutatorian, who talks in terms of memories with a beautiful slide show behind her (created by the senior class students from digital pictures) of their four-year journey. The first pictures are of the students during freshman year with hard hats at a work site, with a microphone at a radio station, with health care workers at a walk-in clinic, with a supervisor at a bean co-op watching laser machinery sort beans, and with pilots and mechanics as they work on planes at an airport. From sophomore year are wonderful pictures of Natalie and her classmates spending a day on the job in a huge assortment of career fields—with a hockey team, at a meat counter, in a photography studio, at a graphic design firm, in a doctor's office, at a pharmacy, at a farm farrowing pigs, and on a construction site. As the slide show continues to click away, reviewing the students' junior year, the audience is treated to pictures of students working side-by-side with adults in various workplaces. There are students drafting, students designing merchandise windows, students building, students fixing engines, students writing at newspapers, and all this along with a collage of many students working at a wide variety of worksites. As Rochelle reviews the senior year, the pictures show the audience a wonderful variety of students involved in creative and meaningful capstone projects—working with children at a hospital, on the job at a wildlife site, working at a police station fingerprinting suspects, on the computers at a water treatment plant, and in a restaurant kitchen garnishing desserts.

Then comes the moment everyone has been waiting for: distribution of the diplomas. As students walk individually to the podium for their moment of glory, two slides are shown. The first is each student's baby picture so everyone can "ohh" and "ahh" over how they have grown. Next to the baby picture is the student's Pathway selection and postsecondary plan. As the student walks across the stage with diploma in hand, the second slide shows what he or she has done to streamline the plan to this point. As Natalie's name is called, she walks proudly to the podium as a picture of her digging into her first birthday cake is marked by the side with the words, Health Science Pathway and Smith College: to pursue a degree in nursing with a specialty in pediatrics. As she walks across the stage and receives her diploma, smiling brilliantly to the crowd, the second slide outlines the path she has taken: Health Science Pathway; Job Shadows: emergency room nurse, pharmacist, and physical therapist; Internship: neonatal unit at Jones Hospital; Senior Project: raised funds for the revamping of the pediatrics playroom at Johnston Rehabilitation Center and volunteered in the playroom (for 30 hours).

Once the diplomas are all distributed, the traditional school slide show plays with pictures of all of the wonderful parts of a high school—sports and activities, classes and friendships, and of course, pictures of the school mascot. Then when the caps are thrown into the air and the students march out, everyone meets in the June sun to celebrate with the graduates. This is a happy day that will be equally enjoyed by everyone who has collaborated in these young people's lives. Natalie is surrounded by teachers, mentors, admissions counselors, community members, classmates, and family who have played vital roles in her success. At a Collaborative Pathways High School, everyone in attendance somehow owns a small piece of each diploma.

SYSTEM CHANGE

As you read Natalie's scenario, it likely becomes evident that more has happened at her high school than simply a structural change. Yes, the structure of the school was changed significantly, but what you see reflected the most in the scenario is the cultural change—those beliefs, practices, and traditions that make a school. That is the difference between program change and systems change. Systems change affects the entire process and every aspect of your school. If you compared it with the human body, it is not just a change in the arm or the foot but in the circulatory system that circulates messages and oxygen to the whole "system."

Structural Change + Cultural Change = SYSTEMS CHANGE

As you read through each chapter of the book, you were examining how to incorporate a specific aspect of your school into the Collaborative Career

Pathways Model. The model then became the "venue" for the systems change, with each component directly addressed and connected to the "blood flow" of the circulatory system. This was done by examining and working with the three main "arteries" of counseling, classroom and community.

Creating a Structure With Purpose, Collaboration, and Support

Any successful systems change must be made within a purposeful structure that is both collaborative and flexible. This is a difficult concept—you must give directions while giving away ownership. Your faculty will first need to be given a structure with purpose: the Collaborative Career Pathways Model. Its purpose is that every student will focus his or her high school education on a realistic postsecondary plan with the skills, knowledge, and experiences needed to successfully complete that plan. Through self-exploration and the practicing of life skills, students also learn to be productive citizens and global residents.

The Pathways system is implemented through learner-centered instruction utilizing the three Cs: counseling, classroom, and community. The system process must allow for structure and collaboration among all stakeholders, and it must be flexible; it also requires a directive from the school leadership, however, that a Collaborative Pathways system *will* be implemented.

The leadership's directive involves moving to a student-centered teaching and learning model, implementing Pathways classes, using businesses and the community, communicating with parents, and so forth. Collaboration can be encompassed by the following question: What is the best way to implement this system? Flexibility within the system can be understood by exploring questions such as, How will we move teaching and learning to a self-directed mode? Where and how will we implement the Pathways classes? How will we use our business partners? How, when, and where will we communicate with parents?

> *To ensure success as you implement the Pathways system at your school, you must supply stakeholders with a clear structure and purpose for the project. With that in hand, stakeholders can develop and implement a system that best fits the needs of the school, of the faculty and staff, and—most important—of the students.*

We are not saying that you alone must give the directive for a systems change. It will be more effective if you have your school board, superintendent, counselors, key teachers, students, parents, and community members—in other words, your Pathways team—behind you. In the end, however, the principal will be the one to give the directive and "stay the course."

The final key to success in systems change after a purposeful structure and collaboration is support. Change is difficult, and your key players must feel support during the change process. Change always produces a certain amount of chaos. It is important that during this period everyone feels supported.

Changing your teaching style, letting students have more control, or using your community in the classroom is not easy, and mistakes can be made. Keep to the positive and make sure the necessary professional development is provided. Protect your change agents because they may get more resistance than expected. Listen, listen, listen and address concerns and conflicts as they arise. Keep your finger on the pulse of the change and defuse myths and "snipers" as they surface. Know who your key supporters are and use them to build a safety net for your change process. They can help you by supporting your structure, helping with collaborative efforts, and lending support to "uncertain" participants.

Creating Cultural Change Through Process and Experience

As you change the structure, you are also changing the culture of your school. Cultural change comes through processes and experiences. The beliefs your staff, students, parents, and community have will change as they become more involved in the processes and the experiences provided by the implementation of their Collaborative Career Pathways system. Only involvement and personal experiences can change mind-sets. These processes may be different for every stakeholder but will include the following:

- Developing vision and goals for your school
- Opening the classroom to counseling processes
- Taking ownership and control of the curriculum
- Implementing Pathways classes at each level
- Experimenting with flexible scheduling and staffing
- Interweaving core and elective classes into the Pathways process
- Taking ownership and control of your school's public relations
- Using the community in all aspects of your instructional process
- Confronting the culture and climate issues facing your school

Outcomes for stakeholders (including students, teachers, parents, and community members) from these processes include the following:

- Stakeholders understand and support the larger purpose of the school.
- Students experience the application of life-and self-management skills.
- Faculty members gain control over identifying and teaching essential skills in the classroom and are able to integrate those skills with the rest of the school's curriculum.
- Students take interest and control of their own learning process.
- The community supports the classroom.
- A connected teaching and learning experience is created by tying together Pathway, core, and elective class objectives.
- Stakeholders gain freedom from rigid schedules and a new openness to creative thinking.
- Stakeholders feel connected instead of isolated.
- Stakeholders have a direct influence on public relations and community involvement.

- Stakeholders have control and ownership of the culture and climate of the school.
- Stakeholders see purpose in their role.

Key Provisions for Successful Systems Change

While this structural and cultural change is happening simultaneously, there are several components you must provide for stakeholders:

- A deep understanding of the Collaborative Pathways Model
- Time
- Team-building processes
- Staff-empowered curriculum
- Facilitation and professional development
- Documentation of effectiveness
- Consistent leadership
- Celebrations

Throughout your journey, your stakeholders must have a deep understanding of the Collaborative Career Pathways Model. Specifically, they must have the depth of understanding that you expect teachers to pass on to students. They must be able not only to know the processes but to do them. They must understand enough to be able to communicate, apply, adjust, and evaluate the concepts without losing the purpose of the system. For this to happen, your stakeholders must understand why the change is necessary, a structure for implementation, the importance of their role, and the outcome. The initial education you must provide is crucial to your success because stakeholders cannot "stay the course" if they do not believe in and understand what they are trying to accomplish. They must also be provided with the armor needed to reach their objective: knowledge and skills. We can accomplish so much if we have a clear direction with purpose, and you must provide that to your forces.

One piece of armor you must provide is time—time for collaboration between administrators and teachers, between school and community, and, most important, among teachers. It is essential to successfully changing the processes in your classrooms that you ensure that teachers have time to collaborate, plan, dialogue, and share with and support each other. You must provide a team-building process. Also, all stakeholders must be trained in a teaming process, and the process must be used religiously. Whenever people feel that teaming is only valued on a superficial level, you will lose support.

Teachers must also be empowered by having control over their curriculum, by being able to sustain academic rigor, and by understanding how their instructional part fits into the whole. If there is a subliminal message in this book, it is *professional development*. Without proper facilitation of professional development for all stakeholders, whatever you are trying to implement will fail. This is especially true for teachers because they need to be able to practice, experiment, learn, expand, retry, coach, and support the changes. Don't ask people to do what they are not trained to do. The changes that must take place may be more comfortable or easier for some but may prove difficult for others. Once they succeed, however, you will have won them forever; to succeed, they need professional development and support.

To keep your momentum going and to make informed decisions, you must measure your results. Start with baseline data and measure consistently each year. You will want to be able to compare and see results in the area of attendance, tardiness, discipline referrals, student achievement in terms of grades and achievement tests, successful transitions to postsecondary plans, accuracy of plans, and wages earned after postsecondary completion. Each year, as you complete more of the components and the system becomes ingrained in your culture, you should see a consistency in your data and a rise in student success from previous years. This success can be divided into two areas: student success during their years at your school and their success after leaving your school. This data should also reflect a rise in the percentage of students achieving success. If you can show all your stakeholders clear data to support what they are doing and if they know their hard work is paying off for students, they will keep going even if the going gets rough. After all, we are working together in this field for the same purpose—the success of students; if your data show student success, people will listen and participate. On the other hand, if parts of your data are not showing student success, examine why this is the case. Use your information to decide where the weak links are and fix problems as soon as they begin to appear. If you are willing to examine your processes honestly, you will prevent more problems, and more people will respect the system.

> *It is crucial for the principal to provide consistent leadership for your system.*

A decision process and program effectiveness based on documentation are only two of the most important areas of effective leadership. Strong research in both business and industry and in education points to the leader as pivotal and key to the entire change process.

The principal must understand and support the interaction of all the arenas and play gatekeeper. Keep all the parts interconnected, and don't let gaps or cracks develop and grow between parties. Be careful that a division doesn't occur between your Pathways and core or elective teachers, your counselor and classroom process, or between your employers and your school district, for example. Keep everyone moving in the same direction—toward the successful transition of students. Keep asking your stakeholders important questions such as the following:

- How will this help students transition to their plans?
- How will this help students achieve?
- How will this help students be better citizens or community members?

Always keep asking yourself these questions:

- What do they need to be successful?
- How can I help?
- What will show my support?
- How can I reward them for their efforts?
- How can I show them that what they are doing is working?

When the road gets tough— and it will— it is important that you keep hope alive and that your belief in the system not falter. Nothing worthwhile is easy, and the Pathways process is no different. When trouble rears its ugly head, your team will look to you for positive input, direction, creative problem solving, flexibility, and support. In other words, your team will look to you for leadership.

Finally, don't forget to celebrate. Celebrations help shape culture and show people what we think is important. Don't just celebrate the "big" successes, celebrate the small steps, too. Celebrate achievement and events with students, such as the Freshman Pathway Selection Parties. Celebrate teachers' growth with awards and celebrations when they complete training or implement a new strategy. Celebrate with parents when their students succeed. Celebrate with employers—give a school luncheon for this year's community participants, for example. Keep the spirit of challenge and conquest alive by rewarding yourselves and having fun together.

CONCLUSION

As we wish you luck and Godspeed on your Collaborative Career Pathways journey, we would like to conclude with just a few words of inspiration. We ourselves have been through this process and are still experiencing phases of it. We have seen how it positively affects the lives and roles of teachers, parents, and the community. The change is greatest seen in, and experienced by, the students. Once you begin to work with students who have taken control of their learning, of their future plans, and of their lives, you, your faculty, and your staff will never go back. You will say what we have heard so many times, once stakeholders begin to see Pathways working for their students: "This is the reason I went into education."

Resource A

Action Plan for Model Implementation

Committee:			
Goal:			
Task 1:			
Action/Outcome:			
Person(s) Responsible:	Time line:	Funding:	Date Completed:
Task 2:			
Action/Outcome:			
Person(s) Responsible:	Time line:	Funding:	Date Completed:

Copyright © 2004 by Corwin Press. All rights reserved. Reprinted from *Career Pathways: Preparing Students for Life,* by Elaine Makas Howard and Pamela J. Ill. Thousand Oaks, CA: Corwin Press, www.corwinpress.com. Reproduction authorized only for the local school site that has purchased this book.

Resource B

Vision Process Action Plan

Steps to Completing Your Vision Process:	Persons	Begun	Completed
1. Pathways Committee investigates the Collaborative Career Pathways Vision/Mission/Goals gaining clarity and understanding			
2. Gather all previous documents and compile information			
3. Pathways Committee presents Career Pathways vision materials and compiled previous vision data to entire staff			
4. Staff breaks into integrated teams and reviews all materials, making recommendations			
5. Entire staff uses team's information to compile new vision, mission, and goal statements			
6. Stakeholder teams are created and value statements developed			
7. New vision document, including value statements, is put together for approval by staff, administration, parent associations, student government, board of education, etc.			
8. Document is published			
9. Pathways Committee (or School Improvement Committee, etc.) sets database and activities for the review and evaluation of the vision, mission, and goals on a yearly basis			
10. Stakeholder groups create database and activities to measure value statements			
11. Yearly evaluation of vision document			

Copyright © 2004 by Corwin Press. All rights reserved. Reprinted from *Career Pathways: Preparing Students for Life*, by Elaine Makas Howard and Pamela J. Ill. Thousand Oaks, CA: Corwin Press, www.corwinpress.com. Reproduction authorized only for the local school site that has purchased this book.

Resource C

Student 4-Year Planning Sheet

Student:	Grade 9　1st　　2nd	Grade 10　1st　　2nd	Grade 11　1st　　2nd	Grade 12　1st　　2nd
Block 1				
Block 2				
Block 3				
Block 4				

Copyright © 2004 by Corwin Press. All rights reserved. Reprinted from *Career Pathways: Preparing Students for Life*, by Elaine Makas Howard and Pamela J. Ill. Thousand Oaks, CA: Corwin Press, www.corwinpress.com. Reproduction authorized only for the local school site that has purchased this book.

Resource D

Sample Career Pathway Educational Development Plan (E.D.P.)

Educational Development Plan: _____
_____ High School _____

Assessment Results:

State Exam:

ACT:

Career Pathway Choice:
    Assessment-Based Recommendation:
    Career Pathway Choice:
    Career Choice:

Career Prep Activities:
    Interviews:
    Job Shadows:
    Internships:
    Work-related experience:

Extra-Curricular Activities/Interests:

Plans and Preparation:

Short-Term Goals:
Long-Term Goals:

Academic Activities: Career Activities:

Postsecondary Plan:

Class Selection   1st semester   2nd semester
Signatures:

Student: _____ Date _____

Parent: _____ Date _____

Counselor: _____ Date _____

Copyright © 2004 by Corwin Press. All rights reserved. Reprinted from *Career Pathways: Preparing Students for Life,* by Elaine Makas Howard and Pamela J. Ill. Thousand Oaks, CA: Corwin Press, www.corwinpress.com. Reproduction authorized only for the local school site that has purchased this book.

Resource E

Department Goal Planning/Action Sheet

Department Goals:_____	Outcome	Time line	Person(s) Responsible

Copyright © 2004 by Corwin Press. All rights reserved. Reprinted from *Career Pathways: Preparing Students for Life*, by Elaine Makas Howard and Pamela J. Ill. Thousand Oaks, CA: Corwin Press, www.corwinpress.com. Reproduction authorized only for the local school site that has purchased this book.

Resource F

Curriculum Planning Tool

Curriculum Process or Step	Yes	No
Have you and your staff developed a curriculum vision statement with goals (life skills) for the student learners who exit your high school?		
Have you and your staff incorporated those goal statements into life skills to be integrated across the curriculum?		
Have you developed curriculum learner statements and goal for each content area in your high school?		
Have you and your staff identified standards and benchmarks for each of your content areas?		
Have you aligned your content standards and benchmarks to grade levels and coursework?		
Have you aligned your standards and benchmarks to your assessment testing program?		
Have you mapped your curriculum?		
Have you developed essential content skills for the reinforcement of academic skills and rigor throughout the curriculum and as a base for developing integrated units?		
Is your staff versed in brain-based teaching and learning?		
Does your staff understand the concept of integrated curriculum and how it can "pull" together learning for students?		
Has your staff been trained in the development and implementation of integrated themes, units, and curriculum?		
Is your staff trained on the use and integration of technology in instruction?		
Does your staff know how to create assessments that can work as predictors of success for mastery of standards and state and national tests?		
Does your staff know how to collect and use data to make instructional decisions?		
Does your staff understand the connection between curriculum processes and implementation of Career Pathways?		
Does your staff understand the connection between curriculum processes and accreditation systems?		

Copyright © 2004 by Corwin Press. All rights reserved. Reprinted from *Career Pathways: Preparing Students for Life*, by Elaine Makas Howard and Pamela J. Ill. Thousand Oaks, CA: Corwin Press, www.corwinpress.com. Reproduction authorized only for the local school site that has purchased this book.

Resource G

Career Pathway 4 × 4 Block Scheduling Planner

Freshman First Semester	**Freshman Second Semester**

Sophomore First Semester	**Sophomore Second Semester**

Junior First Semester	**Junior Second Semester**

Senior First Semester	**Senior Second Semester**

Copyright © 2004 by Corwin Press. All rights reserved. Reprinted from *Career Pathways: Preparing Students for Life*, by Elaine Makas Howard and Pamela J. Ill. Thousand Oaks, CA: Corwin Press, www.corwinpress.com. Reproduction authorized only for the local school site that has purchased this book.

Resource H

Career Pathway Alternative Block (A/B) Scheduling Planner

Freshman First Semester						**Freshman Second Semester**				
Block A: odd days										
Block B: even days										
Sophomore First Semester						**Sophomore Second Semester**				
Block A: odd days										
Block B: even days										
Junior First Semester						**Junior Second Semester**				
Block A: odd days										
Block B: even days										
Senior First Semester						**Senior Second Semester**				
Block A: odd days										
Block B: even days										

Copyright © 2004 by Corwin Press. All rights reserved. Reprinted from *Career Pathways: Preparing Students for Life,* by Elaine Makas Howard and Pamela J. Ill. Thousand Oaks, CA: Corwin Press, www.corwinpress.com. Reproduction authorized only for the local school site that has purchased this book.

Resource I

Career Pathways Traditional Block Scheduling Planner

Freshman First Semester			**Freshman Second Semester**		
Sophomore First Semester			**Sophomore Second Semester**		
Junior First Semester			**Junior Second Semester**		
Senior First Semester			**Senior Second Semester**		

Copyright © 2004 by Corwin Press. All rights reserved. Reprinted from *Career Pathways: Preparing Students for Life*, by Elaine Makas Howard and Pamela J. Ill. Thousand Oaks, CA: Corwin Press, www.corwinpress.com. Reproduction authorized only for the local school site that has purchased this book.

Resource J

Student Goal Planner

Goals today	Goals this week	Goals this year	Goals for ten years

Copyright © 2004 by Corwin Press. All rights reserved. Reprinted from *Career Pathways: Preparing Students for Life*, by Elaine Makas Howard and Pamela J. Ill. Thousand Oaks, CA: Corwin Press, www.corwinpress.com. Reproduction authorized only for the local school site that has purchased this book.

Resource K

Study Skill Planner

September:	October:
November:	December:
January:	

Resource L

Student Teaming Card

Name:

Hartman Personality Profile Colors:

   Primary:

   Secondary:

Holland Hexagon Profile (list first three):

   1.

   2.

   3.

Learning Style:

Multiple Intelligences (first three):

1.   2.   3.

Copyright © 2004 by Corwin Press. All rights reserved. Reprinted from *Career Pathways: Preparing Students for Life*, by Elaine Makas Howard and Pamela J. Ill. Thousand Oaks, CA: Corwin Press, www.corwinpress.com. Reproduction authorized only for the local school site that has purchased this book.

Resource M

Sample Journal Questionnaire

- Do you think the results of your Personality Profile match the real you?

- Is there another personality or hexagon section that better matches who you are?

- Do your skills and interests match your profile?

- What are your future dreams? Are they the same or do they differ from your long-term goals? How, if at all, do your dreams differ from your parents' dreams and goals for you?

Copyright © 2004 by Corwin Press. All rights reserved. Reprinted from *Career Pathways: Preparing Students for Life,* by Elaine Makas Howard and Pamela J. Ill. Thousand Oaks, CA: Corwin Press, www.corwinpress.com. Reproduction authorized only for the local school site that has purchased this book.

Resource N

Pathway Decision-Making Planner

Problem 1: Which is the better Pathway for me?	Short-Term Goal Long-Term Goal

Pathway A:	Pathway B:
Pros:	Pros:
Cons:	Cons:
Skill Emphases:	Skill Emphases:

Decision:

Reasons:

Copyright © 2004 by Corwin Press. All rights reserved. Reprinted from *Career Pathways: Preparing Students for Life*, by Elaine Makas Howard and Pamela J. Ill. Thousand Oaks, CA: Corwin Press, www.corwinpress.com. Reproduction authorized only for the local school site that has purchased this book.

Resource O

Chat Card

Interviewee Name:

Occupation & what you do:

Pathway:

What do you like most about your job?

What are the biggest challenges of your job?

What skills do you use on a daily basis?

What training do you have for this job?

Copyright © 2004 by Corwin Press. All rights reserved. Reprinted from *Career Pathways: Preparing Students for Life,* by Elaine Makas Howard and Pamela J. Ill. Thousand Oaks, CA: Corwin Press, www.corwinpress.com. Reproduction authorized only for the local school site that has purchased this book.

Resource P

Pathway-Integrated Unit Planner

Skills	Unit: Pathway: Emphasis:			Standards
Cognitive:	\multicolumn{3}{c|}{Community Links}	Science:
	Research:	Speakers:	Shadows:	Math:
	Visits:	Internships:	Projects:	
Technical:	Other:			Language Arts:
	\multicolumn{3}{c|}{Assessment}	
	Written:	Video:	Oral:	
People:	Skits:	Portfolio:	Journals:	Social Studies: (Life Management)
Work Ethic:	Other:			(Other)

Notes:

Copyright © 2004 by Corwin Press. All rights reserved. Reprinted from *Career Pathways: Preparing Students for Life*, by Elaine Makas Howard and Pamela J. Ill. Thousand Oaks, CA: Corwin Press, www.corwinpress.com. Reproduction authorized only for the local school site that has purchased this book.

Resource Q

Relationships	Current Status	What We Need	Action Plan	Time line
Staff-to-staff relations				
Staff-student relations				
School-community relations				
School rituals and celebrations				
Student Needs	**Current Status**	**What We Need**	**Action Plan**	**Time line**
Student social and academic support				
Student connectedness				
Self				
Students				
Teachers				
Community				
Student participation				
Student orientations and transitions				
Student avenues to seek help				
Instruction	**Current Status**	**What We Need**	**Action Plan**	**Time line**
Well-managed and facilitated classrooms				
Staff development				
Curriculum Integration of Culture and Climate programs*				
Culturally appropriate/enhanced curriculum				
Structure	**Current Status**	**What We Need**	**Action Plan**	**Time line**
No Tolerance Policies and Procedures for teasing and bullying				
Simple and cohesive rules and procedures (without punitive and tedious discipline policies)				
Conflict resolution and teaming processes				

*Continual practice in the classroom of counseling curriculum skills (e.g., character development, conflict resolution, ethical decision making, listening skills, etc.)

Copyright © 2004 by Corwin Press. All rights reserved. Reprinted from *Career Pathways: Preparing Students for Life*, by Elaine Makas Howard and Pamela J. Ill. Thousand Oaks, CA: Corwin Press, www.corwinpress.com. Reproduction authorized only for the local school site that has purchased this book.

Resource R

Staff First Day of School Questionnaire

QUESTION	YES	NO	Response
How are your students welcomed into the building the first day of school?			
What are the first items they are presented with? Rules? Discipline policies? Positive interactions?			
It is clear that respect, responsibility, and the school environment are a collaborative effort rather than a "them against us" attitude?			
Is it clear that no one will be teased or bullied in your school and is it clear what avenue a student can take who needs help with teasing and bullying?			
Are students made to feel that the school belongs to you, to them, or to everyone?			
Do you help new and transitioning students to get acclimated to your building?			
Do you involve community members and parents in a meaningful way on the first day of school?			
Does each teacher give his or her students a different set of rules and grading procedures?			
Is what you are expecting of them clear and fair for everyone?			
Do you make it clear how conflict and anger are expected to be resolved in your building?			
Is your discipline policy punitive and has a point system so complicated your students have to complete an algebra class just to do the math?			
Do you interact with the students on the first day or do you just "talk" at them?			
Do you learn something special about your students the first day and share something special about yourself?			
Do you give the students a chance to interact positively with each other?			
Do you present your subject and class in a manner the students can relate to and be excited about participating in?			
Does your first day of school really show your students the respect and care you have for them and their future?			
Does your first day reflect a unified staff, good teaming, and care among yourselves?			
Is everyone having fun on the first day of school—even you?			

Copyright © 2004 by Corwin Press. All rights reserved. Reprinted from *Career Pathways: Preparing Students for Life*, by Elaine Makas Howard and Pamela J. Ill. Thousand Oaks, CA: Corwin Press, www.corwinpress.com. Reproduction authorized only for the local school site that has purchased this book.

References

Armstrong, T. (1993). *7 kinds of smart: Identifying and developing your multiple intelligences.* New York: Plume/Penguin.

At Texas school, students try many paths to future. (2001, June 13). *What works in teaching and learning* (pp. 1, 6–8). Alexandria, VA: Aspen.

Bernhardt, V. (2003). No schools left behind. *Educational Leadership, 60*(5), 26–30.

Berrien County Intermediate School District. (2001). *Career Pathways* [annual education report]. Berrien Springs, MI: Lakehouse Evaluation.

Bingham, M., & Stryker, S. (1993). *Career choices* (rev. ed). Santa Barbara, CA: Academic Innovations.

Blum, R. W., McNeely, C. A., & Rinehart, P. M. (2002). *Improving the odds: The untapped power of school to improve the health of teens.* Minneapolis: Center for Adolescent Health and Development, University of Minnesota.

Blum, R. W., & Rinehart, P. M. (2000). *Reducing the risk: Connections that make a difference in the lives of youth.* Minneapolis: Division of General Pediatrics and Adolescent Health, University of Minnesota.

Bossert, R. (n.d.). *Exploring careers: What's right for you?* [video]. Pleasantville, NY: Sunburst Communications.

Caine, G., & Caine, R. (1991). *Making connections: Teaching and the human brain.* Alexandria, VA: Association for Supervision and Curriculum Development.

Campbell, C. A., & Dahir, C. A. (1997). *Sharing the vision: The national standards for school counseling programs.* Alexandria, VA: American School Counselor Association.

Canady, R. L. (1994). High school alternative scheduling to enhance teaching and learning. *The Video Journal of Education, 4*(2). Sandy, UT: TeachStream.

Choosing Success. (1999). *First quarter report summary for Pathways to Professions.* Santa Ana, CA.

Cotton, K. (2000). *The schooling practices that matter most.* Portland, OR: Northwest Regional Educational Laboratory/Association for Supervision and Curriculum Development.

Differential Aptitude Test. (1990). *Form C,* 5th ed. Retrieved September 9, 2001, from http://www.bridgew.edu

Drug Strategies. (1999). *Making the grade: A guide to school drug prevention programs.* Washington, DC: Author. (Available for purchase at http://www.drugstrategies.org/pubs.html)

Dufour, R., & Eaker, R. (1998). *Professional learning communities at work: Best practices for enhancing student achievement.* Bloomington, IN: National Education Service.

Gardner, H. (1983). *Frames of mind: Theory of multiple intelligences.* New York: Basic Books. (Tenth anniversary edition, 1993)

Gibbs, J. (2000). *Tribes, a new way of learning and being together.* Sausalito, CA: Center Source Systems.

Gray, K. (2000). *Getting real: Helping teens find their future.* Thousand Oaks, CA: Corwin.

Harris, K. (1996). *Making connections: Curriculum integration projects.* Sonoma, CA: SRS Associates.

Hartman Color Profile. (1999). Salt Lake City, UT: Color Code Communications.

Holmboe, J., & Malone, D. (1996). *Focus on Freshmen: An energetic, hands-on curriculum for developing successful high school students.* Boston: Jobs for the Future.

Hughes, K. L., Bailey, T., & Mechur, M. (2001). *School-to-work: Making a difference in education. Institute on Education and the Economy.* New York: Teacher's College Press, Columbia University.

Ingham Intermediate School District. (1998). *MOIS: Michigan Occupational Information System.* Mason, MI: Author. Retrieved from http://www.mois.org

Jacobs, H. H. (1997). *Mapping the big picture: Integrating curriculum and assessment K–12.* Alexandria, VA: Association for Supervision and Curriculum Development.

Jensen, E. (1998). *Teaching with the brain in mind.* Alexandria, VA: Association for Supervision and Curriculum Development.

Kendall, J. S., & Marzano, R. J. (2000). *Content knowledge: A compendium of standards and benchmarks for K–12 education* (3rd ed.). Aurora, CO: Mid-continent Research for Education and Learning; Alexandria, VA: Association for Supervision and Curriculum Development.

Kovalik, S. (1994). *ITI: The model.* Kent, WA: Books for Educators.

Kovalik, S. (2001). *Intelligence is a function of experience* [video]. Covington, WA: Author.

Kovalik, S., with Karen Olsen. (1997). *ITI: The model. Integrated Thematic Instruction* (3rd ed., Chapter 11, pp. 139–161). Kent, WA: Books for Educators (distributors).

Masden, P., & Wagner, C. R. (2002). *School culture triage.* Clarksville, TN: Austin Peay State University; Bowling Green: Western Kentucky University.

Michigan Department of Career Development. (2001). *How do our children choose careers?* (Project 0301-225). Retrieved April 2001 from http://www.michigan.gov/mdcd/0,1607,7-122-1678_2568_2578—,00.html.

Michigan Department of Education. (1996). *Michigan curriculum framework.* Lansing, MI: Author.

Michigan Department of Education. (1996, July). *Technology content standards and benchmarks.* Lansing, MI: Author.

Michigan Department of Education. (1990). *Technology, content standards, and benchmarks.* Lansing, MI: Author.

Michigan Department of Education, Office of School Excellence. (2002). *Michigan school climate profile.* Lansing, MI: Author.

Michigan Occupational Information System. (1998). Mason, MI: Ingham Intermediate School District. Retrieved from http://www.mois.org

National Association of Secondary School Principals. (1990). *Comprehensive assessment of school environments information management system.* Reston, VA: Author.

National Commission on the High School Senior Year. (n.d.). *Raising our sites: No high school senior left behind.* Princeton, NJ: Woodrow Wilson National Fellowship Foundation.

Radd, T. R. (2000). *Getting from here to there: Education for the new millennium.* Omaha, NE: Grow With Guidance.

Ross, A. (2000). *ITI advanced curriculum writing workshop.* Tulsa, OK: Susan Kovalik & Associates.

Scales, P., & Leffert, N. (1999). *Developmental assets: A synthesis of the scientific research on adolescent development.* Minneapolis, MN: Search Institute.

Scales, P., & Leffert, N. (1999). *Other adult relationships and caring neighborhoods.* Minneapolis, MN: Search Institute.

Schmoker, M. (1999). *Results: The key to continuous school improvement* (2nd ed.). Alexandria, VA: Association for Supervision and Curriculum Development.

Schmoker, M. (2003). First things first: Demystifying data analysis. *Educational Leadership, 60*(5), 22–23.

School-to-Work Web site. (n.d.) Retrieved from http://www.stw.ed.gov/

Sousa, D. A. (1995). *How the brain learns: A classroom teacher's guide.* Reston, VA: National Association of Secondary School Principals.

South Carolina Governor's Workforce Education Task Force. (2001). *Pathways to prosperity: Success for every student in the 21st-century workplace.* Columbia, SC: The Task Force, 2001. Retrieved from http://www.state.sc.us:80/governor/gwetf.pdf

South Carolina task force calls for mandatory Career Clusters. (2001, October 31). *What works in teaching and learning* [newsletter] (pp. 1, 7–8). Alexandria, VA: Aspen.

Sprenger, M. (1999). *Learning and memory: The brain in action.* Alexandria, VA: Association for Supervision and Curriculum Development.

STW Reporter. (1998). *Research-based information on School-to-Work in New York.* White Plains, NY: Westchester Institute for Human Services Research.

Tuscola Intermediate School District. (2003). *Tuscola County Student Career Pathways/Freshman Focus survey.* Retrieved May 5, 2003, from http:www.tisd.k12.mi.us

U.S. Department of Education/Office of Vocational and Adult Education. (2002). *The sixteen career clusters.* Retrieved August 7, 2002, from http://www.careerclusters.org.

U.S. Department of Labor. (1991). *What work requires of schools: A SCANS report for America 2000.* Washington, DC: Author.

Vocational Biographies. (1999). *Vocational biographies: Career library* (Series A–C, Y, Z). Sauk Centre, MN: Author.

Vocational Biographies. (2000). *Vocational biographies: Career library* (Series D). Sauk Centre, MN: Author.

Vocational Biographies. (2001). *Vocational biographies: Career library* (Series D). Sauk Centre, MN: Author.

Vocational Biographies. (2002). *Vocational biographies: Career library.* Sauk Centre, MN: Author.

Vossekuil, B., Reddy, M., Fein, R., Borum, R., & Modzeleski, W. (2002). *Threat assessment in schools: A guide to managing threatening situations and to creating safe school climates.* Washington, DC: U.S. Secret Service, National Threat Assessment Center.

Vossekuil, B., Reddy, M., Fein, R., Borum, R., & Modzeleski, W. (2000). *U.S.S.S. safe school initiative: An interim report on the prevention of targeted violence in schools.* Washington, DC: U.S. Secret Service, National Threat Assessment Center.

Wonacott, M. (2001). *The highlight zone: Research @ Work*, no. 6. Retrieved August 8, 2002, from http://www.nccte.org/publications/infosynthesis/highlightzone/highlight06/index.asp

Index

Action plans
    department goal, 313
    for model implementation, 309
    vision process, 310
Action research on pathways high
    schools, 19
Agriculture, food, and natural
    resources career cluster, 7
    (table), 11 (table), 191t
Alignment, curriculum, 115
Alternative block (A/B) scheduling
    planner, 316
American College Test (ACT), 35, 85,
    102, 214
American School Counselor Association,
    85–86, 91
Architecture and construction career cluster,
    7 (table)
Armed Services Vocational Aptitude
    Battery, 102
Armstrong, T., 120
Arts, audiovisual technology, and
    communications career cluster, 7
    (table), 10 (table), 191t
Assessment systems, and predictors of
    success, 129–131
ASVAB (Armed Forces Vocational Aptitude
    Battery), 209
Aviation, 192–193

Basic Skills Foundation, 9
Before- and after-school
    programming, 296
Benchmarks, 112–115
Bernhardt, V., 102
Big Picture Plan, 188
Bingham, M., 185
Blum, R. W., 279, 280, 283, 284–285
    (table), 285, 290
Borum, R., 282, 286, 287–289 (table)
Brain-based learning, 16–17, 118–120,
    121–122 (table)
Business, management, and
    administration career cluster, 7
    (table), 10 (table)

Caine, G., 120
Caine, R., 120
Campbell, C. A., 85, 86
Canady, Robert Lynn, 166
Career and employability benchmarks,
    114 (table)
Career Biographies Library, 195
Career clusters, 5–6, 7–8 (table), 10–11
    (table), 65, 105, 203–204, 210
Career Pathways High Schools
    action research on, 19
    brain research supporting, 16–17,
        118–120, 121–122 (table)
    career clusters, 5–6, 7–8 (table),
        10–11 (table), 17, 65, 105
    career paths in, 5
    citizenship and, 40, 43–44
    data collection, 102–104
    defining, 4–5
    Five Competencies and Basic Skills
        Foundation, 9
    flexibility, 104–105
    focus and goals of, 49–51
    funding, 65–69
    graduations, 300–302
    as a great scaffold, 205, 222–223
    guidance programs, 87–90
    myths about, 44–45, 254–255, 257
    national standards and,
        91, 92–94 (table)
    paradigm shifts in, 12 (table)
    purpose of, 11
    results, 19–22
    rural, 9
    scheduling in, 91, 97
    small, 64–65, 284–285 (table)
    stakeholders, 241–242
    state and federal findings on, 17–18
    student web, 40, 41–42 (table)
    students as the center of learning in,
        38–40, 303–304
    village concept of, 15–16
Change process, the, 80–81, 161–162
    cultural, 304–305
    data collection, 57

focus and goals, 49–51
key provisions for success in, 305–307
teaming and collaboration, 51–56
Chat card, 323
Chats, 9th grade, 195–197
Citizenship and Pathways, 40, 43–44
Classrooms
culture and climate issues as part of instruction in, 292
pillar of pathways high school model, 27, 29, 31, 51–53, 54f, 79f
processes that are student centered, 294
well-managed, 284 (table)
Clubs and organizations, student, 296
Codes of silence, 285–289
Collaborative career pathways model, the
action plan for implementation of, 309
as an avenue to good culture and climate, 294–295
citizenship and, 40, 43–44
classroom pillar, 27, 29, 31, 51–53, 54f, 79f
community pillar, 27–28, 31, 32 (table), 51–53, 56f, 79f
complete implementation chart, 38–44, 87–89
comprehensive guidance programs in, 87
core classes, 29, 30 (figure), 41 (table), 117 (table), 233–234
counseling pillar, 26–27, 28 (table), 29, 41 (table), 51–53, 55f, 79f
elective classes, 29, 30 (figure), 41 (table), 235
focus and goals, 49–51
funding, 65–69
grade 9 skills and outcomes, 33, 34f, 179–202
grade 10 skills and outcomes, 34–35
grade 11 skills and outcomes, 35–37
grade 12 skills and outcomes, 37–38
horizontal integration of the three pillars in, 32–38
ideal schedule for, 169–172
implementation timeline, 57–65
integration of curriculum, 120, 124–125
myths about, 44–45
organizer, 191f
parent involvement in, 47–48
pathways classes, 29, 30 (figure)
preparation for internship in, 34–35
rubric, 193f
school size and, 64–65
selection of career pathway in, 33, 34f
skills acquired through, 205, 206 (table)
steps to successful change, 48–57
student web, 40, 41–42 (table)
students as the center of learning in, 38–40, 294
teaming and collaboration, 51–56
vertical implementation of the three pillars in, 28–31
vision process, 310
4 × 4 block scheduling in, 166–169
College students, trends among, 14–15
Communication with teachers, 228–230
Community
attendance at board meetings, 239–241
culture and climate and, 294–295
and Freshman Explorations, 187–189
guest speakers from, 263–267
guest visits by members of, 261, 263
involvement in curriculum, 261–274
involvement in funding, 68–69
and Junior Judgments, 215–216
pillar of pathways high school model, 27–28, 31, 32 (table), 51–53, 56f, 79f, 94 (table), 259–261, 262 (table)
public relations and, 251–252, 253 (table)
role in Pathways, 262 (table)
and Senior Transitions, 221–222
and Sophomore Selections, 209–211
support from the academic, 272, 273–274 (table)
Comprehensive Assessment of School Environments Information Management System, 291
Connectedness, school, 279–285
Content Knowledge: A Compendium of Standards and Benchmarks for K-12 Education, 115
Core classes, 29, 30 (figure), 41 (table), 117 (table), 233–234
Cotton, K., 26
Counseling
channels and outcomes, 88–89
culture and climate and, 294
defining, 86
in the four-year pathways process, 94 (table)
funds, 67
importance of, 85–87
Junior Judgments, 213–214
national standards, 91
peer, 295
pillar of pathways high school model, 26–27, 28 (table), 29, 41 (table), 51–53, 55f, 79f
public relations and, 247–248, 249 (table)
scenario, 83–85
Senior Transitions, 220–221
Sophomore Selections, 209
traditional high school, 87–90
Cross-curricular standards, 111–112
Culture and climate
appropriate and enhanced curriculum, 294

assessment, 291–292
changes, 302–303, 304–305
characteristics of, 277–278
community processes as part of instruction in, 294–295
complementary programs to, 295–296
connectedness in, 279–285
control solutions and suggestions, 289–292
importance of, 278–279
indicators of violence and, 286–289
issues as part of classroom instruction, 292
Pathways as an avenue to good, 294–295
planning sheet, 292, 293 (table)
prejudice and codes of silence in, 285–289
professional development and, 292
school connectedness and, 280–285
teaching strategies, 294
typical, 276–277
working committee for issues in, 290–291
Curriculum
  alignment, 115
  benchmarks, 112–115
  culturally appropriate and enhanced, 294
  defining, 111
  department defined key skills and, 116–118
  focusing, 116–118
  Freshman Explorations, 117 (table), 181–189
  as a great scaffold, 205
  importance of, 110–111
  integrating, 120, 124–125
  Junior Judgments, 211–213
  language arts, 113 (table), 116 (table)
  mapping, 116
  mathematics, 114 (table)
  and Pathways connections, 131, 132 (table)
  placement of Pathways classes, 161–162
  planning tool, 314
  Senior Transitions, 216–220
  social studies, 113 (table)
  Sophomore Selections, 107–109, 207–208
  standards, 112–115
  standards for cross-, 111–112
  technology, 125–127
  vision and outcomes, 111–112

Dahir, C. A., 85, 86
Data collection, 57, 102–104, 306
Decision making, 199–201, 210
  planner, 322
Demographic data, 102, 104 (table)
Department goal planning/action sheet, 313

Developmental Assets: A Synthesis of the Scientific Research on Adolescent Development, 16
Differential Aptitude Test, 146, 184
Dropouts, college, 14–15
Drug prevention programs, 296
Drug Strategies, 296
DuFour, R., 26, 75, 117

Eaker, R., 26, 75, 117
Education and training career cluster, 7 (table)
Educational development plans (EDP), 52, 84, 89, 97–99, 214, 312
  sample junior year, 100 (table)
  web-based, 97, 99
Elective classes, 29, 30 (figure), 41 (table), 235
Embedded technology, 127–129
Extracurricular activities, 42 (table)

Fein, R., 282, 286, 287–289 (table)
Field trips, 67–68, 268–269
Finance career cluster, 7 (table)
First day of school, 296–299
  questionnaire, 326
First Things First, 104
Five Competencies, 9
Flexibility, pathways, 104–105
Focus and goals
  in the change process, 49–51
  key content skills, 116–118
Focus on Freshman, 188
  4 × 4 block scheduling, 107–109, 152, 156, 164, 166–169, 208, 235
  planner, 315
Freshman Explorations, 33, 34f, 39f, 59, 66, 67, 85, 87, 92–94 (table), 138–139, 146–148
  career classes, 183f
  chats, 195–197
  connections to school, 187–189
  connections to self, 181–187
  course blueprints, 140, 141t, 142f
  curriculum, 181–189
  decision making, 199–201
  important connections and, 180–181
  integrated thematic units, 190–193
  Pathways classes, 183f
  public relations, 256 (table)
  site visits, 197–198
  typical student experiences in traditional classes *versus,* 179–180.
  See also 9th grade
Friendship groups, 284 (table)
Funding
  costs, 65–66
  through community involvement, 68–69
  through grants and awards, 68
  through reallocation, 66–68

Gardner, Howard, 120, 184
Getting From Here to There . . . Education for the New Millenium, 87
Getting Real: Helping Teens Find Their Future, 14
Gibbs, J., 187–188
Goals, 49–51, 76 (table)
    defining, 74–75
    department, 116–118, 119 (table)
    educational development plan (EDP), 98 (table)
Government
    and public administration career cluster, 7 (table)
    student, 296
Grants and awards, 68
Gray, Kenneth, 14
Guest visits, 261, 263

Harris, Kathleen, 16, 111
Hartman Personality Profile, 184, 201, 320, 321
Health
    education and drug prevention programs, 296
    science career cluster, 7 (table), 10 (table), 147, 191t
        pathways classes for, 95 (table)
        sample four-year schedule for, 96 (table)
Herriott, Don, 18
History curriculum, 107–109
Holland Hexagon Profile, 184, 201, 320, 321
Holmboe, J., 188, 201
Horizontal testing, 130
Hospitality and tourism career cluster, 7 (table)
How the Brain Learns: A Classroom Teacher's Guide, 120
Human services career cluster, 7 (table), 11 (table), 191t, 203–204, 266

Implementation timeline, 57–65
Improving the Odds: The Untapped Power of Schools to Improve the Health of Teens, 280
Information technology (IT) career cluster, 7 (table)
In-servicing opportunities for staff, 230–232
Integrated Thematic Instruction (ITI) Model, 17, 27, 181
Integrated unit planner, 324
Integration
    curriculum, 120, 124–125
    technology, 125–127
Intelligence Is a Function of Experience, 17
Internships, 35, 36f, 38, 92–94 (table), 153, 271–272. See also Job shadows
Intramural sports, 295

Jacobs, Heidi Hayes, 116, 188
Jefferson, Thomas, 13
Jensen, E., 120
Job shadows, 85, 150, 201, 206, 212, 267, 269–270. See also Internships
Journal questionnaire sample, 321
Journaling, 187
Junior Judgments, 35, 36f, 38, 39f, 60 (table), 66, 87, 92–94 (table), 138–139, 140, 144f, 152–156
    community issues, 215–216
    counseling issues, 213–214
    curriculum issues, 211–213
    public relations, 256–257 (table). See also 11th grade

Kendall, J. S., 115, 126
Kovalik, Susan, 17, 27, 181, 185, 188

Language arts curriculum, 113 (table), 116 (table)
Learning and Memory: The Brain in Action, 120
Learning styles, 320
Leffert, N., 16
Lions Clubs, 69, 295

Making Connections: Curriculum Integration Projects, 16
Making the Grade: A Guide to School Drug Prevention Programs, 296
Malone, D., 188, 201
Manufacturing career cluster, 8 (table), 10 (table)
Mapping, curriculum, 116
Mapping the Big Picture, 116
Marketing, sales, and service career cluster, 8 (table)
Marzano, R., 115, 126
Masden, P., 291
Mathematics curriculum, 114 (table)
McNeely, C. A., 280, 283, 284–285 (table), 285, 290
Mentors and advisory committees, 42 (table)
Michigan career pathways, 5–6, 8 (table), 17, 19, 20–21 (table), 22 (table), 68, 188
Michigan Department of Education, 114, 126, 192, 278, 291
Michigan Occupational Information System, 195
Mission, 74–75, 76 (table)
    public relations as an ongoing, 257–258
Modzeleski, W., 282, 286, 287–289 (table)
Multimedia presentations, 159
Multiple intelligences, 120, 123 (table), 146, 320
Myths about Pathways High Schools, 44–45, 254–255, 257

National Association of Secondary School Principals, 291
National Commission on the High School Senior Year, 218
National Institute of Child Health and Human Development, 279
National Institute of Health Revitalization Act of 1993, 279
National Longitudinal Study of Adolescent Health, 279
National School to Work Office, 13, 14
National standards, 91, 92–94 (table)

Ohio career clusters, 5, 8 (table)
Oregon state pathways, 5, 8 (table)

Parent involvement in pathways, 47–48, 243–244
Pathways classes, 29, 30 (figure), 95 (table)
    as an avenue to good culture and climate, 294–295
    change process, 161–162
    course blueprints, 140, 141–145 (table), 146–160
    curriculum placement of, 161–162
    delivery methods, 160–161
    exploration, 194–201
    field trips, 67–68, 268–269
    groups, 296
    guest speakers in, 263–267
    guest visits to, 261, 263
    instructional purposes of, 138–139
    integrated thematic units, 190–193
    internships, 35, 36f, 38, 92–94 (table), 153, 271–272
    job shadows, 85, 150, 201, 206, 212, 267, 269–270
    key concepts and placement, 139–140, 141–145 (table)
    long-term results, 162
    service learning, 160, 270–271, 296
    site visits, 197–198, 267
Peer counseling, 295
Perception data, 102, 103, 104 (table)
Personal digital assistants (PDAs), 128
Planning sheets
    4 × 4 block scheduling, 315
    action plan for model implementation, 309
    alternative block (A/B) scheduling, 316
    culture and climate, 292, 293 (table)
    curriculum, 314
    department goal, 313
    educational development plan (EDP), 312
    pathway decision making, 322
    pathway integrated unit, 324
    student goal, 318
    study skill, 319
    traditional block scheduling, 317
    vision process action, 310
    4-year, 311
Portfolios, 99–101, 149
Postsecondary transition, 37–38, 39f, 42 (table), 137–138
    educational development plan (EDP), 99 (table)
Prejudice and codes of silence, 285–289
Professional development, 172–173, 230–232, 292
Professional Learning Communities at Work, 26, 75, 117
Public education, purpose of, 13
Public relations
    board meetings and, 239–241
    community, 251–252, 253 (table)
    considerations for the first five years, 256–257 (table)
    counselor, 247–248, 249 (table)
    gathering the stakeholders for, 241–242
    and myths about Pathways, 254–255, 257
    ongoing, 257–258
    school board and administration, 246–247, 248 (table)
    staff, 250–251, 252 (table)
    strategy, 242–243
    by talking to parents, 243–244
    by talking to students, 244–246
    by talking to the school community, 246–252
    teacher, 248–250, 250 (table)
    with technical centers and academic sources, 252–254
Public safety and security career cluster, 7 (table)
Purpose of career pathways high schools, 11

Radd, Tommie, 87
Reallocation of funds, 66–68
Reddy, M., 282, 286, 287–289 (table)
Riley, Richard W., 5
Rinehart, P. M., 279, 280, 283, 284–285 (table), 285, 290
Ross, A., 185
Rotary Clubs, 69, 239–240, 295
Rural high schools, 9

Scaffold, Pathways, 205, 222–223
Scales, P., 16
SCANS (Secretary's Commission on Achieving Necessary Skills Report), 9, 17, 57, 79f, 138, 190, 192, 207
Schedules, 91, 96 (table), 97
    creating, 173–175
    ideal, 169–172
    importance of addressing, 165–166
    major types of, 166–169
    Senior Transitions, 218

teaching styles and professional
 development and, 172–173,
 174 (table)
Schmoker, M., 48, 104
Scholastic Assessment Test (SAT), 35,
 102, 214
School boards
 meetings, 239–241
 talking to, 246–247, 248 (table)
School process data, 102, 103, 104 (table)
School to Work Opportunities Act of 1994,
 17, 68
Science, technology, engineering,
 and mathematics career cluster, 8
 (table), 191t
Senior Transitions, 37–38, 39f, 42 (table),
 60 (table), 66, 87, 92–94 (table),
 138–139, 140, 145f, 156–160,
 203–204
 community issues, 221–222
 counseling issues, 220–221
 curriculum issues, 216–220
 public relations, 257 (table).
  See also 12th grade
Service learning, 160, 270–271, 296
Site visits, 197–198, 267
Small schools, 64–65, 284–285 (table)
Social studies curriculum, 113 (table)
Sophomore Selections, 34–35, 39f, 60
 (table), 65, 66, 85, 87, 92–94 (table),
 105, 138–139, 148–152, 205–206
 community issues, 209–211
 counseling issues, 209
 course blueprints, 140, 141t, 143f
 curriculum, 107–109, 207–208
 public relations, 256 (table).
  See also 10th grade
Sousa, D. A., 120
South Carolina, 18
Speakers, guest, 263–267
Sports, team and intramural, 295
Sprenger, M., 120
Staff
 public relations, 250–251, 252 (table)
 questionnaires, 325, 326
Standards
 curriculum, 111–115
 national, 91, 92–94 (table)
State pathways, 5–6, 8 (table)
Stress management, 149
Structural changes, 302–303
Stryker, S., 185
Students
 centered learning, 38–40, 294, 303–304
 clubs and organizations, 296
 and the community pillar of Pathways,
  259–261
 drug prevention programs for, 296
 goal planner, 318
 government system, 296

intramural sports and, 295
learning data, 102–103, 104
 (table), 306
peer counseling and, 295
personality styles, 184, 201, 320, 321
portfolios, 99–101, 149
talking to, 244–246
team sports and, 295
teaming card, 186, 320
testing and data collection, 102–104
tutoring programs for, 295–296
Study skill planner, 319
Systems change, 302–303
 collaborative and flexible, 303–304
 key provisions for, 305–307
 through process and experience,
  304–305

Teachers
 assessments and, 129–131
 career technology and academy *versus*
  Collaborative Pathways, 233
 communications with, 228–230
 core, 233–234
 elective, 235
 gaining support of, 225–226
 inclusion in the Pathways process,
  226–228
 in-servicing opportunities for, 230–232
 as part of the team, 226–232
 in Pathways *versus* traditional classrooms,
  235–236
 professional development, 172–173,
  230–232, 292
 public relations and, 248–250,
  250 (table)
 role in the four-year pathways
  process, 94 (table)
 scheduling and, 172–173, 174 (table)
 strategies for culture and climate
  skills, 294
 teaming and collaboration among, 232
 transformation to Pathways, 224–225
 work time, 228–230
Teaching with the Brain in Mind, 120
Team sports, 295
Teaming
 card, student, 186, 320
 and collaboration, 51–56
 teacher, 232
Technology
 centers public relations, 252–254
 embedded, 127–129
 funds, 67
 integration, 125–127
 literacy, 125–127
 teachers, 233
Testing, student, 102–104
 assessment systems and predictors
  of success, 129–131

horizontal, 130
vertical, 129–130
Texas, 18
9th grade
　career pathway choice in, 33
　chats, 195–197
　citizenship skills, 43 (table)
　core curriculum, 117 (table)
　decision making, 199–201
　embedded technology in, 127, 129 (table)
　site visits, 197–198
　skills and outcomes, 33, 34f, 186–187. *See also* Freshman Explorations
10th grade
　citizenship skills, 43 (table)
　curriculum, 107–109, 207–208
　embedded technology in, 127–128, 129 (table)
　preparation for internship, 34–35
　skills and outcomes, 34–35. *See also* Sophomore Selections
11th grade
　citizenship skills, 43 (table)
　embedded technology in, 128, 129 (table)
　internships, 35, 36f, 38, 39f, 153
　preparation for senior project, 36–37
　sample educational development plan (EDP) for, 100 (table)
　skills and outcomes, 35–37. *See also* Junior Judgments
12th grade
　citizenship skills, 43 (table)
　embedded technology in, 128, 129 (table)
　senior projects, 37–38, 39f, 42 (table), 60 (table), 66, 87, 92–94 (table), 138–139, 140, 145f, 156–160, 217–220, 271–272
　skills and outcomes, 37–38. *See also* Senior Transitions
Threat Assessment of Schools, A, 282
Time line for implementation of pathways model, 57–65

Time management, 149
Traditional block scheduling planner, 317
Traditional high schools
　counseling programs, 87–90
　teachers, 235–236
Transportation, distribution, and logistics career cluster, 8 (table)
Tribes, a new way of learning and being together, 187–188
Tribes Program, 185
Tutoring programs, 295–296

U. S. Department of Education and Office of Vocational and Adult Education (USDE/OVAE), 5–6
U. S. Department of Labor, 9, 13, 17, 190
Utah state pathways, 5, 8 (table)

Values, 74–75, 77–78 (table), 184–185
Vertical community processes, 32 (table)
Vertical counseling, 28 (table)
Vertical testing, 129–130
Village concept, the, 15–16
Violence, indicators of, 286–289
Vision
　curriculum, 111–112
　defining, 74–75, 75 (table)
　process action plan, 310
　process chart, 81 (table)
Vossekuil, B., 282, 286, 287–289 (table)

Wagner, C. R., 291
Web-based educational development plans (EDP), 97, 99
What Work Requires of Schools: A SCANS Report for America 2000, 9
Wonacott, M., 6
Work-based learning experiences, 42 (table)
Workforce Education and Development Program, Penn State, 14

4-year planning sheet, 311

CORWIN PRESS

The Corwin Press logo—a raven striding across an open book—represents the union of courage and learning. Corwin Press is committed to improving education for all learners by publishing books and other professional development resources for those serving the field of K–12 education. By providing practical, hands-on materials, Corwin Press continues to carry out the promise of its motto: **"Helping Educators Do Their Work Better."**